READING SMARTER!

More than 200 Reproducible Activities
to Build Reading Proficiency in Grades 7-12

PATRICIA OSBORN

**THE CENTER FOR APPLIED
RESEARCH IN EDUCATION**

Library of Congress Cataloging-in-Publication Data

Osborn, Patricia.
    Reading smarter! : more than 200 reproducible activities to build
reading proficiency in grades 7–12 / Patricia Osborn.
        p.   cm.
        ISBN 0-87628-850-6 (spiral wire) — ISBN 0-13-044976-8 (paper)
        1. Reading (Secondary).   2. Education, Secondary—Activity
programs.   3. Teaching—Aids and devices.   I. Center for Applied
Reseach in Education.   II. Title.
LB1632.O83   1995
428.4'071'2—dc20   94-34552
                                                                  CIP

©1987, 1995, 2002 by The Center for Applied Research in Education

Printed in the United States of America

10 9 8 7 (spiral wire)   10 9 8 7 6 5 4 3 2 1 (paper)

ISBN 0-87628-850-6 (spiral wire)   ISBN 0-13-044976-8 (paper)

**THE CENTER FOR APPLIED RESEARCH
IN EDUCATION**
Paramus, NJ 07652

http://www.phdirect.com/education

About The Author

Patricia Osborn is a graduate of Bowling Green State University in Ohio, where she received a B.A. in journalism and earned her teaching credentials. She has also attended the University of Toledo and Instituto Mexicano-Norte Americano in Mexico.

Ms. Osborn has taught English in grades 9-12 at all levels, basic to honors, in Toledo, Ohio. As well as required English courses, she has also taught electives in composition, Russian literature, drama, and journalism; advised high school newspapers; and served as English department chairperson. Ms. Osborn's career choices reflect her love of reading and writing, and she firmly believes that students must know how to read thoughtfully in order to write effectively.

In addition to *Reading Smarter,* Ms. Osborn has written a number of other books and articles concerned with language arts and education. These include *How Grammar Works, A Self-Teaching Guide* (1989, Johny Wiley & Sons, Inc.) for both personal and classroom use; *Poetry by Doing* (1992, National Textbook Company); and *Finding America* (1995, Amsco School Publications, Inc.) a multicultural anthology of literature.

Before becoming a teacher, Ms. Osborn was a general news reporter on the *Marion Star* and an advertising copywriter for a Toledo department store. A writer of fiction and poetry as well as books and articles, her work has appeared in magazines ranging from *Educational Digest* to *TV Guide.*

Acknowledgments and Credits

About This Book

Reading Smarter provides you and your students with easy, step-by-step techniques and activities that build naturally and unstressfully to higher levels of reading proficiency. Containing more than 200 worksheets, it features unique, thorough, and educationally-sound exercises that introduce and reinforce basic literary and reading concepts as well as develop essential thinking and interpretive skills.

Here's the flexibility you seek, with activities ready to suit the needs of your classes and students with varying levels of ability. You can use individual lessons in conjunction with your regular literature assignments—to introduce a concept or reinforce specific skills. Or you may present its units as an integrated program to emphasize areas in which your students need a concentrated approach.

You'll find the progression of activities from basic to more difficult to be exceedingly clear, logical, and sensible. Not only thorough in approach and original in outlook, these lessons also supply proof that learning can be both productive and fun.

Highlights include:

- The Writer/Reader Compact
- Making the Educated Guess
- Activating the Mind's Search Function
- The Reader as Reporter
- Introduction to Imagery
- The Truth in Fiction
- Making Thoughful Inferences

Each of the 12 units is packed with stimulating, effective activities—ready to reproduce and use with your classes. Your students will not only find themselves actively participating in the acquisition of advanced reading skills—but will also discover that writing down their ideas is a natural component of becoming a more thoughtful reader.

Reading is a one-on-one activity in which the good reader must take an active part, adjust to the demands of the text, and react to the voice of the writer.

When you are an accomplished reader, the transaction takes place inside your head. In a real sense, you decode the message. You interpret it. You evaluate it.

When a storyline is involved, you actually stage it in your "mind's eye." Reading provides no director or cameraman to dramatize characters, setting, costumes, and story.

TV and film create shadow images with no depth or inner dimension. Both allow the viewer to separate himself or herself from the action—sitting back to watch as an uninvolved observer, not a participant.

In contrast, the active, productive reader actually enters the book. And, the book enters the reader. This is the one-on-one experience. For the reader, the written details translate into sense and experience strictly through the workings of one's own mind and imagination.

For the good reader, reading is always an active process—to be undertaken by a mind full of questions and purposefully engaged with the words and ideas of another person who has chosen to write them down.

Through the resources in this book, you will discover how to help students develop capacities which will enable them to become better readers. You can also help them discover how to share more fully in the ideas that writers express—the one-on-one activity of writing/reading.

In *Reading Smarter* you'll find a wealth of exercises and ideas that not only prepare students for higher-level reading but also approach reading as a lively art.

Along with more than 200 activities and exercises, *Reading Smarter* includes these additional features:

Reading Selections, containing literary selections and lively introductory background essays, are especially designed to save you time and effort. These selections are distinctively headed so that you need to make just one set instead of duplicating a sufficient number of copies for each individual student. In this way, you can use these selections with more than one class and keep the set in your files for future distribution.

Notes on Activities concerning each unit are conveniently grouped following the unit's introduction. These offer helpful and stimulating suggestions about teaching and enriching the concepts discussed.

Also included is a complete Answer Key at the back of the book.

Patricia Osborn

Contents

UNIT 3
WHEN TO USE A DICTIONARY • 49

UNIT 4
A MEETING OF MINDS • 79

Contents   **ix**

UNIT 7
COMING TO TERMS WITH TECHNIQUES OF LITERATURE • 173

UNIT 8
THE TRUTH IN LITERATURE • 209

UNIT 11
CHARACTER: THE HEART OF THE STORY   •   303

UNIT 12
SOMETHING TO THINK ABOUT   •   331

ANSWER KEY   •   367

UNIT 1

The Good Reader in Action

Why do people read?
A little girl of pre-kindergarten age comes to her father, who's reading the evening paper.

"Look, daddy. I can read." Her eyes, concentrating intently, follow across the lines of type and down the printed column. Her pudgy finger points out each word as she says it.

"The. . .the. . .the. . .the. . .the. . .the. . .

"See, I can read," she cries proudly.

"Why, so you can," her father agrees.

Is this reading? By some definitions, perhaps not, but her delight shows that reading can have many purposes.

This chapter consists of a series of warm-up exercises to help students become more free and flexible in working with words.

First, ask them to list as many different kinds of material a newspaper prints daily that they can think of—news, editorials, entertainment reviews, and sports, of course. Then there are cartoons, display ads, classified ads, the weather, the daily horoscope, and the stock market.

And, what about a crossword puzzle? This is an example of a reading game that involves two players—the writer of the puzzle and the person working it. The writer gives a clue. The reader must guess the exact word that the crossword's creator had in mind to fit the given number of spaces. For certain, the puzzle maker wants to be tricky, but not too tricky. If it were too hard to complete, no one would try to work the puzzles and the newspapers would stop publishing them.

Next, ask students to consider and list as many as possible different kinds of reading that they encounter every day—school work doesn't count. There are can and bottle labels, street signs, team jackets and sweatshirts, telephone books, warnings and directions for a multitude of products, and television listings.

"Oh, I don't read much," people say. What they have in mind is the kind of reading found in schools, libraries, and bookstores.

Television performs for its viewer, who needs only to watch and listen passively. Reading is the original interactive method of acquiring knowledge.

When someone reads, the transaction takes place inside that person's head. In a real sense, the reader decodes the message, interprets it, and evaluates it.

Reading and writing are truly two parts of a whole—and accomplished readers know they have an essential part in the reading/writing process.

The following exercises are designed to help students develop the mind-set needed to take an active part as involved readers. The answers are given at the end of the book.

NOTES ON ACTIVITIES

Filling in Famous Quotations (1–3)

In addition to discovering how the eye "fills in" missing letters when they read, students will have the chance to meet some ageless ideas. Encourage them to discuss the underlying meanings of these quotations, and whether their ideas hold true and have value today. They might also enjoy trying to decide the time period in which they were written, in the hope students will reach the conclusion that good words are ageless.

Playing THE *Game (1–4)*

Begin by telling the students the category: Person, quotation, place, title and author, thing, etc. Make handouts or draw dashes on the chalkboard to represent the spaces to be filled with the correct letters. For example, if the first puzzle was the title *The Call of the Wild*, you would draw on the blackboard:

___ ____ __ ___ ____

Assign one student to list all the letters that have been called on one side of the board. You or another student can fill in the correct letters when they are called. You can have the entire class participate by having students call out letters in order around the room. The first student to raise his or her hand and volunteer the correct answer wins the round. The "prize" might be filling in the letters for the next puzzle.

Or, you may prefer to have three students compete with one another at the front of the room, while the rest "play along" at their desks. The winner of the round becomes "king of the hill," taking on the next two comers.

Here are some possible puzzle answers:

Mark Twain and Samuel Clemens (*Person*)
"A mind is a terrible thing to waste." (*Quotation*)
Stratford on Avon, England (*Place*)
"It is a silly game where nobody wins." (*Quotation*)
A Raisin in the Sun (*Title*)
"If at first you don't succeed . . . cry, cry again." (*Pun on Quote*)

You can add to the list with titles, authors, place names, and quotations from your classes' curriculum.

Guides to Taking Notes:
Australia—A Penal Colony (1–8A)

This reading selection by Mark Twain allows students to practice the skill of picking out key points and organizing them into a brief report.

More Than Just the Facts (1–8B)

Accompanying the Twain reading selection, exercise 1–8B asks students to discover how Twain also reveals his attitude toward the colony's harsh punishments. Your class may also want to discuss whether they agree with Twain that 25 lashes would be an appropriate punishment for those convicted of such crimes as wife-beating and robberies that involve physical assault.

Asking "What Happens?" (1–10)

After they answer the questions about "The Return of Adrian Hopewell," you may want to have your students write their version in finished short-story form. Encourage them to include dialogue and action, as well as description.

Why We Read (1–1)

Directions: The following is a list of reasons you might have for reading. Look them over, and see if you have any additional reasons. If so, write them in the blank spaces at the end of the listings.

1. Assignments
2. Applications
3. News
4. Research
5. Technical Data
6. Enjoyment

7. General Knowledge
8. Advice or Guidance
9. Test-Taking
10. Puzzles, Games
11. Correspondence, Letters
12. "How-to" Directions

13. Self-Improvement
14. Stories, Fiction
15. TV Credits, Commercials
16. Merchandise Tags, Labels
17. _____
18. _____

GETTING YOUR IDEAS IN ORDER

Directions: When you and your classmates have agreed upon a list of 16 to 20 reasons for reading, write them below in alphabetical order.

      What kind of reading do you do? In the box following each item in the list, write the number that best describes the frequency with which you do that type of reading, using the following key:

Frequently—1   *Occasionally*—2   *Rarely*—3   *Never*—4

1. _____ ☐	11. _____ ☐
2. _____ ☐	12. _____ ☐
3. _____ ☐	13. _____ ☐
4. _____ ☐	14. _____ ☐
5. _____ ☐	15. _____ ☐
6. _____ ☐	16. _____ ☐
7. _____ ☐	17. _____ ☐
8. _____ ☐	18. _____ ☐
9. _____ ☐	19. _____ ☐
10. _____ ☐	20. _____ ☐

What's Missing? (1–2)

A good reader does not read word for word, stopping to study each word carefully. To become a better reader, you must form the habit of recognizing words by the way they look—their size and shape—along with the part they play in a sentence.

For example, check out the following:

m _ p = **ma**p or **mo**p   (*Who ever heard of a m**i**p or m**u**p?*)
r _ b = **ro**b, **ri**b, or **ru**b
d _ g = **do**g, **di**g, or **du**g

Without looking at every letter, how do you know which is meant? Consider the sentence below.

The d _ g barked at the mailman.

It certainly wasn't the "dig" barking. In fact, you would probably figure out the following, as well.

Th_ d_g b_rk_d _t th_ m_ _lm_n.

WARM-UP EXERCISE: FAMILIAR SAYINGS

Directions: Just for fun, practice reading the following familiar sayings and adages. You'll notice that all of the missing letters are vowels, with only those needed for clarity included. The five vowels—a, e, i, o, u—represent the "open" sounds that make words pronounceable, while consonants form the structure and "backbone" of words. That's why close attention to vowels is less important when reading silently than when reading orally.

To gain practice in reading words without vowels, first say aloud or "hear" the words in your head so the saying sounds right and makes sense. Then fill in the blank spaces with the correct vowels: *a, e, i, o,* or *u.*

1. A st____tch in t____me s____ves nine.

2. W____ste not, w____nt not.

3. A p____nny s____ved is a p____nny e____rn____d

4. L____ ____k b____f____re you l____ ____p.

5. H____n____sty is the b____st p____l____cy.

6. It's b____tt____r to be s____fe than s____rry.

Filling in Famous Quotations (1–3)

Directions: Following is a series of quotations with which you may be unfamiliar. After filling in the blank spaces to make them read correctly, you and your teacher may want to discuss these words and ideas said by some of the world's greatest writers and thinkers.

1. 'Tis the g__ __d r__ __der that m__kes the g__ __d b__ __k.
   Ralph Waldo Emerson, 1803–1882

2. Alm__st ev__ryth__ng that is gr__ __t has been d__ne by y__ __th.
   Benjamin Disraeli, 1804–1881

3. M__k__ng p__ __ce is h__rder than m__k__ng w__r.
   Adlai Stevenson, 1900–1965

4. The app__tite gr__ws by e__t__ng.   *François Rabelais, 1494(?)–c.1533*

5. After all, t__m__rr__w is another d__y.   *Margaret Mitchell, 1900–1949*

6. A h__use is a l__v__ng-m__ch__ne.   *Le Corbusier, 1887–1965*

7. A riot is at b__tt__m the l__ngu__ge of the unh__ __rd.
   Martin Luther King, Jr., 1929–1968

8. Educ__t__ __n m__k__s us what we __r__.
   Claude Adrien Helvetius, 1715–1771

9. No t__me like the pr__s__nt.   *Mrs. Manley, 1663–1724*

10. You can't st__p tw__ce into the same r__v__r.   *Heraclitus, c. 513 B.C.*

11. There was an __ld __wl l__v'd in an o__k
    The m__re he h__rd, the l__ss he sp__k__;
    The l__ss he sp__k__, the m__re he h__ __rd
    O, if m__n were all l__ke that w__s__ b__rd!
    Punch Magazine, vol. LXVIII, 1875

12. If all the g__ __d p__ __pl__ were cl__v__r,
    And all the cl__v__r p__ __pl__ were g__ __d,
    The w__rld w__ __ld be n__c__r than __v__r
    We th__ __ght that it p__ss__bly c__ __ld . . .
    Elizabeth Wordsworth, 1840–1932

Playing *THE* Game (1–4)

MORE FUN WITH WORDS!

It's the popular word game on television! And, it's a game you'll enjoy playing in class—while you get extra practice in identifying words and sayings before all of the letters are in place.

You start with a series of blank spaces that your teacher will draw on the chalkboard or mark on a handout. For example, if the first puzzle is the title *The Call of the Wild,* the puzzle would look like this:

___ ____ __ ___ ____

After learning the category—person, quotation, place, title, thing, etc.—contestants name a letter they think the puzzle might include. Your practice filling in letters from familiar sayings and famous quotations should make it easier to do.

Remember to make a habit of calling the most-used consonants first. These are *t, n, s,* and *r.* Since the five vowels are used with the greatest frequency, a vowel can't be called until after a set of five consonants are named.

It's not only fun, but will help you learn some of the rules of reading—such as the fact that the majority of words that begin like this, t _ _, turn out to be *the* and wh _ _ h is probably *which.*

Your teacher will give you the category and the number of words and spaces you need to fill in. After that, it's up to you and your classmates to see who can guess the answer first!

Another Kind of Reading . . . For Fun (1–5)

Here's a type of word search that lets you practice spotting the shape and size of words. This skill can help make it easier for you to pick out particular words, facts, and details when you are doing research or studying for a test. Words are printed horizontally, vertically, and diagonally—both backwards and forwards.

TV SPORTS

Directions: Check off each word in the list after you have found and circled its letters on the puzzle. Some letters are used in more than one word, so it is better to circle individual letters, as shown, rather than entire words. When you have finished, all letters should be circled with the exception of those spelling out the Mystery Word, which will tell you something else about the subject. (**Mystery Word = 7 letters**)

```
S  R  A  T  S  E  T  E  L  H  T  A
P  P  N  E  S  C  O  R  E  S  Y  H
O  R  N  A  A  R  E  N  A  V  T  A
N  E  O  M  B  A  S  E  B  A  L  L
S  D  U  S  R  E  F  I  S  L  A  F
O  I  N  S  Y  A  L  P  A  E  N  T
R  C  C  C  E  L  T  B  R  A  E  I
S  T  E (G) K  A  T  F  E  G  P  M
O  I  R (O) C  O  U  A  M  U  W  E
N  O  S (L) O  G  M  M  A  E  I  S
A  N  R (F) H  Y  P  E  C  S  N  O
F  S  B  A  S  K  E  T  B  A  L  L
```

Words to find and circle:

Announcers	Cameras	Golf ✓	Penalty	Sponsors
Arena	Fame	Halftime	Plays	Stars
Athletes	Fan	Hockey	Predictions	Teams
Baseball	Football	Leagues	Ref	Ump
Basketball	Goal	Lose	Scores	Win

About Reading (1–6)

Directions: Underline or check off each word in the list after you have found and circled its individual letters on the puzzle as shown.

```
L  O  G  I  C  H  A  R  A  C  T  E  R  S  S
E  (E)(N)(I)(L) E  A  K  I  Q  U  O  T  E  I
Z  T  I  W  I  R  E  N  O  G  R  O  L  E  S
Y  Y  T  O  M  O  D  T  O  O  R  A  O  P  I
L  H  T  D  A  E  I  R  H  Y  B  M  B  G  R
A  P  E  A  X  S  E  O  H  O  U  A  M  N  C
N  A  S  H  E  M  S  P  O  E  T  R  Y  I  E
A  R  H  S  D  M  N  E  R  C  O  D  S  N  R
R  G  E  E  I  S  E  R  R  S  A  S  S  E  U
R  O  R  R  G  R  P  R  O  Y  E  G  A  P  T
A  I  O  O  E  O  S  N  R  M  O  T  T  O  N
T  L  I  F  S  H  U  N  O  I  T  C  I  F  E
I  B  N  R  T  T  S  L  O  V  E  A  R  T  V
V  I  E  W  S  U  W  R  I  T  E  R  I  E  D
E  B  S  S  D  A  E  R  S  E  U  L  C  S  A
```

Words to find and circle:

Adventure	Drama	Meaty	Report
Analyze	Essay	Motto	Rogue
Art	Fiction	Narrative	Roles
Authors	Foreshadow	Novel	Satiric
Bibliography	Heroes	Opening	Set
Book	Heroines	Page	Setting
Characters	Horror	Plot	Story
Climax	Idea	Poetry	Suspense
Clues	Index	Prose	Symbol
Crisis	Line ✓	Quote	Views
Digests	Logic	Reads	Wit
	Love		Writer

A Crossword with a Difference (1–7)

Directions: Here's a different kind of crossword puzzle that lets you figure out the word by reading a sentence. (It also gives a definition as an extra clue, when it seems necessary.)

Don't worry if you don't know some of the words. Crossword makers tend to choose words because they fit, not because they're common. And, this is where the crossing of one word with others can help you out.

If you form an unfamiliar word, check it in the dictionary to see if its meaning fits.

Crossword Clues for 1-7

Across

1. The miner staked his _ _ _ _ _. (*declaration of a right*)
6. The Jrs. challenged the _ _ _. (*abbr.*)
9. Your _ _ _ _ _ day relates to your birth.
14. The old fur coat looked _ _ _ _ _. (*like a certain rodent*)
15. The team was given a _ _ _ rally. (*liveliness and spirit*)
16. The huge _ _ _ _ _ lifted the heavy beams into place.
17. _ _ _ _ was among the Greek gods as Cupid was among the Roman ones.
18. The football team ran onto the _ _ _ _ _.
20. Who are the team's tight _ _ _? (*linemen farthest from the center*)
21. The doctor said the _ _ _ on his scalp was not dangerous. (*cyst, tumor*)
22. At camp, everyone sang songs and toasted marshmallows around a _ _ _ _ _ _ _.
24. Most students would like to _ _ _ good grades. (*obtain*)
25. The _ _ _ _ _ _ storm struck, with high winds and driving rain. (*harsh*)
27. Only the _ _ _ _ _ _ of the Greek statues were found; the heads were missing. (*trunk of the human body*)
29. Do you _ _ _ the cafeteria food or bring your lunch from home?
30. The rival teams will _ _ _ for the championship. (*compete*)
31. Dropping the mirror caused it to _ _ _ _ _ _ _. (*break into pieces*)
35. The _ _ _ _ _ _ _ paid the rent promptly. (*occupants, renters*)
39. We studied about the _ _ _ in science class. (*electrically charged particle*)
40. The team's star player acts like he's on an _ _ _ trip. (*self-awareness, conceit*)
41. _ is the seventh letter in the alphabet.
42. The fans were in _ _ _ at seeing their idol in person. (*full of wonder*)
43. During the sale, the price was _ _ _ _ _ _ _ by 50 percent. (*made smaller*)
47. A stop sign is the shape of an _ _ _ _ _ _ _. (*eight-sided figure*)
51. Lynn plays the _ _ _ in the school band. (*reed instrument*)
52. The witch in *Hansel and Gretel* was an ugly old _ _ _.
53. The brand _ _ _ _ _ _ the cattles' hides. (*burned the surface of*)

56. Before the prom, the girls got their hair done at their favorite beauty _ _ _ _ _ _.
59. A shoemaker uses an _ _ _ to punch holes.
60. Some students are _ _ _ _ _ _ _ about doing their homework. (*irregular*)
62. Ken can _ _ _ to re-enlist or be discharged. (*choose*)
64. The captain ordered the ship _ _ _ _ with provisions. (*to load with cargo*)
66. You need a _ _ _ _ _ to ride the bus.
67. Please, shut the _ _ _ _.
68. Hockey is usually played in an _ _ _ _ _ _.
70. The yapping dog likes to _ _ _ at people's ankles.
71. Be sure to _ _ _ _ _ the stamps on tightly. (*glue*)
72. The bridesmaids will _ _ _ _ _ flowers as they come down the aisle.
73. In printing, two _ _ _ equal the width of one em.
74. Being _ _ _ _ _ is unhealthy as well as unattractive. (*extremely fat*)

Down

1. The ship's _ _ _ _ was very helpful during the cruise.
2. _ _ _ _ _ are a kind of Roman household spirit.
3. He wanted to _ _ _ _ _ for his bad behavior. (*make up for*)
4. The dog performed _ _ _ tricks. (*form of pronoun*)
5. This is _ _ notebook; that is yours. (*form of pronoun*)
6. The _ _ _ _ _ of a book has the same name as a human backbone.
7. There was a coral _ _ _ _ close to the island.
8. Pioneers had to _ _ _ _ _ _ logs to use for firewood. (*cut in parts*)
9. The abbreviation for North Carolina is _ _.
10. We _ _ _ planning to leave at noon tomorrow.
11. They danced the _ _ _ _ _. (*South American dance*)
12. Llamas are native to the _ _ _ _ _ mountains of South America.
13. Don't hurry, _ _ _ _ you make a foolish mistake. (*for fear that*)
18. Even though the direction called for _ _ _ _ _, I thought the music too loud.
19. He _ _ _ _ _ _ his parents' car. (*operated*)
22. The song has a good _ _ _ _. (*tempo*)
23. _ _ _ _ is another name for Ireland.
26. We took our dog to the _ _ _. (*animal doctor—abbr.*)
28. Can you point out the Mediterranean _ _ _ on the map?

Crossword Clues for 1–7 (continued)

31. Enlisted men call male officers "_ _ _." (*title of respect*)
32. Gardeners _ _ _ the ground before planting seed.
33. Coordinate conjunctions include _ _ _, *but,* and *or.*
34. On a traffic light, the color _ _ _ symbolizes *stop.*
35. _ _ _ means *also* and *excessively.*
36. Parents sometimes _ _ _ about doing homework.
37. _ _ _ is a number; *to* is a preposition.
38. _ _ _ is a monetary unit of Japan, equal to 1/100 of a yen.
44. _ _ _ is the abbreviation for the United States of America.
45. Try to take good _ _ _ _ of your health.
46. You _ _ _ _ _ a great deal of effort working out for a sport. (*put out, apply*)
48. The gate was fastened with a heavy steel _ _ _ _ _.
49. There was a powdery film of _ _ _ _ on the bathroom floor. (*a kind of powder*)
50. Many popular nursery tales were written long _ _ _.

53. _ _ _ _ _ is another form of *swarthy,* meaning dark-skinned.
54. Kim is three years younger than her _ _ _ _ _ brother.
55. In the distance we heard the _ _ _ _ _ of a plane's engines.
56. We climbed the _ _ _ _ _ instead of taking the elevator.
57. The _ _ _ _ _ tightened around the condemned man's neck.
58. The cleaner removed the _ _ _ _ _ from my jacket.
59. She cried, "_ _ _ _," when she realized her sweater was ruined. (*cry of regret*)
61. Although the friends look alike, they are not _ _ _ _.
63. There is an oak _ _ _ _ in their back yard.
65. The wind direction was _ _ _. (*abbr.*)
67. Matt put an extra _ _ _ of color on the painting. (*light touch*)
69. "_ _, no," Steve protested when he spilled the orange juice.
71. The _ _ river is in Italy.

A Question of Speed (*Reading Selection 1–8*)

It's not how fast you read but how well you read. And, reading fast and reading well are not necessarily the same thing. Are you reading to take a test? Reading to memorize facts? Then you might want to keep a notebook handy to jot down the details you want to remember or will be expected to know.

When you know *why* you are reading, you can consciously decide how to vary your speed to read at the pace that best fits each particular purpose.

> **A wise man once said:**
> Some books are to be tasted, others to be swallowed,
>   and some few to be chewed and digested;
>   that is, some books are to be read only parts;
>   others to be read but not curiously;
> and some few to be read wholly,
>   and with diligence and attention . . .
>
> *Francis Bacon, 1561–1626*

In other words, not all books should be read in the same way. It depends upon the book and your purpose in reading it.

Following are several examples of different types of reading, along with hints about how best to approach reading them.

MARK TWAIN—REPORTER

You may know Mark Twain (or Samuel Langhorne Clemens) as a writer of humor and creator of Tom Sawyer and Huckleberry Finn. But he also wrote for newspapers in Virginia City, Nevada, and San Francisco, California.

He wrote books about his travels, too, including *The Innocents Abroad* and an account of his trip around the world in 1893, called *Following the Equator*.

FROM *FOLLOWING THE EQUATOR*

You might choose to read all or part of Twain's book for more than one reason.

One might be because you like Mark Twain's writing, and another because you're interested in learning about a trip around the world.

Here is another reason that requires you to practice a different style of reading from the other two.

Directions: Read this selection as if you were writing a report about the early days of Australia. In this case, you will read it more slowly with "diligence and attention." You will also plan to take notes and, as an active reader, put "two and two" together to select the details you need to include in your report.

13

(*Reading Selection 1–8 continued*)

As you read, refer to the exercise at the end, which will serve as a guide to help you choose the important details to note down.

Australia—A Penal Colony

Captain Cook found Australia in 1770, and eighteen years later the British government began to transport convicts to it. Altogether, New South Wales[1] received 83,000 convicts in 53 years. The convicts wore heavy chains; they were ill-fed and badly treated by the officers set over them; they were heavily punished for even slight infractions of the rules; "the cruelest discipline ever known" is one historian's description of the life.[2]

English law was hard-hearted in those days. For trifling offenses—which in our day would be punished by a small fine or a few days' confinement—men, women, and boys were sent to this other end of the earth to serve terms of seven and fourteen years, and for serious crimes they were transported for life. Children were sent to the penal colonies for seven years for stealing a rabbit.

When I was in London twenty-three years ago there was a new penalty in force for diminishing garroting[3] and wife-beating—twenty-five lashes on the bare back with the cat-o'-nine-tails.[4] It was said that this terrible punishment was able to bring the stubbornest ruffians to terms; and that no man had been found with grit enough to keep his emotions to himself beyond the ninth blow; as a rule the man shrieked earlier. That penalty had a great and wholesome effect upon the garroters and wife-beaters.

Twenty-five lashes! In Australia and Tasmania[5] they gave a convict fifty for almost any little offense; and sometimes a brutal officer would add fifty, and then another fifty, and so on, as long as the sufferer could endure the torture and live. In Tasmania I read the entry, in an old manuscript official record, of a case where a convict was given *three hundred* lashes—for stealing some silver spoons. And men got more than that, sometimes. Who handled the cat? Often it was another convict; sometimes it was the culprit's dearest comrade; and he had to lay on with all his might; otherwise, he would get a flogging himself for his mercy—for he was under watch—and yet not do his friend any good: the friend would be attended to by another hand and suffer no lack in the matter of full punishment.

The convict life in Tasmania was so unendurable, and suicide so difficult to accomplish, that once or twice despairing men got together and drew straws to determine which of them should kill another of the group—this murder to secure death to the perpetrator and to the witnesses of it by the hand of the hangman!

---

[1]State in southeast Australia
[2]*The Story of Australasia* (sic), J. S. Laurie
[3]choking in order to rob
[4]a whip, usually with nine knotted lines attached to its handle
[5]island state, SE Australia

(Reading Selection 1-8 continued)

The incidents quoted above are mere hints, mere suggestions of what convict life was like—they are but a couple of details tossed into view out of a shoreless sea of such.

Some of the convicts—indeed, a good many of them—were very bad people, even for that day; but most of them were probably not noticeably worse than the average of the people they left behind at home. We must believe this; we cannot avoid it. We are obliged to believe that a nation that could look on, unmoved, and see starving or freezing women hanged for stealing twenty-six cents' worth of bacon or rags, and boys snatched from their mothers, and men from their families, and sent to the other side of the world for long terms of years for similar trifling offenses, was a nation to whom the term "civilized" could not in any large way be applied. And we must also believe that a nation that knew, during more than forty years, what was happening to those exiles and was still content with it, was not advancing in any showy way toward a high grade of civilization.

If we look into the characters and conduct of the officers and gentlemen who had charge of the convicts and attended to their backs and stomachs, we must grant again that as between the convict and his masters, and between both and the nation at home, there was a quite noticeable monotony of sameness.

Guide to Taking Notes: Australia—A Penal Colony (1-8A)

Directions: Complete the sample notes by filling in the missing information. Use details in the text to figure out the dates, if not expressed as numbers.

Part I. Fill in the blanks with the information called for.

Date	Act or Event
1. 1770	_____
2. 1788	_____
3. 1788–1831	_____

Examples of Crimes and Punishments

    A. In time of penal colonies

Crime	Punishment
1. _____	_____
2. _____	_____
3. _____	_____
4. _____	_____
5. _____	_____
6. _____	_____

    B. In England during Twain's earlier visit

1. _____	_____
2. _____	_____

Part II. Using the facts from your notes above, write a short, informative report of 5–7 sentences about the penal colonies in Australia. Use the space below and the back of this sheet.

_____

_____

_____

_____

_____

More Than Just the Facts (1–8B)

Directions: In addition to reading for facts and details, you might also have found yourself reading Mark Twain's article about the Australian penal colonies "curi-
ously," meaning with curiosity and interest.

A. After reading or rereading the article, write three or more phrases or sentences
that reveal Twain's attitudes towards using Australia as a penal colony and the
treatment of prisoners there.

1. _____

_____

2. _____

_____

3. _____

_____

4. _____

_____

5. _____

_____

B. With what two words did Twain describe the effect being punished with 25
lashes had on wife-beaters and garroters?

1. _____

2. _____

C. Write a short paragraph explaining your reactions and feelings after reading the
selection by Twain.

_____

_____

The Reader/Writer Compact (*Reading Selection 1–9*)

A compact is a kind of agreement in which both parties promise to do their share. This is how it is between a well-matched writer and reader.

The writer tries to anticipate and answer the reader's questions, not get sidetracked or bogged down in unimportant details, and yet not leave out anything necessary for understanding.

Readers take an active part by asking questions, both of the writer and themselves, being alert for clues to their answers, and staying aware of the point and purpose behind what the writer is saying. In some ways good readers conduct an imaginary dialogue with an author—finding answers to their questions and answering for themselves as they read.

FROM *THE BIG SEA*[1] BY LANGSTON HUGHES

Directions: First, quickly read these opening paragraphs from Hughes' autobiography before you work with the exercise that follows. Since Langston Hughes is known as one of America's leading poets and short-story writers, the selection may surprise and even confuse an inexperienced reader.

Beyond Sandy Hook[2]

Melodramatic[3] maybe, it seems to me now. But then it was like throwing a million bricks out of my heart when I threw the books into the water. I leaned over the rail of the S.S. *Malone* and threw the books as far as I could out into the sea—all the books I had had at Columbia[4], and all the books I had lately bought to read.

The books went down into the moving water in the dark off Sandy Hook. Then I straightened up, turned my face to the wind, and took a deep breath. I was a seaman going to sea for the first time—a seaman on a big merchant ship. And I felt that nothing would ever happen to me again that I didn't want to happen. I felt grown, a man, inside and out. Twenty-one.

I was twenty-one . . .

You see, books had been happening to me. Now the books were cast off back there somewhere in the churn of spray and night behind the propeller. I was glad they were gone.

I went up on the poop[5] and looked over the railing toward New York . . . There were no longer any lights to be seen . . . I was sleepy, so I went down a pair of narrow steps that ended just in front of our cabin—the mess boys'[6] cabins.

---

[1]Hughes, *The Big Sea*, copyright 1940, 1986, by Langston Hughes
[2]a spot at the entrance to New York Bay
[3]overly dramatic, exaggeratedly emotional
[4]Columbia University in New York City
[5]a weather deck at the stern of a ship
[6]Hughes' job was serving the officers' mess and making up their staterooms

Dialogue with an Author (1–9A)

Directions: After reading the quote from Langston Hughes and the imaginary reader's response and questions, fill in the blank spaces, basing your answer on the selection and your own reasoning.

BEYOND SANDY HOOK

Hughes: Melodramatic maybe, it seems to me now. But then it was like throwing a million bricks out of my heart when I threw the books into the water.

Reader: I can think of two other, reasonable ways to get rid of books without destroying them.

1. They are _____ and _____

2. Is that why you now think you were acting melodramatic?
   (Check one)   Yes ____   Probably ____   Possibly ____   No ____

Hughes: I leaned over the rail . . . and threw the books as far as I could . . . all the books I had had at Columbia, and all the books I had lately bought to read.

Reader: You went to Columbia University. How does that help explain why the books felt like "a million bricks out of your heart"?

3. _____

Hughes: The books went down into the moving water in the dark off Sandy Hook.

Reader: Why did you pick nighttime to throw away your books?

4. _____

Hughes: Then I straightened up, turned my face to the wind, and took a deep breath. I was a seaman going to sea for the first time—a seaman on a big merchant ship.

Reader: After becoming a seaman, you felt you wouldn't have to deal with books and studying any more.

5. _____ True or False?

Hughes: And I felt that nothing would ever happen to me again that I didn't want to happen. I felt grown, a man, inside and out. Twenty-one.

I was twenty-one.

Reader: You repeat twice that you were twenty-one at the time. That means you now realize that you weren't really in control of everything that would happen to you.

6. _____ True or False?

(1–9A continued)

Hughes: You see, books had been happening to me. Now the books were cast off back there somewhere in the churn of spray and night behind the propeller. I was glad they were gone.

Reader: Why did you feel books had been "happening" to you? Why would you feel forced to read them?

7. _____

Hughes: I went up on the poop and looked over the railing toward New York . . . There were no longer any lights to be seen . . . I was sleepy, so I went down a pair of narrow steps that ended just in front of our cabin—the mess boys' cabins.

Reader: Why would you have to take a mess boys' job on the ship?

8. _____

More Questions from the Reader:

9. By calling yourself "melodramatic" at age twenty-one, do you want me to realize it's no longer something you'd do, now that you're older?

   Yes or no? _____

10. Why might you think going to sea, as well as college, would be helpful for someone like you who wanted to be a writer?

   _____

   _____

   _____

   _____

ABOUT THIS EXERCISE:

Of course, experienced readers do not actually have to stop reading periodically to make up and answer such questions. They come almost automatically.

As you gain skill and confidence in spotting clues and answers, your awareness of the compact between reader and writer will help you develop the habits you need to read faster and understand more of what you read.

© 1995 by The Center for Applied Research in Education

Asking "What Happens?" (*Reading Selection 1–10*)

One of the fastest kind of reading you do is reading to find out what happens.

This is reading that you swallow in a big gulp—like Stephen King's horror stories, science fiction, romance, and adventures.

Because your interest is to find out what happens, your main goal is to follow the action and catch the clues that point to the outcome. You want to read it fast, and it's possible because you don't need to worry about underlying meanings or information that you have to file in your memory for future use.

Here is the opening of this kind of story:

The Return of Adrian Hopewell

There was a mysterious tapping at the window, and a sudden silence fell over the four people sitting by the fireplace. It was as if a cold chill had invaded the warmly lit room to remind them of the threatening storm and dark outside.

The two brothers and their wives had been talking of Adrian Hopewell, although they did not speak of him often, for they had little enough to say. He had simply walked away two years ago, leaving a cryptic note:

"I will be back when I'm ready. I hope I have forgiven you by then."

What happens next? . . .

This Is a Story Without an Ending . . . Yet! (1–10A)

Directions: As a reader, here are some of the questions you'd want to have answered. Just for fun, try completing the story and answering them yourself.

1. Who or what was tapping at the window?

   _____

2. What had been done to Adrian Hopewell? Who did it?

   _____

3. Does he come back to seek revenge or express forgiveness?

   _____

   To complete the story and answer "what happens?" you will also have to provide additional background. Here are a few more questions:

4. What is the relationship of the people in the room to Adrian Hopewell? Is he a
   brother of the two brothers? Their father? Their brother-in-law?

   _____

   _____

5. What were the four people saying about Hopewell when the mysterious tapping
   began?

   _____

   _____

6. What happens next?

   _____

   _____

Use your imagination!
There is no right or wrong. You may even decide to change the title, too.

When you are finished, you'll want to share and compare your version with those of
your classmates so that everyone can get in on the action and find out how many things
can happen when you start asking questions.

© 1995 by The Center for Applied Research in Education

UNIT 2

All Words Are Not Created Equal

It is possible to read words yet have little or no idea of what a writer is actually saying. At times, good readers even do so intentionally.

Sometimes readers choose to overlook meaning on purpose because it allows them to accomplish their goal more quickly and efficiently. For example, the brain's ability to remember and interpret a piece of writing is not of major importance to someone who is reading for proof, typing, or copying a manuscript. In fact, getting sidetracked by meaning makes the job take longer to get done.

The human brain has remarkable abilities. Perhaps it's an exaggeration to say most human brains can put computers to shame. Yet it's still an irresistible temptation to compare these two types of electronic equipment, one human and one created by humans.

The brain can be highly selective in the information it chooses to process formally. An experiment has shown that two entirely different messages can be directed at a person's ears, one to one side and a second to the other. Instead of being confused or disoriented, the subject can choose to receive and fully comprehend the one, while rejecting and in a true sense, not even hearing the other.

Everyone knows that people also "see" only what they wish to see. In the landscape included in its field of vision, the eye focuses on the area, detail, or details that most interest the beholder.

So it is with reading. Students whose minds wander and who proclaim their boredom are probably merely passing their eyes across a series of words because it is "required reading." Their interest is elsewhere. The purpose is to be done with it. The wandering mind and thoughts of boredom accomplish the purpose, faster than the student may wish to admit. They *do* get out of reading, simply by "turning off."

The blame falls on the boring book, not on minds that chose not to concentrate or did not realize the purpose of their reading.

Yet, like a computer, the human brain is programmable. Practice in various kinds of reading provides helpful exercise in programming one's brain to read for specific purposes and to direct its attention to the goal at hand and the methods for doing it best.

NOTES ON ACTIVITIES

Reading for Proof (2–1)

Exercises in proofreading have two goals: to provide experience in correcting mistakes in spelling, punctuation, and usage, and to help students discover that errors make it difficult for them to read, too. In rewriting this and the following exercise, students may vary in their handling of details. It is most important that they get practice identifying errors and making corrections. Because of the archaic phrasing, students may find the first exercise more difficult than the following one.

Spelling Dosent Madder—Or Dose It? (2–2)

As an outcome of their discussion of this exercise, it is hoped that students will reach the following conclusions:

1. Proofreading, typing, or copying words from a dictionary or an encyclopedia are situations where a page's content barely concerns the reader. In such cases ideas or meanings are not expected to lodge in the brain. Production matters. Finishing the job quickly and correctly matters. The eye/brain/hand connection turns a person into a machine whose job is to function efficiently. Under such conditions, thinking about meaning wastes time.
2. Readers pay minimal attention to spelling so long as the words are spelled correctly, as they have every right to expect them to be. This makes the writer correct in saying that, especially to a reader, spelling doesn't matter so long as it's right.
3. Spelling must be important to a writer who hopes to make a good impression and wants to be read by those given a choice.

Reading Orally (2–3)

Oral and silent reading are two different skills. In a very real sense, the oral reader is actually a stand-in for the writer. The purpose of oral reading is not to receive a message but to deliver it.

Oral reading shows the ability to decode written words into correctly pronounced and emphasized spoken ones. It is possible to pronounce a word correctly without knowing its meaning. And the opposite is equally true.

Oral and silent reading have another difference. A good silent reader can read much faster than someone can read the same number of words aloud. Because they are concentrating on meaning, good readers sometimes make "slips of the tongue" which don't affect meaning—and actually show they're absorbing its sense.

To introduce the differences between silent and oral reading, select one or several students to read "Royal Exile" by Beryl Markam orally to the class. Tell these student readers not to worry whether they pronounce every word correctly. Assure them that if they are unfamiliar with a word and/or its pronunciation, chances are their classmates will be, too. It is more important to read smoothly with proper emphasis so that the sense of what they're reading will come through.

Getting the Idea from Strong Words (2–6)

In addition to illustrating the importance of strong words, this exercise gives students the opportunity to see how small variations in connecting words need not change the essential meaning of a sentence or paragraph.

FOR EXAMPLE, sentence 5 could be written in either of the following two ways:

It is incorrect to speak of them as if they were a single species.
It is incorrect to speak of it as if it were a single species.

Have students compare their papers, not only to discover their errors, if any, but also to see their different ways of solving the same problem of missing words while maintaining the same meaning.

Not Equal, but Genuinely Needed (2–7)

Students should be encouraged to have fun with this assignment and see that they should not be impressed, just because someone uses big words. Writing must make good sense (and some doesn't)—or it forces a reader to waste time puzzling out something that could and should have been written more clearly.

A woman who knew a number of geniuses, including Joseph Salk and Pablo Picasso, said a sign of a true genius was having the ability to explain his or her ideas so that the average person could understand them.

Discussion: From Forewords & Afterwords (2–8A)

Students need to complete activity 2–6 to understand how to do this exercise. You may want to give this question as a composition assignment after your students have discussed the first four questions in class.

How Good Writers Use Strong Words (2–8B)

If you plan to provide students with their own copies of this reading selection, ask them to underline the strong words in the paragraph itself. However, if you intend them to be used in more than one class, have students list the strong words as they were in Reading Selection 2–6. For the Auden selection, the first words might read: – modern books – bringing – children warn parents – , etc.

Student choices may vary in some instances. It is more important that students understand the principle of strong words than that they agree on every detail.

When they have finished, ask them to compare the number of strong words to the number they did not underline or list. If there are 80 strong words, there will be 102 left unmarked, more than half.

Then ask them to compare the number of strong words in "A Case of Selling Too Hard" with connectors and determiners. They should count about 18 strong words and 3 others—or almost 90% strong words! This comparison should help them have a better idea about what actually constitutes good writing.

When students have finished underlining or identifying the strong words, ask them to reread the paragraph orally and/or silently. Ask them to notice how it seems natural to allow a stress to fall upon the underlined words and how such emphasis makes the paragraph easier to understand than when all words are stressed equally.

Activitating the Mind's "Search" Function (2–9)

In addition to the items given, you may want to assign students other elements to search out for extra practice or have them exercise their scanning abilities on other materials and with other elements—such as characters' names, strong words, or parts of speech.

It is important for students to realize that a good reader knows his or her purpose for reading and sets the right pace to accomplish it.

Reading for Proof (*Reading Selection 2-1*)

When your purpose is proofreading—looking for and correcting mechanical errors—it's possible to finish your task and have only a foggy idea of content or meaning. And, that's exactly how it should be. Your aim is to correct spelling, punctuation, and grammatical errors. Reading for ideas distracts you from this goal.

Directions: Tackle this entry by Sarah Kemple Knight, whose journal was written in 1704, when standard spelling was less important than it is now. Many people thought themselves lucky to be able to read and write! Today her way of spelling and capitalizing words presents a stumbling block for almost every reader.

Read the selection and see how many "misteaks" you find, judging by modern standards. You may wish to circle or underline each one you spot. Then write a corrected version, and see how reading for sense becomes much easier once the changes are made. You may also wish to edit or change some of the phrasing to make the selection read more smoothly.

Strange Customs of Connecticut

Saturday, Oct. 7th, wee set out early in the Morning, and being something unacquainted with the way, having ask't it of some wee mett, they told us wee must Ride a mile or two and turne down a Lane on the right hand; and by their Direction wee Roade on but not Yet comeing to the turning, wee mett a Young fellow and ask't him how farr it was to the Lane which turn'd down towards Guilford. Hee said wee must Ride a little further, and turn down by the Corner of uncle Sams Lott.

by Sarah Kemble Knight, writing of a stop on her journey by horseback from the colony of Massachusetts to New York

Strange Customs of Connecticut (2–1A)

Directions: Write a corrected copy of Knight's selection in the space below.

_____

_____

_____

_____

_____

_____

_____

_____

_____

_____

_____

_____

_____

_____

_____

_____

_____

_____

_____

Name _____ Date _____ Period _____

Spelling Dosent Madder—Or Dose It? (2–2)

Proofreading is one means of decoding language. But its main purpose is to make a manuscript correct and clear for easier reading. When there is a large number of errors, the message gets lost, even for expert readers.

Directions: Proofread the following essay. First, underline all of the mistakes in spelling, capitalization, punctuation, and usage that you may find.

Then, make a "fair" copy, correcting all errors. You should find a total of 67 mistakes.

The Proof Is in the Proofreeding

Spelling dosent madder so long as its rite.

Most of the time when your reeding, nuthing cud be farther from your mine then lookng for errers in spelling, punchuashun, and grammer, thats becuz you except it too bee correck

A peace of writting isn't really reddy too reed until its proofred.

Thats becuz slopy or even unintenshunal misteaks creat a bad impreshun rite from the start.

If the writter dosent care enuff to correck his or her errers, the reeder will deside that he or she cant have much wurth saying. someone who dosent care about the detales that mak it posible too reed more easier also probly hasnt bother to get facts strait, hasnt thot thru his or her ideas, and dont no how to express them intrestingly & well.

Directions: Write a corrected copy of the essay on another sheet of paper..

For Discussion:

1. When you were correcting and copying this selection, were you aware of what the writer was saying or did the process of copying make you ignore meaning?
2. When you are reading a book, magazine, or other printed material, do you pay much, little, or no attention to the way words are spelled? Explain your choice. Do you agree that, to a reader, spelling doesn't matter as long as it's right?
3. Do you believe spelling should be important to a writer? Why or why not?

Reading Orally (*Reading Selection 2–3*)

Reading orally and reading silently have two different purposes. When you read orally, your aim is to make someone else understand what you are reading. For that reason, it is best to read aloud in a natural pace and tone. Don't worry if you mispronounce or "fluff" a word, and don't bother to go back to correct yourself. Even if you miss a word, your listeners will get the sense better if you continue to read on.

Royal Exile[1]

To an eagle or to an owl or to a rabbit, man must seem a masterful and yet a forlorn animal; he has but two friends. In his almost universal unpopularity he points out, with pride, that these two are the dog and the horse. He believes, with an innocence peculiar to himself, that they are equally proud of this alleged confraternity.[2] He says, "Look at my two noble friends—they are dumb, but they are loyal." I have for years suspected that they are only tolerant.

Suspecting it, I have nevertheless depended on this tolerance all my life, and if I were, even now, without either a dog or a horse in my keeping, I should feel I had lost contact with the earth. I should be as concerned as a Buddhist monk having lost contact with Nirvana.

Horses in particular have been as much a part of my life as past birthdays. I remember them more clearly. There is no phase of my childhood I cannot recall by remembering a horse I owned then, or one my father owned, or one I knew. They were not all gentle and kind. They were not all alike. With some my father won races and with some he lost. His black-and-yellow colours have swept past the post from Nairobi to Peru, to Durban. Some horses he brought thousands of miles from England just for breeding.

Camciscan[3] was one of these.

When he came to Njoro,[4] I was a straw-haired girl with lanky legs and he was a stallion bred out of a stud book[5] as big as a tome—and partly out of fire. The impression of his coming and of the first weeks that followed are clear in my mind.

But sometimes I wonder how it seemed to him.

by Beryl Markham

Note: Be sure to save your copy of Beryl Markham's selection or return it to your teacher. You will need it for a future exercise.

---

[1] from *West with the Night,* copyright 1942, 1983 by Beryl Markham
[2] supposed brotherhood
[3] a horse brought from England by the author's father
[4] a place in East Africa where Markham's father, a horse breeder, brought her to live when she was four
[5] a book giving the pedigree of horses

© 1995 by The Center for Applied Research in Education

Discussing "Royal Exile" (2–3A)

Directions: Write your answers to the following questions.

1. Why would man or humans be unpopular with such animals as the eagle and rabbit? Name two other animals you think would have especially good reasons for disliking or fearing human beings, and explain why.

   _____

   _____

   _____

   _____

2. According to Markham, human beings believe dogs and horses are "dumb but loyal." Does this mean dumb in the sense of stupid or being unable to talk?

   _____

   _____

3. Markham believes that dogs and horses merely "tolerate" or put up with humans. What advantages does their association with humans have for dogs and horses? What disadvantages?

   _____

   _____

   _____

   _____

4. For what reasons would Markham wonder whether Camciscan felt differently about his coming and first weeks in Africa from the way she did?

   _____

   _____

   _____

   _____

   _____

What's the Difference? (2–3B)

Oral reading and silent reading are two different skills. Slips of the tongue that indicate basic understanding are sometimes made by good silent readers who are mainly concentrating on the sense of what they read.

For example, a good silent reader might say "in" instead of "into" when reading aloud, "I looked into the box." Such "errors" simply replace one word with another close in meaning. They reveal someone who is reading to understand.

Sometimes students, reading orally, hear their own mistake, go back to correct it, and start again from there. If it doesn't affect the meaning, a good silent reader might not even notice making such a substitution.

Directions: Read the following pairs of sentences, including several from "Royal Exile," and decide whether the changes have made a difference in their meanings or kept them essentially the same.

FOR EXAMPLE, here are two versions of the first sentence of Markham's work:

  a. To an eagle or to an owl or to a rabbit, man must seem a masterful and yet a forlorn animal; he has but two friends.

  b. To an eagle, an owl, or a rabbit, man must seem a masterful yet forlorn animal; he has but two friends.

Even though some words have been omitted, the meaning is the same.

Read the following pairs of sentences. If the changes have made their meanings **differ,** write **D** in the blank space. If they stay the **same,** write **S.**

_____ 1. a. He says, "Look at my two noble friends—they are dumb but loyal."

  b. He says, "Look at my two noble friends—they are dumb, but they are loyal."

_____ 2. a. I have for years suspected that they are only tolerant.

  b. I have for years suspected they are only tolerant.

_____ 3. a. There is no phase of my childhood I can't recall by remembering a horse I owned, one my father owned, or one I knew.

  b. There is no phase of my childhood I cannot recall by remembering a horse I owned then, or one my father owned, or one I knew.

_____ 4. a. The impression of his coming and the first weeks followed are clear in my mind.

  b. The impression of his coming and of the first weeks that followed are clear in my mind.

_____ 5. a. The cat was lying, curled up beneath the sofa.

  b. The cat was lying, curled up under the sofa.

_____ 6. a. A letter postmarked London arrived from Terry's father.

b. A letter postmarked London arrived for Terry's father.

_____ 7. a. I figured out the answer to the riddle that had us all so confused.

b. I figured out the answer to the riddle had us all so confused.

_____ 8. a. After all of our warnings, Mark still risked skating on the thin ice and ended up falling into the icy water.

b. In spite of all our warnings, Mark still risked skating on thin ice and ended up falling into the icy water.

_____ 9. a. By noting the direction where the sun had set, the campers knew they were heading west.

b. By noting the direction where the sun had set, the campers knew they were heading toward the west.

_____ 10. a. Cliff felt he deserved a bonus since he finished the job early.

b. Cliff felt he deserved a bonus if he finished the job early.

The Importance of Strong Words (*Reading Selection 2–4*)

Good readers do not read word for word. Instead, their eyes take in groups or clusters of words. And, of course, they are aware of the strong words that carry most of the weight or meaning of a sentence.

- What are the **strong words**? They are the ones that together can form sentences all by themselves:

    Airplanes fly.   The *strong words* are nouns (which answer Who or
    Chickens lay eggs.   What?) and verbs (Did what? Is or Are What?)
    Kids like pizza.
    Vanessa is president.

- Next come the *qualifiers:*

    Adjectives*, though not so strong as nouns or verbs, can change a *weak* man into a *strong* man, while **adverbs** can turn walking *slowly* to walking *fast*.
- And, don't forget the *pronouns,* which "stand in" for nouns:

    They like pizza.   *She is president.*
- Finally, the *connectors,* words such as *and, after, over* and *or,* the prepositions and conjunctions, as well as determiners such as *the, a,* and *an.*
- Oh, the *interjections!* Well, since dropping them usually does not change the meaning of the rest of a sentence, words like "oh" and "well" come last on the list.

© 1995 by The Center for Applied Research in Education

---

* Descriptive adjectives are such words as *pretty, big, little,* and *loyal.* Do not include pronoun forms, such as *my* and *this,* or the articles *the, a,* and *an.*

Counting on Strong Words (2–4A)

Both good writers and readers depend upon strong words. Nouns and verbs answer a reader's key question: Who or what did what?

A clutter of qualifiers tends to get in the way of the answer. By choosing precise nouns and verbs, writers don't need to rely on a lot of descriptive adjectives and so can get their meaning across more quickly and directly.

Directions: To prove the point, reread the first four paragraphs of "Royal Exile" by Beryl Markham, and list the nouns, verbs, and descriptive adjectives you find there in the three columns below. Because some words might be labeled in more than one way, your count might differ slightly from that of your classmates. Your goal is to discover for yourself the importance of strong words, not do a grammar exercise.

Nouns	Verbs	Adjectives
1.	1.	1.
2.	2.	2.
3.	3.	3.
4.	4.	4.
5.	5.	5.
6.	6.	6.
7.	7.	7.
8.	8.	8.
9.	9.	9.
10.	10.	10.
11.	11.	11.
12.	12.	12.
13.	13.	13.
14.	14.	14.
15.	15.	15.
16.	16.	16.
17.	17.	17.
18.	18.	18.
19.	19.	19.
20.	20.	20.
21.	21.	21.
22.	22.	22.

Nouns	Verbs	Adjectives
23. _____	23. _____	23. _____
24. _____	24. _____	24. _____
25. _____	25. _____	25. _____
26. _____	26. _____	26. _____
27. _____	27. _____	27. _____
28. _____	28. _____	28. _____
29. _____	29. _____	29. _____
30. _____	30. _____	30. _____
31. _____	31. _____	31. _____
32. _____	32. _____	32. _____
33. _____	33. _____	33. _____
34. _____	34. _____	34. _____
35. _____	35. _____	35. _____
36. _____	36. _____	36. _____

Comparison of Totals: Nouns _____ Verbs _____ Adjectives _____

Counting on Poetry (*Reading Selection 2–5*)

What kind of writer uses more adjectives than other kinds of word?

Chances are, your guess would be a poet. Especially one writing a love poem . . . especially a poet from a long time ago. Yet, you will discover for yourself that good poets also use fewer adjectives than nouns or verbs.

Read the following poem about a shepherd who was willing to promise anything to a young woman if she would only be his love. Could she believe him? Maybe that hasn't changed either.

Directions: After reading the poem, list the nouns, verbs, and descriptive adjectives you find in the three columns on sheet 2–5A.

The Passionate Shepherd to His Love

Come live with me, and be my love;
And we will all the pleasures prove
That hills and valleys, dales and fields,
Woods, or steepy mountain yields.

And we will sit upon the rocks,
Seeing the shepherds feed their flocks
By shallow rivers, to whose falls
Melodious birds sing madrigals[1].

And I will make thee beds of roses,
And a thousand fragrant posies;
A cap of flowers, and a kirtle[2]
Embroidered all with leaves of myrtle.

A gown made of the finest wool
Which from our pretty lambs we pull;
Fair-lined slippers for the cold,
With buckles of the purest gold.

A belt of straw and ivy-buds
With coral clasps and amber studs;
And if these pleasures may thee move,
Come live with me, and be my love.

The shepherd-swains shall dance and sing
For thy delight each May morning;
If these delights thy mind may move,
Then live with me, and be my love.

Christopher Marlowe, 1564–1593

---

[1] a song for five or six parts or voices

[2] a gown

Counting Strong Words in
"A Passionate Shepherd to His Love" (2–5A)

Directions: List the nouns, verbs, and descriptive adjectives in Christopher Marlowe's poem.

Nouns	Verbs	Adjectives
1. _____	1. _____	1. _____
2. _____	2. _____	2. _____
3. _____	3. _____	3. _____
4. _____	4. _____	4. _____
5. _____	5. _____	5. _____
6. _____	6. _____	6. _____
7. _____	7. _____	7. _____
8. _____	8. _____	8. _____
9. _____	9. _____	9. _____
10. _____	10. _____	10. _____
11. _____	11. _____	11. _____
12. _____	12. _____	12. _____
13. _____	13. _____	13. _____
14. _____	14. _____	14. _____
15. _____	15. _____	15. _____
16. _____	16. _____	16. _____
17. _____	17. _____	17. _____
18. _____	18. _____	18. _____
19. _____	19. _____	19. _____
20. _____	20. _____	20. _____
21. _____	21. _____	21. _____
22. _____	22. _____	22. _____
23. _____	23. _____	23. _____
24. _____	24. _____	24. _____
25. _____	25. _____	25. _____
26. _____	26. _____	26. _____
27. _____	27. _____	27. _____
28. _____	28. _____	28. _____

(2–5A continued)

Nouns	Verbs	Adjectives
29. _____	29. _____	29. _____
30. _____	30. _____	30. _____
31. _____	31. _____	31. _____
32. _____	32. _____	32. _____
33. _____	33. _____	33. _____
34. _____	34. _____	34. _____
35. _____	35. _____	35. _____
36. _____	36. _____	36. _____
37. _____	37. _____	37. _____
38. _____	38. _____	38. _____

Comparison of Totals: Nouns _____ Verbs _____ Adjectives _____

Getting the Idea from Strong Words (*Reading Selection 2-6*)

When reading for meaning, good readers generally realize that all words should not be considered equal. Nor should they be given equal attention.

The "shorthand" version below of an article about kangaroos contains only its strong words, mostly nouns and verbs. There are a few adjectives—often those formed from nouns, such as *aboriginal, national,* and *rain*—and some pronouns, such as *all, those,* and *others.* It contains almost no connectors or determiners, but dashes are used to show where such words are missing.

Read the following paragraph to discover how much you can understand of what you're reading when only the strong words are present.

Kangaroo: Symbol of Australia

Australia – land – kangaroo. – Centuries aboriginal tribes –
depicted kangaroos – totems, – used – subject – rituals. Today – image –
national coat of arms. – Foreigners – kangaroo – symbol – Australia.
Incorrect – speak – single species. – 90 varieties. Some – no larger – rats.
Others – tall – humans. Some – essentially inhabitants – deserts. Others
live – eastern rain forests. All – vegetarians, except musky rat kangaroo –
also feeds – insects.

*Adapted from "The Kangaroo: Symbol of Pride and
Prejudice," Chapter 97 of* Animals of Australia,
translated by John Gilbert

Kangaroo: Symbol of Australia (2–6A)

Directions: Write your own version of "Kangaroo: Symbol of Australia" below, supplying the words you believe should be added. When you have finished, compare your version with those of your classmates.

_____

_____

_____

_____

_____

_____

_____

_____

_____

_____

_____

_____

_____

_____

_____

_____

_____

_____

_____

_____

_____

Not Equal, but Genuinely Needed (2–7)

Although good readers do not give equal attention to every word in a sentence, the extra, less important words—*the, and, but, of, however,* and so on—serve as needed links and signposts. They clear the way by pointing out connections between ideas and help you weigh words correctly.

They also give you a chance to think and to fix the important words and ideas in your mind. When too many strong words are poured into one sentence, it becomes necessary to read haltingly and puzzle out the meaning with great difficulty—sometimes only to discover the message may be very simple at its heart.

Directions: The following paragraph is an example of weak writing, caused by too many strong words clustered too closely together. Try to "translate" it into clear, understandable English. Your teacher may wish you to tackle it as a group project or work together on it as a class because it crowds so many multi-syllable words together in one sentence that it's hard for anyone to comprehend.

A Case of Selling Too Hard

Innumerable modern multinational corporations encourage increased consumption by underdeveloped countries' populations of quick-fix convenience products more appropriately formulated for technologically advanced societies.

Rewritten Version:

_____

_____

_____

_____

_____

_____

_____

_____

The Proper Balance (*Reading Selection 2–8*)

Good writing balances strong words with those that clarify their connection and guide the reader to the writer's main points. This has been known and practiced by the world's finest writers, past and present.

In fact, the percentage of multi-syllable to one-syllable words has not changed greatly from the days of Charles Dickens to the present. The difference is that today's writers use shorter sentences. Perhaps this is because fewer of today's readers are aware of the relationships existing among different kinds of words.

In the following paragraph, observe how poet and essayist W. H. Auden uses words of lesser impact to bridge the ideas expressed by stronger words and to balance his writing by allowing the reader to put a greater emphasis on the important ones.

From Forewords & Afterwords

Most modern books on bringing up children warn parents against projecting their own ambitions onto their children and demanding of them a high standard of achievement. It seems to me that this warning is merited only in cases where there is no relation between the parents' ambition and the child's actual endowments[1]. If the child is stupid, it is obviously harmful to show anger or shame because he is not at the top of the class, just as it is wrong for a father to try to force a son with a talent for, say engineering, into the family grocery business. But there are many cases in which a parent's ambition is quite justified—if his child is *talented* in the way which the parent believes. From my own experience, I would say that, in the majority of cases, the children of parents who were ambitious for them are successful and, whatever the conflicts and mistakes may have been, they recognize in later life how much they owe their success to the high standards of achievement which was demanded from them at home.

by W. H. Auden

---

[1] natural talents, abilities, capabilities

Discussion: From Forewords & Afterwords (2–8A)

Directions: Write your answers to the following questions.

1. Although Auden uses a father/son as an example, what shows he means his words to apply to girls as well as boys?

   _____

   _____

   _____

2. When does Auden believe it would be harmful for a parent to expect a child to be a top student?

   _____

   _____

   _____

3. Does Auden feel it is right or wrong to encourage sons or daughters to follow in their parents' footsteps? Explain.

   _____

   _____

   _____

4. Does Auden believe it is helpful or harmful for parents to demand high standards for their children? What proof does he give to support his opinion?

   _____

   _____

   _____

5. Do you believe the standards set by today's parents or schools are too high or too low? Explain the reasons for your opinion, giving examples from your experience, reading, or other media.

   _____

   _____

   _____

   _____

   _____

How Good Writers Use Strong Words (2–8B)

Identify the strong words that you find in the paragraph by Auden to discover how good writers balance strong words with those that clarify their connection and help readers absorb important points.

You should find no more than 80 strong words in all. There may be some differences of opinion between you and your classmates, but it is not necessary to agree on every word. Realizing the importance of strong words is what really matters.

NOTE THOSE LITTLE "NOT'S" AND "NO'S"

It is always important for the reader's eye to catch the little words "no" and "not" that completely change the meaning of a sentence.

FOR EXAMPLE: Steve was prepared for the test. *Vs.* Steve was *not* prepared for the test. There will be track practice after school. *Vs.* There will be *no* track practice . . .

It is a good idea to include *no* and *not* along with the strong words.

Directions: List the strong words as they were given in the exercise 2–6, "Kangaroo: Symbol of Australia." For the Auden selection, the first words might read: – modern books – bringing – children warn parents – , etc.

_____

_____

_____

_____

_____

_____

_____

_____

_____

_____

_____

_____

Note: Your teacher may prefer that you underline words in the selection itself.

Activating the Mind's "Search" Function
(*Reading Selection 2–9*)

Imagine that you are taking notes for a paper, studying for a test, or concentrating on just one element of a piece of writing. What individual areas might you program your brain to search for?

Here is a partial listing:

1. People's Names	6. Spelling Errors
2. Dates	7. Mistakes in Usage and Punctuation
3. Place Names	8. Key Words
4. Parts of Speech	9. Placement of Words in Alphabetical Order
5. Numerical Data	10. Others

As you exercise your own "search" function, be sure to keep in mind exactly what you wish to spot. Don't concern yourself with the subject or sense. Ignore everything but the details you have programmed yourself to find.

Your goal is to achieve both speed and accuracy.

The following example contains many kinds of data that might make it the object of a research project. After picking the element you wish to search, you may choose to scan the paragraph downward from the center of each line, letting your eye catch and note the details it seeks. Or, by experimenting, you may find a better method of your own.

An important by-product of this exercise is to show that you need not focus on each word, one by one, in lines or blocks of type. Concentrate on "getting out" what you seek, not just "getting it done."

Expansion and Business

The treaty of Utrecht inaugurated an era of peace and expansion for England's continental colonies. Their population had grown from about 85,000 in 1670, to 360,000 in 1713. By 1734 it had quadrupled again to about 1,500,000. This increase owed much to heavy migration of non-English people—Irish and Scots, Germans and French—favored by a liberal naturalization act of the British Parliament in 1740. Only two new continental colonies, Nova Scotia and Georgia, were founded between 1713 and 1754, but the area of settlement almost tripled. In the North it spread into the hilly interior of New England, the region west of the lower Hudson, and central Pennsylvania. In the Southern colonies it spread into Piedmont, the area between the fall line of the rivers and the Blue Ridge and Smoky Mountains. And the manner of settlement, as we shall see, created new tensions.

High prices prevailed in Europe for colonial products, especially tobacco, rice, and sugar. The last-named primarily helped the West Indies, but the continental colonies, which provided the islands with lumber, live-stock, and provisions, indirectly profited.

Before 1713 there had not been a real town on the continent between Philadelphia and Charleston. Norfolk now grew up as an outlet for the lumber and naval stores of North Carolina. Baltimore, founded in 1730, soon became a principal point of export for the wheat of Maryland and Pennsylvania. Philadelphia countered in 1733 by building the "Great Road" to the mouth of the Conestoga river, Lancaster County. For wagon traffic over this road in farm products, draft horses were bred from the Dutch and Flemish stock brought over by early settlers; and the Conestoga wagon, which eventually became the covered wagon of the Oregon trail, was developed.

The Oxford History of the American People
by Samuel Eliot Morison
chapter 10, volume one

Search and Scan Exercise (2–9A)

Directions:

1. List in order each of the dates included in the selection.
   (List more than once, if repeated.)

   _____

   _____

   Now, go back to the passage and scan for any of the following items your teacher asks you to find.

2. Capitalized words that refer to or name specific colonies or states in North America. (List more than once, if repeated.)

   _____

   _____

3. Numbers giving the population of the American colonies, along with their dates.

   _____

   _____

4. Capitalized words naming colonial cities. (List more than once, if repeated.)

   _____

   _____

5. Count the number of sentences in these two paragraphs. There are _____.

UNIT 3

When to Use a Dictionary

The exercises in this chapter are designed to help students understand when to use a dictionary—and when not to use it.

When they spot an unfamiliar word, many students feel they should immediately look it up in the dictionary. By doing so, they risk losing the thread of what they are reading, and definitions sometimes use additional unfamiliar words that leave them as lost as before. In this chapter you will find exercises to help your students become more proficient at determining meaning from context.

Students might also be surprised to discover that many really don't know the exact meanings of supposedly simple words like *too*, for example. Although they may use it easily and correctly in everyday speech, a single synonym can pop into their heads when they're reading. Thus, when they see a sentence like "The king's subjects thought him *too* demanding," they may jump to the conclusion that *too* must mean *also* because that's what they "learned." Such confusion also occurs with homographs like *corporal*. Here, too, context is the key, although students will learn that checking the dictionary is an important way to refine their understanding of words they have acquired through context or thought they already knew.

One of the most valuable lessons for students to learn is that reading itself is the best way to gain new words in their vocabularies, for it allows them to meet words "at work" and discover how writers actually use them, instead of trying to memorize lists of imposing words and definitions, which they find difficult to remember because they were learned out of context.

NOTES ON ACTIVITIES

Making the Educated Guess (3–1)

Explain to your students that context simply means the sense of a word as it is used in a sentence or printed "with" the text. Tell students that dictionary definitions try to give them the meanings of a word as they apply in a variety of different contexts. To show students how they already determine meaning through context, ask them to think of sentences containing a common word like *cap*. Though its meaning can range from a *cap* on a bottle to a baseball *cap* to a *cap* shot off to startle or surprise someone, they automatically know its meaning by how it's used in a sentence.

Although answers are given in matching form at the end of this exercise, encourage students to make educated guesses about all the sentences first—and discover how easy and natural it is to get meaning from context.

Words with Two Meanings (3–5)

As well as concentrating on words that are homographs, this exercise also illustrates the close relationship between context and meaning. You may want to introduce the exercise by writing the word *well* on the chalkboard. Ask several students to give some of its definitions. Then explain that it's impossible to choose which definition is wanted until you see the word in context, since *well* is an example of a homograph—words spelled alike with different meanings.

When they have gone over the exercises, ask students if they can think of other familiar words that are also homographs. Or, list others—such as *beat, plant, calf, grain,* and *close*—for them. Then have students make up original sentences, either orally or in writing, to illustrate their multiple meanings.

What's in a Name? (3–12A)

The aim of this exercise is to help students discover the three types of words in most people's vocabularies. The words were specifically chosen to represent a range from familiar, everyday words like *face* to their rarely used synonyms, such as *physiognomy.* Students should not feel they "ought" to know a certain number of these unfamiliar words since a major factor in word recognition is context, while choosing from a list requires prior familiarity with a word's meaning.

If students do not have access to dictionaries, you may ask them to write "(3)" after the words they do not know, instead of randomly adding them to one of the lists.

Because each synonym has a different shade of meaning, you might also want to do an additional activity, which requires a set of dictionaries. Assign the different lists as group work, and ask students to determine the shades of differences that give each word on the list a special meaning of its own.

Discussing "Discontent" (3–13A)

Invite your class to discuss the meaning of this story and compare its moral to the American Indian saying that you should not envy another person until you have walked a mile in his moccasins.

Also, ask students to discuss some individual traits shown in this selection that are still recognizable in people they know today.

Discontent: Understanding Meaning
Through Context (3–13B)

Although students are asked to underline the vocabulary words in the reading selection, you may want them to omit this step if you are using the copies in more than one class.

The advantage to underlining is that it makes it easy for students to find the right word and ponder it in context before writing their definition. Underlining will also make it easier to go over the answers in class. However, the exercise lists the words in order, so the step may easily be omitted.

Making the Educated Guess (3–1)

What should you do when you come across an unfamiliar word in your reading? Most of the time the best choice is—just read on.

The rest of the sentence or paragraph often contains important clues to the meaning of unfamiliar words. When you learn words this way, it is called determining meaning from context.

EXAMPLE: The *bobolink*, holding an insect in its beak, flew towards its nest. Because of "beak," "flew," and "nest," it's obvious a *bobolink* is some type of bird. And it's usually not important to know anything more.

Part A. Directions: Step One. First, read through each of the following sentences. Then make an educated guess about what the underlined word means, and complete the statement that follows. You need not be more specific than "a type of bird."

Step Two. When you have finished, try to match the definitions that follow these sentences, and write the correct key letter before each number to see how closely your educated guess matches your choice of definition.

_____ 1. The garden was abloom with larkspur, roses, <u>delphiniums</u>, and daisies.

<u>Delphiniums</u> means _____.

_____ 2. After barking twice softly, the <u>Dalmatian</u> stood at the door, showing his desire

to go outside. A <u>Dalmatian</u> means _____.

_____ 3. Students' grades may suffer a <u>retrogression</u> when they begin working after

school and buy a car. <u>Retrogression</u> means _____.

_____ 4. There is no question of Mr. Stone's <u>integrity</u>, so you can believe what he says.

<u>Integrity</u> means _____.

_____ 5. The <u>diminutive</u> child could not reach the countertop without standing on a

chair. <u>Diminutive</u> means _____.

_____ 6. Some people fear the deserted house is haunted by a <u>malevolent</u> spirit seeking

revenge. <u>Malevolent</u> means _____.

_____ 7. Worried and upset, Lisa's mother <u>upbraided</u> her for coming home later than

expected. <u>Upbraided</u> means _____.

© 1995 by The Center for Applied Research in Education

(3–1 continued)

____ 8. The startled guest tried to hide the <u>transitory</u> look of astonishment that crossed his face. <u>Transitory</u> means _____.

____ 9. The teacher expressed <u>incredulity</u> when the boy claimed his dog ate his homework. <u>Incredulity</u> means _____.

____ 10. Jerry is full of <u>caprice</u> and always does what's least expected. <u>Caprice</u> means _____.

____ 11. The first robin is often considered a <u>harbinger</u> of Spring. <u>Harbinger</u> means _____.

____ 12. Although the teacher looked funny when she tripped over the wastebasket, the students thought it best to hide their <u>mirth</u>. <u>Mirth</u> means _____.

____ 13. Sarah was concentrating so hard that she was <u>oblivious</u> to the noise in the next room. <u>Oblivious</u> means _____.

____ 14. During the <u>interim</u> between exams, the students compared notes about them. <u>Interim</u> means _____.

____ 15. The <u>meager</u> supply of firewood in the cabin would last for only one more night. <u>Meager</u> means _____.

Part B. Directions: Among the definitions below, choose the one that best fits the meaning of each underlined word. Write its key letter in the blank space before each sentence.

a. poor; lacking fullness
b. very small, tiny
c. unmindful, unaware
d. act of going backward, getting worse
e. soundness of moral character, including honesty
f. a breed of dog
g. doubt or disbelief
h. to scold severely
i. a kind of flower
j. wishing evil or harm to others
k. amusement and/or laughter
l. acting on sudden impulse
m. period of time between
n. a sign, one that announces
o. temporary, lasting only briefly

How Writers Help You Make Educated Guesses (3–2)

Directions: Read the selections below to see how professional writers provide you with clues to the meaning of unfamiliar words. Then complete the sentences that follow each selection, indicating your educated guesses about the underlined words.

1. He dressed underlined stealthily, making sure that the coast was clear before crossing the hall to the bathroom. He tried not to creak the floorboards as he descended the stairs. — from *The Accidental Tourist* by Ann Tyler

   Someone who moves stealthily does not want to be _____

   or _____.

2. Once he'd said the car was sold, he said he was waiting for the money; he did pay me back three quid, but he borrowed again a day or so later. — from "Good Climate, Friendly Inhabitants" by Nadine Gordimer

   A quid must be some type of foreign _____.

3. His caution and inquisitiveness did not foresake him, for with a face as sharp and cunning as ever, he often stopped . . . and stood listening for any conversation in the next room, of which he was the theme. — from *The Old Curiosity Shop* by Charles Dickens

   "Listening for any conversation" is a clue that inquisitiveness means

   _____.

4. That constant pacing to and fro, that never-ending restlessness, the incessant tread of feet wearing the rough stones smooth and glossy—is it not a wonder how the dwellers in narrow ways can bear to hear it. — from *The Old Curiosity Shop* by Charles Dickens

   Incessant must be close in meaning to constant and _____.

5. She feels a kiss, . . . within the general pandemonium. Cars drive up blaring their horns. Firecrackers go off. Dogs come from under the house and begin to yelp and bark. — from "Roselily" by Alice Walker

   Pandemonium is a place or scene where there is _____.

(3–2 continued)

6. We had no children, for I had been <u>apprehensive</u> about begetting children for fear they would look like her. — from "The Doctor's Divorce" by S. Y. Agiron

   The word _____ is the clue to the meaning of <u>apprehensive</u>.

7. Everything falls into place . . . <u>dissonance</u> becomes harmony, and nonsense wears a crown of meaning. — from *Sweet Thursday* by John Steinbeck

   <u>Dissonance</u> must be the opposite of the word _____.

8. The canneries themselves fought the war by getting the limit taken off the fish and catching them all. It was done for patriotic reasons, but that didn't bring the fish back . . . Cannery Row was sad when all the <u>pilchards</u> were caught and canned and eaten. — from *Sweet Thursday* by John Steinbeck

   <u>Pilchards</u> must be a type of _____.

9. He tried to recall everything he had heard about Doc's frustration, and it was all <u>nebulous</u>, all vague, except for one thing: Mack had said Doc couldn't write his paper. — from *Sweet Thursday* by John Steinbeck

   The word _____ serves as a clue to the meaning of <u>nebulous</u>.

10. This (the landscape) has a bland <u>homogeniety</u>, dominated by <u>cupola</u>-shaped crowns of umbrella trees. Variation, no matter how rich, would in any case be disguised by the cloud of dry-season dust that billows up from the road when traffic passes and that settles like dull, red powder . . . To travel down this red corridor is dismally monotonous. — from *One Dry Season* by Caroline Alexander

    Is something that has <u>homogeniety</u> essentially varied or alike? _____

    A <u>cupola</u> must have a shape similar to that of an _____

    _____.

Turning to the Dictionary for Help (3–3)

Here's what you find in most dictionary entries:

1. The word being defined, showing its division into syllables
2. A key to the word's pronunciation and stress
3. Parts of speech: n. (noun), v. (verb), adj., adv., prep., pron., and conj.
4. Spelling of irregular plurals and other irregular endings
   a. Dictionaries only show the plurals of words if they are not regular.
   b. If no plural ending is given, you may assume the plural simply takes an added -s or an -es if the plural creates an extra syllable.
5. Word backgrounds
   Found within brackets are the word and language from which the defined word was derived (OE = Old English, Gk = Greek, etc.). Also included are synonyms for the background word, often given as prefix + root. (Sometimes may follow the definition or be omitted if these elements seem obvious.) This information is called a word's etymology.
6. Definition
   A listing of one or more senses of each word, including its standard, general senses; technical usages in special fields such as Music and Pyschology; and slang and familiar meanings used in everyday speech, but not formally, if any.

Directions: Look up the following words, and write the correct form of each one's plural in the blank space.

1. fair _____

2. calf _____

3. monkey _____

4. moose _____

5. tomato _____

6. sky _____

7. witch _____

8. empress _____

9. fish _____

10. human _____

© 1995 by The Center for Applied Research in Education

All Dictionaries Are Not Alike (*Reading Selection 3–4*)

By just glancing at these three entries from three different dictionaries, all defining the same word, you can easily tell that each is different from the others in length and placement of some of its parts. Scan the entries quickly to check the number of senses included in each. Then answer the questions on activity 3-4A.

A. **fan ta sy** (fan' t se) *n., pl.* -sies [<Gr. *phainein,* to show] 1. imagination or fancy. 2. an illusion or reverie. 3. an imaginative poem, play, etc.

> *Webster's New World Dictionary of the American Language,*
> Paperback pocket-size edition   Simon & Schuster, 1979

B. **fan ta sy** (fan' t si, fan' t zi) *n.,* [*pl.* FANTASIES (-siz, -ziz)] [ME. & OFr. *fantasie;* LL. *phantasia,* idea, notion; Gr. *phantasia,* look or appearance of a thing, lit., a making visible <*phainein,* to show.] 1. imagination or fancy, especially wild, visionary fantasy. 2. an unreal mental image; illusion; phantasm. 3. a whim; queer notion; caprice. 4. an imaginative poem, play, etc. 5. in *music,* a fantasia. 6. in *psychology,* a mental image, as a daydream, usually pleasant and with some vague continuity. Also spelled **phantasy**.

> *Webster New World Dictionary, College Edition of the American Language*
> The World Publishing Company, 1957

C. **fan ta sy** (fan' t se, -ze) *n., pl.* -sies. 1. imagination, esp. when extravagant and unrestrained. 2. the forming of grotesque mental images. 3. a mental image, esp. when grotesque. 4. *Psychol.* an imaginative sequence, esp. one in which desires are fulfilled, a daydream. 5. a hallucination. 6. a supposition based on no solid foundation. 7. caprice; whim. 8. an ingenious or fanciful thought or creation. 9. *Music,* fantasia. Also, **phantasy.** [ME *fantasie* imaginative faculty, mental image, <L *phantasia,* <Gr: idea, notion, image, lit. a making visible.] —Syn. 1. See **fancy**

> *The Random House College Dictionary*
> Random House, 1984

Finding It in the Dictionary (3–4A)

Directions: Write your answers to each of the following questions after scanning the three dictionary entries defining the word *fantasy* to find the information you need.

1. Write the number of different senses of *fantasy* given by each dictionary entry.

   A. _____   B. _____   C. _____

2. a. Which dictionary's placement of the word's background or etymology is different from the others? _____

   b. How does it differ? _____

3. Unless you are doing scholarly research, you have little reason for remembering the background words or their spelling. It is more important to notice the earlier meaning of the word being defined. (Given within brackets [ ])

   a. How many other languages are listed in each of the three examples?

   A. _____   B. _____   C. _____

   b. Write the words denoting the meaning of an earlier word that are alike in examples A and B. _____

   c. Write the words denoting the meaning of an earlier word that are alike in examples B and C. _____

4. a. The example that gives no technical or specialized senses is

   b. The two fields in which fantasy has a specialized sense are _____

   and _____.

5. a. Write the alternate spelling of fantasy. _____

   b. What example does not give this spelling? _____

6. What example does not include "imaginative poem, play, etc." as part of its definition? _____

7. Example C refers to fantasy as often being a "grotesque" mental image. Explain how this differs from an "unreal" mental image. _____

   _____

8. When you are using a dictionary, you must be careful not to take the first sense given as the right one. With that in mind, write the sense that best fits each of the following sentences. Include the key letter of the source example.

   a. Stories, movies, and TV shows about Superman are a type of fantasy.

   Sense _____ Source _____

   b. In his fantasies, he imagines himself as a new Elvis Presley.

   Sense _____ Source _____

   c. During severe illnesses, people sometimes lose their awareness of reality and their minds are invaded by weird fantasies.

   Sense _____ Source _____

Words with Two Meanings (3–5)

Directions: The following words are called homographs, which means each pair has the same spelling but different meanings. Use the dictionary to check the senses of those you are not sure of. Some will be given as more than one entry, some in the list of senses, and others in the background or etymology. Pocket-size dictionaries may not contain the full information. *Write the meaning of each word, as used in its sentence, on the line following it.*

Example: a. If you <u>hide</u> your money, don't forget where you put it.

<u>to put or keep out of sight, conceal</u>

b. The <u>hide</u> was ready to be tanned.
<u>an animal skin or pelt</u>

1. a. My brother received a promotion to <u>corporal</u> in the U.S. Marines.

_____

b. Some people do not believe <u>corporal</u> punishment creates better behavior as satis-

factorily as other methods do. _____

2. a. After not being emptied for a week, the garbage can smelled <u>rank</u>.

_____

b. The highest <u>rank</u> in the U.S. Army is five-star general.

_____

3. a. Can you name the <u>capital</u> of Virginia?

_____

b. There are varying opinions about the value of <u>capital</u> punishment.

_____

4. a. In the past, a man used to <u>sue</u> a girl for her hand in marriage and was called her

suitor. _____

b. The film company plans to <u>sue</u> the actor for breaking his contract.

_____

5. a. Talcum powder is made from a purified, finely <u>ground</u> mineral.

_____

b. During the earthquake the <u>ground</u> shook for only a few seconds, but it seemed to

last much longer. _____

(3–5 continued)

6. a. The collars of men's shirts used to have <u>stays</u> to keep their points neat and firm.

   _____

   b. We enjoyed our trip to Florida and wished we could <u>stay</u> longer.

   _____

7. a. With its big eyes and a delicate look, a <u>fawn</u> is a gentle, shy, and harmless creature. _____

   b. The two-faced man always <u>fawns</u> on rich people, trying to win their favor.

   _____

8. a. The look of <u>gravity</u> on his face let us know the situation was a tense one.

   _____

   b. It is impossible to successfully defy the law of <u>gravity</u> without the proper technological equipment. _____

9. a. Carla's rudeness was not <u>deliberate</u>, and she apologized for hurting her friend's feelings. _____

   b. How much longer must the jury <u>deliberate</u>*?

   _____

10. a. The lumberman <u>cleaved</u> the log in two with powerful strokes of his ax.

    _____

    b. It is important to <u>cleave</u> to your standards and beliefs, even though others urge you to go against them. _____

_____
*differs in pronunciation from *a*.

Words with a Past (3–6)

Part A Directions: Sometimes words that you use every day have older or other meanings that might surprise you. For example, have you ever thought that using the term *horsepower* to measure the power of modern cars actually goes back to the days when the horseless carriage replaced coaches and carriages pulled by horses? Knowing the history and additional senses of a word adds to your understanding of the way it is used and its underlying meaning.

Step 1: Match the definitions that follow to the underlined word, used in its modern meaning.

Step 2: Look up the word to discover its other sense, sometimes based on farming or life in earlier time. Then complete the statement about it. (You may need to check related words, such as crest in addition to crestfallen.)

_____ 1. Many Americans pay taxes to their local, county, state, and federal governments.

Earlier, county was the office or territory belonging to _____.

_____ 2. The family made the trip via turnpikes in Indiana, Ohio, and Pennsylvania.

According to its etymology, a turnpike was _____.

_____ 3. Shelly browsed through several interesting-looking books, trying to decide which appealed to her the most.

With reference to animals, browse means _____.

_____ 4. I thought the film was simply awful, although some of my friends liked it.

In another sense, awful can also mean inspiring _____ or _____.

_____ 5. The homecoming queen candidates rode in convertibles as part of the car caravan in Saturday's parade.

In its broader terms, a caravan is a group of _____ or _____ going together for safety or common interest.

_____ 6. The television station broadcast the news that school would be closed because of bad weather conditions.

With reference to seeds, broadcast means _____.

_____ 7. Rick was crestfallen to learn that he got the problem wrong because of a simple mistake in addition.

Crestfallen also means having a drooping crest, such as the crest of a

_____ or a _____.

(3–6 continued)

_____ 8. The man sat, <u>ruminating</u> about his future course of action.

With reference to animals, <u>ruminate</u> means _____

as animals like _____, _____, and _____ do.

_____ 9. The <u>pastor</u> has many responsibilities to members of his congregation, who are called his flock.

With reference to farming, a <u>pastor</u> is _____.

_____ 10. Traci tried to <u>glean</u> as much information as she could about the topic of her term paper.

With reference to farming, <u>glean</u> means _____.

Part B Directions. Write the letter of the correct definition before each numbered sentence.

a. minister, clergyman

b. to meditate, ponder, think deeply

c. a line of vehicles following one another

d. to transmit via the airwaves

e. to examine casually

f. to collect gradually

g. dejected, with drooping spirits

h. a toll road, especially an expressway

i. a governmental district of a state

j. very bad

Context Clues to "Little, But Tricky" Words (3–7)

You might be surprised to look in the dictionary at the definitions of some easy, everyday words you're sure you know well. Take *down*, for example. Isn't it just the opposite of *up*? It's that, too, of course. But some dictionaries list over 20 different senses for this "simple" little word.

For example, consider the following sentences:

a. After their recent loss, the team is feeling <u>down</u>. (*dejected*)

b. The man asked him to slow <u>down</u>. (*to a lower level*)

c. Jennie ran <u>down</u> the stairs. (*descending*)

When you are reading, you must determine the meaning of these words from context, judging by the strong words around them, or you might become confused.

Directions: Each sentence in the following sets of sentences contains the same "little, but tricky" word used in different ways. Choose the right sense from the partial list of correct definitions following, and write its key letter in the blank space.

A. Over

_____ 1. The captain showed us <u>over</u> the ship.

_____ 2. Can you tell me what time the play will be <u>over</u>?

_____ 3. A big dog can easily jump <u>over</u> that fence.

> ***Senses:*** a. during; b. upside down; c. throughout; d. more than; e. finished; f. across

B. Through

_____ 1. It was difficult to get the piano <u>through</u> that narrow door.

_____ 2. Jimmy is not <u>through</u> yet.

_____ 3. I got my new job <u>through</u> a recommendation from my counselor.

> ***Senses:*** a. as a result of; b. in one side and out the other; c. among; d. finished; e. around; f. completely

C. Up

_____ 1. Excited about the game, Diana got <u>up</u> early.

_____ 2. When the President entered, everyone stood <u>up</u>.

_____ 3. Squirrels are said to store <u>up</u> nuts so they have food for the winter.

> ***Senses:*** a. to a standing position; b. to a later period; c. aside, away; d. above the ground; e. completely; f. out of bed

(3–7 continued)

D. For

_____ 1. Jan asked me to help her choose a present <u>for</u> her sister.

_____ 2 There is no reason for Denny to be angry, <u>for</u> I didn't mean to insult him.

_____ 3. Mona was trying to use her shoe <u>for</u> a hammer.

> ***Senses:*** a. in favor of; b. in place of; c. suitable to; d. at the price of; e. meant to be received by; f. because

E. By

_____ 1. Grandparents often like to talk about time gone <u>by</u>.

_____ 2. My little sister was sitting <u>by</u> the television.

_____ 3. Judging <u>by</u> the look on her face, I'd say Rosita is really surprised.

> ***Senses:*** a. in or during; b. following in series; c. beside, near; d. past; e. aside, away; f. according to

F. Along

_____ 1. Alex's younger brother always wants to tag <u>along</u> with him.

_____ 2. <u>Along</u> the road to Louisville they saw many beautiful horse farms.

> ***Senses:*** a. in conformity (with); b. together (with); c. lengthwise; d. in a line; e. on or beside the length of

G. Too

_____ 1. I'm sure you'll like their new album, <u>too</u>.

_____ 2. Sometimes Bert can be <u>too</u> stubborn for his own good.

> ***Senses:*** a. belonging with; b. more than enough; c. very; d. also; e. until

H. Off

_____ 1. Would you please turn the light <u>off</u> before you leave?

_____ 2. Felix, the team's star player, seemed a little bit <u>off</u> his game last night.

_____ 3. At the beginning of the school year, vacation seems a long way <u>off</u>.

> ***Senses:*** a. so as to no longer be in operation; b. relieved from; c. not attached; d. at a distance; e. from the substance of; f. not up to the usual standard

© 1995 by The Center for Applied Research in Education

Recognizing Shades of Meaning (3–8)

It's close to impossible to find any two words that mean exactly the same thing, even though you find them listed together in a book of synonyms. The differences between words that have similar meanings but differ in vital details are called their **shades** or **variations of meaning.** You get more out of reading by being aware of subtle differences between synonyms, and, when writing, you should be careful about freely substituting one word for one of its synonyms unless you're sure it's the word you really want.

FOR EXAMPLE, *frigate, yacht,* and *liner* are all ships, but they are very different in type and description.

Directions: You can find the following sets of synonyms in lists of words under the heading of the first word given. To understand the precise sense of each word, you need to know its special shade of meaning. For each set, read the first sentence and the base word's definition. Then match its synonyms to the definitions below, which contain the variations of meaning. Write out the correct synonym in the blank space. You may wish to check the dictionary for this exercise.

A. Journey

The Stewarts enjoyed their journey but were glad to be home.
    (journey: a traveling from place to place)

Synonyms: a. outing   b. voyage   c. trek
                  d. tour   e. expedition   f. pilgrimage

_____ 1. a journey for a purpose such as exploration or battle

_____ 2. a journey made slowly and with difficulty

_____ 3. a long journey, especially by sea or air

_____ 4. a pleasure trip, such as an outdoor ride, walk, picnic, etc.

_____ 5. a trip, as for sightseeing, inspection, or performance

_____ 6. a journey made to a shrine or other sacred place

(3–8 continued)

B. Slow

The runner had a <u>slow</u> start but managed to overtake his opponents.
> (<u>slow</u>: not fast; taking a longer time than is usual)

Synonyms: a. sluggish   b. deliberate   c. gradual
                  d. lackadaisical   e. dawdling   f. leaden

_____ 1. unhurried; steady in movement; not rash or hasty

_____ 2. taking place by degrees; little by little; one step at a time

_____ 3. showing lack of interest or spirit; listless

_____ 4. lacking energy; lazy; not acting with normal vigor

_____ 5. heavy in action, feeling, etc.

_____ 6. wasting time; spending time idly

C. Produce

The playwright is seeking someone to <u>produce</u> his new script.
> (<u>produce</u>: to bring into view; show; make or manufacture)

Synonyms: a. assemble   b. compose   c. construct
                  d. develop   e. generate

_____ 1. to build; devise; to form by putting together parts

_____ 2. to bring into being; cause to be; create

_____ 3. to make up by combining things, parts or elements; to put in proper form or order

_____ 4. to gather into a group; to put or fit together

_____ 5. to make fuller, bigger, better, etc.

Choosing the Right Synonym (3–9)

Directions: From each set of synonyms, choose the one with a shade of meaning that best fits the rest of the sentence, and write it in the blank space. Add endings such as *-s* or *-ed* where needed.

A. Synonyms for Journey

    Choices: a. outing   b. voyage   c. trek

                d. tour   e. expedition   f. pilgrimage

1. According to the pamphlet, the _____ includes stops in London, Paris, and Rome.

2. Most religions have holy places that believers visit on _____.

3. The explorers planned their _____ carefully and made sure of having sufficient supplies.

4. On our last _____, we decided to picnic at Pearson Park.

5. After the exhausting _____ through the jungle heat, the two men wanted rest and water, most of all.

6. Do you think you would enjoy taking a _____ on an ocean liner like the *Queen Elizabeth II?*

B. Synonyms for Slow

    Choices: a. sluggish   b. deliberate   c. gradual

                d. lackadaisical   e. dawdling   f. leaden

1. Eager to go out, Joe did his math homework in a _____ way.

2. Moving with _____ steps, the tired runner could hardly push himself onward.

3. On TV the forecaster predicted a _____ change in the weather, with more sunshine and less rain for the weekend.

4. Letitia tends to be very _____ about making decisions, and she usually makes good ones.

5. Not eating the right foods and being overweight can cause a person to feel _____.

6. The small child, _____ over his meal, was wasting time by pushing peas around his plate with his spoon instead of eating them.

(3–9 continued)

C. Synonyms for Produce

Choices: a. assemble   b. compose   c. construct
              d. develop   e. generate

1. Scientists are working to _____ cures for most major diseases.

2. The builder plans to _____ a new home for himself when he finishes our neighbor's.

3. Everyone in the student body will _____ in the gym tomorrow morning for the rally.

4. The poet _____ a sonnet dedicated to his baby daughter.

5. It is hoped that the suggestion box and bonuses will _____ creative new ideas for operating the business more efficiently.

More Practice with Synonyms (3–10)

Directions: Look up the words that follow the base word in each set of synonyms. On the line that follows, write the special sense that makes each word's shade of meaning different from its synonyms.

A. Clear

All the pictures Bev took with her new camera turned out sharp and <u>clear</u>.
　　(**clear**—easily seen or heard; free from darkness; bright; transparent, etc.)

1. noticeable　_____

2. obvious　_____

3. unmistakable　_____

4. visible　_____

5. distinct　_____

6. limpid　_____

B. Flow

The river <u>flows</u> right through the heart of the city's downtown.
　　(**flow**—to move as liquid does; pour out; move gently and smoothly, etc.)

1. pour　_____

2. gurgle　_____

3. swirl　_____

4. surge　_____

5. circulate　_____

C. Ordinary

It started out as an <u>ordinary</u> day, but it suddenly turned exciting.
　　(**ordinary**—customary, usual, unexceptional, common)

1. humdrum　_____

2. habitual　_____

3. expected　_____

4. routine　_____

5. typical　_____

6. traditional　_____

Putting Synonyms in Their Places (3–11)

Directions: From each set of synonyms, choose the one with a shade of meaning that best fits the rest of the sentence, and write it in the blank space. Add endings such as *-s* or *-ed* where needed.

A. Synonyms for Clear
   Choices: a. obvious   b. noticeable   c. visible
                  d. distinct   e. limpid   f. unmistakable

1. Because of the clouds, the sun was not _____ all day long.

2. Each partner has her own _____ idea about how her business should be run.

3. I'm sure I would recognize the man if I saw him again, for his great height and scarred forehead made his appearance _____.

4. If you know the secret, the solution to the puzzle seems _____.

5. The tiny spot on your sweater is barely _____.

6. The little girl has blonde hair and _____ blue eyes.

B. Synonyms for Flow
   Choices: a. surge   b. swirl   c. gurgle
                  d. pour   e. circulate

1. The wind caused the dry leaves to _____ around in the yard.

2. The small, swift-moving stream seemed to _____ as it flowed over the pebbles on its bed.

3. Would you please _____ me another cup of hot chocolate?

4. Ceiling fans help to _____ the air.

5. During a storm, electrical power can suddenly _____ and cause damage to computers, television sets, and other appliances.

C. Synonyms for Ordinary
   Choices: a. typical   b. expected   c. humdrum
                  d. habitual   e. traditional

1. The _____ snowstorm did not hit last night.

2. If you keep to a regular schedule, soon daily exercise becomes _____.

3. People are always talking about _____ teenagers, but there is really no such thing.

4. The planning committee hopes to make our _____ school festival bigger and better this year.

5. Wishing to escape her _____ life, she dreamed of taking a trip to Paris.

Three Kinds of Words in a Typical Vocabulary
(*Reading Selection 3–12*)

No matter what their age or degree of education, most people's vocabularies are made up of three kinds of words. See if the words in your vocabulary also fit into the following three categories:

1. Words you know well and use freely in everyday conversation and writing.
2. Words you understand, can define, and would use in formal writing—perhaps double-checking first—but do not use in ordinary conversation, sometimes because you aren't sure how to pronounce them and sometimes because they don't seem to fit everyday speech.
3. Words that you recognize and that make sense to you in context, although you can't define them precisely when they stand alone and so don't use them in conversation or writing.

ALL THREE TYPES OF WORDS ARE VALUABLE TO YOU

When you first meet an unfamiliar word in context, you can't be sure when you'll come across it again or how often it's used by people with good vocabularies. When you encounter the same word a number of times, you begin to have a better idea of its shades of meaning and the way that it's used by experienced writers.

As recently-read words become more familiar to you, they will progress from words you know on a "recognition" level to words you understand more fully and use more confidently.

All three types of words are important to your vocabulary. To know a word well, you need to see and/or hear it in a variety of settings so that you understand its various shades of meaning and its proper usage.

What's in a Name? (3–12A)

Directions: Each of the sentences used in this activity has eight different synonyms that correctly complete its meaning. Some will be obvious. Some words are probably unfamiliar. They represent the three types of words in your vocabulary.

On the lines following each sentence, write the words from the list below that sensibly complete its meaning. First, write the words you know well and use freely and label them (1). Next, write the words you understand and can define but do not use in ordinary conversation, labeled (2). If you do not know the meaning of a word and need to find its meaning in the dictionary, write (3) after it.

1. He has the _____ of a classic hero—a strong chin, a direct gaze, and well-shaped lips.

   _____   _____

   _____   _____

   _____   _____

   _____   _____

2. Although their _____ is nice, it seems too small for such a large family.

   _____   _____

   _____   _____

   _____   _____

   _____   _____

3. Feel free to ask her advice, for there's no doubt of her _____.

   _____   _____

   _____   _____

   _____   _____

   _____   _____

Word Choices:

abode	acumen	look	countenance
judgment	domicile	visage	dwelling
face	wisdom	features	house
home	mien	good sense	kisser
prudence	habitation	household	intelligence
sagacity	residence	perspicacity	physiognomy

© 1995 by The Center for Applied Research in Education

Meeting "New" Words in Context (*Reading Selection 3–13*)

Read the following selection, titled "Discontent." When you meet an unfamiliar word, do not stop to look it up, but make an educated guess about its sense in the sentence if it seems obvious to you. If not, continue reading to discover whether additional clues to its meaning follow, or if you can understand the rest of the passage without knowing what this one word means.

Discontent by Joseph Addison (*adapted and abridged*)

According to Socrates[1], if all the misfortunes of mankind were cast into a public stock in order to be distributed equally among everybody, those who now consider themselves most unhappy would prefer the share they already have to that which would be theirs through such a division.

Horace[2] has carried the idea farther and supposes our own hardships or misfortunes are easier to bear than someone else's if we would exchange places.

While sitting in my chair, ruminating about these two remarks, I fell asleep and dreamed that Jupiter[3] proclaimed that every human being should bring his griefs and calamities and throw them in a heap. A large plain was chosen for this purpose. I stood in its center and saw every human being marching one after another, each throwing down his or her load, which immediately grew into a prodigious mountain that seemed to rise above the clouds.

There was a certain lady of thin, airy shape who was very active in this ceremony. She carried a magnifying glass and wore a loose, flowing robe embroidered with weird designs. There was something wild and distracted in her looks. Her name was Fancy.

She led every mortal to the chosen spot, after helping each to choose what to discard. I felt great pity to see my fellow-creatures groaning under their troubles and misfortunes.

Several persons, however, gave me diversion. One brought a fardel, very carefully concealed in an old embroidered cloak. After he threw it into the heap, I discovered it was poverty. Another, after much puffing, threw down his burden. Upon examination, I discovered it to be his wife.

A multitude of lovers were saddled with whimsical burdens, made up of cupid's arrows and flames. Oddly, though they sighed as if their hearts would break under such calamities, they could not talk themselves into throwing them into the heap. After a few faint efforts, they shook their heads and marched away, as heavily laden as they were before.

---

[1]an ancient Greek philosopher
[2]Roman poet and satirist
[3]Supreme god of the Romans

I saw multitudes of old women throw down their wrinkles, and there were great heaps of red noses, large lips, and rusty teeth. I was surprised to see the greatest part of the mountain was made up of bodily deformities . . .

There were also distempers of all sorts, though I could not but note that many were more imaginary than real. One little packet was a complication of all the diseases incident to human nature, and it was in the hand of many fine people. It was called the spleen—containing ill will, peevish temper, and grudges.

What surprised me most was that not a single vice or folly was thrown into the whole heap. I had thought that everyone would take this opportunity to get rid of passions, prejudice, and frailities.

I particularly noticed one profligate fellow who, I did not question, came loaded down with his crimes. Upon searching his bundle I found that, instead of throwing away his guilt, he only laid down his memory. Another worthless rogue flung away immodesty instead of his ignorance.

When the whole race of mankind had cast down their burdens, the phantom Fancy, seeing me an idle spectator, came near and held her magnifying glass before my eyes. I no sooner saw my face than I was startled by its shortness compared to its breadth. This made me very out of humor with my own countenance, which I threw from me like a mask. Luckily, the man before me had just thrown down his visage, which it seems was too long for him. I believe the very chin was, modestly speaking, as long as my whole face. We both had the opportunity to mend ourselves. All the contributions were now brought in, and everyone was free to exchange misfortunes for those of another.

As we stood around the heap, there was scarcely a person who did not discover what he thought pleasures and blessings of life, and wondered how their owners ever came to see them as burdens or grievances. As we were regarding this confusion of miseries, Jupiter issued a second proclamation. Everyone was free to exchange his affliction and return to his habitation with whatever other bundle was delivered to him.

Upon this, Fancy began to hand out the whole heap with incredible activity, recommending to everyone a particular choice. The hurry and confusion was too great to express, yet here are some observations I made at the time.

An old, grey-headed man who had laid down a stomach ailment and who, I found, wanted an heir to his estate, snatched up an undutiful son that had been thrown in the heap by an angry father. The graceless youth, in less than a quarter hour, pulled the old gentleman by the beard and had liked to have knocked his brain out. Upon meeting the true father, who came toward him with a bad pain in his stomach, the old gentleman begged him to take his son again and give him back his ailment. But they were incapable, either of them, to recede from the choice they had made.

The female sex were very busy bartering for features. One was trucking a lock of grey hairs for a pus-filled boil. Another was trading a short waist for a pair of rounded shoulders. But, in every case, everyone thought the new blemish, as soon as she had it in her possession, was more disagreeable than the old one.

I must not omit my own experience. My friend with the long visage had no sooner taken upon him my short face, but he looked so grotesque in it that I could not help laughing at myself. The poor gentleman was so sensible of the ridicule that I found he was ashamed of what he had done.

On the other hand, I found I had no great reason to triumph. When I went to touch my forehead, I missed its place and clapped my fingers upon my upper lip. Besides, as my nose was exceedingly prominent now, I gave it two or three unlucky knocks as I was aiming at some other part of my face.

I saw two other gentlemen in similar ridiculous circumstances. These had made a foolish swap between a pair of thick bowed legs and two long trapsticks that had no calves on them. One man looked like a man walking on stilts while the other made such awkward circles as he attempted to walk that he scarcely knew how to move forward on his new supporters.

The heap was at last distributed among the two sexes who made a most piteous sight. The whole plain was filled with murmurs and complaints, groans and lamentations.

Jupiter, at length taking compassion on the poor mortals, ordered everyone a second time to lay down their loads with a design to give everyone his own again. They discharged this with a great deal of pleasure.

Then Jupiter commanded Fancy to disappear and sent in her stead a goddess of a quite different figure. Her motions were steady and composed, her aspect serious but cheerful. Her name was Patience.

She had no sooner placed herself by the Mount of Sorow than, remarkably, the whole sunk to such a degree that it did not appear a third as big as before. She afterward returned to every man his own proper calamity and, teaching him how to bear it in the most commodious manner, he marched off contentedly, being well pleased that he had not been left to his own choice of the kind of evil which fell to his lot.

Beside the several morals to be drawn from this vision, I learned never to repine at my own misfortunes or envy the happiness of another.

It is impossible to make a right judgment of a neighbor's suffering, for which reason I have determined never to think too lightly of another's complaints, but to regard the sorrows of my fellow creatures with sentiments of humanity and compassion.

Discussing "Discontent" (3–13A)

Directions: Write your answers to the following questions.

1. Why would the poor man want to hide his poverty in an embroidered cloak?

   _____

   _____

   _____

   _____

2. What would make the lovers decide not to give up their burdens?

   _____

   _____

   _____

   _____

3. Why did one man want to get rid of his memory? Why would another choose to

   get rid of his modesty but keep his ignorance? _____

   _____

   _____

   _____

4. What do you find humorous about this selection? What serious point is its au-

   thor trying to make? _____

   _____

   _____

5. One definition of *fantasy* lists *fancy* as one of its synonyms, and it was also the
   name of the first goddess. In what way does imagination play a part in the people's attitudes towards their misfortunes and miseries?

   _____

   _____

   _____

© 1995 by The Center for Applied Research in Education

Discontent: Understanding Meaning Through Context
(3–13B)

Directions:

Step One. Find the words in the story that are listed below and underline each. Some words will be underlined more than once because unfamiliar words are easier to understand when seen in more than one context.

Step Two. Reread the story, and write the meaning of each word, as you determine it from context, on the first line following it. Be sure that you judge a word by its present context, not by another meaning you happen to know. (*Note:* Place a dash after a word if you have previously defined it.)

Step Three. Save the second line for a comparison with one of the word's dictionary senses.

1. cast _____ _____

2. stock _____ _____

3. ruminating _____ _____

4. proclaimed _____ _____

5. calamities _____ _____

6. prodigious _____ _____

7. distracted _____ _____

8. mortal _____ _____

9. diversion _____ _____

10. fardel _____ _____

11. multitude _____ _____

12. whimsical _____ _____

13. calamities _____ _____

14. multitudes _____ _____

15. distempers _____ _____

16. complication _____ _____

17. incident _____ _____

18. spleen _____ _____

19. peevish _____ _____

20. folly _____ _____

21. frailities _____ _____

22. profligate _____ _____

23. rogue _____ _____

24. breadth _____   _____
25. humor _____   _____
26. countenance _____   _____
27. visage _____   _____
28. proclamation _____   _____
29. affliction _____   _____
30. habitation _____   _____
31. ailment _____   _____
32. graceless _____   _____
33. bartering _____   _____
34. trucking _____   _____
35. visage _____   _____
36. grotesque _____   _____
37. sensible _____   _____
38. prominent _____   _____
39. trapsticks _____   _____
40. calves _____   _____
41. piteous _____   _____
42. lamentations _____   _____
43. discharged _____   _____
44. stead _____   _____
45. aspect _____   _____
46. commodious _____   _____
47. repine _____   _____
48. compassion _____   _____

UNIT 4

A Meeting of Minds

The aim of this unit is to show students that good reading involves more than recording, storing, and regurgitating information—a computer is better at doing that than the human brain.

The activities in "A Meeting of Minds" require students to be mentally active participants. They ask students to make decisions about what they are reading and to become aware that writers also make many choices and decisions that readers should learn to recognize. One example is how a writer may purposely choose a single word to affect the reader's attitude towards a subject, and good readers need to be alert for such slanted words when they're reading.

Throughout the unit, students will become engaged in looking beyond the surface to discern the writer's meaning, whether it is seeing how use of high-flown vocabulary is not the same as profundity of thought or discovering how to recognize the difference between fact and opinion.

Humor is one of the most difficult kinds of literature to teach because many students fail to recognize it as wit. "A Meeting of Minds" also takes up the difference between serious and humorous writing, arming students with knowledge of the techniques that let readers know a writer doesn't intend to be taken seriously.

NOTES ON ACTIVITIES

Identifying a Writer's Point of View (4–1A)

As a result of their introductory work with point of view, students need to develop the habit of determining whether a selection is written in first person or third person. Although the examples do not distinguish between fiction and nonfiction, such awareness is needed to understand the subtleties in point of view, which will be discussed later and which are an integral part of higher level reading of short stories, novels, and poetry.

A Matter of Opinion (4–5)

To help students make their decisions about whether a statement is fact or opinion, advise them that such attributions as "Ted remarked" and "according to Sue" should be accepted as accurate. Since some students may be confused by this detail, it may need additional emphasis and explanation.

In Other Words: Familiar Sayings in Disguise (4–9)

Students can have more fun with this exercise if they break the sayings down to manageable phrases. For example, "the person's manual appendage" becomes "hand." They may also enjoy doing this exercise as a group activity.

If most members of your class seem unfamiliar with these sayings, you may want to write them on the chalkboard and allow students to match these, too.

A Taste of Humor (4–10A)

To someone who doesn't understand it, humor can seem "stupid." The purpose of these activities is to show that humorous writing need not be uproariously funny . . . just should not be taken seriously.

Encourage students to realize that, when something is humorous, the writer *doesn't* mean what he or she says . . . and expects (or hopes) the reader to know this. It is not important for students to memorize the possible techniques of humor. It is important for them to be aware that both writers and readers have a part in making humor "work."

Serious or Humorous? Determining the Difference (4–12) and (4–13)

In assessing answers to part 3 of each set of questions, allow for individual differences in descriptions of the subjects of serious paragraphs. If humorous, variation may be possible, as noted. However, be sure students use each technique of humor only once per exercise.

Students may want to discuss some of the ideas expressed in these examples, especially those concerning the attitude of a mother toward her obviously teenaged son in Part II, Example 4, by Nikki Giovanni.

Saying It the "Nice" Way: Euphemisms (Class Activity)

A valuable class project is to share students' funds of euphemisms—which they'll discover they have, even though they're unfamiliar with the term itself.

They'll see that euphemisms are different from doublespeak in one sense, because they are a way of avoiding saying something bothersome to the speaker.

Concerning someone they care about, many people avoid making a reference to dying or death. Since this is such a common feeling, students should be able to share many different expressions they've heard used in place of being straight forward. They will also discover how and why people use euphemisms.

Have students volunteer expressions they know. List them on the chalkboard, and then ask class members to group together those euphemisms that reveal a similar attitude towards the subject.

Among the possibilities:

- pass away, go to one's reward—*expressing a respectful or reverent attitude*
- kick the bucket, bought the farm—*trying to affect a joking manner*
- blown away, terminated—*acting tough and unfeeling*

(Students should have many additional examples of their own, both familiar and some perhaps surprising.)

You may wish to continue by discussing euphemisms used for various occupations, such as janitor, garbageman, housewife, waiter, and others.

NOTE: No reproducible activity sheet accompanies this activity.

From the Writer's Point of View
(Reading Selection 4–1)

A writer can only write about what he or she knows, believes, or has imagined—whether it comes from personal experience, independent research, or what someone else has written or said.

That's why one of America's most honored writers, Henry David Thoreau, reminded his readers at the beginning of his most famous book, *Walden,* that it is always the first person speaking, whether or not a writer chooses to speak as "I."

Skillful readers need to be aware of writers' choice of point of view, whether they decide to use a personal approach, speaking directly to the reader and calling themselves "I" or "We," or to choose an objective approach, omitting these words unless quoting someone else.

There are two basic points of view:

First Person: The writer uses *I, we,* or one of the other forms such *me, my, mine, myself, us, our,* or *ourselves* outside of quotation marks.

EXAMPLE: During my travels through the Orient, I discovered that people are people, no matter how strange their customs seemed to me at first.

Third Person: The writer distances him- or herself from the subject, omitting the first-person pronouns unless directly quoting someone else.

EXAMPLE: A traveler through the Orient will discover that people are people no matter how strange their customs seem at first.

Explain why the following is also third person: On his return from a trip through the Orient, Bruce Snyder said, "I discovered that people are people, no matter how . . ."

Identifying a Writer's Point of View (4–1A)

Part A Directions: On the line, indicate the writer's point of view by writing the words **first person** or **third person.** (*NOTE:* The words *first* and *third* are not the complete or correct terms, so do not accurately describe the point of view.)

_____ 1. During the lengthy trial, members of the jury were not supposed to read newspaper accounts or listen to radio or TV reports about it.

_____ 2. I will never forget the thrill of going downhill skiing for the first time in my life.

_____ 3. As Americans, we owe it to ourselves and our country to remember the ideals on which our nation was founded.

_____ 4. Even though you love the sun, don't forget that its rays are dangerous and can lead to unwelcome consequences.

_____ 5. Although a used book sale seemed like a good idea to me, the rest of the committee disagreed.

_____ 6. The audience was enthusiastic at first, but the performance did not live up to its expectations.

_____ 7. Students should not be surprised if their career goals change many times as they progress from childhood to adulthood.

_____ 8. Some fashion designers want to turn people into walking billboards for their styles, in my opinion.

_____ 9. "It was not my intention to mislead you," the television interviewer assured her guest.

_____ 10. "I could see that you wondered what was up, but I wanted to surprise you," Jill told me at the party.

A Note About You

Since it is "always the first person speaking," writers must be careful about using the word *you,* and readers should be aware of its different effects.

(4–1A continued)

Part B Directions: Consider the examples below, and write out your answers to the question or questions following each.

1. If you are planning a trip abroad, you should coordinate your wardrobe carefully before beginning to pack.

   Question: Who is the "you" in this sentence? _____

   _____

2. When you enter a classroom, the first thing you do is look to see if the teacher is there.

   Question: What is wrong with this use of "you"?_____

   _____

3. a. You have an important choice to make, and you're having trouble deciding. What do you do next?
   b. When someone has an important choice to make, it's sometimes difficult to decide what to do next.
   c. When there's an important choice to make, I sometimes have trouble deciding what to do next.

   Questions:

   (1) Which of the three statements above is written in first person? _____

   (2) Which sounds as if it would offer the most expert advice? _____

   (3) Do you find it easy or difficult to identify with the "you" in example **a**?

   Why or why not? _____

   _____

   _____

Name _____ Date _____ Period _____

Writing in First- and Third-Person Points of View (4–1B)

Directions: Write 10 original sentences of at least 12 words each, five using the first-person point of view and five in third person. Vary your choices of first-person pronouns, and include at least four direct quotations. Be sure to label each sentence clearly to show the point of view you chose.

1. _____

   _____

   Point of view: _____

2. _____

   _____

   Point of view: _____

3. _____

   _____

   Point of view: _____

4. _____

   _____

   Point of view: _____

5. _____

   _____

   Point of view: _____

6. _____

   _____

   Point of view: _____

7. _____

   _____

   Point of view: _____

8. _____

   _____

   Point of view: _____

9. _____

   _____

   Point of view: _____

10. _____

    _____

    Point of view: _____

Always the First Person (4–2)

Using first-person forms of the pronoun "I" are always necessary when someone is writing about such topics as personal experiences and plans. Although not necessary, good writers also sometimes use such first-person expressions as "it seems to me" when they want to emphasize the fact that others might disagree or because they wish everyone to recognize the idea as their own.

On the other hand, beginning writers may add "in my opinion" as if to say, "Well, it's just my own personal opinion, and I'm really not sure whether it's right or wrong." This weakens their writing, since writers can only speak for themselves and good readers know this.

Directions: In each of the following examples, indicate whether the use of first-person forms are necessary or weaken the sentence. Write **W** in the blank space if use of first-person pronouns weakens the example and **N** if necessary to it.

_____ 1. The way I see it, it would be hard to drive in a snowstorm if your windshield wipers weren't working.

_____ 2. It is difficult for me to imagine what it would be like to be colorblind.

_____ 3. The books of Charles Dickens, it seems to me, are some of the most-admired novels ever written in English.

_____ 4. Some people expect more of others than they do of themselves, I think.

_____ 5. To be fair, in my view, the laws should treat everyone equally.

_____ 6. Since I left, my friends write that there have been many changes in my former school.

_____ 7. My advice is to consider the possible effect before accusing someone of being unfair.

_____ 8. What to me seems obvious might confuse someone else.

_____ 9. In my opinion, American teens need to have a healthy, well-balanced diet and avoid eating too much junk food.

_____ 10. I think the answer is right, but it was marked wrong.

© 1995 by The Center for Applied Research in Education

Name _____ Date _____ Period _____

A Meeting of Minds (4–3)

Part A Directions: Compare the following:

      a. The world is flat.
      b. I believe that the world is flat.
      c. In times gone by, many people believed that the world was flat.

1. Which one or more of the above statements would you classify as true? (Identify by key letter.) _____
2. Which seems most obviously untrue? _____
3. Which, if true, would make someone today seem foolish? _____

A good reader should always remember that, whether or not a writer uses the first person "I," he or she is always responsible for choosing words, examples, the order of presentation, and so on, down to every detail written.

Skillful readers do not base their decisions about the truth of a piece of writing upon whether or not it is labeled nonfiction. They depend upon their own judgment and opinion, resulting from thoughtful attention to the words, ideas, and proof the writer presents.

Part B Directions: Read the following examples and decide which are backed up with adequate proof and which merely express opinion. A statement that provides a source, such as "According to the Principal, Mr. Harding, Easton High is the best in town," can be considered to have sufficient proof—the fact being that he said it, not that what he said is necessarily true. Write **O** if the sentence simply expresses an opinion, and **SP** if it offers satisfactory proof.

_____ 1. This year's homecoming queen was beautiful.

_____ 2. This year's homecoming queen was blonde, blue-eyed Margi Macy.

_____ 3. The audience gave the performers a standing ovation.

_____ 4. The audience enjoyed every moment of the performance.

_____ 5. Four members of the audience fainted during the preview showing of the horror film, "The Glob of Glu."

_____ 6. "The Glob of Glu" is the most frightening and exciting horror film ever made.

_____ 7. Pete Contos said, "'The Glob of Glu" was the most exciting horror film I've ever seen."

_____ 8. Most Americans are against the new education bill proposed by Senator Bacon.

_____ 9. Senator Bacon stated, "Letters received in my office show the voters favor my education bill, five to one."

_____ 10. Trailing by 16 points at halftime, the team closed the gap in the second half and lost by a single point.

_____ 11. According to Brutus, Caesar might become an evil tyrant if he became king.

_____ 12. Caesar might become an evil tyrant if he became king and therefore had to be assassinated.

Providing Satisfactory Proof (4–4)

Directions: Using examples from the news, your reading, or your own imagination, write a total of ten original sentences about five different topics. Have one that represents opinion and one containing satisfactory proof for each subject. In the blank space in front of each sentence, label **O** or **SP** to indicate your intention.

_____   1. _____

               _____

_____   2. _____

               _____

_____   3. _____

               _____

_____   4. _____

               _____

_____   5. _____

               _____

_____   6. _____

               _____

_____   7. _____

               _____

_____   8. _____

               _____

_____   9. _____

               _____

_____   10. _____

               _____

Name _____ Date _____ Period _____

A Matter of Opinion (4–5)

Directions: In the following groups of sentences, decide whether each statement should be considered true or whether it is a matter of opinion. Write the letter **T** for True or **O** for Opinion in the blank space.

1.
   _____ a. I don't believe in ghosts.
   _____ b. People in many parts of the world believe that the spirits of dead people return as ghosts.
   _____ c. The belief in ghosts is superstitious nonsense.
   _____ d. To deny the existence of ghosts shows a lack of imagination and insufficient research.

2.
   _____ a. Senator Nolan declared that the President's new foreign trade policy would prove disastrous.
   _____ b. The President assured voters that his new foreign trade policy means increased economic growth.
   _____ c. The President's new foreign trade policy looks promising on the surface but has a number of shortcomings.
   _____ d. In a poll taken yesterday, the majority of Senators expressed themselves in favor of the President's new foreign trade policy.

3.
   _____ a. School is not fun; it's hard work.
   _____ b. Kids will only learn in school when they have fun doing it.
   _____ c. Today's parents are overly involved in their children's lives, according to family psychologist John Rosemond.
   _____ d. The average American child comes to school not possessing the habit of respecting adults.

VOICE YOUR OPINION

You might wish to discuss some of the statements made in this exercise that you think are matters of opinion. Explain the ideas on both sides of the topic, and provide proof and examples to back up the views with which you agree.

Discuss the chosen topics as a class or in groups. Your teacher might ask you to write about one of these subjects later.

Recognizing "Charged" Words (4–6)

A "charged" word is one that carries an extra kick with it and that can subtly influence a reader, sometimes without his or her being aware of it.

FOR EXAMPLE, notice the difference between the following two sentences:
a. The teacher <u>demanded</u> that we read our compositions orally.
b. The teacher <u>asked</u> that we read our compositions orally.
Which underlined word makes the teacher seem mean and bossy? Is there any question about its being "demanded"?

Part A. Directions: Often the change of one or two words in a sentence will serve to create a different impression in the reader's mind. Read the following pairs of sentences, and answer the question or questions concerning each.

1. a. The suspect <u>claimed</u> that he was visiting friends at the time of the robbery.
   b. The suspect <u>stated</u> that he was visiting friends at the time of the robbery.

   Question: Which underlined word plants a doubt in the reader's mind about

   the suspect's truthfulness? _____

2. a. The <u>mob</u> gathered outside the auditorium began to grow restless when the doors did not open on time.
   b. The <u>crowd</u> gathered outside the auditorium began to grow restless when the doors did not open on time.

   Question: Explain how <u>crowd</u> and <u>mob</u> create different effects on a reader.

   _____

   _____

3. a. Some people <u>have the belief</u> that money is the root of all evil.
   b. Some people <u>take the attitude</u> that money is the root of all evil.

   Question 1: Explain the difference between an <u>attitude</u> and a <u>belief</u>.

   _____

   _____

   Question 2: Which underlined phrase more clearly reveals the writer's dis-

   agreement with such people's feelings about money? _____

   _____

(4–6 continued)

4. a. Hank <u>said</u> that he was <u>responsible</u> for the error.
   b. Hank <u>admitted</u> that he was <u>guilty</u> of the error.

   Question 1: Which pair of underlined words makes the error seem more serious?

   _____

   Question 2: Explain the difference between being <u>responsible</u> and being <u>guilty</u>.

   _____

   _____

CHOOSING BETWEEN WORDS

Part B. Directions: From the pair of choices in parentheses following each sentence, select the one that will add <u>less</u> of a negative charge to the meaning. Write your choice on the line.

1. The scholarship committee _____ Alex's application.
   (rejected; did not accept)

2. Such expressions are _____ and should not be used in a classroom setting. (inappropriate; tasteless)

3. After a while, you forget how _____ Deidra looks and only remember how nice she is. (plain; ugly)

4. The teacher said Brad was _____ to let his friend copy his paper. (unwise; foolish)

5. Opponents of the plan _____ the accuracy of some of the (attacked; questioned) details presented as facts resulting from thorough research.

Dealing with Doublespeak (4–7)

Doublespeak is the use of words and phrases that, at first glance, seem to mean one thing but really mean something else. It's the sometimes unintentional but more often deliberate misuse of words to mislead, cover up, or impress, rather than explain.

Directions: Read the following "Doublespeak" words and phrases, and try to figure out what they really mean. See how many you can understand on your own, and write their meanings on the line. Then match the rest to their definitions at the bottom of the second sheet.

1. behavior modification _____
   _____
   _____

2. physically challenged _____
   _____
   _____

3. gender neutral _____
   _____
   _____

4. correctional facilities _____
   _____
   _____

5. inoperative _____
   _____
   _____

6. inner city _____
   _____
   _____

7. corporate downsizing _____
   _____
   _____

8. ethnic cleansing _____
   _____

9. culminating activity _____

_____

_____

10. free gift _____

_____

_____

11. disadvantaged _____

_____

_____

12. job termination _____

_____

_____

13. scholastic facilitator _____

_____

_____

14. exceptional child _____

_____

_____

15. politically correct _____

_____

_____

a. a teacher
b. broken; not working
c. firing workers to increase profits
d. handicapped; having a disability
e. method of discipline; ways to make kids behave
f. an item not free because you must buy another item to get it
g. a word or words not found offensive by a member of the group it refers to
h. not favoring either sex, male or female
i. one well above or below average
j. poor, needy
k. prisons
l. a test
m. the act of being fired from a workplace
n. the poor section of a town
o. people getting rid of a group of people they hate

Fancy Words, Simple Ideas (4–8)

The clearest, most direct way of stating an idea is best. Yet sometimes a reader must puzzle out the simple idea hidden within a complicated piece of writing.

For example, a writer, trying to impress readers with his originality and vocabulary, wrote "an equine quadruped of a variegated color and shade," instead of "a horse of a different color," which says the same thing much better!

Directions: Each of the following sentences has a very ordinary meaning, once you get past its attempt to say something simple in an excessively complex way. Choose from the simply written versions at the bottom of the page, and write the key letter that matches its overly fancy restatement.

_____ 1. He responded to the interrogatory in the affirmative.

_____ 2. The malfunction of my requisite recollective mental process culminated in the unintentional unfulfillment of my obligator scholastic requirements.

_____ 3. A manifestation of unbridled enthusiasm emanated from the assembled multitude.

_____ 4. The protective overstructure of the multi-compartmented private domicile failed to eliminate the infiltration of precipitation.

_____ 5. At this particular point in time the full ramifications of the subject under consideration make it impossible for me to give a definitive response.

    a. The house's roof leaked.
    b. He is hard to understand.
    c. I can't give you a definite answer right now.
    d. I forgot to do my homework.
    e. The crowd cheered.
    f. He said yes.

In Other Words: Familiar Sayings in Disguise (4–9)

Directions: See if you can figure out the well-known sayings rewritten in too fancy, overly complicated versions. It will help to read the entire sentence and begin from what you know.

Write the original version on the line that follows each sentence. The number of words in the original is written in parentheses.

1. A solitary plumed, warm-blooded vertebrate with organs of flight in the person's manual appendage deserves an evaluation equivalent to double that quantity in a low, woody organism with spreading branches.

   (11 words)_____

   _____

2. A member of the species commonly designated Homo Sapiens who exhibits an insufficiency of normal sagacity faces imminent separation from his spendable financial assets.

   (8 words)_____

   _____

3. One one-hundreth of a basic American paper monetary unit preserved for future eventualities is synonymous with an identical amount acquired through purposeful effort.

   (7 words)_____

   _____

4. A representative of the fluttering feathered tribes that exceeds the expectations of timely arising acquires the possession of the long and slimy, soft-bodied, creepy, crawly creatures.

   (6 words)_____

   _____

5. Preference attaches itself to the advisability of failing to adhere to the prescribed limits of promptitude as a superior alternative to an act's everlasting omission.

   (4 words)_____

   _____

A Sense of Humor *(Reading Selection 4–10)*

Did you hear about the eyeglass maker who was arrested for making a spectacle of himself?

If you recognize something that's meant to be humorous, you "get the point." If not, you don't "get it," and you might think it stupid.

He said, "I wuz framed."

Humor is not meant to be taken seriously, and it's not always intended to make you laugh out loud. Humor can include body language and verbal wit—and much of its success depends upon doing or saying the unexpected on purpose as a surprise.

Humor can be *slapstick*—when a guy in baggy pants whacks his buddy with a specially-made stick that cracks like a pop gun—and startles an audience into laughing.

Humor can make you chuckle or simply enjoy seeing the clever twist it puts on something familiar by using a pun—or play upon the two meanings of a word like *spectacle*.

Written humor is not always easy to "catch," for the signals of a smiling jokester or baggy pants comedian are missing. But, good writers of humor are not trying to throw a verbal curve or fool their readers. As participants in the writer/reader compact, humorists offer their readers a fresh and original way of looking at the world. And, readers in humor take an active part by being alert to its signals, noting the writers' clever ways of saying the unexpected and "getting the point" of written humor.

A Taste of Humor (4–10A)

Directions: Following are five examples of humorous writing, along with one or more techniques of humor the writer has used.

Read each selection and answer the question or questions concerning it. Plan to keep a list of the techniques that signal humor in your English notes or notebook for future reference.

A. People often say to me: "Dave, as a professional columnist, you have a job that requires you to process large quantities of information on a timely basis. Why don't you get a real haircut?" — "Learning About Life on the Internet" by Dave Barry

Technique: seemingly senseless change of subject (*non sequitur*)

Questions:

(1) Write a question that would more logically follow the first statement, "People often say . . ." _____

_____

(2) What is also humorous about Barry's use of the word "often"?

_____

_____

B. For more than a quarter of a century I have been a high school English teacher—an unrepentant inmate in the house of correction of composition. — *Anguished English* by Richard Lederer

Technique: play on words

Questions:

(1) What is the usual meaning of "house of correction"? _____

_____

(2) What play on words allows Lederer to claim he is an inmate of one?

_____

_____

C. Animals talk to each other, of course. There can be no question about that; but I suppose there are very few people who can understand them. I never knew but one man who could. I knew he could, however, because he told me so himself . . . This was Jim Baker . . . — "Blue Jays" by Mark Twain, from *A Tramp Abroad*

Technique: flaws in logic; unbelievable proof

Questions:

(1) What is the only proof given that Jim Baker understands animals' language?

_____

(2) Why isn't this proof good? _____

(3) Is it truth or opinion to "There can be no question about" animals having the ability to talk? Explain the reasons for your choice. _____

_____

D. *(More about Jim Baker)*
According to Jim Baker, some animals have only a limited education and use only very simple words and scarcely ever a comparison or a flowery figure, whereas certain other animals have a large vocabulary, a fine command of language, and a ready and fluent delivery; consequently these latter talk a great deal, they like it, they are conscious of their talent, and they enjoy "showing off." — "Blue Jays" by Mark Twain, from *A Tramp Abroad*

Technique: exaggeration; making fun of human traits by giving them to animals

Questions:

(1) Although animals communicate, why wouldn't they really have a "large vocabulary"? _____

_____

(2) Give two other ways Jim Baker says animals use language that are better fitted to describing human speech. _____

_____

(3) What negative qualities, also typically human, are shown by those with "a fine command of language"? _____

_____

(4–10A continued)

E. Do you love me or do you not?
   You told me once but I forgot. — Author Unknown

Technique: an unexpected twist or contradiction

Questions:

   (1) What is the usual reason for asking someone if he or she loves you?

       _____

   (2) What does saying "I forgot" seem to indicate about the asker's feelings towards the

       other person? _____

       _____

   (3) Why does this seem contradictory? _____

       _____

   (4) Do you feel that many people, at times, would like to express this same attitude

       toward someone? Explain why or why not. _____

       _____

A Taste of Humor (4–10B)

Directions: Read each selection and answer the question or questions concerning it. Plan to keep a list of the techniques that signal humor in your English notes or notebook for future reference.

A. Sonnets are of two types: (1) Shakespearean and (2) Petrarchan. Another way of classifying them is (1) Good and (2) Bad. Sonnets may be easily recognized,* because they contain fourteen lines. Occasionally a poet has written a sonnet that was a little shorter, because he could think of nothing more to say, or a little longer, because he was being paid by the line. — "The Sonnets" by Richard Armour, from *Twisted Tales from Shakespeare*

---

* By anyone who can count.

Technique: ridiculous statements; flaws in logic

Questions:

   (1) Considering the first method of classifying sonnets, why is the second way obviously meant to be humorous? _____

      _____

   (2) Why can't the footnote be taken seriously either? _____

      _____

      _____

   (3) Why wouldn't it be logical for some sonnet to be longer or shorter than others?

      _____

      _____

   (4) What humorous twist is there in a sonnet writer's being paid by the line?

      _____

      _____

B. A few weeks ago I turned down an opportunity to worry about litter in space. It happened when a man who was being interviewed on television said that as many as 7,200 objects, most of them the sort of thing that a good citizen might drop in the nearest trash receptacle, are orbiting the earth. Just as soon as I heard the man say that, I heard myself say, "Well, none of them belong to me."

    I think you could call it an instinctive response, familiar to anyone who grew up with a sibling—a sister in my case—and thus became accustomed to using as his first line of defense "I'm not going to clean up her mess!" . . . — "Space Mess" by Calvin Trilling, from *Enough's Enough*

Technique: clever, unexpected twists of language; a sense of the ridiculous

Questions:

(1) Is an opportunity usually something good or bad? _____

Give an example of something you would consider an opportunity _____

_____

(2) Does the first sentence refer to a genuine opportunity? Why or why not?

_____

_____

(3) Why isn't most of the litter in space the "sort of thing" someone would just drop in

a trash bin? _____

_____

(4) How does the author relate the problem of litter in space to family life?

_____

_____

C. *(to be read solemnly)*
Mister Thomas Jones
Said to James, his son:
"Never swallow bones,
Never point a gun.

Never slam a door,
Never play with flames,
Never shun the poor."
"Dull old fool!" said James. — "Bringing Him Up" by Lord Dunsany

Technique: surprise; making fun of typical human behavior

Questions:

(1) Why does the repetition of "never" seem typical of adult and parent behavior to-

wards young people? _____

_____

(2) Why does "swallow bones" create a humorous impression? _____

_____

(3) a. Why is "flames" a surprising choice of words? _____

_____

b. Why did the poet "have" to choose "flames"? _____

(4–10B continued)

(4) Why is James' response considered typical of young people? _____

_____

(5) Is the advice basically good or bad? Explain your choice. _____

_____

_____

D. "The most ferocious, relentless and bloodthirsty American predator isn't the wolf, or the bear, or the bob-cat," said Tim. "It's the mosquito . . ."

"Today there probably isn't a mosquito in the Upper Peninsula of Michigan that measures more than four inches from wing tip to wing tip," continued Tim. "But in the old days . . . there were times when all hands had to stay in camp with the doors and windows barred. Outdoors, folks had to kick a hole in the swarms before they could spit.

"Every mosquito weighed two pounds or more and had a wing spread of up to fifteen inches . . ." — "Lake Superior Wild Life" by Stanley D. Newton, from *Paul Bunyan of the Great Lakes*

Technique: exaggeration; ridiculous examples

Questions:

(1) How does Tim exaggerate the size of the mosquitoes found in the old days? _____

_____

(2) Is he accurate in reporting the wingspan of mosquitoes in Michigan today? Explain

why or why not. _____

_____

(3) What humorous reason is given for the folks daring to go outside in spite of the

mosquitoes? _____

(4) The stories about Paul Bunyan are called tall tales. How does the very beginning

show that Tim is telling a whopper? _____

_____

(4–10B continued)

E. *Qu.*—How fast duz sound travel?

Ans.—This depends a good deal upon the natur ov the noise yu are talking about. The sound ov a dinner horn, for instance, travels a half a mile in a sekoned, while an invitashun tew git up in the morning I hav known to be 3 quarters ov an hour going up two pair ov stairs, and then not hav strength enuff left tew be heard. — Josh Billings, from *Mark Twain's Library of Humor*

Technique: dialect or misuse of language; making fun of human nature

Questions:

(1) Why is this an obviously wrong answer to the question?

_____

_____

(2) Why does the answer given fit the typical attitude of many people?

_____

_____

(3) Why does the misspelling seem appropriate for this type of answer?

_____

_____

10 SIGNALS OF HUMOR

1. Exaggeration
2. Intentional flaws in logic
3. Surprise; unexpected twists
4. Dialect; misuse of language
5. *Nonsequitur* (something that doesn't fit or follow)
6. A sense of the ridiculous
7. Play on words; puns
8. Unbelievable proof
9. Obvious contradictions
10. Making fun of typical human traits or behavior

Note: Humor often contains a number of techniques, some closely related, so opinions on those used may vary. As you become familiar with reading humor, you will discover other approaches to add to this list.

103

22
2

In All Seriousness (4–11)

When writers wish to be taken seriously, there are no special signals needed. They simply take a straightforward approach and say what they have to say. Although their subjects are different and their purposes vary, they have no need to alert their readers as humorists do.

Directions: Following are five examples of paragraphs that have a serious approach, although their points of view and purposes vary. Read each and answer the questions.

A. It began with the dream of a boat. At a certain moment in my life (I was thirty-two), I was struck with what seemed an irresistible urge to become a sailor—or more accurately, to acquire a boat . . . I had no fantasy of sailing to the South Seas. Still, every boat dream has some suggestion of escape—in my case, escape from responsibilities, from the security of a university career, from the perils of everyday life.

My dream had another component . . . not simply owning but building a boat. I ought to have known better. — "Wind and Water" by Witold Rybcznski, from *The Most Beautiful House in the World*

Questions:

(1) What is the point of view? _____

(2) What two words give a clue to the type of work the author does?

_____

(3) What are the first two parts of the author's dream? _____

_____

(4) What is the final part or component? _____

(5) What words suggest that the final part was more difficult than he'd dreamed?

_____

B. It was sheep-shearing time in Southern California; but sheep-shearing was late at the Señora Moreno's. The Fates had seemed to combine to put it off. In the first place, Felipe Moreno had been ill. He was the Señora's eldest son, and since his father's death, had been at the head of his mother's house. Without him, nothing could be done on the ranch, the Señora thought . . . — from Chapter One of *Ramona* by Helen Hunt Jackson

Questions:

(1) What is the point of view? _____

(2) What is a clue that this story concerns an earlier time in American history?

_____

(4-11 continued)

(3) Who was considered the head of the ranch? _____

Why? _____

_____

(4) What had forced the annual sheep-shearing to be delayed?

_____

C. "Beauty is truth, truth beauty,"—that is all
Ye know on earth, and all ye need to know. — The final two lines of "Ode on a Grecian
Urn" by John Keats

Questions:

(1) What is the point of view? _____

(2) a. Does the "Ye" or *you* most probably represent *everyone* or *one specific person*?

_____

b. Explain the reasons for your choice. _____

_____

(3) The final two lines of the poem sum up the poet's response after admiring an ancient Greek urn or decorated vase. From the choices below, pick the one that best expresses the poet's attitude and circle its key letter.
   a. You must study an artist's life in order to understand the truth of what he or she creates.
   b. A sense of truth, like a sense of beauty, lies deeper than facts.
   c. Education is generally a waste of time.

D. Without water the desert is nothing but a grave, and is useless either as a dwelling-place or even as a high-road for the living. If the traveller's food is poor he will go hungry, if his road is long he will be weary, if his lot is hard he will be lonely, but to all these things he can become inured. No one, however, can be inured to thirst. When the craving for water assails a man he will forget all else in his frantic search for it, knowing that life itself depends on finding it . . . — from *The Gobi Desert* by Mildred Cable and Francesca French

Questions:

(1) What is the point of view? _____

(2) Judged from context, what must be the meaning of the word *inured?*

_____

(3) What must be the meaning of *assails?* _____

(4) List the three things the authors say a traveller can endure more easily than a lack of water.

a. _____

b. _____

c. _____

E. When shall I forget the night I first set foot on African soil? I am the sixth generation in descent from forefathers who left this land. The moon was at the full and the waters of the Atlantic lay like a lake. All the long slow afternoon as the sun robed herself in her western scarlet with veils of misty cloud, I had seen Africa afar. Cape Mount—that mighty headland with its twin curves, northern sentinel of the realm of Liberia—gathered itself out of the cloud at half past three and then darkened and grew clear. On beyond flowed the dark low undulating land quaint with palm and breaking sea . . . — from "What Is Africa to Me" by W. E. Burghardt Du Bois

Questions:

(1) What is the point of view? _____

(2) The "realm of Liberia" must be a _____ in Africa.

(3) As a black American, what is the probable reason the author's forefathers left

their African homeland? _____

(4) What phrase proves the visit made a lasting impression on the author?

_____

Name _____ Date _____ Period _____

Serious or Humorous? Determining
the Difference—Part I (4–12)

Directions: Following are five paragraphs, including both serious and humorous writing. *For each paragraph:*

(1) Indicate whether it is *serious* or *humorous*.

(2) Give its point of view.

(3) a. If *humorous,* write the technique that signals it as humor. Choose from the following, and use each only once: making fun of human nature; flaws in logic; exaggeration; surprise or unexpected twists.

   b. If *serious,* write a short phrase telling its subject, such as "a first visit to Africa."

A. It is customary to place the date for the beginnings of modern medicine somewhere in the mid-1930s, with the entry of sulfonamides and penicillin into the pharmacopoeia, and it is usual to ascribe to these events the force of a revolution in medical practice. This is what things seemed like at the time. Medical practice was upheaved, revolutionized indeed. Therapy had been discovered for great numbers of patients whose illnesses had previously been untreatable. Cures were now available . . . — by Lewis
Thomas

Questions:

   (1) Serious or Humorous? _____

   (2) Point of view? _____

   (3) Signal, if Humorous; or Subject, if Serious: _____

   _____

B. A baseball weighted your hand just so, and fit it. Its red stitches, its good leather and hardness like skin over bone seemed to call forth a skill both easy and precise. On the catch—the grounder, the fly, the line drive—you could snag a baseball in your mitt, where it stayed, *snap,* like a mouse locked in its trap . . . You could curl your fingers around a baseball, and throw it in a straight line. When you hit it with a bat it cracked—and your heart cracked, too, at the sound. It took a grass stain nicely, stayed round, smelled good, and lived lashed in your mitt all winter, hibernating. — From *An American Childhood* by Annie Dillard

Questions:

   (1) Serious or Humorous? _____

   (2) Point of view? _____

   (3) Signal, if Humorous; or Subject, if Serious: _____

   _____

C. **Principles of Legal Writing**

1. Never use one word where ten will do.
2. Never use a small word where a big one will suffice.
3. Never use a simple statement where it appears that one of substantially greater complexity will achieve comparable goals.
4. Never use English where Latin, *mutatis mutandis,* will do . . . — by Fred Rodell, from *Virginia Law Review*

Questions:

(1) Serious or Humorous? _____

(2) Point of view? _____

(3) Signal, if Humorous; or Subject, if Serious:_____

_____

D. How do I love thee? Let me count the ways.
I love thee to the depth and breadth and height
My soul can reach . . . — XLIII, *Sonnets from the Portuguese* by Elizabeth Barrett Browning

Questions:

(1) Serious or Humorous? _____

(2) Point of view? _____

(3) Signal, if Humorous; or Subject, if Serious: _____

_____

E. I have done things and had things happen to me and nobody knows about it. So I am writing about it so people will know. Although there are a lot of things I could tell about, I will just tell about the jumping because that is the most important. It gave me the biggest thrill. I mean high jumping, standing and running. You probably never heard of a standing high jumper but that's what I was. I was the greatest jumper ever was. — "That's What Happened to Me" by Michael Fessier

Questions:

(1) Serious or Humorous? _____

(2) Point of view? _____

(3) Signal, if Humorous; or Subject, if Serious: _____

_____

Serious or Humorous? Determining the Difference—Part II (4–13)

Directions: Following are five paragraphs, including both serious and humorous writing. *For each paragraph:*

(1) Indicate whether it is *serious* or *humorous.*

(2) Give its point of view.

(3) a. If *humorous,* write the technique that signals it as humor. Choose from the following, and use each only once: making fun of human nature; flaws in logic; exaggeration; surprise or unexpected twists.

   b. If *serious,* write a short phrase telling its subject, such as "a first visit to Africa."

A. The first grand discovery was time, the landscape of experience. Only by marking off months, weeks, and years, days and hours, minutes and seconds, would mankind be liberated from the cyclical monotony of nature . . . — Introduction to Book 1, *Time,* of
The Discoverers by Daniel Boorstin

Questions:

(1) Serious or Humorous? _____

(2) Point of view? _____

(3) Signal, if Humorous; or Subject, if Serious: _____

_____

B. . . . Said Eugene Oliver, "Ah was travellin' in Texas and laid down and went to sleep. De skeeters bit me so hard till Ah seen a ole iron wash-pot, so Ah crawled under it and turned it down over me good so de skeeters couldn't git to me. But you know dem skeeters bored right thru dat iron pot . . . — *Mules & Men* by Zora Neale Hurston

Questions:

(1) Serious or Humorous? _____

(2) Point of view? _____

(3) Signal, if Humorous; or Subject, if Serious: _____

_____

C. Lie on! While my revenge shall be,
   To speak the very truth of thee. — by Lord Nugent

(4–13 continued)

Questions:

    (1) Serious or Humorous? _____

    (2) Point of view? _____

    (3) Signal, if Humorous; or Subject, if Serious: _____

    _____

D. Everyone says babies are difficult; it's just not true. Changing diapers, wiping pabulum from chins, heating bottles in the middle of the night are a snap compared to picking up your own telephone . . . and never hearing a familiar voice, either friend or relative, but rather a barbarian girl or boy demanding, "Tom home?" I was at first annoyed by the question and then by the tone, but I've trained myself to respond only to the question asked: "Why, yes, he is. How kind of you to call and inquire. I must go now." I then hang up. The barbarian response next was, "Can I speak to Tom?" to which I replied, again, as sweetly as possible: "It appears you are quite capable. I hear you very well. I must go now." Finally they reached the desired question: "May I speak to Tom?" which, unfortunately, elicits, "I'm sorry, dear, but Thomas may not use the telephone until his grades improve." . . . — "In Sympathy with Another Motherless Child" by Nikki Giovanni, from *Sacred Cows . . . and Other Edibles*

Questions:

    (1) Serious or Humorous? _____

    (2) Point of view? _____

    (3) Signal, if Humorous; or Subject, if Serious: _____

    _____

E. Swimming in a summer pond, we notice how natural it is to use all four limbs to travel along. We are a quadruped again; even the stroke we do is called "the crawl." Opening our eyes underwater, we look instead ahead or up. A log sunk on the bottom looms like a snapping turtle. The stems of the pond lilies, rising five feet, tangle one's arms a little frighteningly . . . — by Edward Hoagland

Questions:

    (1) Serious or Humorous? _____

    (2) Point of view? _____

    (3) Signal, if Humorous; or Subject, if Serious: _____

    _____

UNIT 5

The Reader as Reporter

Before beginning to write, reporters must gather the right information for their stories. To do so, they must be sure to ask the right questions first.

A reporter's five W's and an H—and Rudyard Kipling's "six serving men"—are Who, What, When, Where, Why, and How. Together they ask—and elicit the answers to—almost all the questions anyone needs to ask, except those involving a matter of choice or decision.

Like reporters, good readers develop the habit of looking for, noting, and filing away the answers to these questions in their memories as they read.

The exercises in "The Reader as Reporter" first take up the 5 W's and an H in newspaper-style leads, first paragraphs written especially to present the answers in a readily determinable form. Additional exercises allow students to refine their skills on selected passages from various literary authors and works.

A sense of organization is also important—both for the reporter and the reader—and this unit also takes up the subject of outlining, not only as a means for making clear notes as a preliminary step in writing a report or studying for a text, but also as a practical way to train students to organize ideas logically.

Much has been said about the importance of grammar to writing, but almost nothing about its value to reading. Yet, an understanding of grammar is of enormous help in getting to the heart of difficult sentences and passages—not only when reading prose but also when reading poetry.

In fact, the 5 W's and an H answer the questions of grammar, too.

Who or What? finds the subject noun or pronoun.

Did or Does What? finds the verb.

When? Where? Why? How? elicit responses that are adverbs or adverbial phrases and clauses.

Since some students are resistant to the teaching of grammar, you may want to delay introducing this quality of the 5 W's and an H until students are comfortable with the idea of reader as reporter and have successfully completed a number of exercises.

The ability to draw correct conclusions is another attribute of good reporters and good readers, so this unit will provide practice in distinguishing between valid and invalid conclusions to be drawn from a variety of passages.

NOTES ON ACTIVITIES

The Five W's and an H (Reading Selection 5–1)

In finding "Who or What?" and "Did or Does What?" make sure that students get to the actual action in the lead. Point out that, in the example, the "Who or What" is not the *blaze* and the "Did What" is not *destroyed an Ashland Street carryout.* Explain that all parts must fit together to form a complete answer to these key questions. Some leads provide no answer for "How" or "Why," as in the example, which doesn't specifically state "Why."

Writing Original Leads (5–3)

Writing leads helps students practice brevity and appreciate the worth and placement of words. When they have finished writing, you may want them to exchange papers or work in groups to identify the five W's and an H in one another's papers.

The 5 W's and an H in Prose Literature (5–5)

If students are not familiar with the word *prose,* you may need to define the term and its relationship to literature. You may also want to list types of literary prose, in addition to short stories, novels, and essays, such as biography and autobiography.

In going over the directions, explain to students that they need only identify an unnamed narrator as "the first-person speaker," if his or her name is not actually given in the paragraph itself. They should not assume narrator and author are always the same.

When discussing the answers, you might explain that Lincoln was giving Stowe credit for increasing public aversion to slavery by writing the antislavery novel, *Uncle Tom's Cabin,* and so "made the war." You may want students to find a summary of its plot, if they are not familiar with its story of Little Eva and Simon Legree.

Using the 5 W's and an H in Poetry, Too (5–7)

One reason for students' difficulties with poetry is they have trouble figuring out what the words mean on the most basic level. This is often because poets frequently do not state their ideas in a straightforward Subject-Verb-Complement order. When they reach a confusing or contorted statement, good readers almost automatically look for Who? and Did What?

Although this and the following exercise do not attempt to get to the underlying meaning, they endeavor to show students how to feel less lost when approaching poetry.

Identifying the "You's" in Poems (5–8A)

In going over the answers to this exercise, you might also want students to identify the When's, Where's, Why's, and How's, when given.

The Need for Organization (Reading Selection 5–9)

The exercises given in this unit include subtopics down to the Arabic numerals 1, 2, 3, 4, etc.; and the use of small letters a, b, c, etc., is also noted. If you teach advanced classes or students express curiosity, you may want to tell them that the next set of subtopics would be Arabic numerals in parentheses, (1), (2), (3), etc., followed by small letters, (a), (b), (c), etc.

Outlining "The Background of Mythology" (5–11A)

When completing the outline, students should be reminded to look for the key words that serve as subtopics relating to the main one. Subtopics at the same level, such as A, B, and C, should also be related to each other in some way. For example, the Hyperboreans, Ætheopians, and peoples of the Elysian Plain were all races imagined by the Greeks to live at Earth's edge.

Students need not copy out exact phrases, but should be encouraged to be both accurate and concise. Answers will necessarily vary, but they should touch on the points given in the answer key.

The 5 W's and an H (*Reading Selection 5–1*)

Just as good newspaper reporters know the basics of every story they write, so does the good reader want to be sure of the basics when reading.

Both begin with the six basic questions reporters learn to include in their leads—the first paragraph of a news story.

They are **Who? What? When?**
Where? Why? and **How?**

Reporters call them the five W's and an H.
When reading, you might think of them as:

Who? (or What?)
Did or Does What?
When? Where? Why? How?

Not every sentence or paragraph will answer every one of the final four questions, but by the time you have finished an entire story or selection, you should be able to answer them all.

EXAMPLE:

Fire investigators have determined arson caused an estimated $150,000 blaze that destroyed an Ashland Street carryout yesterday. Empty gas cans were found discarded at the scene.

Who or What?	Fire investigators
Did what?	determined arson caused fire
Where?	on Ashland Street
When?	yesterday
Why?	by discovery of empty gas cans at scene
How?	Not stated, but logically as a result of their discovery.

In the News: The 5 W's and an H (5–1A)

Directions: Following are leads or opening paragraphs of five newspaper stories. Read each, and fill in the answers to the 5 W's and an H that it contains. If one is not included, mark a dash on the line for its answer. Each includes at least five of the six. You need not copy all the exact words.

1. Benson High's Xavier Powers was named Athlete of the Year at the all-city sports banquet Friday in recognition of his record-breaking scoring in basketball this year.

   Who or What? _____

   Did What? _____

   When? _____

   Where? _____

   Why? _____

   How? _____

2. In her recent book, *Fads and Fantasies,* psychologist Betina Everett warns teenagers against setting false goals, by exposing twisted standards of beauty and behavior in TV and films.

   Who or What? _____

   Did What? _____

   When? _____

   Where? _____

   Why? _____

   How? _____

3. Armed with signed petitions, opponents of a new sports arena plan to stage a protest at tonight's city council meeting. They hope to convince members to vote it down.

   Who or What? _____

   Did What? _____

   When? _____

   Where? _____

   Why? _____

   How? _____

(5–1A continued)

4. By non-stop barking, whining, and pawing, their pet dog Spunky alerted the Garcia family members of fire in their Sloane Avenue home early this morning. All escaped unharmed.

Who or What? _____

Did What? _____

When? _____

Where? _____

Why? _____

How? _____

5. Eastgate's 86–85 win Tuesday night over chief rival Bayfield strengthens the home team's chance for the league championship, putting Eastgate in a tie for first with Henley.

Who or What? _____

Did What? _____

When? _____

Where? _____

Why? _____

How? _____

In the News: The 5 W's and an H (5–1B)

Directions: Following are leads or opening paragraphs of five newspaper stories. Read each, and fill in the answers to the 5 W's and an H that it contains. If one is not included, mark a dash on the line for its answer. Each includes at least five of the six. You need not copy all the exact words.

1. Rayman Webster, Farmingdale junior, was awarded top honors in this year's statewide Young Artists contest at ceremonies today in Capital City. His painting was named best of 2,000 entries.

   Who or What? _____

   Did What? _____

   When? _____

   Where? _____

   Why? _____

   How? _____

2. "Somebody had to do it," said Toni Grace, 14, who saved 4-year-old Sheryl Wayne from drowning in a neighbor's pool yesterday. The toddler fell in, after straying from home.

   Who or What? _____

   Did What? _____

   When? _____

   Where? _____

   Why? _____

   How? _____

3. Sought as treasure and history, a sunken Spanish galleon was discovered Saturday off Mexico's coast. Divers credit the find to an ancient map, scientific diving equipment, and luck.

   Who or What? _____

   Did What? _____

   When? _____

   Where? _____

   Why? _____

   How? _____

(5–1B continued)

4. In order to prevent further robberies, police today issued a warning against con men now operating in Carlton, who identify themselves as furnace inspectors to gain entry into homes.

   Who or What? _____

   Did What? _____

   When? _____

   Where? _____

   Why? _____

   How? _____

5. TV star Clarissa Kraft said her job "looks more glamorous than it is," when interviewed today by local media. The young actress described long hours and grueling rehearsals.

   Who or What? _____

   Did What? _____

   When? _____

   Where? _____

   Why? _____

   How? _____

Checking Out Leads (5–2)

Directions: In your local or school newspaper, find three examples of well-written leads, each containing at least five of the six elements of the five W's and an H.

Either cut out and mount, or copy the leads on your own paper. Then list the Who or What? Did or Does What? When? Where? Why? How? contained in each.

Writing Original Leads (5–3)

Directions: Because reporters must learn to get ideas across without wasting words, one rule for writing leads limits each to no more than 28-30 words. You may wish to check the leads in previous exercises and your local newspapers to see how closely they follow this count.

Then, write five original leads, based on school activities, a scene in a story you've read, or your own imagination. Include at least five of the six W's and an H in each. Rewrite and polish your work to cut out unnecessary words and deliver the facts clearly in fewer than 30 words.

Textbook Topics: The 5 W's and an H (5–4)

Directions: It's important to be aware of the five W's and an H when reading factual information in textbooks, encyclopedias, and other reference books, too. After reading each of the following paragraphs, fill in the answers to the 5 W's and an H that it contains. If one element is not included, mark a dash on the line for its answer. Each includes at least five of the six. You need not copy all the exact words.

1. Calvin Coolidge became the 30th President of the United States in 1923. He was the vice president of Warren G. Harding, who died suddenly in August 1923, amidst rumors of government scandal and corruption. As Harding's successor, Coolidge was known for his personal honesty and his belief in a sound economic policy and tax cuts.

   Who or What? _____

   Did What? _____

   When? _____

   Where? _____

   Why? _____

   How? _____

2. Founded in the U.S. in 1874, osteopathic medicine treats patients through the manipulation of their affected bones and muscles. Osteopathy is based on the theory that most ailments are due to the misalignment of bones or other conditions involving muscles and cartilage.

   Who or What? _____

   Did What? _____

   When? _____

   Where? _____

   Why? _____

   How? _____

3. In spite of the association in many people's minds, the Eskimos, though natives of the cold far north, rarely spend their winters in igloos or snow huts like those so often pictured in storybooks. Instead, in winter Eskimos traditionally build shelters of sod, wood, or stone, while in summer they live in tents of caribou or seal skin.

   Who or What? _____

   Did What? _____

   When? _____

(5–4 continued)

Where? _____

Why? _____

How? _____

4. Part of a short but glorious period of American history, pony express riders carried the mail from Saint Joseph, Missouri, to Sacramento, California. Traveling some 2,000 miles in about eight days, they attained this speed by riding in a series of relays, changing horses and riders on each leg. Begun in 1860, the pony express was no longer needed in October 1881 when a transcontinental telegraph line offered even better communication.

Who or What? _____

Did What? _____

When? _____

Where? _____

Why? _____

How? _____

5. Based on the theory of continental drift proposed by German meteorologist Alfred Wegener in 1912, plate tectonics envisions the Earth consisting of a single super-continent, called Pangaea, 100 million years ago, instead of the seven continents and many islands we know today. Wegener based his theory on the apparent jigsaw fit of the coastlines of continents on opposing sides of the Atlantic Ocean.

Who or What? _____

Did or Does What? _____

When? _____

Where? _____

Why? _____

How? _____

The 5 W's and an H in Prose Literature (5–5)

You may not find the answers in the first sentence or even paragraph of short stories, novels, essays, and other kinds of literature. Yet, keeping the reporter's questions in mind can help you discover the writer's purpose when you are reading literature.

Ask yourself: **Who** or **What** is doing the action? **Did What? When? Where? How?** And, of great importance, **Why?**

Directions: After reading each of the following selections, fill in the answers to the 5 W's and an H that it contains. If "Who?" is identified only as "I," write "first-person speaker." Add name or other identification, if given. If one is not included, mark a dash in its space.

1. It was a hot August morning, Saturday, six o'clock, and Mr. and Mrs. Delahanty still lingered at the breakfast table. Six-thirty is midmorning for a rancher in summer; but Mrs. Delahanty hadn't finished talking about the hat. — "The Hat" by Jessamyn West, from *Cress Delahanty*

   Who or What? _____

   Did What? _____

   When? _____

   Where? _____

   Why? _____

   How? _____

2. There was no hurry, except for the thirst, like clotted salt, in the back of his throat, and Durante rode on slowly, rather enjoying the last moments of dryness before he reached the cold water in Tony's house. There was really no hurry at all. He had almost twenty-four hours' head start, for they would not find his dead man until this morning . . . — "Wine in the Desert" by Max Brand

   Who or What? _____

   Did What? _____

   When? _____

   Where? _____

   Why? _____

   How? _____

3. Over a century ago, in November, 1863, Harriet Beecher Stowe[1] wrote that she was going to Washington to satisfy herself that "the Emancipation Proclamation was a reality and a substance not to fizzle out. . ." She meant to talk to "Father

---

[1] Author of *Uncle Tom's Cabin*

© 1995 by The Center for Applied Research in Education

Abraham himself." When she was ushered into his study, her frailty startled President Lincoln. As his big knotted hand took her small one, he quizzed: "So this is the little lady who made this big war." Pressed by her eagerness, Lincoln assured Harriet Beecher Stowe that he was determined to issue the Emancipation Proclamation on New Year's Day. — "A Century of Negro Portraiture in American Literature" by Sterling A. Brown

Who or What? _____

Did What? _____

When? _____

Where? _____

Why? _____

How? _____

4. It was a bright frosty morning when I bade adieu to the farm, the birthplace of my little Agnes, who, nestled beneath my cloak, was sweetly sleeping on my knee, unconscious of the long journey before us into the wilderness. The sun had not as yet risen. Anxious to get to our place of destination before dark, we started as early as we could . . . — "A Journey to the Woods" by Susannah Moodie

Who or What? _____

Did What? _____

When? _____

Where? _____

Why? _____

How? _____

5. There were times in early autumn—in September—when the greater circuses would come to town—the Ringling Brothers, Robinson's, and Barnum and Bailey shows, and when I was a route-boy on the morning paper, on those mornings when the circus would be coming in I would rush madly through my route in the cool and thrilling darkness that comes just before the break of day, and then I would go back home and get my brother out of bed. — "Circus at Dawn" by Thomas Wolfe

Who or What? _____

Did What? _____

When? _____

Where? _____

Why? _____

How? _____

More Practice with Prose Literature (5–6)

Directions: Some of the sentences below may concern more than one person or thing. When you are filling the 5 W's and an H, make sure that your answers relate to the one "Who" or "What" that the entire selection is really about and the main action that is involved.

1. On his way to the station William remembered with a fresh pang of disappointment that he was taking nothing to the kiddies. Poor little chaps! . . . Their first words always were as they ran to greet him, "What have you got for me, daddy?" and he had nothing . . . — "Marriage a la Mode" by Katherine Mansfield

   Who or What? _____

   Did What? _____

   When? _____

   Where? _____

   Why? _____

   How? _____

2. On the 19th of December in 1949, when I had been living in Paris for little over a year, I was arrested as a receiver of stolen goods and spent eight days in prison. My arrest came about through an American tourist whom I had met twice in New York, who had been given my name and address and told to look me up . . . — "Equal in Paris" by James Baldwin from *Notes of a Native Son*

   Who or What? _____

   Did What? _____

   When? _____

   Where? _____

   Why? _____

   How? _____

3. The moment Krueger stepped aboard the steamer he was aware of a vague sense of something gone wrong. He had never understood the atavism behind these instinctive warnings, but he had had them before and usually he had been right.
   He paused at the head of the gangplank . . . Down in the well, the Brazilian stevedores were just finishing with the last of the cargo. The steward was standing just inside a door marked *De Segunda Clase* . . . — "A Habit for the Voyage" by Robert Edmond Alter

(5–6 continued)

Who or What? _____

Did What? _____

When? _____

Where? _____

Why? _____

How? _____

4. The winter found a cowboy in southwestern Nebraska who had just ended a journey from Kansas City, and he swore bitterly as he remembered how little boys in Kansas City followed him about in order to contemplate his wide-brimmed hat. — "Galveston, Texas, in 1895" by Stephen Crane

Who or What? _____

Did What? _____

When? _____

Where? _____

Why? _____

How? _____

5. He has changed, Molly thought, the instant she glimpsed her husband in the station at Montreal. He has changed . . . The thought thudded hollowly through her mind, over and over during the long train ride into northern Quebec.

   It was more than the absence of uniform. His face seemed so still, and there was something about his mouth—a sort of slackness . . . — "The Old Woman" by
Joyce Marshall

Who or What? _____

Did What? _____

When? _____

Where? _____

Why? _____

How? _____

Using the 5 W's and an H in Poetry, Too (5–7)

To understand poetry, you first need to know its "Who's" and "What's." That's why a reporter's questions are helpful when you're reading poetry. Often you'll find that the subject—the "Who?" or "What?"—doesn't come at the beginning. That's true of such sentences as:

EXAMPLE 1: *From a great distance came a faint cry for help.*

EXAMPLE 2: *After crying and fussing for almost an hour and refusing to be soothed or quieted, the baby finally fell asleep.*

Directions: Given are the opening lines from some of the world's best-known poems. After each, write the "Who or What?" and "Did or Does What?" where indicated. If the lines also answer one of the other key questions—When, Where, Why, or How—first indicate the question and then give its answer on the lines that follow.

1. In Xanadu did Kubla Khan
    A stately pleasure-dome decree
   Where Alph, the sacred river, ran,
   Through caverns measureless to man,
      Down to a sunless sea. — from "Kubla Khan" by Samuel Taylor Coleridge

   Who or What? _____

   Did or Does What? _____

   _____

   _____

2. By the rude bridge that arched the flood,
     Their flag to April's breeze unfurled,
   Here once the embattled farmers stood,
     And fired the shot heard 'round the world. — from "The Concord Hymn" by
                                                         Ralph Waldo Emerson

   Who or What? _____

   Did or Does What? _____

   _____

   _____

3. The harp that once through Tara's halls
     The soul of music shed,
   Now hangs as mute on Tara's walls
     As if that soul were fled . . . — "The Harp That Once Through Tara's Walls"
                                                          by Thomas Moore

(5–7 continued)

Who or What? _____

Did or Does What? _____

_____

_____

4. By a route obscure and lonely,
   Haunted by ill angels only,
   Where an Eidolon, named Night,
   On a black throne reigns upright,
   I have reached these lands but newly . . . — from "Dream-land" by Edgar Allan
   Poe

   Who or What? _____

   Did or Does What? _____

   _____

   _____

5. Between the dark and the daylight,
   When the light is beginning to lower,
   Comes a pause in the day's occupations,
   That is known as the Children's Hour . . . — "The Children's Hour" by Henry
   Wadsworth Longfellow

   Who or What? _____

   Did or Does What? _____

   _____

   _____

6. Weary of myself, and sick of asking
   What I am, and what I ought to be,
   At this vessel's prow I stand, which bears me
   Forwards, forwards, o'er the starlit sea. — "Self-Dependence" by Matthew Arnold

   Who or What? _____

   Did or Does What? _____

   _____

   _____

A Word About "You" in Poetry (*Reading Selection 5–8*)

"O world, I cannot hold thee close enough!"

In this line by Edna St. Vincent Millay, who or what does the poet mean by her use of "thee," which is an older, polite form of the word *you*?

The answer is found in the first two words. By "thee," Millay means "world." In other words, she cares so much for the earth and its life that she's saying, "I cannot hold you, the world, close enough."

Poets use the word *you*—and its older forms *thee, thy, thou,* and *thine*—in a variety of ways. The reader must look for the clues and judge each poem for itself. Here are examples of several different meanings *you* can have.

1. **You** can be someone the poet loves or know.

   EXAMPLE: *"How do I love thee, let me count the ways . . ."*

2. **You** can be an object, a part of nature, or even one's own heart or soul.

   EXAMPLE: *"Thou blossom bright with autumn dew . . ."*

3. **You** can be the reader or listener.

   EXAMPLE: *"Ask not what your country can do for you . . ."*

4. **You** can also be the average person or people in general.

   EXAMPLE: *"You would think the fury of aerial bombardment
   Would rouse God to relent . . ."*

5. **You** may not be openly stated, but simply understood.

   EXAMPLE: *Please listen to my story.*
   Understood as: *(You) please listen to my story.*

Identifying the "You's" in Poems (5–8A)

Directions: After reading the following lines of poetry, explain whether the poet's use of "you" or one of its older forms is stated or unstated, and also give its meaning. Also supply the answers to "Who or What?" and "Did What?" in the spaces provided.

1. Have you heard of the wonderful one-hoss shay,
   That was built in such a logical way
   It ran a hundred years to a day . . . — "The One-Hoss Shay" by Oliver Wendell
   Holmes

   Who or What? _____

   Did or Does What? _____

   Is *you* stated or unstated? _____

   What does *you* mean? _____

2. When I am dead, my dearest,
   Sing no sad songs for me . . . — from "Song" by Christina Georgina Rosetti

   Who or What? _____

   Did or Does What? _____

   Is *you* stated or unstated? _____

   What does *you* mean? _____

3. Hear the mellow wedding bells—
   Golden bells!
   What a world of happiness their harmony foretells! — from "The Bells" by Edgar
   Allan Poe

   Who or What? _____

   Did or Does What? _____

   Is *you* stated or unstated? _____

   What does *you* mean? _____

© 1995 by The Center for Applied Research in Education

4. Good people all, of every sort,
    Give ear unto my song,
And if you find it wondrous short,
    It cannot hold you long. — from "Elegy on the Death of a Mad Dog" by Oliver
                                                                    Goldsmith

Who or What? _____

Did or Does What? _____

Is *you* stated or unstated? _____

What does *you* mean? _____

5. Tiger, Tiger, burning bright
In the forest of the night,
What immortal hand or eye
Could frame thy fearful symmetry? — from "The Tiger" by William Blake

Who or What? _____

Did or Does What? _____

Is *you* stated or unstated? _____

What does *you* mean? _____

6. Sigh no more, ladies, sigh no more,
    Men were deceivers ever;
One foot in sea, and one on shore,
    To one thing constant never . . . — from *Much Ado About Nothing* by William
                                                                    Shakespeare

Who or What? _____

Did or Does What? _____

Is *you* stated or unstated? _____

What does *you* mean? _____

7. It was many and many a year ago,
    In a kingdom by the sea,
That a maiden lived whom you may know
    By the name of Annabel Lee.
And this maiden she lived with no other thought
    Than to love and be loved by me. — from "Annabel Lee" by Edgar Allan Poe

Who or What? _____

Did or Does What? _____

Is *you* stated or unstated? _____

What does *you* mean? _____

The Need for Organization (*Reading Selection 5–9*)

Reporters need to organize their facts and ideas before writing. And you, as a reader, need to form an idea of how you want to "store" the ideas and information you get from your reading.

One way to store it is in your memory. Another is on paper, in outline form. An outline is most convenient if you need to refer to the information later to study for a test or give a report.

Some writers do not like to write from outlines, believing they get in the way of the creative process and might "block out" fresh ideas. Yet a good outline should not attempt to include every detail. It should serve mainly to "jog" your memory and preserve the factual names, numbers and data that are difficult to retrieve from your memory alone.

Practice with outlines can also help you learn to pick out and organize thoughts, ideas, and facts while you are reading.

Here is a sample outline. You may check paragraph 1 of activity 5–4 "Textbook Topics" to find the source of part I.

Calvin Coolidge

I. Became 30th U.S. President
   A. Took office in 1923
      1. Was vice president to Warren G. Harding
      2. Became President upon Harding's death
   B. Known for personal honesty
      1. Replaced scandal-ridden Harding administration
      2. Believed in sound economic policy
      3. favored tax cut
II. Opposed government interference in business, etc. . . .

SUGGESTIONS FOR WRITING GOOD OUTLINES

1. Use short phrases or sentences, but avoid mixing both in the same outline.
2. Number the main topics with Roman numerals: I, II, III, IV, etc.
3. Use capital letters for their subtitles: A, B, C, D, etc.
4. Number the next set of subtopics, if any, with Arabic numerals: 1, 2, 3, 4, etc.
5. If other subtopics are needed, use small letters: a, b, c, etc.
6. All topics, if given subtopics, should have no fewer than two.
7. Indent subtopics as shown in the examples.
8. Use periods at end *only* if entries are written in sentence form.

Specialists in Sleep (*Reading Selection 5–10*)

Some students at Bowling Green State University major in sleep, but they don't earn their degrees by dozing in class. In fact, these doctoral candidates, who are studying to be sleep specialists in the field of psychology, are likely to spend their nights in the speech lab, wide awake, discovering what happens while others are sleeping.

According to speech lab director Dr. Pietro Badia, scientists still don't understand enough about sleep to specify in great detail what is normal and abnormal. And sleepers themselves can't say what happens because everyone experiences a total loss of memory when actually asleep. As a result, some people can honestly believe they didn't sleep a wink all night when, in fact, scientific monitoring equipment shows they slept soundly. On the other hand, some people report having a normal night's sleep although monitors prove they've actually awakened as many as 500 times.

To obtain accurate information, students working in the Sleep Lab learn to score and evaluate the results from sleep-monitoring instruments, which record 1,000 to 1,500 feet of paper from just one night's sleep. A camera that "sees" in total darkness is focused on volunteer sleepers, paid up to $20 per night to be videotaped and observed from the control center. As the first step, student researchers must "wire" the volunteers to a series of electrodes that record their wave patterns in six distinct areas. Sleep specialists must know not only the proper placement of electrodes but also the meaning of the curves, peaks, and waves scribbling across multi-tiered graphs and creating mounds of paperwork, each with its own story to tell . . .

Outlining "Specialists in Sleep" (5–10A)

Directions: Read the selection "Specialists in Sleep," and then complete its outline. Match the answers provided at the end, and write each in the blank space after the correct letter or numeral. The information in the outline should closely follow the order in which it is given in the selection.

Specialists in Sleep

I. Major in sleep offered Bowling Green State University students
  A. _____
    1. _____
    2. _____
  B. _____
    1. _____
    2. _____

II. Sleep not fully understood, according to lab directior Dr. Pietro Badia
  A. _____
  B. _____
  C. _____
    1. _____
    2. _____

III. How lab and students obtain accurate information
  A. _____
    1. _____
    2. _____
  B. _____
    1. _____
    2. _____
  C. _____
    1. _____
    2. _____

Choose from the following:

Able to "see" in total darkness

Are candidates for doctoral degree

Difference between scientific results and people's honest beliefs

Knowledge needed of proper placement and interpretation of results

Likely to spend nights in speech lab

1,000–1,500 feet of paper recorded in one night

Others reporting sound sleep monitored awakening up to 500 times

Don't earn degree dozing in class

Graphs, mounds of paperwork—with own stories to tell

Scientists unable to specify what is normal and abnormal

Scored and evaluated by students

Seek to discover what happens during sleep

Videotapes allow observation from control center

Some monitored as sleeping soundly contrary to their opinions

Stay awake while others are sleeping

Volunteers "wired" to electrodes recording wave patterns in six areas

Total loss of memory experienced during sleep

Studying to be sleep specialists in field of psychology

Cameras also focused on volunteer sleepers

Sleepers recorded by sleep-monitoring instruments

The Background of Mythology
(*Reading Selection 5–11*)

The religions of ancient Greece and Rome are extinct. The so-called divinities or gods of Olympus have not a single worshipper among living men. They belong now not to the department of theology or religion, but to those of literature and thought. There they still hold their place and will continue to hold it, for they are too closely connected with the finest productions of poetry and art, both ancient and modern, to pass into oblivion.

The Greeks thought the earth was a flat and circular disk. They believed that their own country occupied the middle of it and that its central point was either Mount Olympus, the abode of the gods, or Delphi, so famous for its oracle, who answered them with utterances coming from the gods.

As pictured by the Greeks, the circular disk of the Earth was crossed from west to east and divided into two equal parts by the *Sea,* as they called the Mediterranean, and its continuation . . . Around the earth flowed the *River Ocean,* its course being from south to north on the western side of the earth, and in a contrary direction on the eastern side. It flowed in a steady, equable current, unvexed by storm or tempest.

According to the Greeks, special races of people lived near the edge of the earthly disk. The northern portion was supposed to be inhabited by a happy race named the Hyperboreans, who dwelt in everlasting bliss and spring. On the south side of the Earth, close to the stream of Coacean, lived a happy and virtuous people named the Ætheopians, whom the gods favored so highly that they at times left their Olympian homes and went to share their sacrifices and banquets. On the western side, by the stream of Ocean, lay a happy place named the Elysian Plain. From there, mortals favored by the gods were transported without tasting of death, to enjoy an immortality of bliss. This happy region was also called the "Fortunate Fields" and the "Isles of the Blessed."

The Greeks of early ages knew little of any real people except those to the east and south of their own country, or near the coast of the Mediterranean. Their imagination meantime peopled the western portion of this sea with giants, monsters, and enchantresses; while they placed around the disk of the Earth . . . nations enjoying the special favor of the gods, and blessed with happiness and longevity.

Adapted from the introduction to *Mythology of Greece and Rome*
by Thomas Bullfinch

© 1995 by The Center for Applied Research in Education

Name_____ Date _____ Period _____

Outlining "The Background of Mythology" (5–11A)

Directions: Reread the selection, and fill in the subtopics that will form a clear and informative outline, usable either for studying or giving a report.

        Notice that topics I through V are already given. Since they are written as phrases, not sentences, you should keep to this same form. Some of the subtopics may consist of only a few key words. Of main importance is that these words capture the idea of the selection "in a nutshell."

THE BACKGROUND OF MYTHOLOGY

I. Religions of Greece and Rome now extinct
    A. _____
        1. _____
        2. _____
    B. _____
        1. _____
        2. _____

II. Earth a flat, circular disk to Greeks
    A. _____
    B. _____
        1. _____
        2. _____

III. Greeks' picture of the Earth
    A. _____
    B. _____
        1. _____
        2. _____
        3. _____

IV. Special races at Earth's edge
    A. _____
        1. _____
        2. _____
    B. _____
        1. _____
        2. _____
        3. _____
    C. _____
        1. _____
        2. _____
        3. _____

V. Knew little of real peoples other than Greeks
    A. _____
    B. _____

Drawing Conclusions (*Reading Selection 5–12*)

Learning to draw valid conclusions is an essential skill for reporters. After gathering a great deal of information and details, they need to decide what has the most importance, what needs to be included, and what left out so the finished story makes sense to their readers.

That requires drawing conclusions. And it's a skill necessary for good reading, too.

What does it mean to draw a conclusion?
When you see this much of a circle, your mind tells your eye how to fill in the rest. That's close to what is meant by drawing conclusions as you read. You take the amount of information that's given you, and use your knowledge and understanding to fill in the details that naturally follow.

Of course, you can't go too far—and jump to conclusions or make wild guesses about what a writer "might" have had in mind. Yet, writers often expect readers to take the information given, put two and two together, and draw a thoughtful conclusion about it.

Then, the next step is keeping that conclusion in mind while reading—testing for additional proof of its validity and adjusting it, if necessary, when further information is known.

EXAMPLE: I wish I had known then what I know now. Yet, when you're in school, I guess it's not unusual to think you know a lot more than you actually do.

Possible conclusions: (1) The speaker regrets something about the past.
(2) The speaker is a recent high school graduate.

The first sentence makes the first statement (1) a likely or valid conclusion. Although statement (2) is possible, there is nothing in the paragraph to serve as its support so it must be considered an open question.

Drawing Valid Conclusions (5–12A)

Directions: Read the paragraphs below and the five sentences giving possible conclusions to be drawn from each. Mark + if you feel it is a valid conclusion based on the information given. Mark 0 if it does not seem to fit or follow logically from what was written or suggested in the paragraph it's based on. Be able to point out the details in the passage that support a conclusion as being valid.

A. The day was bright and sunny, the lake calm and inviting. It bore no signs of its treachery when wild winds and violent waves held no mercy for any sailor who dared to defy it, thought Marcia as she walked along its shore.

_____ (1) This is not the woman's first trip to the lake.

_____ (2) The story will likely concern a carefree summer vacation.

_____ (3) The woman is making plans to go sailing.

_____ (4) The story will include details of a disaster or near-disaster on the lake.

_____ (5) The woman is worrying about someone out on the lake now.

B. Prescott opened his eyes and tried to focus on his surroundings. The pressure in his head prevented clear thinking.

    There were three people—two men and a woman—standing over him, looking down upon where he lay.

    "They left you for dead," the woman said. "Luckily, we found you and brought you here. The enemy are all around."

    It was hard to think clearly. After the sudden impact, he could remember nothing of the attack. It was best to say nothing, too.

_____ (1) A war or rebellion serves as the story's background.

_____ (2) Prescott has been shot or wounded.

_____ (3) Prescott is on the same side as the two men and a woman.

_____ (4) Prescott suspects the woman of lying.

_____ (5) A bump on the head has caused Prescott to hallucinate.

(5–12A continued)

C. It wasn't my fault. Why don't adults ever listen to you? I mean, either they start yellin' at you right away. Or else they start on that "I'm trying to understand" kind of stuff. And you can tell all this stuff is just an act, and they're yellin' at you inside, just tryin' not to show it.

_____ (1) The speaker is a pre-teen or teenager.

_____ (2) The speaker was blamed for doing something wrong.

_____ (3) By "you" the speaker means himself or herself.

_____ (4) It is unusual for the speaker to be in trouble with adults.

_____ (5) The speaker knows that he or she really deserves the blame.

D. Everyone should have the right to his or her own opinion. Anyone who thinks that theirs is the only opinion that has genuine value just happens to be wrong. It's hard to see how anyone could be so narrow-minded.

Nobody should be allowed to claim theirs is the only right way or try to force their beliefs on others. Nobody has the right to express such an attitude in a country like ours, which stands for freedom of speech and opinion.

_____ (1) The speaker opposes narrow-mindedness.

_____ (2) The speaker is likely a professor or law student.

_____ (3) The belief of the speaker allows freedom of opinion for everyone.

_____ (4) The speaker has expressed a narrow-minded view.

_____ (5) This is an example of clear and independent thinking.

Drawing Conclusions About Literature (5–13)

Directions: Read the paragraphs below and the five sentences giving possible conclusions to be drawn from each. Mark + if you feel it is a valid conclusion based on the information given. Mark 0 if it does not seem to fit or follow logically from what was written or suggested in the paragraph it's based on. Be able to point out the details in the passage that support a conclusion as being valid.

A. The more I see of children—and I am thankful to say I do manage to see more of them now—the more I realize that their world is quite unlike ours. It is so different from ours that, it seems to me, to describe it needs a peculiar kind of imagination and understanding. And I think any real account of a childhood would necessarily be long, for how much happens in an hour or a day of a child's life, and what changes come in a year. — "Notes on Virginia's Childhood" by Vanessa Bell

_____ (1) The speaker probably has many brothers and sisters.

_____ (2) By *children,* the speaker must mean children in general.

_____ (3) The speaker feels adults lead fuller lives than children.

_____ (4) By *their world,* the speaker means the world of childhood.

_____ (5) By *ours,* the speaker means the world of her own childhood.

B. Looking back, I guess me and Granpa was pretty dumb. Not Granpa, when it come to mountains or game or weather or any number of things. But when you got into words and books and such, well, me and Granpa took the decision to Granma. She straightened it out. — from *The Education of Little Tree* by Forrest Carter

_____ (1) The speaker sounds young and not well educated.

_____ (2) Granpa was knowledgeable about nature and wildlife.

_____ (3) Granma made most important family decisions.

_____ (4) The speaker feels his grandfather is no smarter than he is.

_____ (5) The speaker admired Granma more than Granpa.

(5–13 continued)

C. Chicken Hawk stayed high pretty much all the time and he was nineteen years old limping down academic corridors trying to make it to twelfth grade.

Unlike his good sidekick Wine, whose big reason for putting up with school was to please his mother, Chicken Hawk just loved the public school system and all the advantages that came with it. He could go on boarding at home, didn't have to work, and could mess over a whole year and not feel he'd lost anything. — "Chicken Hawk's Dream" by Al Young

_____ (1) Chicken Hawk was lame and may have walked with a limp.

_____ (2) Chicken Hawk had probably failed a number of classes.

_____ (3) Wine did not like school as well as Chicken Hawk did.

_____ (4) Both boys saw school as a stepping stone to a better future.

_____ (5) Chicken Hawk felt school work was too challenging.

D. Inquiries as to the physical law or mechanical principle that underlay a phenomenon or operation came frequently from Lincoln. "Unless very much preoccupied," wrote Brooks[1], "he never heard any reference to anything that he did not understand without asking for further information." He would ask, "What do you suppose makes that tree grow that way?" and was not satisfied until he had found out. Or he would take one of his boy's toys to pieces, find out how it was made, and put it together again. Tad had occasion more than once, said Brooks, to bewail his father's curiosity. — Chapter 18, "The Man in the White House," from *Abraham Lincoln* by Carl Sandburg

_____ (1) Lincoln was interested in why and how things worked.

_____ (2) During his presidency, Lincoln wasted valuable time asking unnecessary questions.

_____ (3) Tad, Lincoln's son, didn't always appreciate his father's curiosity.

_____ (4) Lincoln didn't hesitate to admit not understanding something.

_____ (5) The incidents quoted come from official government records.

---

[1] Noah Brooks, a newspaper correspondent

Drawing Conclusions About Literature (5–14)

Directions: Read the paragraphs below and the five sentences giving possible conclusions to be drawn from each. Mark + if you feel it is a valid conclusion based on the information given. Mark O if it does not seem to fit or follow logically from what was written or suggested in the paragraph it's based on. Be able to point out the details in the passage that support a conclusion as being valid.

A. You know, we were so young that we didn't know we were supposed to be poor. We were so young and excited with the life we knew that we had not yet learned we were the ones who were supposed to be deprived. We were even so young that sometimes we forgot we were supposed to be hungry, because we were just too busy living. —
"We Who Came After" by Ronald L. Fair

_____ (1) The speaker was considered an underprivileged child.

_____ (2) As a child, the speaker wasn't aware of living differently from others.

_____ (3) The speaker had everything needed for growing up strong and healthy.

_____ (4) As an adult, the speaker now feels cheated of a decent childhood.

_____ (5) By "supposed to be," the speaker means by the standards of others, such as welfare and social workers.

B. Janus was the porter of heaven. He opens the year, the first month being named after him. He is the guardian deity of gates, on which account he is commonly represented with two heads, because every door looks two ways. His temples at Rome were numerous. In war time, the gates of the principal one were always open. In peace, they were closed; but they were shut only once between the reign of Numa and that of Augustus.
— from *Mythology of Greece and Rome* by Thomas Bullfinch

_____ (1) Numa and Augusta must have been Roman rulers or emperors.

_____ (2) Janus is sometimes two-headed because doors look both in and out.

_____ (3) In wartime, Janus's temples were fortified for war.

_____ (4) January is named for Janus because it opens the door to the new year.

_____ (5) Between the reign of Numa and Augustus, Rome must have mostly been at peace.

(5–14 continued)

C. Coming home from school that day (well, it was not really home from school because he had met Totoy on the way to school in the morning and went with him instead of continuing to school and in spite of his mother's constant warning against Totoy's company), Amador sensed an ominous silence in the house as he opened the screen door. Like the silence of a vast shell put close to the ear. — "Dark Fiesta" by Oscar Penaranda

_____ (1) Amador arrived home after school had left out.

_____ (2) Totoy was a dropout from school.

_____ (3) Amador had skipped school and gone with Totoy.

_____ (4) Amador's mother disapproved of his friendship with Totoy.

_____ (5) To Amador, the silence in the house was a sign no one was at home.

D. Beside the open fire I sat within our tepee. With my red blanket wrapped tightly about my crossed legs, I was thinking of the coming season, my sixteenth winter. On either side of the wigwam were my parents. My father was whistling a tune between his teeth while polishing with his bare hand a red stone pipe he had recently carved. Almost in front of me, beyond the center fire, my old grandmother sat near the entranceway.

She turned her face toward her right and addressed most of her words to my mother. Now and then she spoke to me, but never did she allow her eyes to rest upon her daughter's husband, my father. It was only upon rare occasions that my grandmother said anything to him. Thus, his ears were open and ready to catch the smallest wish she might express . . . — "The Soft-Hearted Sioux" by Zitkala-Sa

_____ (1) The story must take place in earlier days of life in America.

_____ (2) The speaker's family must be native Americans.

_____ (3) The speaker is a sixteen-year-old girl.

_____ (4) Because her husband is dead, the grandmother may not look at or speak to a man.

_____ (5) The father evidently resents the way his mother-in-law treats him.

UNIT 6

When Complications Arise

The exercises in this unit concern advanced problems in reading, such as those that students are likely to encounter when reading standard selections in most literature courses.

Writers such as Hawthorne, Dickens, Brontë, Conrad, and Shakespeare often confuse and bewilder inexperienced readers. Students' bewilderment is not solely caused by the depth of these major writers' thinking. It is also caused by the length and complications of their sentences.

Before learning how to read for underlying meaning, students need to learn how to approach the kind of sentences great writers often favor.

Of course, there is an infinite variety of ways to combine sentences, so this unit can only introduce students to some of the most usual ones. However, by becoming aware of the fact that long, complicated sentences are formed by combining shorter ones, students will learn how to approach such passages in their reading and gain confidence in their ability to "break them down" into understandable units.

By working with combined sentences, students will, of course, be dealing with the grammatical structure of the English language. However, such terms as *subject, verb, clause, complex or compound sentence,* and *conjunction* have been carefully avoided since the subject is reading, not grammar itself. In addition, celebrated writers combine sentences in ways that go far beyond the skills of the average grammar student to parse or diagram.

You may nevertheless discover a carryover from this approach to reading that will make students more proficient in grammar.

The reading exercises in this unit are especially useful as introductory work before assigning selections by major authors who favor complicated sentences and elevated language, while the skill of paraphrasing is of great value in "translating" passages of Shakespeare and other writers.

You will find the exercises in this unit most convenient as a way to prepare students for reading literary masterpieces that might otherwise overwhelm them.

NOTES ON ACTIVITIES

Making Sense of Busy Sentences (Reading Selection 6–1)

In the example given, parentheses show the type of phrases that you may want to accept as optional in student answers. Although "to the phone" actually answers the question "Where?" it is vital to complete the basic meaning.

When students do the following exercises, encourage them to include words that would make sense standing alone, punctuated as complete sentences. You may want to allow students to eliminate some descriptive words in long phrases by indicating the omission with three dots, such as "on . . . an impulse," instead of "on a sudden and mischievous impulse."

Breaking Up Busy Sentences (6–1A and 6–1B);
The Real Meanings of There and It (6–2A and 6–2B);
Supplying Understood Words (6–3A, 6–3B, and 6–3C);
A Challenge for "Understanding" Readers (6–4)

In their answers, some students may include words that do not actually answer the basic questions of "Who or What?" and "Do or Did What?" For example, in passage "C" of 6–1A, they might include "to a happy ending" which actually answers the question "Where?" It is best to allow credit as long as such answers include nothing that changes the meaning or belongs outside the given clause.

When discussing these exercises, it will be helpful to have students also identify answers to When, Where, How, and Why. At times, of course, the answers will be provided by one of the other elements or clauses, as discussed in Reading Selection 6–1. Becoming aware of this fact will help students realize the value of combining sentences.

After completing each exercise, encourage students to reread the originals to see that they now seem easier to understand.

Note: In "Supplying Understood Words" (6–6A through C), you may need to explain that it is also sometimes necessary to add helping verbs in parentheses. For example: *(were) coming home from Florida.*

Shorter, but Not Always Better (6–5)

As a culminating activity, you may want students to rewrite a paragraph from a previous exercise or a passage from a current or upcoming literature assignment as a series of simple sentences. Students may need to use adverbs or adverbial phrases to maintain the meaning of adverbial clauses, if possible. If not, it will help students understand why combined sentences add to meaning.

When they have finished the exercise, encourage students to compare the rewritten version with the original and discuss their reactions. This comparison should help them see the advantage of sentences that may at first seem involved and difficult to read. They should note that such sentences avoid repetition and clearly show the relationship of one idea to another in a way that is impossible with shorter ones.

Practice in Paraphrasing (6–6A)

When students write paraphrases, encourage them to follow the word order of the original as closely as possible. In a few instances, a change to standard subject/verb (or Who or What? Did What?) order may be advisable to clarify meaning.

Unless the meaning of a word would be obvious to the average reader in its context, students should put the passage in simpler language that shows their understanding of the original and is clear and correctly written. However, they should avoid the use of slang and colloquial expressions.

You may want to work out one or two paraphrases with students at the chalkboard before having them finish the exercises on their own. Paraphrasing is also suited to group work.

Making Sense of Busy Sentences
(*Reading Selection 6–1*)

EXAMPLE: As soon as she heard the bell, Sarah hurried to the phone because she was expecting an important call.

Who?	Did What?
Sarah	hurried (to the phone)
She	was expecting an important call

Often more than one thing is "happening" in a sentence. For instance, the example could easily be written as three different sentences: Sarah heard the bell. She hurried to the phone. She was expecting an important call.

But that wouldn't make it clear that "as soon as. . . the bell" answers the question "When?" and "she hurried to the phone" answers the question "Why?"

Good writers often combine sentences to show how their ideas are connected with one another and make it clear that one is more important. Those of lesser importance often begin with introductory words such as:

after   although   as soon as   because   before   since   when

until   unless   so   that   whether   while

Sentences can also link related but equal sentences together to show how closely they are related. FOR EXAMPLE: Sarah hoped to hear Rick's voice on the line, but she was greatly disappointed, for someone wanted to talk to her brother.

Words that join equal sentences include: **and   but   or   nor   for.**

Writers sometimes join closely related sentences with the semicolon (;). FOR EXAMPLE: The process of driving a car is simple; the job of driving safely and well is complicated.

A correctly written sentence can be any length the writer thinks necessary—as long as its ideas are properly connected and joined. A sentence can be as short as one word. FOR EXAMPLE: Look!

Or, it can extend to a paragraph, a page, or even longer—and still be correct. It is the job of a good reader to spot the relationships and find the "Who's?" and "Did What's?" that serve as the controlling ideas in long, complicated sentences.

Breaking Up Busy Sentences (6–1A)

Directions: Each of the following examples consists of several sentences, joined together to show the relationship of their ideas. To help you gain awareness of how sentences can be joined, divide each one into its separate parts. Write **Who or What?** and **Did or Does What?** for each part.

The correct number of spaces are provided for each example. Remember that *and* can join individual words and phrases as well as independent parts of sentences.

A. Soon we saw the first faint blushes of morning in the east, where the sun would rise, and the day promised to be a good one for beginning our journey.

Who or What?	Did or Does What?
(1) _____	_____
(2) _____	_____
(3) _____	_____

B. Tony waited outside of the room while Cindy asked the teacher about tomorrow's assignment, and then they headed for the cafeteria and lunch.

Who or What?	Did or Does What?
(1) _____	_____
(2) _____	_____
(3) _____	_____

C. When we left the movie, both Chet and I agreed that we expected it to end differently because everything pointed to a happy ending.

Who or What?	Did or Does What?
(1) _____	_____
(2) _____	_____
(3) _____	_____
(4) _____	_____

(6–1A continued)

D. Coach Andrews is well-respected, he treats everyone fairly and, even though he demands discipline, he cares about his players.

Who or What?	Did or Does What?
(1) _____	_____
(2) _____	_____
(3) _____	_____
(4) _____	_____

E. I believe that most people want to do well, but that they often become confused and discouraged when they don't get the kind of results that they want so they just quit trying.

Who or What?	Did or Does What?
(1) _____	_____
(2) _____	_____
(3) _____	_____
(4) _____	_____
(5) _____	_____
(6) _____	_____

Breaking Up Busy Sentences (6–1B)

Directions: Following are examples of how well-known writers join sentences together to show the relationship of their ideas. To gain a better sense of the elements such sentences contain, divide each one into its separate parts. Write **Who or What?** and **Did or Does What?** for each part.

The correct number of spaces are provided for each example. Remember that *and* can join individual words and phrases as well as independent parts of sentences. (Underlined words are not part of the sentence but are added to clarify its meaning.)

A. Daisy stood, a little left out and solitary, there in the kitchen, as Billy, the older of the babies, climbed frantically over Elmer (his father) . . . , and the little one toddled smilingly about. — "A Start in Life" by Ruth Suckow

Who or What?	Did or Does What?
(1) _____	_____
(2) _____	_____
(3) _____	_____

B. At length we began to see symptoms of vegetation; occasional palm-trees and flowers, and by the time we had reached a pretty Indian village, where we stopped to change mules, the light had broke in, and we seemed to have been transported, as if by enchantment, from a desert to a garden. — from *Life in Mexico* by Frances Calderon de la Barca

Who or What?	Did or Does What?
(1) _____	_____
(2) _____	_____
(3) _____	_____
(4) _____	_____
(5) _____	_____

C. . . .Very many people . . . read with difficulty. I mean by this that they read slowly and with effort, that it tires them—that they do not read as easily as they breathe . . . Many people think they can read, but they can't. — "On Reading Books" by John Maynard Keynes

Who or What?	Did or Does What?
(1) _____	_____
(2) _____	_____
(3) _____	_____
(4) _____	_____
(5) _____	_____

(6–1B continued)

D. <u>Ishmael Bush had passed the whole of a life of more than fifty years on the skirts of society</u>. He boasted that he had never dwelt (in a place) where he might not safely fell every tree he could view from his own threshold, that the law had rarely been known to enter his clearing, and that his ears had never willingly admitted the sound of a church bell. — from *The Prairie* by James Fenimore Cooper

Who or What?	**Did or Does What?**
(1) _____	_____
(2) _____	_____
(3) _____	_____
(4) _____	_____
(5) _____	_____
(6) _____	_____

E. We hold these truths to be self-evident: that all men are created equal; that they are endowed by their creator with certain unalienable rights; that among these are life, liberty, and the pursuit of happiness. — from the "Declaration of Independence" by Thomas Jefferson

Who or What?	**Did or Does What?**
(1) _____	_____
(2) _____	_____
(3) _____	_____
(4) _____	_____

A Note About Introductory "There" and "It"
(*Reading Selection 6–2*)

Poets, writers, and speakers sometimes use sentences such as these:

> It was a bright and sunny day.
> There was nothing left to do.

In many cases, "it" and "there" are used merely to introduce or fill out a sentence. The words that really answer the question "Who or What?" in the examples given are *day* and *nothing*. The sentences could also be written:

> The day was bright and sunny.
> Nothing was left to do.

When you are reading, be sure to note the difference between *it* being used as an introduction and its use the following way:

> My elbow hit the glass, and it fell off the table.

In this case, *it* is a personal pronoun, which takes the place of "glass."

In a similar way, *there* sometimes answers the question "Where?" as in the following sentence:

> Put your books right there.

When you see an introductory *there* or *it* in your reading, be sure to determine the real answer to the question "Who or What is the sentence about?"

The Real Meanings of "There" and "It" (6–2A)

Directions: Each of the following examples consists of several sentences, joined together to show the relationship of their ideas. To help you gain awareness of how sentences can be joined, divide each one into its separate parts. Answer **"Who or What?"** and **"Did or Does What?"** for each part.

    If a sentence or part of a sentence begins with *there* or *it,* check to determine the exact words that correctly state Who or What is doing the action. The correct number of spaces are provided for each example.

    Note: In long sentences, the words *who, that,* or *which* often take the place of another word in order to show the relation of one part of a sentence to another. If one of these words or a personal pronoun (*he, she, it,* or *they*) answers "Who or What?", write the word or words it replaces after it, enclosed in parentheses.

A. There were no satisfactory answers given to the questions that had been bothering us for weeks, and we left the meeting angrily because our time had been wasted by attending.

Who or What?	Did or Does What?
(1) _____	_____
(2) _____	_____
(3) _____	_____
(4) _____	_____

B. It was a time of celebration because everyone was awaiting the return of our hometown hero who won two gold medals in Olympic skiing.

Who or What?	Did or Does What?
(1) _____	_____
(2) _____	_____
(3) _____	_____

C. When the explorers started off on their expedition, there were many well-wishers on hand to cheer them on, for everyone knew they faced a journey that was bound to be both long and dangerous.

Who or What?	Did or Does What?
(1) _____	_____
(2) _____	_____
(3) _____	_____
(4) _____	_____
(5) _____	_____

(6–2A continued)

D. Although the snake looked harmless, there was no sense in taking chances and, unless there was a good reason for doing so, the woodsman did not wish to disturb a creature that was hurting no one.

Who or What?	**Did or Does What?**
(1) _____	_____
(2) _____	_____
(3) _____	_____
(4) _____	_____
(5) _____	_____

E. There is no way to tell which method will work out best so you will just have to try one and, if that isn't successful, you can try the other.

Who or What?	**Did or Does What?**
(1) _____	_____
(2) _____	_____
(3) _____	_____
(4) _____	_____
(5) _____	_____

The Real Meanings of "There" and "It" (6–2B)

Directions: For each of the following examples, divide each sentence or poem into its separate parts. Write **Who or What?** and **Did or Does What?** for each part.

If a sentence or part of a sentence begins with *there* or *it,* write the exact words that correctly state Who or What is doing the action. The correct number of spaces are provided for each example.

If *who, that,* or *which* answers "Who or What?", write the word or words it replaces after it. (Underlined words are not part of the sentence but are added to clarify its meaning.)

A. Old Caesar seldom lifted up his voice in a growl or a bark; he was fat and sleepy; there were yellow rings which looked like spectacles around his dim old eyes; but there was a neighbor who bore on his hand the imprint of several of Caesar's sharp, white, youthful teeth, and for that he had lived at the end of a chain, all alone in a little hut, for fourteen years. The neighbor . . . had demanded either Caesar's death or complete ostracism. . . — from "A New England Nun" by Mary E. Wilkins Freeman

Who or What?	Did or Does What?
(1) _____	_____
(2) _____	_____
(3) _____	_____
(4) _____	_____
(5) _____	_____
(6) _____	_____
(7) _____	_____

B. There were three sisters fair and bright,
    Jennifer, Gentle, and Rosemary,
And they three loved one valiant knight—
    As the dove flies over the mulberry-tree. — from "The Riddling Knight," an old,
                                                          anonymous ballad

Who or What?	Did or Does What?
(1) _____	_____
(2) _____	_____
(3) _____	_____

(6–2B continued)

C. It was a summer evening;
    Old Kaspar's work was done,
And he before his cottage door
    Was sitting in the sun;
And by him sported on the green
    His little grandchild Wilhelmine. — from "The Battle of Blenheim" by Robert Southey

Who or What?	Did or Does What?
(1) _____	_____
(2) _____	_____
(3) _____	_____
(4) _____	_____

D. At one time the whole town took a lively interest in the hunger artist; from day to day of his fast the excitement mounted; everybody wanted to see him at least once a day; there were people who bought season tickets for the last few days and sat from morning till night in front of his small barred cage; even in the nighttime there were visiting hours, when the whole effect was heightened by torch flares; on fine days the cage was set out in the open air, and then it was the children's special treat to see the hunger artist; for their elders he was often just a joke that happened to be in fashion, but the children stood open-mouth . . . — from "A Hunger Artist" by Franz Kafka

Who or What?	Did or Does What?
(1) _____	_____
(2) _____	_____
(3) _____	_____
(4) _____	_____
(5) _____	_____
(6) _____	_____
(7) _____	_____
(8) _____	_____
(9) _____	_____
(10) _____	_____
(11) _____	_____
(12) _____	_____

What Good Readers Need to Understand
(*Reading Selection 6–3*)

Look out! Everyone knows that when someone says, "Look out!" the subject is *you*. Although not actually stated, "you" is *understood*—its meaning is actually supplied by the listener or reader.

You are probably less aware of how many other meanings are automatically supplied by an accomplished reader or good listener. To understand complicated sentences, you need to know how to "put in" the words that a writer or speaker expects you to understand. Here are some of the most important ones:

1. WORDS ENDING IN "-ING" ALWAYS SPELL ACTION

Running, swimming, flying, coming, and *going*—because *-ing* words are generally involved in action, writers use them to add life and a sense of immediacy. And, they can be used in many different ways:

- **In answer to Who or What?** *Swimming* is my favorite sport.
- **As part of the answer to "Does What?"** The relay team *is running*. We *must be going* soon.
- **To describe another word:** Have you ever seen a *flying* fish?

Of course, in each of these examples, all of the words are expressed openly. As a reader, you don't need to supply anything more.

The following sentence works in the same way.

> We were coming home from Florida during Spring vacation.

But what about this one?

> Coming home from Florida during Spring vacation, we were delayed because of a snowstorm which struck the Smoky Mountains.

When two ideas or sentences are joined like this, the reader must make a mental note that "we were" belongs to "coming home" as well as delayed.

And, it's also true with past forms of verbs or action words:

> A sweater was sent me by Aunt Fred.

> Gold was discovered in 1849.

Joined with other sentences or ideas and they become:

> The sweater sent me by Aunt Fred didn't fit.

> Discovered in 1849, gold brought a flood of fortune hunters to California.

(6–3 continued)

2. THE UNDERSTOOD "WHO OR WHAT?"

Our team won the district finals and goes on to play for the state championships.

Who goes on to the state championships? *Our team, of course!*

When parts of a sentence are linked by *and, but, or,* or *nor,* it's not always necessary to repeat "Who or What" is doing the action. Good readers mentally supply the missing word. But, they also learn to be careful when the parts are separated by another element. For example:

> The fans cheered the Grammy-winning star, and when he sang his final number, begged for an encore.

Whom did they beg for an encore? *The star, of course!*

3. WHO OR WHAT IS *HE, SHE, IT,* OR *THEY?*

> Although Lisa has never been in an airplane, she plans to fly to Colorado this summer.

Who is "she"? *Lisa, of course!*
It's always important to know who or what a personal pronoun stands for—and this sometimes can seem confusing.

> Our science teacher, Mr. Graves, told Bart that he had been named to the Student/Faculty Advisory Board.

Who is "he"? It's correct to assume that a personal pronoun—*he, she, it,* or *they*—is taking the place of the word that it could logically replace and that comes closest to it. In the example, both "Mr. Graves" and "Bart" are obviously "he's," but, in the sentence Bart is nearer to "he." Then, who's "he"? *Bart, of course.*

As you read, be aware of the importance of "filling in" the words that the writer expects you to supply so that communication between writer and readers flows smoothly.

Supplying Understood Words (6–3A)

Directions: Answer **"Who or What?"** and **"Does or Did What?"** for each thought element in the following sentences. Add words that are understood but necessary to complete each thought and include them in parentheses.

If "Who or What?" is answered by a personal pronoun (*he, she, it,* or *they*), by *who, which,* or *that,* or if it is not restated, supply the correct word in parentheses. For example:

Though Lisa has never been in an airplane, she plans to fly to Colorado this summer.

Who or What?	Did or Does What?
she (Lisa)	plans to fly

A. When I thought of the clean, tidy, comfortable surroundings in which I had been reared, a wave of homesickness swept over me that made me feel faint . . . — from *The Autobiography of an Ex-Colored Man* by James Weldon Johnson

Who or What?	Did or Does What?
(1) _____	_____
(2) _____	_____
(3) _____	_____
(4) _____	_____

B. I looked at the cot in which I was to sleep and suspected, not without good reasons, that I should not be the first to use the sheets and pillow-case since they had last come from the wash. — from *The Autobiography of an Ex-Colored Man* by Jame Weldon Johnson

Who or What?	Did or Does What?
(1) _____	_____
(2) _____	_____
(3) _____	_____
(4) _____	_____
(5) _____	_____

C. The trapper did not allow his companions time to hesitate, but dragging them both after him, he nearly buried his person in the fog of the prairie while he was speaking.
— from *The Prairie* by James Fenimore Cooper

Who or What?	**Did or Does What?**
(1) _____	_____
(2) _____	_____
(3) _____	_____
(4) _____	_____

D. The three (companions) were scarcely bowed to the ground when their ears were saluted with the well-known, sharp, short reports of the western rifle, and instantly the whizzing of the ragged lead was heard, buzzing within dangerous proximity of their heads. — from *The Prairie* by James Fenimore Cooper

Who or What?	**Did or Does What?**
(1) _____	_____
(2) _____	_____
(3) _____	_____
(4) _____	_____

Supplying Understood Words (6–3B)

Directions: Answer **"Who or What?"** and **"Does or Did What?"** for each thought element in the following sentences. Add words that are understood but necessary to complete each thought and include them in parentheses.

If "Who or What?" is answered by a personal pronoun (*he, she, it,* or *they*), or by *who, which,* or *that,* or if it is not restated, supply the correct word in parentheses. For example:

Though Lisa has never been in an airplane, she plans to fly to Colorado this summer.

Who or What?	**Did or Does What?**
she (Lisa)	plans to fly

A. It was in 1868, when nine years old or thereabouts, that while looking at a map of Africa of the time and putting my finger on the blank space then representing the unsolved mystery of that continent, I said to myself with absolute assurance and an amazing audacity which are no longer in my character now: "When I grow up I shall go *there.*" — from *A Personal Record* by Joseph Conrad

Who or What?	**Did or Does What?**
(1) _____	_____
(2) _____	_____
(3) _____	_____
(4) _____	_____
(5) _____	_____
(6) _____	_____
(7) _____	_____

B. I wandered lonely as a cloud
That floats on high o'er vales and hills,
When all at once I saw a crowd,
A host, of golden daffodils;
Beside the lake, beneath the trees,
Fluttering and dancing in the breeze. — from "Daffodils" by William Wordsworth

Who or What?	**Did or Does What?**
(1) _____	_____
(2) _____	_____
(3) _____	_____
(4) _____	_____
(5) _____	_____

(6–3B continued)

C. Once upon a midnight dreary, while I pondered, weak and weary,
   Over many a quaint and curious volume of forgotten lore,
   While I nodded, nearly napping, suddenly there came a tapping,
   As of some one gently rapping, rapping at my chamber door . . . — from "The Raven"
   by Edgar Allan Poe

Who or What?	Did or Does What?
(1) _____	_____
(2) _____	_____
(3) _____	_____
(4) _____	_____
(5) _____	_____

D. Bailey didn't look up from his reading so she (the grandmother) wheeled around then and faced the children's mother, a young woman in slacks, whose face was as broad and innocent as a cabbage and was tied around with a green head-kerchief that had two points on the top like rabbit's ears. — from "A Good Man Is Hard to Find" by Flannery O'Connor

Who or What?	Did or Does What?
(1) _____	_____
(2) _____	_____
(3) _____	_____
(4) _____	_____
(5) _____	_____
(6) _____	_____

Supplying Understood Words (6–3C)

Directions: Write the **"Who or What?"** and **"Does or Did What?"** for each thought element in the following sentences. Supply the words that are understood but necessary to complete each thought.

If "Who or What?" is answered by a personal pronoun (*he, she, it,* or *they*), by *who, which,* or *that,* or if it is not restated, supply the correct word in parentheses.

A. He (Frederic Woolley) was not without wit, he had great knowledge and considerable taste and even in the full movement of the "new" literature he had won a certain respect for his refusal to accept it. — "Of This Time, Of That Place" by Lionel Trilling

Who or What?	Did or Does What?
(1) _____	_____
(2) _____	_____
(3) _____	_____

(4) What does "it" stand for in this sentence? _____

B. It was altogether a picturesque and striking scene; the huts composed of bamboo, and thatched with palm-leaves, the Indian women with their long black hair standing at the doors with their half-naked children, the mules rolling themselves on the ground, according to their favorite fashion, snow-white goats browsing amongst the palm-trees, and the air so soft and balmy, the first breath of morning; the dew-drops still glittering on the broad leaves of the banana and palm, and all around (was) so silent, cool, and still. — from *Life in Mexico* by Frances Calderon de la Barca

Who or What?	Did or Does What?
(1) _____	_____
(2) _____	_____
(3) _____	_____
(4) _____	_____
(5) _____	_____
(6) _____	_____
(7) _____	_____
(8) _____	_____
(9) _____	_____

(6–3C continued)

C. Sometimes I heard the foxes as they ranged over the snow crust, in moonlight nights, in search of a partridge or other game, barking raggedly and demoniacally like forest dogs, as if laboring with some anxiety, or seeking expression, struggling for light and to be dogs outright and run freely in the streets; for if we take the ages into our account, may there not be a civilization going on among brutes as well as men? — from "Winter Animals," *Walden* by Henry David Thoreau

Who or What?	**Did or Does What?**
(1) _____	_____
(2) _____	_____
(3) _____	_____
(4) _____	_____
(5) _____	_____
(6) _____	_____
(7) _____	_____
(8) _____	_____

D. When I heard the learned astronomer,
When the proofs, the figures, were ranged in columns before me . . .
When I sitting heard the astronomer where he lectured with much applause in the
    lecture-room,
How soon unaccountable I became tired and sick,
Till rising and gliding out I wandered off by myself,
In the mystical moist night-air, and from time to time,
Looked up in perfect silence at the stars. — "When I heard. . ." by Walt Whitman

Who or What?	**Did or Does What?**
(1) _____	_____
(2) _____	_____
(3) _____	_____
(4) _____	_____
(5) _____	_____
(6) _____	_____
(7) _____	_____
(8) _____	_____
(9) _____	_____
(10) _____	_____

A Challenge for "Understanding" Readers (6–4)

Directions: When a paragraph or passage contains a long, complicated sentence, there is often a shorter, more direct sentence before or after it that clarifies the meaning, as in the underlined sentences in the examples that follow.

Write the **"Who or What?"** and **"Does or Did What?"** for each thought element in the sentences that is not underlined. Supply the words that are understood but necessary to complete each thought. If "Who or What?" is answered by a personal pronoun *(he, she, it,* or *they)*, or by *who, which,* or *that,* or if it is not restated, supply the correct word in parentheses.

A. Paul Bunyan, the mythical hero of the lumber jacks, is the supreme figure of American folklore. Paul was a Herculean logger who combed his beard with a young tree; who skidded his timber with Babe the Blue Ox, a creature so vast that he measured forty-two ax handles and a plug of chewing tobacco between the horns; who operated a camp cook house where the flapjack griddle was greased by twenty-four Arabs—imported from the Sahara Desert because they could stand the heat—skating to and fro with slabs of bacon strapped to their feet; who tamed the Mississippi when it was young and wild . . . ; who ruled the American country in the period when it was only a timberland . . . — from "An American Hercules" by James Stevens

Who or What?	**Did or Does What?**
(1) _____	_____
(2) _____	_____
(3) _____	_____
(4) _____	_____
(5) _____	_____
(6) _____	_____
(7) _____	_____
(8) _____	_____
(9) _____	_____
(10) _____	_____
(11) _____	_____
(12) _____	_____
(13) _____	_____
(14) _____	_____

(6–4 continued)

B. <u>How exciting they were, those little ships of the Great Plain!</u> The prairie schooners, rigged with canvas tops which gleamed whitely in the shimmering light, first became visible as tiny specks against the eastern sky; one might almost imagine them to be sea gulls perched far, far away on an endless green meadow; but as one continued to watch, the white dots grew; they came drifting across the prairie like the day; after long waiting, they gradually floated out of the haze, distinct and clear; then, as they drew near, they proved to be veritable wagons, with horses hitched ahead, with folk and all their possessions inside, and a whole herd of cattle following behind. — from *Giants in the Earth* by O. E. Rolvaag

Who or What?	Did or Does What?
(1) _____	_____
(2) _____	_____
(3) _____	_____
(4) _____	_____
(5) _____	_____
(6) _____	_____
(7) _____	_____
(8) _____	_____
(9) _____	_____
(10) _____	_____
(11) _____	_____
(12) _____	_____
(13) _____	_____

Shorter, but Not Always Better (6–5)

Directions: Rewrite a long, complicated sentence or passage as a series of correctly-written simpler sentences. Write each element that contains **"Who or What/Did or Does What"** as a separate sentence, being sure to include all of the When's, Where's, Why's, and How's that relate to each. You will sometimes need to supply words naming Who or What when they are understood, and omit linking words, such as *before, while,* and *because,* if used to combine sentences.

Your teacher will tell you whether to use an example from a previous exercise or work with a sentence from another reading selection.

_____

_____

_____

_____

_____

_____

_____

_____

_____

_____

_____

_____

_____

_____

_____

_____

_____

_____

Paraphrasing: A Help to Readers
(*Reading Selection 6–6*)

Some reading is difficult, even for the best of readers. That's especially true of writers from the past—like William Shakespeare. Their use of unfamiliar words and unexpected phrasing can make a reader feel lost at first—and miss the richness of such writers' ideas and the truth of their words.

That's why the skill of paraphrasing is worthwhile to learn.

Paraphrasing is rewording part or all of a text or passage, stating its meaning in another way. Its purpose is to reveal a clear understanding of the original.

Paraphrasing is more than just trying to tell what an author or poet meant by putting his or her ideas in your own words.

Paraphrasing is a word that should remind you of the word *parallel*. Like two parallel lines that run side by side, a good paraphrase should follow alongside the original so they are easy to compare. For a paraphrase is not intended to be better than the original. Its purpose is to help the reader understand the original more fully.

Here is how someone might paraphrase the opening passage of the "Declaration of Independence," penned by Thomas Jefferson. Of course, another person paraphrasing this sentence could do it somewhat differently and still capture its meaning.

Original Version by Thomas Jefferson

We hold these truths to be self-evident: that all men are created equal; that they are endowed by their creator with certain unalienable rights; that among these are life, liberty, and the pursuit of happiness.

Paraphrased Version

We believe and maintain that these things are true and need no proof or additional evidence: that all people are equal from their origin or birth; that God gives them certain rights that cannot be taken away or transferred; and that these rights include the right to life, the right to freedom, and the right to seek happiness.

Original Version from "To a Louse" by Robert Burns

O, wad some Power the giftie gie us
To see oursels as ithers see us.

Paraphrased Version

If only someone or something would give us the ability
To see ourselves as we look to other people.

Notice that it's sometimes necessary to use more words in the paraphrased version than in the original. The tempo and sound are also lost. Yet paraphrasing can be an important tool for proving to yourself—as well as someone else—that you've understood a difficult piece of writing.

Once you have mastered the skill of paraphrasing, you can use it not only for writing out a paraphrased version of a difficult passage, but also for mentally paraphrasing a tricky phrase or confusing sentence as you read.

Practice in Paraphrasing (6–6A)

Directions: Paraphrase the following passages and poems. Try to restate the meaning in your own words in a way that shows your understanding of the original. You may first want to think about how you would "break up" the sentences into their individual elements to make paraphrasing them easier.

   Use a dictionary if you wish to check the shade of meaning to use in paraphrasing some words in the original versions.

1. The possible quantity of play depends upon the possible quantity of pay. — John Ruskin

 _____

 _____

2. Four score and seven years ago, our fathers brought forth upon this continent a new nation, conceived in liberty and dedicated to the proposition that all men are created equal. — opening of "The Gettysburg Address" by Abraham Lincoln

 _____

 _____

 _____

3. It was a summer evening;
  Old Kaspar's work was done,
And he before his cottage door
  Was sitting in the sun;
And by him sported on the green
His little grandchild Wilhelmine. — from "The Battle of Blenheim" by Robert Southey

 _____

 _____

 _____

 _____

 _____

4. We (human beings) are composite creatures, made up of soul and body, mind and spirit. When men's attention is fixed upon one to the disregard of the others, human beings result who are only partially developed, their eyes blinded to half of what life offers and the great world holds. — from *The Greek Way* by Edith Hamilton

 _____

 _____

 _____

 _____

Practice in Paraphrasing (6–6B)

Directions: Paraphrase the following passages and poems. Try to restate the meaning in your own words in a way that shows your understanding of the original. You may first want to think about how you would "break up" the sentences into their individual elements to make paraphrasing them easier.

Use a dictionary if you wish to check the shade of meaning to use in paraphrasing some words in the original versions.

1. Breathes there the man with soul so dead,
   Who never to himself hath said,
   "This is my own, my native land!" — "Breathes There the Man with Soul So Dead" by Sir Walter Scott

   _____

   _____

   _____

   _____

2. In reading, we do well to propose to ourselves definite ends and purposes. The more distinctly we are aware of our own wants and desires in reading, the more definite and permanent will be our acquisitions . . . — "A Definite Aim in Reading" by Noah Porter

   _____

   _____

   _____

   _____

3. The private history of every self-educated man, from Franklin onwards, attests that they all were uniformly not only earnest but *select* in their reading . . . Indeed, the reason why self-trained men so often surpass men who are trained by others in the effectiveness and success of their reading, is that they know for what they read and study, and have definite aims and wishes in all their dealings with books. — "A Definite Aim in Reading" by Noah Porter

   _____

   _____

   _____

   _____

(6–6B continued)

4. My heart leaps up when I behold
   A rainbow in the sky;
   So was it when my life began,
   So is it now I am a man,
   So be it when I shall grow old,
   Or let me die! — from "The Rainbow" by William Wordsworth

_____

_____

_____

_____

_____

_____

5. The theory of politics which has possessed the mind of men and which they have expressed the best they could in their laws and in their revolutions, considers persons and property as the two objects for whose protection government exists. Of persons, all have equal rights, in virtue of being identical in nature. This interest of course with its whole power demands a democracy . . . — from "Politics" by Ralph Waldo Emerson

_____

_____

_____

_____

_____

_____

A Challenge in Paraphrasing (6–7)

Directions: Paraphrase the following passage from "The Crisis" by Thomas Paine. Try to restate the meaning in your own words in a way that shows your understanding of the original. You may first want to think about how you would "break up" the sentences into their individual elements to make paraphrasing them easier.

Use a dictionary if you wish to check the shade of meaning to use in paraphrasing some words in the original versions.

These are the times that try men's souls. The summer soldier and the sunshine patriot will, in this crisis, shrink from the service of their country; but he that stands it now, deserves the love and thanks of man and woman. Tyranny, like hell, is not easily conquered; yet we have this consolation with us, that the harder the conflict, the more glorious the triumph. What we obtain too cheap, we esteem too lightly: it is dearness only that gives everything its value.

from *The Crisis* by Thomas Paine
(*Written during gloomy hours of the Revolutionary War*
to encourage American freedom fighters)

_____

_____

_____

_____

_____

_____

_____

_____

_____

_____

_____

_____

Name_____ Date _____ Period _____

Paraphrasing a Speech by Shakespeare (6–8)

Directions: Paraphrase the following passage from the play *Julius Caesar* by William Shakespeare. Try to restate the meaning in your own words in a way that shows your understanding of the original. You may first want to think about how you would "break up" the passage into its individual elements to make paraphrasing it easier.

Use a dictionary if you wish to check the shade of meaning to use in paraphrasing some words in the original versions.

The opening lines have been paraphrased to assist you.

But 'tis a common proof,
That lowliness is young ambition's ladder,
Whereto the climber upward turns his face;
But when he once attains the upmost round,
He then unto the ladder turns his back,
Looks in the clouds, scorning the base degrees
By which he did ascend.

from *Julius Caesar* by William Shakespeare
(*Brutus, deciding it was necessary
to assassinate Rome's ruler, Julius Caesar*)

_____Yet it is commonly accepted as true,_____

That being in a low position makes a young person want to climb the ladder of success,

_____

_____

_____

_____

_____

_____

_____

_____

_____

© 1995 by The Center for Applied Research in Education

UNIT 7

Coming to Terms with Techniques of Literature

Literary techniques and terms can be confusing to students and difficult to present, especially when incidentally encountered in the midst of other reading assignments.

In the course of studying major selections or units of poetry, appropriate examples appear too infrequently for students to grasp their purpose and meaning—or to realize that merely being able to recognize their use and apply the right terms is not enough. Students need to discover that the key techniques of literature add significantly to the substance and sense, as well as the style, of what they are reading.

To become accomplished readers, it is essential that students know how to approach literature that contains figurative and allusive language. It is the goal of this unit to show students how and why writers use special techniques to convey and amplify their meaning—and help them discover the part that active, involved readers play to achieve a fuller benefit from their usage.

As an introduction to the terms of literature, this unit contains eighteen key techniques used by writers of prose and poetry. Included are a wealth of examples, which will allow your students to concentrate on individual techniques, their purposes, and definitions—along with ample exercises illustrating their use and the kinds of questions good readers ask to discover how figurative and allusive language complements and illuminates a work's underlying meaning.

Students gain proficiency via reading selections and exercises addressing related techniques. In this way, students can hone their interpretive skills and are better prepared when major techniques are used in higher-level reading.

At the end of this unit, you'll find a glossary of terms plus a pair of quizzes designed to test acquired knowledge. The culminating activities include a humorous reading selection, illustrating techniques of metaphor, irony, satire, and implication/inference, which enables students to apply their skills profitably and enjoyably.

NOTES ON ACTIVITIES

Colloquial, Colorful, or Cliché (7–2)

You might also want to discuss the literal sense of some of these clichés and explain the reasons for avoiding them in formal writing or speaking. When clichés lose their sense of freshness through overuse, they also lose much of their impact and fullness of meaning. So, although there is nothing really "wrong" with clichés, they show a lack of originality on the part of those who use them.

Making Thoughtful Inferences (7–3)

Making inferences is a form of drawing conclusions, but it requires more than putting two and two together from evidence given in the text itself. It involves a higher level of thinking, so students need to apply their own knowledge and ideas in their attempts to infer what an author had in mind. Emphasize the importance of determining the writer's underlying intent before allowing personal opinions, biases, and ideas to intrude.

Introduction to Imagery (Reading Selection 7–4)

When students respond to the stimulus of imagery, advise them to avoid giving synonyms for the word itself. Instead, they are to describe their mental picture of the image—how it looks, feels, smells, sounds, and tastes as they envision it in their imaginations—or explain its effect.

In presenting imagery, encourage students to "brainstorm" and volunteer their responses to the metaphors given as examples. Students should come up with a variety of responses; accept all that seem fitting and meaningful.

Seeing the Logic in an Analogy (7–7)

After classes discuss why the writer chose to make each analogy, these examples should also stimulate spirited discussions of their ideas. You may want to introduce the *syllogism,* especially in connection with question 5 and the word *idiot.* A typical form for stating this manner of deductive reasoning is as follows: All cocker spaniels are dogs; Sparky is a cocker spaniel; therefore, Sparky is a dog. Warn students against the logical fallacy that results from reversing the terms in the following way: All cocker spaniels are dogs; Sparky is a dog; therefore, Sparky is a cocker spaniel.

After being introduced to syllogisms, students might enjoy writing their own examples, illustrating both logical truths and fallacy. You may want to assign them to work in pair or groups, then share their results with the entire class.

Identifying Literary Techniques (7–15)

Students should be able to give good reasons for labeling these examples according to the literary techniques they illustrate. If students can explain their reasons for alternate choices, you may want to accept variations from the answer key; for example, metaphor as well as simile when "like" or "as" is used in a comparison.

How You *Infer* What Others *Imply*
(*Reading Selection 7–1*)

Jeremy described what he planned to do with the prize money he saw himself winning.

"Don't count your chickens before they're hatched," Michelle warned him.

"But, I'm not a chicken farmer," he replied.

Jeremy was taking Michelle's words *literally,* as if they meant exactly what they seemed to mean on the surface. Michelle used this familiar expression figuratively, to express her ideas indirectly. And, since both knew he didn't raise chickens, Jeremy should have realized this.

If this were a real-life incident, he probably did—and was simply joking. In everyday situations, most people use the same techniques found in literature without even being aware of it.

"Don't count your chickens before they're hatched" actually makes good sense on two different levels:

- On a **literal** level it means: If you raise chickens, you can't be sure how many eggs laid by your hens will actually hatch as healthy chicks.
- On a **figurative** level it means: In the same way, you shouldn't count on something to happen until you are sure it will come true.

Since Jeremy knew the saying didn't fit on a literal level, he should *infer* Michelle was speaking *figuratively* and meant to *imply* he shouldn't plan how to spend money before winning the prize.

Here are definitions of the terms that fit this imaginary situation:

1.	**figurative**	stating ideas indirectly, such as by a comparison or other expressive manner of speech
2.	**literal**	meant to be taken as given, to be accepted at face value or by its primary meaning, not figuratively
3.	**imply**	to put or "weave" in an underlying meaning that is intended to be understood though not directly stated –*implication:* something that is implied –*implicit:* contained within a statement or situation, though unstated
4.	**infer**	to "take out" or to draw a conclusion based on that which is implied, but not directly stated –*inference:* something that is inferred

What Others Imply, You Infer (7–1A)

Directions: Each of the popular sayings given below can be taken both on a literal and figurative level. On the first line, write the meaning if taken literally. On the second, write what you should infer to be its meaning if the saying was intended figuratively.

EXAMPLE: "Don't count your chickens before they're hatched."

On a literal level: If you raise chickens, you can't be sure how many eggs laid by your hens will hatch as healthy chicks.

On a figurative level: You shouldn't count on something unless you are sure of its happening.

1. It's no use crying over spilt milk.

   On a literal level: _____

   _____

   On a figurative level: _____

   _____

2. You can catch more flies with honey than you can with vinegar.

   On a literal level: _____

   _____

   On a figurative level: _____

   _____

3. A stitch in time saves nine.

   On a literal level: _____

   _____

   On a figurative level: _____

   _____

4. It's a long road that has no turning.

   On a literal level: _____

   _____

   On a figurative level: _____

   _____

5. Let sleeping dogs lie.

   On a literal level: _____

   _____

   On a figurative level: _____

   _____

Colloquial, Colorful, or Cliché (7–2)

colloquial: an expression proper for everyday conversation but not for standard or formal writing or speech

cliché: an expression that seems dull, trite, and unimaginative because of long overuse, such as "brave as a lion"

Directions: Each of the following clichés is also an example of figurative use of language, which some people use to add a colorful flavor to colloquial conversation. On the lines, write what each means on a figurative level.

1. to be "in the chips" _____

_____

2. to have "a chip on your shoulder" _____

_____

3. to be "under the weather" _____

_____

4. to be "off your feed" _____

_____

5. to feel "in the pink" _____

_____

6. to describe something as "water under the bridge" _____

_____

7. to say something has "fallen by the wayside" _____

_____

8. to "take forty winks" _____

_____

9. to avoid something "like the plague" _____

_____

10. to be "out on a limb" _____

_____

Making Thoughtful Inferences (7–3)

Directions: Writers often purposely try to state their ideas in a way that will capture readers' attentions and make them stop and think. They expect thoughtful readers to infer their underlying meaning by using their own knowledge, ideas, and judgment. Read and think carefully about the following quotations, then write your answers to the questions that follow. Show your understanding by stating your ideas in your own words.

A. The fashion wears out more apparel than the man. — from *Much Ado About Nothing* by William Shakespeare

Inference: More people throw out clothes because they are (1) _____

_____ than because they are (2) _____.

B. What does it matter if we have a new book or an old book, if we open neither? —

Jesse Jackson

Inference: (1) Concerning education, Jackson implies that some people worry too

much about children having to _____

_____.

(2) Instead, Jackson believes those interested in schools should put more emphasis on

_____.

C. We are what we eat.

Inference: (1) From a physical standpoint, what people eat affects both their

_____ and their _____.

(2) From an emotional standpoint, people's eating habits can also show _____

_____.

D. "I think her eagerness to plead guilty to a lesser charge speaks for itself," said the prosecutor.

Inference: (1) The prosecutor is implying that the defendant is _____.

(2) His implication also is that she agreed to a lesser charge because she knew

_____.

(7–3 continued)

E. Today's common sense is yesterday's science. — Niels Bohr

Inference: (1) Science is often considered something known mainly by people who

_____

and do their work in _____.

(2) Common sense includes whatever ought to be known by _____

_____ and used in _____.

(3) By "today" and "yesterday" the writer means _____

and _____.

(4) When scientific knowledge becomes widespread, it seems like something

_____.

F. Can it be, I wonder, that children are happier when they are made to obey orders and
are sent to bed at six o'clock than when allowed to regulate their own conduct; that
bread and milk is more favourable to laughter and soft childish ways than beefsteaks
and pickles three times a day; that an occasional whipping, even, will conduce to rosey
cheeks? It is an idea which I should never dare to broach to an American mother; but
I must confess that after my travels on the western continent my opinions have a ten-
dency in that direction . . . — from *North America* by Anthony Trollope

Inference: (1) The writer implies that children should not be allowed to

_____ or _____.

(2) The writer must not be a citizen of _____.

(3) The reader should infer this because _____

_____.

(4) In writing of "an occasional whipping" and "rosey cheeks," the writer implies

_____

_____.

Introduction to Imagery (*Reading Selection 7–4*)

My luve is like a red, red rose
That's newly sprung in June . . .

"A Red, Red Rose" by Robert Burns

Like most techniques of literature, imagery is commonly used in everyday conversation. It simply means language that invites you to "see" or mentally picture the scene, person, or object in question. *Imagery* calls to mind one of the five senses: something you can hear, touch, smell, or taste as well as see.

When you picture a "red, red rose" that's just begun to bloom in June, what words come to mind to describe your mental image of it? Of course, you will only want to think of the good things, because it's being used to describe someone's loved one.

fresh	bright	beautiful
delicate	dewy	sweet-smelling
petal-soft	dainty	brilliant

. . . and you might think of others

When you say something happened "as quick as a wink" or someone is a "real lamb," you're actually using a *figure of speech,* an expressive use of language meant to be taken in a figurative, not literal sense. The figures of speech given as examples are called metaphors and similes.

1. **metaphor:** A figure of speech that compares one object to another that is not obviously similar in an attempt to show the reader qualities that the secondary one shares with the subject of the comparison. For example, Romeo expresses the power of his love with this comparison: "Juliet is the sun." The words *metaphor* and *metaphorical* refer both to a direct comparison, as in the example, and the type of comparison also known as a *simile.*

2. **simile:** A type of comparison or metaphor using *like* or *as.* For example, "His muscles were like a bionic man's" or "She was as quiet as a shadow."

When you read, identifying metaphors and similes is relatively easy. But good readers know that their purpose goes beyond adding color and variety to writing. Their real purpose is to give you a clearer mental image of the subject being described.

By using metaphors, writers invite you to picture something familiar and apply its description to the subject you're reading about. In this way, metaphorical comparisons help you understand how writers want you to "see" their subject in your imagination— and sometimes how it sounds, feels, smells, and even tastes, as well!

Creating Mental Pictures with Metaphors (7–4A)

Directions:

Step 1. Name the subject that serves as the basis for the comparison, followed by the metaphor used to help you picture it more clearly.

Step 2. Indicate whether the comparison is made as a metaphor or simile.

Step 3. List at least two descriptive words or phrases that come to mind when you picture the metaphorical words or phrases and that make them a fitting comparison.

A. The road was a ribbon of moonlight . . . — from "The Highwayman" by Alfred Noyes

(1) The subject _____ is being compared to _____

_____. (2) Type of comparison: _____

(3) Two reasons for this being a fitting comparison: _____

_____

and _____

_____

B. My heart is like a singing bird. — Christina Rossetti

(1) The subject _____ is being compared to _____

_____. (2) Type of comparison: _____

(3) Two reasons for this being a fitting comparison: _____

_____

and _____

_____

C. Truth is a shadow. — Stephen Crane

(1) The subject _____ is being compared to _____

_____. (2) Type of comparison: _____

(3) Two reasons for this being a fitting comparison: _____

_____

and _____

_____

D. Oh for a poet—for a beacon bright . . . — "Oh for a Poet" by Edward Arlington Robinson

    (1) The subject _____ is being compared to _____

    _____ . (2) Type of comparison: _____

    (3) Two reasons for this being a fitting comparison: _____

    _____

    and _____

    _____

E. The Assyrian* came down like the wolf on the fold . . . — from "The Destruction of Sennacherib" by George Gordon, Lord Byron

    (1) The subject _____ is being compared to _____

    _____ . (2) Type of comparison: _____

    (3) Two reasons for this being a fitting comparison: _____

    _____

    and _____

    _____

*enemy army

F. Shame is Pride's cloak. — William Blake

    (1) The subject _____ is being compared to _____

    _____ . (2) Type of comparison: _____

    (3) Two reasons for this being a fitting comparison: _____

    _____

    and _____

    _____

Creating Mental Pictures with Metaphors (7–4B)

Directions:

Step 1. Name the subject that serves as the basis for the comparison, followed by the metaphor used to help you picture it more clearly.

Step 2. Indicate whether the comparison is made as a metaphor or simile.

Step 3. List at least two descriptive words or phrases that come to mind when you picture the metaphorical words or phrases and that make them a fitting comparison.

A. Like two cathedral towers these stately pines
Uplift their fretted summits tipped with cones . . . — Henry Wadsworth Longfellow

(1) The subject _____ is being compared to _____

_____. (2) Type of comparison: _____

(3) Two reasons for this being a fitting comparison: _____

_____

and _____

_____

B. She was a phantom of delight
When first she gleamed upon my sight;
A lovely apparition, sent
To be a moment's ornament . . . — William Wordsworth

(1) The subject _____ is being compared to _____

_____. (2) Type of comparison: _____

(3) Two reasons for this being a fitting comparison: _____

_____

and _____

_____

C. She walks in beauty, like the night
Of cloudless climes and starry skies;
And all that's best of dark and bright
Meet in her aspect and her eyes . . . — George Gordon, Lord Byron

(1) The subject _____ is being compared to _____

_____. (2) Type of comparison: _____

(3) Two reasons for this being a fitting comparison: _____

_____

and _____

_____

(7–4B continued)

D. Good prose is like a window pane. — George Orwell

(1) The subject _____ is being compared to _____

_____. (2) Type of comparison: _____

(3) Two reasons for this being a fitting comparison: _____

_____

and _____

_____

E. Where fog trails . . .
The whistle of a boat
Calls and cries unendingly,
Like some lost child . . . — Carl Sandburg

(1) The subject _____ is being compared to _____

_____. (2) Type of comparison: _____

(3) Two reasons for this being a fitting comparison: _____

_____

and _____

_____

Quotations with More Than One Metaphor (7–5)

Directions: Each of the following uses two or more metaphors, some that refer to the same subject and others with different subjects as their basis for comparison. Identify each metaphor and fill in the answers concerning it.

1. The house of every one is to him as his castle and his fortress. — Sir Edward Coke

   a. (1) The subject _____ is first compared to _____.

   (2) Two reasons for this being a fitting comparison: _____

   _____

   and _____

   _____

   b. (1) The subject, _____, is then compared to _____.

   (2) Two reasons for this being a fitting comparison: _____

   _____

   and _____

   _____

   (3) Both comparisons are examples of _____.

2. A brain of feathers, and a heart of lead. — Alexander Pope

   a. (1) The first subject _____ is being compared to _____.

   (2) Two reasons for this being a fitting comparison: _____

   _____

   and _____

   _____

   b. (1) In the second example, _____ is compared to _____.

   (2) Two reasons for this being a fitting comparison: _____

   _____

   and _____

   _____

   (3) Both comparisons are examples of _____.

3. After "The First Snowfall" . . .
The snow had begun in the gloaming,
   And busily all the night
Had been heaping field and highway
   With a silence deep and white.

Every pine and fir and hemlock
   Wore ermine too dear for an earl,
And the poorest twig on the elm tree
   Was ridged inch deep with pearl. — by James Russell Lowell

a. (1) The first subject _____ is compared to _____

_____. (2) Two reasons this is a fitting comparison:

_____

_____

and _____

_____

b. (1) In the second example, _____ is compared to _____

_____. (2) Two reasons this is a fitting comparison:

_____

_____

and _____

_____

c. (1) The third comparison is _____ to _____

_____. (2) Two reasons this is a fitting comparison:

_____

_____

and _____

_____

(3) All three comparisons are examples of _____.

4. It was the spring of hope, it was the winter of despair. — Charles Dickens

a. (1) The first subject, _____, is being compared to _____.

(2) Two reasons this is a fitting comparison: _____

_____

and _____

_____

b. (1) In the second example, _____ is being compared to _____.

(2) Two reasons for this being a fitting comparison: _____

_____

and _____

_____

(3) Both comparisons are examples of _____.

Name _____ Date _____ Period _____

Finding Your Own Metaphors (7–6)

There are many familiar metaphors you hear every day:

Sly as a fox . . . strong as an ox . . . as quiet as a mouse . . .
. . . the foot of the bed . . . the hands of a clock . . .

Although some of them may be clichés, our everyday conversation could hardly do without them!

Directions: List at least ten familiar metaphors or similes, and explain the mental image that makes each a fitting comparison. If you prefer, you may wish to add some original metaphors of your own on the back of this sheet.

Metaphor	**Why it is fitting**
1. _____	_____
	_____
2. _____	_____
	_____
3. _____	_____
	_____
4. _____	_____
	_____
5. _____	_____
	_____
6. _____	_____
	_____
7. _____	_____
	_____
8. _____	_____
	_____
9. _____	_____
	_____
10. _____	_____
	_____

Seeing the Logic in an Analogy (7–7)

analogy: A comparison of one thing to another, based on their having similar characteristics in certain respects; *for example,* a hummingbird's wing and a bee's wing, or a human heart and a pump. Analogies appeal mainly to a person's logic or intelligence, not the emotions or senses. Writers use analogies to help readers develop a better understanding of the subject discussed.

Directions: Carefully read the following analogies and answer the questions concerning each. Try to restate the ideas in your own words. Except for the terms of the analogy, avoid copying parts of the passage exactly.

A. Serious sport has nothing to do with fair play. It is bound up with hatred, jealousy, boastfulness, disregard of all rules and sadistic pleasure in witnessing violence: in other words, it is war minus the shooting. — George Orwell

    (1) Orwell is making an analogy between _____ and _____.

    (2) Why would both involve each of the following?

        a. jealousy _____

        _____

        b. boastfulness _____

        _____

        c. disregard of all rules _____

        _____

        d. sadistic pleasure _____

        _____

    (3) In what way do the parts of the analogy differ? _____

    _____

B. Crimes, like virtues, are their own rewards. — George Forquer

    (1) Forquer's analogy compares _____ and _____.

    (2) How can virtue be its own reward in regard to the way it makes people feel about

    themselves? _____

    _____

    (3) What, then, must Forquer expect you to infer about the other element in his anal-

    ogy? _____

    _____

(7–7 continued)

C. (To the Japanese) work is a form of beauty, in the sense that it matters less what one does than how one is seen to do it. Japanese, more than any other people I know, have made work into a spectacle, if not a fine art. — Ian Buruma

   (1) Buruma is making an analogy between _____ and

       _____.

   (2) Explain the main reason for their being alike.

       _____

       _____

   (3) Why would it be difficult for work to be a "fine art"? _____

       _____.

       _____.

   (4) In what sense might it be a "spectacle"? _____

       _____.

D. The electronic computer is a moron whose total imbecility can often be quite exasperating . . . If you punch the number three as "3" when it should have been "3.", it will refuse to work the program and instead it will print some gobbledegook like this:
     ERROR IN LINE 123. ILLEGAL MIXING OF MODES.
     EXECUTION DELETED. TIME 23 SECS.
     If the computer is so smart, why does it not put in the one dot instead of churning out all this gibberish? Ask it; but it will just sit there, a moronic heap of wire, semiconductors and tape, and say nothing . . . — from *The Story of Pi* by Petr Backmann

   (1) Backmann makes an analogy between _____ and _____.

   (2) What error was made when punching in the number? _____

       _____.

   (3) In what three ways did the computer respond, making the author believe his analogy is fitting?

      a. _____

        _____

      b. _____

        _____

      c. _____

        _____

   (4) What are two ways the writer implies an intelligent human being would respond to a similar situation?

      a. _____

      b. _____

(7–7 continued)

E. Know how to read? You *must*
    Before you can write. An idiot
    Will always talk a lot. — Marie Francoise-Catherine de Beauveau, la Marquise de Boufflers

(1) An analogy is made between _____ and _____.

(2) In order to write well, the author implies _____
     _____.

(3) The author states, "An idiot will always talk a lot." Why doesn't this mean some-
     one who talks a lot is always an idiot? _____
     _____.

(4) To complete the analogy, what is the idiot lacking? _____
     _____.

Personification Makes *Things* Almost Human—Part I (7–8A)

personification: to give human qualities to a thing or creature that is not human. Writers can personify persons or things through the use of personal pronouns such as *she* and *he* or by describing them as having human emotions, appearance, or abilities. FOR EXAMPLE, "The house waited patiently for its family to return, missing the sound and bustle of its normal life."

Directions: After reading the following examples, tell what is being personified and the phrases used to show personification. Be able to point out the specific words that influenced your decision.

A. April, April,
      Laugh thy girlish laughter;
   Then, the moment after,
   Weep thy girlish tears . . . — "Song" by William Watson

   (1) _____ is being personified.

   (2) Two phrases that show this personification are:

       a. _____

       b. _____

B. I heard the trailing garments of the Night
      Sweep through her marble halls;
   I saw her sable skirts all fringed with light
      from the celestial walls. — "Hymn to the Night" by Henry Wadsworth Longfellow

   (1) _____ is being personified.

   (2) Three phrases that show this personification are:

       a. _____

       b. _____

       c. _____

C. When Freedom, from her mountain height,
       Unfurled her standard to the air,
    She tore the azure robe of night,
       And set the stars of glory there! — "The American Flag" by Joseph Rodman Drake

(1) _____ is being personified.

(2) Three phrases that show this personification are:

    a. _____

    b. _____

    c. _____

(3) The phrase "azure robe" seems to personify _____.

D. The merry brown hares came leaping
       Over the crest of the hill,
    Where the clover and corn lay sleeping,
       Under the moonlight still. — "A Rough Rhyme on a Rough Matter" by Charles Kingsley

(1) The first example of personification is _____.

(2) This is indicated by the poet's use of _____.

(3) The second example of personification is _____.

(4) This is indicated by the poet's use of _____.

Personification Makes *Things* Almost Human—Part II (7–8B)

personification: to give human qualities to a thing or creature that is not human. Writers can personify persons or things through the use of personal pronouns such as *she* and *he* or by describing them as having human emotions, appearance, or abilities. FOR EXAMPLE, "The house waited patiently for its family to return, missing the sound and bustle of its normal life."

Directions: After reading the following examples, tell what is being personified and the phrases used to show personification. Be able to point out the specific words that influenced your decision.

A. Wee, modest, crimson-tippe´d flow'r,
Thou's met me in an evil hour . . . — "To a Mountain Daisy" by Robert Burns

   (1) _____ is being personified.

   (2) This is shown by the poet's use of _____ and

   _____.

B. The toad beneath the harrow knows
Exactly where each tooth-point goes,
The butterfly upon the road
Preaches contentment to that toad. — "Pagett M.P." by Rudyard Kipling

   (1) The first example of personification is _____.

   (2) This is indicated by the poet's use of _____.

   (3) The second example of personification is _____.

   (4) This is indicated by the poet's use of _____.

C. But four young Oysters hurried up,
   All eager for the treat;
Their coats were brushed, their faces washed,
   Their shoes were clean and neat—
And this was odd, because, you know,
   They hadn't any feet. — from "Through the Looking Glass" by Lewis Carroll

   (1) _____ are being personified.

   (2) Five phrases that show this personification are:

      a. _____

      b. _____

      c. _____

      d. _____

      e. _____

D. Shame is Pride's cloak. — William Blake

   (1) _____ is being personified.

   (2) This is shown by the poet's having _____.

   (3) What other figure of speech does this illustrate? _____.

How Antithesis Attracts Attention (7–9)

antithesis: the contrast of two ideas, often done by placing their two opposing parts side by side, or against one another, such as "Give me liberty or give me death." Writers who express themselves well and gracefully use antitheses in a way that offers their readers fresh, original views and that gives them ideas worth thinking about.

Directions: Read the following examples of antithesis, and write your answers to the questions that follow. Carefully think through your answers to make sure they are clearly stated.

A. The farm is a piece of the world, the school-house is not. — Ralph Waldo Emerson

   (1) In what sense is a farm an actual "piece of the world"? _____

   _____

   _____

   (2) What do you infer that school lacks in comparison? _____

   _____

   _____

B. Winning is not the most important thing; it's everything. — Vince Lombardi

   (1) If it stood alone, what mistaken idea would you infer from the first half of the antithesis? _____

   _____

   (2) Restate Lombardi's ideas in the fewest words possible, without using antithesis or using the word "everything." _____

   _____

   (3) Why does the use of antithesis make Lombardi's statement so effective?

   _____

C. Not that you won or lost—
But how you played the game. — Grantland Rice

   (1) What does Rice imply is more important that winning when he uses the phrase "how you played the game"? _____

   _____

   _____

(7–9 continued)

(2) In what way is this quotation the antithesis of quotation "B"?

_____

_____

_____

D. The boys throw stones at the frog in sport, but the frogs die not in sport but in earnest. — Bion

   (1) The contrast in this antithesis is between the _____ attitude of the

   boys and the _____.

   (2) Explain what the writer is implying about some of the things young people do

   "just for fun." _____

   _____

   _____

E. Whether the children rolled in the grass, or waded in the brook, or swam in the salt ocean, or sailed in the bay, or fished for smelts in the creeks, or netted minnows in the salt-marshes, or took to the pine-woods and the granite quarries, or chased muskrats and hunted snapping-turtles in the swamps, or mushrooms or nuts on the autumn hills, summer and country were always sensual living, while winter was always compulsory learning. <u>Summer was the multiplicity of nature; winter was school</u>. — from
The Education of Henry Adams by Henry Adams

   (1) How are the opposing ideas in the underlined antithesis clearly illustrated in the

   sentence before it? _____

   _____

   _____

   (2) Restate the underlined sentence in your own words. _____

   _____

   _____

   (3) Write the part of the first sentence that states an antithesis of its own.

   _____

   _____

Antithesis: Cause for Discussion (7–10)

Directions: Because they present two opposing ideas, antitheses offer thought-provoking ideas that invite further discussion. Working in pairs or groups, first decide the underlying meaning of the quotations you choose or those your teacher assigns you. Then discuss your reactions to it.

Plan to present your findings to the class, and invite them to add their ideas to yours. You may also like further discussion of some of the antitheses in the foregoing exercise.

For Discussion:

1. One should eat to live, and not live to eat. — Molière

2. People ask you for criticism, but they only want praise. — Somerset Maugham

3. Economy is going without something you do want in case you should, someday, want something you probably won't want (if you get it.) — Antony Hope

4. A man is known by the books he reads, by the company he keeps, by the praise he gives, by his dress, by his tastes, by his distastes, by the stories he tells, by his gait, by the motions of his eye, by the look of his chamber; <u>for nothing on earth is solitary, but every thing hath affinities infinite</u> . . . — Ralph Waldo Emerson

5. For a city consists in its men, not in its walls nor ships empty of men. — Nicias, c. 470–413 B.C.

6. The entire object of true education is to make people not merely *do* the right thing but *enjoy* the right thing. — John Ruskin

7. The first and wisest of them all professed
   To know this only, that he nothing knew. — John Milton, from *Paradise Regained*

Three Useful Literary Terms (7–11)

Study the definitions of three different ways of using words that you may encounter in your reading. Then, write your answers to the questions concerning the examples following each.

A. **hyperbole:** obvious exaggeration that is intended for effect; an extravagant statement not meant to be taken literally; another type of figure of speech. ***Example:*** *"I've been waiting here for an eternity."*

Directions: In the blank space after each example of hyperbole, write the key word or words creating a hyperbolic effect.

1. Toussaint, the most unhappy man of men! — William Wordsworth

   Key word or words of hyperbole: _____

2. The atrocious crime of being a young man . . . I shall neither attempt to palliate or deny. — William Penn, Earl of Chatman

   Key word or words of hyperbole: _____

3. "This was the most unkindest cut of all . . ." said by Mark Antony of the stab wound given Julius Caesar by his supposed friend, Brutus. — *Julius Caesar* by William Shakespeare

   Key word or words of hyperbole: _____

4. These, in the day when heaven was falling,
   The hour when earth's foundation fled . . .
   . . . took their wages and are dead. — "Epitaph on an Army of Mercenaries" by A.E. Housman

   Key word or words of hyperbole: _____

B. **apostrophe:** to address or speak directly to a personified thing or idea; also to directly address someone or something not present. ***Example:*** *Rain, rain, go away. Come again some other day!* Words of direct address are *"Rain, rain."*

Directions: In the blank space, write the key word or words used in direct address, which thereby show apostrophe.

1. O, World, I cannot hold thee close enough. — Edna St. Vincent Millay

   Key word or words showing apostrophe: _____

2. Age of Gold, I bid thee come
   To this Earth, was erst thy home! — Pietro Metastasio

   Key word or words showing apostrophe: _____

(7–11 continued)

3. Western wind, when will thou blow
   The small rain down can rain? — Anonymous

   Key word or words showing apostrophe: _____

4. Roll on, thou deep and dark blue ocean, roll! — George Gordon, Lord Byron

   Key word or words showing apostrophe: _____

C. **ambiguous:** having two or more possible meanings or interpretations, with the correct choice difficult to determine. Some *ambiguity* is intentional and is meant to mislead the reader or hearer. ***Example:*** *Do I turn left here? Right!*

Directions: In the first blank spaces, write the ambiguous word or words; then explain the double meaning that creates the ambiguity.

1. Give me a ring sometime.

   (1) Ambiguous word or words: _____

   (2) Cause of ambiguity: _____

   _____

2. "I ran into someone you know today," the teenager told his mother when he came home after borrowing her car.

   (1) Ambiguous word or words: _____

   (2) Cause of ambiguity: _____

   _____

3. "She told me to pass it to her, and I did," explained the quarterback who got in trouble for throwing a book at the teacher.

   (1) Ambiguous word or words: _____

   (2) Cause of ambiguity: _____

   _____

4. I never tell the truth, I always lie.

   (1) Ambiguous word or words: _____

   (2) Cause of ambiguity: _____

   _____

Irony Is Not What You'd Expect
(*Reading Selection 7–12*)

"Have you any more brilliant ideas?"

In some ways, it might seem a surprising question to ask when someone's big plans have turned out wrong. Yet, not if you recognized by the tone of voice or turn of phrase that the question was asked *ironically* and "brilliant" meant the opposite of what was actually said.

As with many figures of speech, irony adds an element of surprise and a note of humor. This often makes it more effective than stating the question plainly as "Have you any more dumb ideas?"

Be careful not to confuse irony and sarcasm. Although some sarcastic remarks contain an element of irony, not all irony is used sarcastically.

Here are definitions of irony you should know:

Irony is a figure of speech that always contains the element of being the opposite of what someone would normally expect. There are three types of irony: verbal, dramatic, and situation irony.

Verbal irony is a statement that means the exact opposite of what is said. The speaker or writer intentionally uses a word or expression that is contrary to what is really meant—and expects the reader or listener to recognize his or her actual intention. *Example:* "Have you any more brilliant ideas?"

Situation irony occurs when an event or situation has an outcome that is the exact opposite of what was hoped for or would be expected—as if a twist of fate had intervened to make it turn out wrong. *Example:* A teacher warns a student to be careful not to drop a vial in chemistry class, then drops it himself.

Dramatic irony involves a situation in which the speaker or person involved does not realize that his or her words or actions have an ironic twist that the reader or observer recognizes. *Example:* After Gwen's fashion-conscious friend, Susie, told her, "You really ought to pay more attention to how you dress," Gwen noticed the price tag Susie forgot to remove from the collar of her new jacket.

Recognizing Irony in Words and Situations (7–12A)

Directions: First, write the key word or words that are used ironically in each example. Then, explain why they create an ironic effect that is the opposite of what you would normally expect.

A. "I knew this was my lucky day," cried Meg when she discovered she forgot her lunch money after a morning when everything had gone wrong.

    (1) Key word or words indicating irony: _____

    (2) Reason for this being ironic: _____

    _____

B. Snubbed by his supposed friends after losing all his money, the former millionaire said, "Now I know how loyal and faithful my friends were."

    (1) Key word or words indicating irony: _____

    (2) Reason for this being ironic: _____

    _____

C. Around me are the two hundred and forty men of B Company
Mud-coloured
Going about their avocations,
Resting between their practice of the art
Of killing men . . . — "What the Orderly Dog Saw" by Ford Maddox Ford

    (1) Key word or words indicating irony: _____

    (2) Reason for this being ironic: _____

    _____

D. The law, in its majestic equality, forbids the rich as well as the poor to sleep under the bridges, to be in the streets, and to steal bread. — Anatole France

    (1) Key word or words indicating irony: _____

    (2) Reason for this being ironic: _____

    _____

    _____

    _____

(7–12A continued)

E. King Edward's new policy of peace was very successful and culminated in the Great War to End War. [It was followed by] the Peace to End Peace. — W. C. Sellar and R. J. Yeatman, *1066 and All That*

    (1) Key word or words indicating irony: _____

       and _____

    (2) Reason for this being ironic: _____

    _____

F. He took castles and towns; he cut short limbs and lives;
He made orphans and widows of children and wives;
This course many years he triumphantly ran,
And did mischief enough to be called a great man. — "Lines from Crotchet Castle"
by Thomas Love Peacock

    (1) Key word or words indicating irony: _____

       and _____

    (2) Reason for their being ironic: _____

    _____

    _____

    _____

Dramatic Irony: "The Blind Men and the Elephant"
(*Reading Selection 7–13*)

Directions: Read the following poem for the first time to enjoy its humor. On your second reading, look for literary techniques used by the poet, including irony and metaphors.

It was six men of Indostan,
To learning much inclined,
Who went to see the elephant,
(Though all of them were blind,)
That each by observation   5
Might satisfy his mind.

The first approached the elephant,
And, happening to fall
Against his broad and sturdy side,
At once began to bawl: 10
"God bless me! but the elephant
Is very like a wall!"

The second, feeling of the tusk,
Cried: "Ho! what have we here,
So very round, and smooth, and sharp?   15
To me 't is very clear,
This wonder of an elephant
Is very like a spear!"

The third approached the animal,
And, happening to take   20
The squirming trunk within his hands,
Thus boldly up he spake:
"I see," quoth he, "the elephant
Is very like a snake!"

The fourth reached out his eager hand,   25
And fell about the knee:
"What most this wondrous beast is like,
Is very plain," quoth he;
"'T is clear enough the elephant
It very like a tree!"   30

The fifth, who chanced to touch the ear,
Said: "E'en the blindest man
Can tell what this resembles most;
Deny the fact who can,
This marvel of an elephant   35
Is very like a fan!"

The sixth no sooner had begun
About the beast to grope,
Than, seizing on the swinging tail
That fell within his scope,   40
"I see," quoth he, "the elephant
Is very like a rope!"

And so these men of Indostan
Disputed loud and long,
Each in his own opinion   45
Exceeding stiff and strong,
Though each was partly in the right,
And all were in the wrong!

by John Godfrey Saxe

Dramatic Irony: "The Blind Men and the Elephant" (7–13A)

Directions: Apply your knowledge of literary techniques in answering the following questions about "The Blind Men and the Elephant."

Part I. A Humorous Use of Metaphors

Each of the six blind men used a different simile to describe what an elephant was *really* like. List in order the six different comparisons that were made.

1. The first compared the elephant's _____ to a _____.

2. The second compared the elephant's _____ to a _____.

3. The third compared the elephant's _____ to a _____.

4. The fourth compared the elephant's _____ to a _____.

5. The fifth compared the elephant's _____ to a _____.

6. The sixth compared the elephant's _____ to a _____.

7. Explain the way in which all were making the same mistake.

   _____

   _____

Part II. Examples of Dramatic Irony

1–6. In lines 1-33, the poet has the men use six expressions that will seem ironical to the reader because of men's known blindness. List them below.

   Stanza 1. _____   Stanza 3. _____

   Stanza 4. _____   Stanza 5. _____

   Stanza 5. _____   Stanza 6. _____

7. Explain why saying "Deny the fact who can" is ironical in line 31.

   _____

   _____

8. This poem contains dramatic irony because _____

   _____

(7–13A continued)

Part III. A Sample of Satire

Satire is a type of humor that makes fun of a serious situation. Although the tale of "The Blind Men and the Elephant" is meant to be humorous in itself, it has a serious side when you apply it to other people and situations. You will discover the poem's satire as you answer the following questions.

1. Why was each of the men "partly in the right"? _____

_____

2. Why were "all . . . in the wrong"? _____

_____

3. In spite of the fact that "all were in the wrong," what attitude did all of them

have about their own opinion? _____

4. How is their attitude typical of the way people sometimes behave in real-life sit-

uations? (Include an example.) _____

_____

_____

_____

5. From this kind of behavior, what serious situation can result? _____

_____

_____

6. By having readers laugh at others through satire, what purpose is the poet also

trying to accomplish? _____

_____

_____

_____

Terms for Talking About Literature:
A Glossary (*Reading Selection 7–14*)

1. **ambiguous** having two or more possible meanings or interpretations, with the correct choice difficult to determine. *Example:* "Give me a ring." Some *ambiguity* is intentional and is meant to mislead the reader or hearer.

2. **analogy** a comparison of one thing to another, based on their similarities in certain respects. Analogies appeal mainly to a person's logic or intelligence, not the emotions or senses. *Example:* comparing the heart to a pump

3. **antithesis** the contrast of two ideas, often done by placing the two opposing parts side by side, or against one another, such as "Give me liberty or give me death."

4. **apostrophe** to address or speak directly to a personified thing or idea; also to directly address someone or something not present. *Example:* Rain, rain, go away. Come again some other day!

5. **cliché** an expression that seems dull, trite, and unimaginative because of long overuse, such as "brave as a lion." Some clichés are accepted as colorful, colloquial sayings.

6. **colloquial** an expression proper for everyday conversation but not for standard or formal writing or speech.

7. **figurative** expressing ideas indirectly, such as by a comparison, metaphor, or other figure of speech

8. **figure of speech** any expressive use of language, such as metaphor, simile, antithesis, irony, and so on, that consists of words used in other than their literal sense

9. **hyperbole** obvious exaggeration that is intended for effect; an extravagant statement not meant to be taken literally; another type of figure of speech. *Example:* "I've been waiting here for an eternity."

10. **imagery** the use of language that directs its appeal to the five senses, asking readers to "see" or mentally picture the scene, person, or object written about. *Imagery* may also appeal to the senses of hearing, touch, smell, and taste. *Image:* a kind of imagery; a figure of speech.

11. imply   to put or "weave" in an underlying meaning that is intended to be understood but is not openly expressed. *Implication:* something that is implied. *Implicit:* contained within a statement or situation, though not stated.

12. infer   to "take out" or to draw a conclusion based on that which is implied, but not openly stated. *Inference:* something that is inferred.

13. irony   a figure of speech that always contains the element of being the opposite of what someone would normally expect. There are three types of irony: verbal, dramatic, and situation irony.

14. literal   meant to be taken as given; to be accepted at face value or primary meaning, not in a figurative sense.

15. metaphor   a figure of speech that compares one object to another that is not obviously similar in an attempt to show the reader qualities that the secondary one shares with the subject of the comparison. *Example:* "Juliet is the sun." The words *metaphor* and *metaphorical* refer both to the example, and the type of comparison also known as a *simile*.

16. personification   to give human qualities to a thing or creature that is not human. *Example:* "The house waited patiently for its family to return, missing the sound and bustle of its normal life."

17. satire   humor that makes fun of a serious situation

18. simile   a type of comparison or metaphor using *like* or *as*. *Example:* "His muscles were like a bionic man's."

© 1995 by The Center for Applied Research in Education

Name _____ Date _____ Period _____

Identifying Literary Techniques (7–15)

Directions: Here are examples of various figures of speech. In the blank spaces, write the term or terms that apply to each. Choose from the following:

ambiguity	analogy	antithesis	apostrophe	cliché
hyperbole	irony	metaphor	personification	simile

1. The island dreams under the dawn. — "An Indian to His Love" by William Butler Yeats

   This illustrates _____.

2. The ruthless destruction of our national forests is a war against nature. — Anonymous

   This illustrates _____ and _____.

3. Time, you old gypsy man,
       Will you not stay,
   Put up your caravan
       Just for one day? — "Time, You Old Gypsy Man" by Ralph Hodgson

   This illustrates _____, _____,

   and _____.

4. The night has a thousand eyes,
       And the day but one . . . — from "Light" by F. W. Bourdillon

   This illustrates _____, _____,

   and _____.

5. The heart has its reasons which reason knows nothing of. — Blaise Pascal

   This illustrates _____ and _____.

6. "This place is going to the dogs."

   This illustrates _____ and _____.

7. Little fly,
   Thy summer's play
   My thoughtless hand
   Has brush'd away. — William Blake

   This illustrates _____, _____,

   and _____.

8. It was roses, rose all the way . . .
   The church-spires flamed, such flags they had,
   A year ago on this very day. — Robert Browning, "The Patriot"

   This illustrates _____ and _____.

9. "Would you like an Hawaiian punch?" — Advertising slogan

   This illustrates _____.

10. That's for me to know, and you to find out. — Colloquial

   This illustrates _____ and _____.

Matching Test: Literary Terms (7–16)

Directions: From the words listed below, choose the term that matches the definition and write the correct letter key in each blank space.

a. ambiguous   f. colloquial   k. imply   p. personification
b. analogy   g. figurative   l. infer   q. satire
c. antithesis   h. figure of speech   m. irony   r. simile
d. apostrophe   i. hyperbole   n. literal
e. cliché   j. imagery   o. metaphor

_____ 1. expressing ideas indirectly, such as by a comparison, metaphor, or other figure of speech

_____ 2. meant to be taken as given; to be accepted at face value or primary meaning, not figuratively

_____ 3. the contrast of two ideas, often done by placing the two opposing parts side by side

_____ 4. humor that makes fun of a serious situation

_____ 5. to address or speak directly to a personified thing or idea; also to directly address someone or something not present

_____ 6. obvious exaggeration intended for effect; an extravagant statement not meant to be taken literally; another type of figure of speech

_____ 7. any expressive use of language, such as metaphor, simile, antithesis, irony, and so on, that consists of words used in other than their literal sense

_____ 8. a comparison of one thing to another, logically based on their similarities in certain respects

_____ 9. having two or more possible meanings or interpretations, with the correct choice difficult to determine

_____ 10. language that appeals to the readers' senses, asking them to form a mental picture of a person, object, or scene

_____ 11. a figure of speech comparing one object to another not obviously similar for the purpose of showing the qualities that the second shares with the first

_____ 12. a figure of speech always with an element of being the opposite of what someone would normally expect; there are three types: verbal, dramatic, and situation

_____ 13. an expression proper for everyday conversation, but not standard for formal writing or speech

_____ 14. to give human qualities to a thing or creature that is not human; for example, "The house waited patiently for its family to return, missing the sound and bustle of its normal life."

_____ 15. a type of comparison or metaphor using *like* or *as*

_____ 16. to put or "weave" in an underlying meaning that is intended to be understood but not openly expressed

_____ 17. an expression that seems dull, trite, and unimaginative because of long overuse

_____ 18. to "take out" or to draw a conclusion based on that which is not openly stated

UNIT 8

The Truth in Literature

After learning the superficial definitions of *fiction* and *nonfiction*, students find it all too easy to remember nonfiction is "true" and therefore, by logical extension, fiction is "untrue" or "false." And so they often dismiss fiction as a waste of time, not on a par with nonfiction, and therefore not worth reading.

Offering fiction as a source of enjoyment and entertainment does no better. What's to enjoy? TV and other media seem to offer more—with far less effort.

The exercises in this unit will show students that the easy definitions of fiction and nonfiction do not go far enough. In fact, this unit leads students to discover that the real purpose of fiction, for good readers and writers alike, is to explore the truth in fiction's one great subject: people. What is human nature? What are people like? Who am I? Who are we?

In previous units, there has purposely been no attempt to distinguish between fiction and nonfiction in prose examples. Although students are encouraged to become aware of the difference between fact and opinion, the insinuation of truth in nonfiction and untruth in fiction has been carefully avoided.

The exercises in this unit are designed to allow students to develop an understanding of differences and similarities between nonfiction and fiction that go beyond labeling one true and one untrue. By comparing the two types of prose, students will discover that the essential difference is the way each is written:

In nonfiction, the writer speaks for him- or herself.

In fiction, the writer speaks through characters.

Further exercises in this unit will refine students' understanding of fiction and introduce major concepts that underlie fiction of literary value and significance.

When introducing basic concepts, such as conflict, it is necessary to use relatively obvious and unsophisticated examples. Space limitations also require that most be brief excerpts. After achieving awareness of the possibilities and truth of fiction, students will be better prepared for their subtler presentation in complete and longer selections.

As you work with these exercises, you may want to emphasize that, when reading literature, all of a reader's questions cannot and should not be answered until someone has read the complete work since only it expresses the writer's intention fully.

NOTES ON ACTIVITIES

Defining Fiction and Nonfiction (Reading Selection 8–3)

Instead of handing out this selection to the class, you might want to guide students to work out the definitions for themselves. Basing their conclusion on the paragraphs in Reading Selection 8–2 and its accompanying exercise, they should consider, step by step, how each element of fiction and nonfiction differs.

Students also should note how fiction and nonfiction can be alike. Both can be serious or humorous; both can be written in first or third person; and both can be true or false to their subjects.

Identifying Fiction and Nonfiction—Part I (8–5A)

Encourage students to become aware of the differences in tone and approach that distinguish fiction and nonfiction. For example, paragraph 4 by its tone creates a distance between reader and subject. In addition, it merely tells about the incident instead of making it seem to be unfolding as a story.

Explain that it would also be possible to write a novel or short story about William James, using the facts of his life as background.

Although paragraph 4 is nonfiction, it does contain elements that seem more appropriate to fiction. For example, how could the writer know what James had said to himself when shaken out of bed by an earthquake? This provides one example for illustrating to students why all nonfiction cannot be accepted as strictly factual.

Identifying Fiction and Nonfiction—Part II (8–5B)

Paragraph 3 could serve as the springboard for a worthwhile discussion or writing assignment. If some students disagree about the writer's premise that adult amusements are similar to children's, it will support the definition of nonfiction as a type of writing in which the writer speaks for her- or himself, leaving the reader to decide its truth or untruth. If students agree with the writer's premise, you may want them to consider certain areas labeled "adult" entertainment, and ask them to discuss whether these all should be made available to children and adults alike.

Is It Fiction or Nonfiction? (*Reading Selection 8–1*)

According to some definitions, *nonfiction* is factual and true. And, since *fiction* is known to be its opposite, that makes *fiction* untrue, made up, or little more than lies—to be read merely for fun and entertainment.

Yet, definitions don't tell the entire story. Sometimes nonfiction is untrue—or little more than lies. And, many excellent readers look to fiction when seeking the truth!

How can this be? Thoughtful readers can draw conclusions and discover that the easy definitions of nonfiction and fiction do not work. Consider these possibilities found in writing about religion or philosophy:

1. One writer states there is only one God, the God of Christianity.
2. A Mohammedan writer declares, "There is no God but Allah."
3. An atheist would write that there is no god at all.

From these few examples, you can see that all can't equally be regarded as factual and true. They contradict one another. How can you tell which is fiction and which is nonfiction?

You might say it depends on what you believe. But that isn't good enough. If it were, no one would know how to file or identify books properly. All three belong to the same class—and, in this case, all could be correctly classed as nonfiction.

With a little thought, you should also be able to give other examples of contradictory "facts" from the fields of history, science, and politics—writings generally classed as nonfiction. You can see for yourself that defining nonfiction simply as "true" doesn't go far enough.

It's possible, in fact, to write about any subject in the world—from predicting the future to out-and-out fantasy—and have it properly labeled nonfiction, whether or not it is true.

And it's also possible to treat the very same subjects in fiction.

Because good readers don't automatically accept something as true, simply because it's written in a textbook or labeled nonfiction, it's important to weigh the evidence and decide for yourself.

Begin by doing an exercise in contradictions—to discover some of the subjects with two or more sides that might be written about in nonfiction.

An Exercise in Contradictions (8–1A)

Directions: In groups or in pairs, choose one of the topics listed below.

1. First list two or more different sides of the topic that might be supported by writers with opposing ideas.

FOR EXAMPLE, one controversial subject with conflicting views is gun control. One writer might claim the need for strict control of all weapons. Another might claim the Constitutional right to bear arms of any type. There are many shades of opinion between. And, all can be written about and accurately labeled as nonfiction.

2. List three or more supporting ideas or arguments that someone writing in favor of each side of the topic might logically include.

Try to find as much valid evidence for all sides of the topic as you can. Do not try to decide which one is right or true, even if you support one side or another. One mark of good readers is their willingness to learn the logic behind opinions that differ from their own, in order to have a firm basis for upholding and presenting their own beliefs.

Plan to report on the various sides and contradictory conclusions relating to the topic to the rest of your class.

Topics to Choose From

Environment	Abortion	Ecology
Equal Rights	Global Warming	Governmental Power
Censorship	Control of Crime	The Value of History
Education	The Future	A Topic of Your Choice

One Topic: Two Approaches (*Reading Selection 8–2*)

If you accept the fact that it's possible to write about any subject in the world and have it properly labeled nonfiction, whether or not it's proved true, then you need to refine your definition of fiction and nonfiction.

How can readers tell whether a selection is fiction or nonfiction? How should they approach the two different types of literature? What should they expect to gain from reading each?

Good readers probably already have a sense of differences that go beyond the common, incomplete definitions. Read the following two paragraphs, both covering the same topic, and decide which is fiction and which nonfiction. Try to discern the differences that help you form your decisions.

Example I

In the year 2500, most people will no longer live in Earth-based houses but in Hover Homes, moored in cities in the sky above their own garden plots. Artificial sunlight from energy plants in the body of each craft will allow each family to grow its own fresh fruits and vegetables, no matter what the weather. Everyone in the family will have a personal space coupe for travel to business or school, for shopping, or pleasure. For vacation trips or changes of residence, it will be a simple matter to fly the Hover Home anywhere in the world on a moment's impulse.

Example II

Dale and Andrea had their noses pressed against the front viewglass of their Hover Home as their father steered it towards the family's new space-lot in Agrocropolis. Below them were the shining, silver domes of other Hover Homes, row upon row of them, each with its own pool of artificial sunlight casting a warm glow on the fertile garden plots beneath.

Dale was filled with impatience, wanting to get into his own space coupe and zoom on ahead, but his father refused to allow him to go, for fear that he would become lost in the strange airways.

Name _____ Date _____ Period _____

One Topic: Two Approaches (8–2A)

Directions: Answer the following questions concerning examples I and II to discover how they are both alike and different.

1. Examples I and II are alike because both involve _____

   and are concerned with a time in _____.

2. Tell the point of view of each example: first person or third person.

   Example I: _____

   Example II: _____

3. Explain the purpose of Example I. _____

   _____

4. Why does the purpose of Example II differ? _____

   _____

5. Is Example I written in present, past, or future tense? _____
   Write three examples of verbs used in the selection to support your answer.

   _____, _____, and _____

6. Is Example II written in present, past, or future tense? _____
   Write three examples of verbs used in the selection to support your answer.

   _____, _____, and _____

7. Which example clearly states the writer's opinion? _____

   Write the word or words on which you base your answer. _____

   _____

8. Which seems to be happening in the present and invites the reader to participate?

   _____ Explain why you believe your choice has this effect.

   _____

   _____

© 1995 by The Center for Applied Research in Education

(8–2A continued)

9. Which involves a typical human reaction? _____

   Explain the proof from the example that determined your choice. _____

   _____

10. Why can neither of these examples really be called true and factual?

   _____

   _____

   _____

11. In what way can each of these examples have elements of truth?

   Example I : _____

   _____

   Example II : _____

   _____

12. The writer is speaking for himself or herself in Example _____ and is speak-

   ing through characters in Example _____. The example of fiction is

   _____.

Defining Fiction and Nonfiction (*Reading Selection 8–3*)

Memorizing definitions is never enough. It's more important to understand how and why they are true. After a comparison between examples of fiction and nonfiction, here are conclusions you can draw about each.

Special qualities of fiction:

1. The writer speaks through characters, telling their story.
2. Fiction is usually written in the past tense, but seems to happen in the present.
3. When reading fiction, the good reader seems to take part in the story—identifying with the characters and sharing in the action.
4. Fiction can be true in its answers to such questions as: What are people like? Why do they behave as they do? What do human beings have in common?

Special qualities of nonfiction:

1. The writer of nonfiction speaks for him- or herself, directly addressing the reader.
2. Nonfiction can be written about any subject, real or imaginary, and can contain information, theories, ideas, and opinions that may or may not be true.
3. Nonfiction puts readers and writers in a one-on-one relationship, with good readers asking questions and drawing their own conclusions.
4. The truth of nonfiction depends upon the knowledge and intent of the individual writer and cannot be taken for granted by a reader.

To state these differences more simply:

In **nonfiction,** the writer speaks for himself on a topic that's informative or personal, giving facts, ideas, or opinions that may or may not be true.

In **fiction,** the writer presents a world that the reader seems to enter as an active participant. All fiction has one basic subject—and that is people, characters or a character—human beings.

Just as the nonfiction writer speaks for herself or himself, while the fiction writer presents a ready-made world, creating what we call and feel as a story, so the reader must take different approaches to each type of writing.

Compare these approaches to the difference between reading an ad about a product and testing it yourself, following directions.

When reading an ad, thoughtful readers would pose questions, compare its claims with what they know about similar products, and be doubtful of its promises.

On the other hand, when testing the product, intelligent users would follow directions as carefully as possible and wait until finishing the test to pass final judgment on the product's effectiveness. They also would want to be sure they had done exactly as directed before declaring the product to be bad or ineffective.

Good readers of fiction are like someone testing a product. They pay close attention to clues and details, waiting till the end to judge its effectiveness and truth.

In literature, this playing by the rules of the writer's fictional world is referred to as the *willing suspension of disbelief*. It means the reader's willingness to share the writer's world, to hold or suspend doubt until the end, and to have a real-seeming experience through reading that otherwise would be impossible to have.

© 1995 by The Center for Applied Research in Education

Once Upon a Time (8–4)

Part I. A Vicarious Experience

Even when the main characters of fiction are animals and things, they still show human emotions and characteristics. For example, although a fairy tale may seem to be "about" three little pigs, the animals talk in human language and have feelings that both children and adults can share. This allows readers to have what is called a *vicarious experience*—which simply means it seems to be happening to them. And, as long as you know you're safe from harm, being scared by the Big Bad Wolf is fun—as fans of Stephen King should know!

Directions: Working individually or in groups, briefly retell the story of one of the following children's tales with which you are familiar. Then, list and explain ways its characters (1) exhibit common human characteristics, (2) go through experiences, and (3) express feelings that most people share. Give at least one example of each.

The Three Little Pigs	*Goldilocks and the Three Bears*
Peter Rabbit	*The Ugly Duckling*
Henny Penny	*Winnie the Pooh*
The Hobbitt	*Curious George*
Babar the Elephant	A story of your choice

Part II. The Present, Past, and Future

Many children's tales take place in a "never-never" land of imagination and fantasy—everyone knows that! Yet these stories, like all fiction, seem to be happening in the present. It's not only the way that it's written. It's also because, although fashions and ways of living may change, writers of fiction attempt to show how human nature stays the same.

Directions: Choose a story or a television show that concerns a time other than the present. It may be a tale of the Old West, of World War II, or another period of history. Or, you may wish to choose a story or program about the future, like "Star Trek," or even a fantasy, like "Superman."

Explain how the characters express typical qualities of human nature and emotions people have in common, which enable the reader or viewer to share in their experiences, as if happening in the present.

First, give a brief summary of the story or show. Then list three or more examples to support your opinion.

Identifying Fiction and Nonfiction—Part I (8–5A)

Directions: Based on your understanding of the differences between fiction and nonfiction, identify the following opening paragraphs of literary selections and answer the questions concerning each. Give the following for each paragraph:

(1) Decide whether the writer is speaking *for himself or herself* directly to the reader or *through characters.*

(2) Identify the specific subject or characters the paragraph concerns.

(3) Tell whether the point of view is first or third person. (If fiction, a first-person narrator is not the writer, but a character.)

(4) Identify the paragraph as fiction or nonfiction.

1. This quick tour of the universe will begin with superstrings and end with butterflies. There will be a couple of intermediate stops on the way. . . . I will not explain what butterflies and superstrings are. To explain butterflies is unnecessary because everyone has seen them. To explain superstrings is impossible because nobody has seen them. But please do not think I am trying to mystify you. Superstrings and butterflies are examples illustrating two different aspects of the universe and two different notions of beauty. Superstrings come at the beginning and butterflies at the end because they are extreme examples . . . — "Butterflies and Superstrings" by Freeman Dyson from *Infinite in All Directions*

   (1) The writer is speaking _____.

   (2) The paragraph is about _____.

   (3) The point of view is _____.

   (4) This is an example of the type of writing called _____.

2. Julio lay as quietly as he could. Only his eyes kept moving, turning toward the open door that led into the other room, as if by looking there he could hear better what the women were saying. His brother Luis was asleep beside him. The same blanket of catskins covered them both. Luis could sleep no matter what happened. The firelight on the walls and the ceiling was enough to keep Julio awake, even if his mother were not weeping in the next room. It was a silent night outside, like all the other nights in this place of home. — "To the Mountains" by Paul Horgan

   (1) The writer is speaking _____.

   (2) The paragraph is about _____.

   (3) The point of view is _____.

   (4) This is an example of the type of writing called _____.

© 1995 by The Center for Applied Research in Education

3. Tom and Grace Carter sat in their living-room on Christmas Eve, sometimes talking, sometimes pretending to read and all the time thinking things they didn't want to think. Their two children, Junior, aged nineteen, and Grace, two years younger, had come home that day from their schools for the Christmas vacation. Junior was in his first year at the university and Grace attended a boarding-school that would fit her for college. — "Old Folks' Christmas" by Ring Lardner

   (1) The writer is speaking _____.

   (2) The paragraph is about _____.

   (3) The point of view is _____.

   (4) This is an example of the type of writing called _____.

4. The earthquake that shook San Francisco at 5:30 in the morning of April 18, 1906, had caught William James in bed. Since January, James had been living in nearby Stanford, where he was giving a series of lectures at Leland Stanford University. Just before he had left Cambridge, a friend had said to him half-jokingly: "I hope they'll treat you to a little bit of an earthquake while you're there. It's a pity you shouldn't have that local experience." Now, as he lay startled, in a quaking bed, the pictures dropping from the walls, the bureaus crashing to the floor, James said to himself: "Here's Bakewell's earthquake after all." — from *Charmed Circle* by James R. Mellow

   (1) The writer is speaking _____.

   (2) The paragraph is about _____.

   (3) The point of view is _____.

   (4) This is an example of the type of writing called _____.

Identifying Fiction and Nonfiction—Part II (8–5B)

Directions: Based on your understanding of the differences between fiction and nonfiction, identify the following opening paragraphs of literary selections and answer the questions concerning each. Give the following for each paragraph:

(1) Decide whether the writer is speaking *for himself or herself* directly to the reader or *through characters.*

(2) Identify the specific subject or characters the paragraph concerns.

(3) Tell whether the point of view is first or third person. (If fiction, a first-person narrator is not the writer, but a character.)

(4) Identify the paragraph as fiction or nonfiction.

1. About eight o'clock one evening in April 1927 it occurred to me that I was out of a job, that I had a little money, and that I had long wanted to go to France. At noon the next day I was aboard the S.S. *President Harding* steaming down the Hudson, outward-bound. I had no definite plans. If anyone had asked me how long I expected to be away, I suppose I would have said a few weeks, possibly a few months. I stayed thirteen years, and it took a world war to send me home. — from *The Paris Edition* by Waverly Root

   (1) The writer is speaking _____.

   (2) The paragraph is about _____.

   (3) The point of view is _____.

   (4) This is an example of the type of writing called _____.

2. The drying east wind, which always brought hard luck to Eastern Oregon at whatever season it blew, had combed down the plateau grasslands through so much of the winter that it was hard to see any sign of grass ever having grown on them. Even though March had come, it still blew, drying the ground deep, shrinking the watercourses, beating back the clouds that might have delivered rain, and grinding coarse dust against the fifty-odd head of work horses that Pop Apling, with young Beech Cartwright helping, had brought down from his homestead to turn back into their home pasture while there was still something left of them. — "Open Winter" by H . L. Davis

   (1) The writer is speaking _____.

   (2) The paragraph is about _____.

   (3) The point of view is _____.

   (4) This is an example of the type of writing called _____.

(8–5B continued)

3. Of all the changes that have altered the topography of childhood, the most dramatic change has been the disappearance of childhood play. Whereas a decade or two ago children were easily distinguished from the adult world by the very nature of their play, today children's occupations do not differ greatly from adult diversions. — "The End of Play" by Marie Winn

    (1) The writer is speaking _____.

    (2) The paragraph is about _____.

    (3) The point of view is _____.

    (4) This is an example of the type of writing called _____.

4. Father was in the army all through the war—the first war, I mean—so, up to the age of five, I never saw much of him, and what I saw did not worry me. Sometimes I woke and there was a big figure in khaki peering down at me in the candlelight. Sometimes in the early morning I heard the slamming of the front door and the clatter of nailed boots down the cobbles of the lane. These were Father's entrances and exits. Like Santa Claus he came and went mysteriously. — "My Oedipus Complex by Frank O'Connor

    (1) The writer is speaking _____.

    (2) The paragraph is about _____.

    (3) The point of view is _____.

    (4) This is an example of the type of writing called _____.

Taking Sides in Conflict (*Reading Selection 8–6*)

Why do people read fiction? One answer might be to discover the truth about human nature and life . . . to learn about people other than themselves.

A simpler answer might be: To find out what happens.

And, that's a good answer, too. No one wants to read to the end of a particular selection without caring about the characters in the story and wondering what happens to them.

Good readers also take sides because characters in fiction are involved in conflict. And, good readers want their side to win. "Their side" is the side of the main character or the "good guy" the writer causes you to choose.

Although the right side doesn't always win at the end, good readers get more out of a story by *identifying* with the character facing the conflict.

Here are 5 major conflicts of fiction:

Note: In stated conflicts, "Man" represents the character, male or female, with whom the writer wants you to side. *Vs.* is an abbreviation of *versus,* which means "against."

1. Man vs. Nature: The main character is attempting to overcome the forces of nature, such as severe weather, an erupting volcano, forest fire, or wild beast.

2. Man vs. Man: The main character must struggle against another individual, male or female, in a one-to-one conflict that may involve a test of courage, character, or strength.

3. Man vs. Society: "Society" is an entire group of like-minded people, usually upheld by custom or laws, against whom the main character often stands alone, seeking justice and truth. It is a more intense conflict than the previous ones because the main character is outnumbered in the struggle against such forces as prejudice, a group's unfairness, or government's power and tyranny.

4. Man vs. Self: This is one of the most difficult conflicts, asking the reader to side with the "right" course for a character to take. *Man vs. Self* may involve a conflict of loyalties or a character who is "brainwashed" by society and finds it hard to trust his or her own instincts.

5. Man vs. Fate: Most usually associated with Greek or Shakespearean tragedies, it is a conflict that the main character can't win when opposing with a god or gods, and the only hope of the main character is attaining their favor.

Taking Sides in Conflict (8–6A)

Directions: Read the following paragraphs and complete the statements following each.

(1) First, state the specific terms of the conflict by naming the character who faces the struggle, along with the thing or person who is on the opposing side.

(2) Explain why the conflict seems difficult for the character to overcome.

(3) Identify the type of conflict: *Man vs. Nature, Man vs. Man, Man vs. Society,* or *Man vs. Self.*

1. For a while she (Jerry Armytage) could see no sign of any change at all; then, faint at first but growing more frequently as her eyes became accustomed to watching for it, she discerned what might have been a heliograph—faint highlights reflected in rapid flashes against a billowing plume of smoke: FIRE.

   Her heart leaped to her throat, and a sickening hot sensation stabbed her through the stomach. . . . A bush fire! Most sinister of all the dire curses Nature held like naked swords suspended above her creatures. A bush fire! And she alone to meet the terror of its passage. Red death to all life trapped within its glowing boundaries. Home, children, livelihood—ashes within its greedy maw. — "Fire in the Bush" by James Warwick

   (1) The conflict is the main character, _____, versus _____
   _____.

   (2) The conflict seems difficult for the character to overcome because _____
   _____.

   _____.

   (3) The type of conflict is _____.

2. As his father-in-law walked heavily across the gravelled lot, Chee was reminded of a statement his mother sometimes made: "When you see a fat Navaho, you see one who hasn't worked for what he has."

   Old Man Fat was fattest in the middle. There was indolence in his walk . . . in his cheeks so plump they made his eyes squint, eyes now smoldering with anger. . . .

   The old man said belligerently, "Why do you come here? . . ."

   "I came to talk with you," Chee answered, trying to keep his voice steady as he faced the old man. . . .

   "It's about the Little One." Chee settled his daughter more comfortably against his hip as he weighed carefully the words he had planned to say. "We are going to miss her very much. It wouldn't be so bad if we knew that *part* of each year she was going to be with us. That might help you too . . ."

   Chee's words did not have the expected effect. Old Man Fat was enraged. . . .
   — "Chee's Daughter" by Juanita Platero and Siyowin Miller

   (1) The conflict is the main character, _____, versus _____
   _____.

(8–6A continued)

(2) The conflict seems difficult for the character to overcome because _____

_____.

_____.

(3) The type of conflict is _____.

3. The Brazilian official threw up lean and lanky arms and clawed the air with wildly distended fingers. "Leiningen!" he shouted. "You're insane! They're not creatures you can fight—they're an elemental—an 'act of God'! Ten miles long, two miles wide— ants, nothing but ants! And every single one of them a fiend from hell; before you can spit three times they'll eat a full-grown buffalo to the bones. I tell you if you don't clear out at once, there will be nothing left of you but a skeleton picked as clean as your own plantation."

   Leiningen grinned. "Act of God, my eye! Anyway . . . I'm not going to run for it just because an elemental's on the way. And don't think I'm the kind of fathead who tries to fend off lightning with his fist, either. I use my intelligence, old man. . . ."
— "Leiningen Versus the Ants" by Carl Stephenson

(1) The conflict is the main character, _____, versus _____

_____.

(2) The conflict seems difficult for the character to overcome because _____

_____.

_____.

(3) The type of conflict is _____.

4. The sleeping sentinel in the clump of laurel was a young Virginian named Carter Druse. He was the son of wealthy parents, an only child, and had known such ease and cultivation and high living as wealth and taste were able to command in the mountain country of western Virginia. His home was but a few miles from where he now lay. One morning he had risen from the breakfast table and said, quietly but gravely, "Father, a Union regiment has arrived at Grafton. I am going to join it."

   The father lifted his leonine head, looked at the son a moment in silence, and replied, "Well, go, sir, and whatever may occur, do what you conceive to be your duty. Virginia, to which you are a traitor, must get on without you. Should we both live to the end of the war, we will speak further of the matter . . ." — "A Horseman in the Sky" by Ambrose Bierce

(1) The conflict is the main character, _____, versus _____

_____.

(2) The conflict seems difficult for the character to overcome because _____.

_____.

_____.

(3) The type of conflict is _____.

Taking Sides in Conflict (8–6B)

Directions: Read the following paragraphs and complete the statements following each.

(1) First, state the specific terms of the conflict by naming the character who faces the struggle, along with the thing or person who is on the opposing side.

(2) Explain why the conflict seems difficult for the character to overcome.

(3) Identify the type of conflict: *Man vs. Nature, Man vs. Man, Man vs. Society,* or *Man vs. Self.*

1. When war came, Spook was my most serious problem. The Army would take care of me, but who would take care of Spook? For weeks I wrestled with the problem and could find no solution. In desperation—for it was almost time to go—I put the setter in the car and drove to a little town upstate where I spent my summers. . . . —"The Red Dog" by Howard Maier

   (1) The conflict is the main character, _____, versus _____

   _____.

   (2) The conflict seems difficult for the character to overcome because _____

   _____.

   _____.

   (3) The type of conflict is _____.

2. Ellie looked up at her mother but her eyes were straight ahead. She knew that Tommy only read the Uncle Wiggily book by himself when he was unhappy. She got up and walked to the kitchen cabinet. . . .

   She pulled open the drawer . . . reached for the knife and at the same time a pile of envelopes caught her eye.

   "Any more come today?" she asked. . . .

   The white people had been threatening them for the past three weeks. Some of the letters were aimed at the family, but most of them were directed to Tommy himself. About once a week in the same handwriting somebody wrote that he'd better not eat lunch at school because they were going to poison him.

   They had been getting those letters ever since the school board had made Tommy's name public. — "Neighbors" by Diane Oliver

   (1) The conflict is the main character, _____, versus _____

   _____.

(8–6B continued)

(2) The conflict seems difficult for the character to overcome because _____

_____.

_____.

(3) The type of conflict is _____.

3. In a forest of mixed growth somewhere on the eastern spurs of the Carpathians,* a man stood one winter night watching and listening as though he waited for some beast of the woods to come within the range of his vision and, later, of his rifle. But the game . . . was none that figured in the sportsman's calendar as lawful and proper for the chase; Ulrich von Gradwitz patrolled the dark forest in quest of a human enemy.

    . . . The neighborhood feud had become a personal one since Ulrich had come to be head of his family; if there was a man in the world whom he detested and wished ill to it was George Znaeym, the inheritor of the quarrel and the tireless game-snatcher and raider of the disputed border forest . . . and this wind-scourged winter night Ulrich had banded together his foresters to watch the dark forest, not in quest of four-footed quarry, but to keep a lookout for the prowling thieves whom he suspected of being afoot from across the land boundary. — "The Interlopers" by Saki (H.H. Munro)

    * a mountain range in central Europe, including northern Czechoslovakia and Rumania

    (1) The conflict is the main character, _____, versus _____

    _____.

    (2) The conflict seems difficult for the character to overcome because _____

    _____.

    _____.

    (3) The type of conflict is _____.

4. Jean Valjean listened, but there was not a sound; he pushed the door with the tip of his finger lightly and with the furtive, restless gentleness of a cat that wants to get in. . . .

    He waited a moment and then pushed the door again more boldly.

    The first danger had passed, but still there was fearful tumult within him. But he did not recoil . . . he only thought of finishing the job as speedily as possible, and entered the bedroom . . . Jean Valjean advanced cautiously and carefully. . . .

    Suddenly he stopped, for he was close to the bed. . . .

    At (this) moment a moonbeam passing through the tall window suddenly illumined the Bishop's pale face. He was sleeping peacefully. . . .

    Jean Valjean was standing in the shadow with his crowbar in his hand, motionless and terrified by the luminous old man. . . . No one could have said what was going on within him, not even himself. In order to form any idea of it we must imagine what is the most violent in the present of what is gentlest. . . .

(8–6B continued)

His eye was not once removed from the old man, and the only thing clearly revealed by his attitude and countenance was a strange indecision. It seemed as if he were hesitating between two abysses, the one that saves and the one that destroys; he was ready to dash out the Bishop's brains or kiss his hand. — from *Les Miserables* by Victor Hugo

(1) The conflict is the main character, _____, versus _____

_____.

(2) The conflict seems difficult for the character to overcome because _____

_____.

_____.

(3) The type of conflict is _____.

Considering Conflict (8–7)

The conflicts facing main characters in literature are not always obvious—but, of course, they are the same conflicts that all human beings may face in life. That's another reason for seeking truth in fiction. And, sometimes, writers can create conflicts that take un-usual twists and turns—just as life can!

Directions: To increase your understanding of the ideas behind the conflicts in fiction, consider the following questions about those most commonly used in fiction: *Man vs. Nature, Man vs. Man, Man vs. Society,* and *Man vs. Self.* Write your answers in the spaces provided.

A. **Man vs. Nature** is the most basic conflict.

1. When engaged in such a conflict, what are three qualities of a person that do not matter to Nature?

   (a) _____

   (b) _____

   (c) _____

2. Name three destructive forces of Nature a person might be forced to struggle against.

   (a) _____

   (b) _____

   (c) _____

3. Against such destructive forces, why can't a human being really defeat Nature?

   _____

   _____

   In what way, then, does a person "win" such a conflict? _____

   _____

   _____

4. Describe two ways in which a person might purposely go seek a conflict with Nature.

   (a) _____

   (b) _____

(8–7 continued)

5. List three characteristics or traits that could help a person in a conflict with Nature.

   (a) _____

   (b) _____

   (c) _____

B. **Man vs. Man** is a conflict between one person facing another.

   1. Name three kinds of family relationships that could create this type of conflict in fiction.

      (a) _____ vs. _____

      (b) _____ vs. _____

      (c) _____ vs. _____

   2. Why is a conflict between two people usually more equal than a conflict between a human being and the forces of Nature? _____

      _____

      _____

   3. Name three human emotions that might be at the root of conflicts between two people.

      (a) _____

      (b) _____

      (c) _____

C. **Man vs. Society** pits one person against the majority in a clearly-defined group.

   1. Explain why Man vs. Society often involves a conflict of ideas. _____

      _____

      _____

   2. Give an example of two opposing ideas that might underlie such a conflict.

      _____

      _____

(8–7 continued)

3. How can Man vs. Society be both an intellectual and a physical struggle?

   (a) Intellectual: _____

   _____

   (b) Physical: _____

   _____

4. Why is this a more complex conflict than the previous two? _____

   _____

   _____

D. **Man vs. Self** involves two opposing sides of a single person.

   1. Why does Man vs. Self often also involve a person's relationship to society?

   _____

   _____

   2. Why, in many situations, doesn't the choice between Good vs. Bad or Right vs. Wrong create a satisfying Man vs. Self or inner conflict? _____

   _____

   _____

   _____

   3. Describe how a conflict of Man vs. Self can involve a character torn between two courses that both have elements of Right and Wrong.

   _____

   _____

   4. Give an example of such a situation. _____

   _____

   _____

   _____

   _____

Also a Hero (*Reading Selection 8–8*)

The main character in fiction—the person whose side the reader takes in a conflict—is also often called a *hero*.

This hero, who may be male or female, man or woman, boy or girl, does not need to win a medal, defeat an enemy in a battle, beat a rival on a playing field, or even perform a death-defying deed.

In fact, people in everyday circumstances often turn out to be heroes—as you'll discover by learning of the heroic qualities they show by winning—and sometimes losing—the conflicts they face in fiction.

What make a hero? It's more than just willingness to fight and the ability to overpower the opposition. The main character in fiction can be called a hero if he or she possesses or honors the qualities most people admire: *courage, determination, loyalty, thoughtfulness, understanding, pride, concern for other.*

And, there are two kinds of courage.

Physical Courage: when a person risks bodily harm or death and is willing to fight or face danger to uphold his or her values or beliefs

Moral Courage: when a person is willing to speak out and express his or her beliefs, feelings or views, even at the risk of being disgraced, humiliated, shunned, or penalized in other ways

The true hero of good fiction isn't perfect. This is one reason why readers can identify themselves with his or her conflict and struggle. While admiring the good traits, readers can sympathize with the difficulties the hero faces, recognize the weaknesses as being those that many people share, and understand the hero's desire and efforts to be better. All are elements of how truth about human nature is found in fiction.

Also a Hero (8–8A)

Part A. In Everyday Life

Directions: Using someone you know or a real-life situation as an example, explain how an average person can be called upon to show one of the following characteristics of a hero in everyday life. All of the characteristics need not pertain to the same person or situation.

Moral Courage	Thoughtfulness
Physical Courage	Understanding
Determination	Pride
Loyalty	Concern for Other

Part B. Heroes You Might Read About

Directions: Choose two examples from fiction, history, or present times, and explain how each was or is called upon to display at least five characteristics of a hero. Use the back of this sheet if you need more space to write.

_____

_____

_____

_____

_____

_____

_____

_____

_____

_____

_____

_____

_____

_____

_____

Creating Conflicts (8–9)

Directions: The following examples present four characters and their backgrounds that could serve as the basis for a fictional conflict. Use your imagination, and develop them as you wish. When you have finished, compare your answers with your classmates' to discover the similarities and differences in the stories you'd tell.

1. After being warned by police, Tully promises his mother he will not get into any more trouble.

   (a) Describe a situation the character now faces that causes the conflict.

   _____

   _____

   (b) Explain what makes it difficult to overcome. _____

   _____

   (c) The conflict is between: (Who?) _____ versus

   (Who or What?) _____

   (d) The type of conflict is _____ vs. _____.

2. Alyson is confident she knows how to handle the sailboat alone, so, when the rest of the family goes to town, she takes it out on the lake by herself.

   (a) Describe a situation the character now faces that causes the conflict.

   _____

   _____

   (b) Explain what makes it difficult to overcome. _____

   _____

   (c) The conflict is between: (Who?) _____ versus

   (Who or What?) _____

   (d) The type of conflict is _____ vs. _____.

(8–9 continued)

3. Before Raoul's friend was imprisoned for treasonable acts, he gave Raoul a sealed envelope for safe-keeping.

   (a) Describe a situation the character now faces that causes the conflict.

   _____

   _____

   (b) Explain what makes it difficult to overcome. _____

   _____

   (c) The conflict is between: (Who?) _____ versus

   (Who or What?) _____

   (d) The type of conflict is _____ vs. _____.

4. Kathie has been going with Judd for over a year now, but lately he has been making excuses for not calling every night as he used to.

   (a) Describe a situation the character now faces that causes the conflict.

   _____

   _____

   (b) Explain what makes it difficult to overcome. _____

   _____

   (c) The conflict is between: (Who?) _____ versus

   (Who or What?) _____

   (d) The type of conflict is _____ vs. _____.

© 1995 by The Center for Applied Research in Education

"The Blanket" (*Reading Selection 8–10*)

Petey hadn't really believed that Dad would be doing it—sending Granddad away. "Away" was what they were calling it. Not until now could he believe it of Dad.

But here was the blanket that Dad had that day bought for him and in the morning he'd be going away. And this was the last evening they'd be having together. Dad was off seeing that girl he was to marry. He'd not be back till late, and they could sit up and talk.

It was a fine September night, with a silver moon riding high over the gully. When they'd washed up the supper dishes they went out on the shanty porch, the old man and the bit of a boy, taking their chairs. "I'll get me fiddle," said the old man, "and play ye some of the old tunes." But instead of the fiddle he brought out the blanket. It was a big, double blanket, red, with black cross stripes.

"Now, isn't that a fine blanket!" said the old man, smoothing it over his knees. "And isn't your father a kind man to be giving the old fellow a blanket like that to go away with? It cost something, it did—look at the wool of it! And warm it will be on these cold winter nights to come. There'll be few blankets there the equal of this one!"

It was like Granddad to be saying that. He was trying to make it easier. He'd pretended all along it was he that was wanting to go away to the great brick building—the government place, where he'd be with so many other old fellows having the best of everything . . . But Petey hadn't believed Dad would really do it, until this night when he brought home the blanket.

"Oh, yes, it's a fine blanket," said Petey, and got up and went into the shanty. He wasn't the kind to cry, and, besides, he was too old for that, being eleven. He'd just come to fetch Granddad's fiddle.

The blanket slid to the floor as the old man took the fiddle and stood up. It was the last night they'd be having together. There wasn't any need to say, "Play all the old tunes." Granddad tuned up for a minute, and then said, "This is one you'll like to remember."

The silver moon was high overhead, and there was a gentle breeze playing down the gully. He'd never be hearing Granddad play like this again. It was as well Dad was moving into that new house, away from here. He'd not want, Petey wouldn't, to sit here on the old porch of fine evenings, with Granddad gone.

The tune changed. "Here's something gayer." Petey sat and stared out over the gully. Dad would marry that girl. Yes, that girl who'd kissed him and slobbered over him, saying she'd try to be a good mother to him, and all . . . His chair creaked as he involuntarily gave his body a painful twist.

The tune stopped suddenly, and Granddad said: "It's a poor tune, except to be dancing to." And then: "It's a fine girl your father's going to marry. He'll be feeling young again, with a pretty wife like that. And what would an old fellow like me be doing around their house, getting in the way, an old nuisance, what with my talk of aches and pains! And then there'll be babies coming, and I'd not want to be there to hear them crying at all hours. It's best that I take myself off, like I'm doing. One more tune or two, and then we'll be going to bed to get some sleep against the morning, when I'll pack up my fine blanket and take my leave. Listen to this, will you? It's a bit sad, but a fine tune for a night like this."

They didn't hear the two people coming down the gully path, Dad and the pretty girl with the hard, bright face like a china doll's. But they heard her laugh, right by the porch, and the tune stopped on a wrong, high, startled note. Dad didn't say anything, but the girl came forward and spoke to Granddad prettily: "I'll not be seeing you leave in the morning, so I came over to say good-bye."

"It's kind of you," said Granddad, with his eyes cast down; and then, seeing the blanket at his feet, he stooped to pick it up. "And will you look at this," he said in embarrassment, "the fine blanket my son has given me to go away with!"

"Yes," she said, "it's a fine blanket." She felt of the wool, and repeated in surprise. "A fine blanket—I'll say it is!" She turned to Dad, and said to him coldly, "It cost something, that."

He cleared his throat, and said defensively. "I wanted him to have the best . . ."

The girl stood there, still intent on the blanket. "It's double, too," she said reproachfully to Dad.

"Yes," said Granddad, "it's double—a fine blanket for an old fellow to be going away with."

The boy went abruptly into the shanty. He was looking for something. He could hear that girl reproaching Dad, and Dad becoming angry in his slow way. And now she was suddenly going away in a huff . . . As Petey came out, she turned and called back, "All the same, he doesn't need a double blanket!" And she ran up the gully path.

Dad was looking after her uncertainly.

"Oh, she's right," said the boy coldly. "Here, Dad"—and he held out a pair of scissors. "Cut the blanket in two."

Both of them stared at the boy, startled. "Cut it in two, I tell you, Dad!" he cried out. "And keep the other half!"

"That's not a bad idea," said Granddad gently. "I don't need so much of a blanket."

"Yes," said the boy harshly, "a single blanket's enough for an old man when he's sent away. We'll save the other half, Dad; it will come in handy later."

"Now, what do you mean by that?" asked Dad.

"I mean," said the boy slowly, "that I'll give it to you, Dad—when you're old and I'm sending you—away."

There was a silence, and then Dad went over to Granddad and stood before him, not speaking. But Granddad understood, for he put out a hand and laid it on Dad's shoulder. Petey was watching them. And he heard Granddad whisper, "It's all right, son—I knew you didn't mean it. . ." And then Petey cried.

But it didn't matter—because they were all three crying together.

"The Blanket" by Floyd Dell

"The Blanket"—Questions of Conflict and Heroism (8–10A)

Directions: After reading the short story, "The Blanket," write thoughtful answers to
the following questions.

1. The conflict is the main character, _____, versus _____.

2. The conflict seems difficult for the character to overcome because _____
   _____.

3. The type of conflict is _____ vs. _____.

4. In what ways did both sides of the conflict "win" at the end? _____
   _____
   _____

5. What was an early clue that the girl Dad was to marry was uncaring? (Write the
   exact word or words.) _____

6. Explain how Petey showed each of the following qualities of a hero:

   a. Moral courage _____
   _____
   _____

   b. Thoughtfulness _____
   _____
   _____

   c. Caring _____
   _____
   _____

   d. Understanding _____
   _____

   e. Pride _____
   _____
   _____

f. Determination _____

_____

_____

7. Explain whether you believe the main character needed physical courage to meet this conflict, and why or why not. _____

_____

_____

_____

_____

_____

_____

_____

_____

_____

_____

_____

_____

_____

_____

_____

_____

Setting the Stage for Action:
Setting & Point of View

First paragraphs of fiction deserve special attention. Whether of short stories or novels, opening paragraphs may not only give the setting—time and place—but also set the tone of the story through obvious foreshadowing or subtle hints and suggest the story's probable direction.

It is the mark of good fiction that the end is in the beginning. And, likewise, the beginning is in the end. Good readers need to develop sensitivity to the subtle clues that enable them to respond to a well-written short story or novel as a seamless piece of workmanship that fits together perfectly. In that way, they become able to see how every detail of plot, action, characterization, and dialogue—from title to closing sentence—contribute to the whole.

Units 9 and 10 will concentrate on some of the elements that accomplished readers can absorb from first paragraphs. These include setting and point of view. Getting the right impression from the opening paragraph helps the reader visualize the story unfolding as it's read.

In order for students to fully appreciate the difference between fiction and nonfiction, an awareness of point of view is of immense importance. While both fiction and nonfiction can be written in first or third person, the writer of fiction uses point of view in a far different fashion, one integral to the story. One of the first lessons for the student of fiction to learn is never to confuse the first-person narrator of fiction with its writer. They may not even be of the same sex or species!

Because short stories are, by necessity, more concentrated, most of the examples in this unit are taken from short pieces of fiction. Since students cannot determine their full development from these excerpts, you may want to encourage them to be aware of the title as a "telling" part of the story and assign them to read some of the complete stories as associated assignments.

NOTES ON ACTIVITIES

Creating a Time Line (9–2)

You may want to assign finding the effects of the nine historical periods on the time line as a research project or group work for well motivated average and above average students. For classes that need extra help, you may find it advantageous to provide students with the additional worksheet (9–3), listing the effects as stated above.

Working with Opening Paragraphs (9–8A)

You may prefer to do practice work with your class on the first set of three paragraphs before students "go out on their own" individually or for a cooperative learning assignment.

For those who need extra help, you might wish to give the assignment as a matching exercise, along with a worksheet of the suggested answers.

"Seeing" Where You're Going: Setting (9–1)

Directions: What difference would it make in your packing plans, whether you were planning a trip to Alaska or one to a South Seas island? The obvious answer, of course, is—a lot!

Setting affects a story, just as your destination affects your expectations when you travel. What happens to someone often depends—directly or indirectly—on the *place* a person lives and the period in *time* that he or she was born into.

To become a better reader, try to combine your mental picture of a place with the details that the writer gives about setting.

FOR EXAMPLE, what do you "see" when you think about **Paris**?

Possibilities: Eiffel Tower, designer fashions, can-can dancers, sidewalk cafes, broad tree-lined avenues

Be sure to name specific things, instead of vague feelings like "full of excitement," "glamorous," or "sophisticated." Instead, list something that makes it this way. And, don't think too hard—there is no right or wrong as long as your answer fits the given place.

PLACE		WHAT YOU "SEE" THERE
1. Florida	(1)	_____
	(2)	_____
	(3)	_____
2. New York City	(1)	_____
	(2)	_____
	(3)	_____
3. Texas	(1)	_____
	(2)	_____
	(3)	_____
4. Alaska	(1)	_____
	(2)	_____
	(3)	_____
5. London, England	(1)	_____
	(2)	_____
	(3)	_____

(9–1 continued)

PLACE	WHAT YOU "SEE" THERE
6. Mexico	(1) _____
	(2) _____
	(3) _____
7. Japan	(1) _____
	(2) _____
	(3) _____
8. An Alien Planet	(1) _____
	(2) _____
	(3) _____
9. _____	(1) _____
Any Other Place You Choose	(2) _____
	(3) _____

COMPARING YOUR MENTAL PICTURES

Combine your list of words describing each place with those of your classmates—to see how closely they match and to discover how complete a picture you can put together.

When you read, you'll also want to compare your "mind's eye" view of a place with the picture the author presents. Sometimes a writer expects you to "fill in" the details of a setting from what you've read about or seen on TV, films, or photos. In other cases, writers want to show you an unexpected side of a well-known place and let you make the comparison.

Either way, it's always important for you to bring what you know to what you read.

JUST FOR FUN: WHERE IN THE WORLD?

Play a guessing game, using the key words describing the place of your choice as clues. If the spot is a less familiar one, you may have to think up some additional hints to help identify it. But, remember, the point is to capture its essence as precisely as possible. The winner, of course, is the person who makes the most correct guesses.

Creating a Time Line (9–2)

Directions: To have a clear understanding of what you read, you need to know *when* an event takes place as well as *where*. These are the two elements that make up **setting,** and together affect what happens.

In determining setting, the time that concerns you first should be the period in history. Imagine the difference between crossing America in pioneer days and going coast to coast today. It's an entirely different story!

In setting up a time line—either to keep in your memory or put in your notebook for reference—you'll want to concentrate on those times that changed the way people looked at the world. Knowing *when* people lived helps explain both their actions and ideas.

A. **Set Up a Time Line.** List the following major events in the order in which they occurred. Copy them in order under "Event."

American Civil War	The Great Depression
World War II	Age of Knights and Chivalry
Turn of 20th Century	American Revolutionary War
Discovery of America	World War I
Viet Nam to Present	

TIME LINE FOR READERS

Event   **Effect**

1. _____   _____

2. _____   _____

3. _____   _____

4. _____   _____

5. _____   _____

6. _____   _____

7. _____   _____

(9–2 continued)

Event	Effect
8. _____	_____
	_____
9. _____	_____
	_____

B. **Chart the Effect of Time on People's Lives.** When reading, it's helpful to remember some of the key periods in time that changed the way people look at the world. Following are suggested ways of stating the effects that different periods in history had on people's lives. Write them on your time line after the period that each matches or restate them in your own words. (*For example:* Resulted in an end to slavery and a reunited country.)

Called "the war to end all wars," but brought disillusionment to many

Resulted in the end of slavery and a reunited national government

A world divided into royalty and peasants, glorifying courage in battle and noble behavior

Opened up a new continent of hope and opportunity to the world's people

Sought to "make the world safe for democracy," led to greater awareness of international interdependence

A time of hopelessness, lost jobs, and bread lines

An era marked by technological change and social questions

A period when the effects of the industrial revolution brought visible changes to life

Brought home the idea that people's voices, ideas, and happiness ought to matter in their governing

Then and Now (9–3)

Directions: An important part of picturing setting is having a mental picture of *how* people's lives are affected by *when* as well as *where* they live. To exercise your ability to visualize setting, think of ten commonplace elements or inventions that make today's life easier. List each and opposite it, write how people accomplished the same purpose 100 to 150 years ago, before its discovery or invention. An example is given.

	NOW	**THEN**
	electric and fluorescent lighting	candlelight and oil lamps
1.	_____	_____
2.	_____	_____
3.	_____	_____
4.	_____	_____
5.	_____	_____
6.	_____	_____
7.	_____	_____
8.	_____	_____
9.	_____	_____
10.	_____	_____

Picturing Yourself in Another Time (9–4)

Choose one of the periods included on your time line, or another of your choosing, and use what you know about it, together with your imagination, to picture what it would be like to spend the rest of your life in that time period.

To make your paper more accurate and interesting, you can do additional research on the period of your choice.

Directions: Write a paper on the following topic:

"If I were to live in another time of history, how would life be different for me?"

Compare specific elements common to the way of life then with how life is today. Consider both of the following points:

1. What you find appealing about that particular time period
2. What difficulties you see about living at that time

Try to choose details and examples that enable someone reading your paper to share in your feelings.

You may use the space below for your notes.

_____

_____

_____

_____

_____

_____

_____

_____

_____

_____

_____

Word Clues to Setting (9–5)

Writers sometimes make an open statement of setting, such as "The stagecoach pulled up at the inn in London shortly before midnight . . ." or "The plane from Seattle landed at the New York airport . . ."

Yet, often settings aren't directly expressed, and, as an alert reader, you must be on the lookout for clues that invite you to make associations and fill in the picture.

A. Natural Habitat

Directions: Following each phrase, write the place or places that you associate with it. Remember, the good reader starts from "educated guesses," but doesn't make wild ones. A response of "northwestern United States" is better than "Oregon" if you don't have accurate proof to pinpoint your answer more closely. An example is given.

Dense jungle _____ South America, Africa, South Pacific _____

PLACE | **LIKELY LOCATION IN U.S.A.**

1. Snow-capped mountains

2. Open range _____

3. Pine-covered mountains _____

4. Bayou country _____

5. Palm trees, sandy beaches _____

B. Growing Properties

Directions: As terms for a country setting, many words not only indicate what is grown there but also serve as clues to setting. If you are not sure of any words, you may want to seek help from the dictionary. An example is given.

PROPERTY	PRODUCT	LIKELY LOCATION IN U.S.A.
Grove	Oranges, grapefruit	California, Florida
1. Plantation		
2. Ranch		
3. Pasture		
4. Orchard		
5. Plowed fields		

(9–5 continued)

C. *At Home in the Wild*

Directions: Writers often expect you to associate certain animals with their natural habitat in a specific part of the world. For example, you would expect to meet an elephant in the wild only in Africa or Asia.

    After the name of each animal, write the place you think of as its natural environment. In blank spaces 7 and 8, add your own examples of animals and their probable homes.

ANIMAL	HOME IN WILD
1. Kangaroo	_____
2. Coyote	_____
3. Moose	_____
4. Armadillo	_____
5. Tiger	_____
6. Lion	_____
7. _____	_____
8. _____	_____

Places People Live (9–6)

Directions: You can often get a good idea of someone's background and customary surroundings from the word a writer chooses to call the place that person lives. For each of the following, write a list of three to five associated words that pop into your mind.

1. Penthouse _____

2. Dormitory _____

3. Cottage _____

4. Hut _____

5. Plantation _____

6. Tenement _____

7. Cabin _____

8. Farmhouse _____

9. Condo _____

OTHERS: How many other words can you think of that name places people live? List five or more below, and be prepared to discuss how any two of them differ from one another.

_____

_____

_____

_____

_____

_____

_____

_____

_____

_____

"How You Say It"— Clue to Setting
(*Reading Selection 9–7*)

"Dag-nabbit! That's a real knee-slapper!"

"Where's he coming from?" is a likely reaction to a remark like the one above. And, that's just what you ought to think. The use of outdated slang is one way to tell that a piece of writing concerns a time other than one's own.

Often a writer doesn't bother to mention a setting's time, and, in that case, it's generally safe to assume that the story concerns what, for the writer, is the present time. But what if you don't know when the writer lived? You still have ways of telling. Writers today tend to use shorter words and sentences, along with less formal language, than writers of the past.

Use of language sometimes reveals both time and place, as: *The cowpokes left their gear at the stable and moseyed down to the Long Horn saloon.* It could hardly be anywhere but the American Old West!

Here's another: *". . . and whether he had made his fortune or whether he had not, no one could be knowing for certain."* Can you hear the special lilt to those words, which make the setting most probably Ireland? How would you rewrite the sentence in colloquial American English?

Each of the following examples contains language clues to setting that will help you answer the questions in exercise 9–7A.

A. There is a certain place where dumb-waiters boom, doors slam, dishes crash; every window is a mother's mouth bidding the street shut up, go skate somewhere else, come home. My voice is the loudest. — "The Loudest Voice" by Grace Paley

B. Yesterday morning, Mr. Horace A. Hurlbut took formal possession of *The Chicago Times,* in compliance with the mandate of justice making him receiver of that institution. Bright and early he was at his post in *The Times* building; and the expression that coursed over his mobile features, as he lolled back in the editorial chair and abandoned himself to pleasing reflections, was an expression of conscious pride and ineffable satisfaction. — "His First Day at Editing" by Eugene Field

C. She had been going to Preacher Gordon for counseling a good two months when the car wreck happened and killed the little boy. She had been a member of the church for about a year. I guess she found out she needed some counseling—first with the divorce and child custody and all that . . . She's sweet in a way, but a little flighty, and don't keep herself up like she should. And I do wish she'd wear a little less makeup, but you know how the styles are. — "Changing Names" by Clyde Edgerton

D. Miss Sharp's father was an artist, and in that quality had given lessons of drawing at Miss Pinkerton's school. He was a clever man; a pleasant companion; a careless student; with a great propensity for running into debt, and a partiality for the tavern. When he was drunk, he used to beat his wife and daughter; and the next morning, with a headache, he would rail at the world for its neglect of his genius . . . — from *Vanity Fair* by William Makepeace Thackeray

"How You Say It"—Clue to Setting (9–7A)

Directions: Answer the following questions concerning examples A-D from the Reading Selection, basing your responses on the clues given in each paragraph.

1. Choose two examples that you think concern the most recent time periods, and briefly explain what influenced your decision. Include specific words or phrases.

   Key letter _____ Reason _____

   _____

   _____

   Key letter _____ Reason _____

   _____

   _____

2. Two of these examples were written before the turn of the century. List their key letters and your reason for choosing each.

   Key letter _____ Reason _____

   _____

   _____

   Key letter _____ Reason _____

   _____

   _____

3. One example takes place in the Southern United States. Indicate its key letter and write the phrases that identify a southern narrator.

   Key letter _____ Reason _____

   _____

   _____

4. One takes place in England, not the United States. Try to identify it, and include reasons for your choice.

   Key letter _____ Reason _____

   _____

   _____

Working with Opening Paragraphs—Part I (9-8A)

Directions: Identify the settings of the following opening paragraphs of short stories as precisely as you can. Use the underlined words to help guide your decisions about where the story takes place and what clues indicate its time period. Base your conclusions on evidence given in the example.

Sample Answer: *Place:*   a campsite in the northern United States
                    Clues to time: The campers' arrival by truck shows modern times.

1. On Saturday afternoon Billy Buck, the <u>ranch-hand</u>, <u>raked</u> together the last of the old year's haystack and pitched small forkfuls over the wire fence to a few mildly interested cattle. High in the air small clouds like puffs of <u>cannon</u> smoke were driven eastward by the March wind. The wind could be heard whishing in the brush on the <u>ridge crests</u>, but no breath of it penetrated down into the <u>ranch</u> cup. — "The Leader of the People" by John Steinbeck

   (1) The story takes place in _____

   (2) Clues to time are _____

2. I met him first in a <u>hurricane</u>; and though we had gone through the hurricane on the same <u>schooner</u>, it was not until the schooner had gone to pieces under us that I first laid eyes on him. Without doubt I had seen him with the rest of the kanaka crew on board, but I had not consciously been aware of his existence, for the *Petite Jeanne* was rather overcrowded. In addition to her eight or ten kanaka seamen, the white captain, mate and supercargo, and her six cabin passengers, she sailed from <u>Rangiroa</u> with something like <u>eighty-five deck passengers</u>—<u>Paumotans</u> and <u>Tahitians</u>, men, women, and children each with a trade box, to say nothing of sleeping-mats, blankets, and clothes bundles. — "The Heathen" by Jack London

   (1) The story takes place in _____

   (2) Clues to time are _____

3. Earl lives next door in Edna's basement, behind the flower boxes Edna paints green each year, behind the dusty geraniums. We used to <u>sit on flower boxes</u> until the day Tito saw a <u>cockroach with a spot of green paint</u> on its head. Now we sit on the steps around the <u>basement apartment</u> where Earl lives. — "The Earl of Tennessee" by Sandra Cisneros

   (1) The story takes place in _____

   (2) Clues to time are _____

4. The boy who resided at <u>Agathox Lodge, 28, Buckingham Park Road, Surbiton</u>, had often been puzzled by the old <u>sign-post</u> that stood almost opposite. He asked his mother about it, and she replied that it was a joke, and <u>not a very nice one</u>, which had been made many years back by some <u>naughty young men</u>, and that the police ought to remove it. For there were two strange things about this sign-post: first, it pointed up a blank alley, and, secondly, it had pointed on it, in faded characters, the words, "To Heaven." — "The Celestial Omnibus" by E. M. Forster

   (1) The story takes place in _____

   (2) Clues to time are _____

Working with Opening Paragraphs—Part II (9–8B)

Directions: Identify the settings of the following opening paragraphs of short stories as precisely as you can. Use the underlined words to help guide your decisions about where the story takes place and what clues indicate its time period. Base your conclusions on evidence given in the example.

Sample Answer: *Place :* <u>a campsite in the northern United States</u>
Clues to time: <u>The campers' arrival by truck shows modern times.</u>

1. Did you ever hear of racing caterpillars? No? Well, it used to be a great thing <u>on the canal</u>. My <u>pa</u> used to have a lot of <u>them insects</u> on hand every fall, and the way he could get them to run would make a man have his eyes examined. — "The Death of Red Peril" by Walter D. Edmonds

   (1) The story takes place in _____

   (2) Clues to time are _____

2. The <u>bus</u> turning the corner of Patterson and Talford Avenue was dull this time of evening. Of the four passengers standing in the rear, she did not recognize any of her friends. Most of the people tucked neatly in the double seats were women, maids and cooks on their way from work or secretaries who had worked late and were riding from the <u>office building</u> at the mill. The <u>cotton mill</u> was out from <u>town</u>, near the house where she worked. She noticed that a few men were riding, too. They were obviously just working men, except for one gentleman dressed very neatly in a dark grey suit and carrying what she imagined was a <u>push-button umbrella</u>. — "Neighbors" by Diane Oliver

   (1) The story takes place in _____

   (2) Clues to time are _____

3. I knew him from the days of my extreme youth, because he made my father's <u>boots</u>; inhabiting with his elder brother two little shops <u>let into one</u>, in a small <u>bystreet</u>—now no more, but then most <u>fashionably placed</u> in the West End. — "Quality" by John Galsworthy

   (1) The story takes place in _____

   (2) Clues to time are _____

(9–8B continued)

4. It was late in the afternoon, and the light was waning. There was a difference in the look of the tree shadows out in <u>the yard</u>. Somewhere in the <u>distance cows</u> were lowing and a little <u>bell was tinkling</u>; now and then a <u>farm-wagon</u> tilted by, and the dust flew; some blue-shirted laborers with shovels over their shoulders <u>plodded past</u>; little swarms of flies were dancing up and down before the <u>people's faces</u> in the soft air. There seemed to be a gentle stir arising over everything for the mere sake of subsidence—a very premonition of rest and hush and night.
 — "A New England Nun" by Mary Wilkes Freeman

(1) The story takes place in _____

(2) Clues to time are _____

5. Henry Cooper had been on the <u>Moon</u> for almost <u>two weeks</u> before he discovered that something was wrong. At first it was only an ill-defined suspicion, the sort of hunch that a hardheaded <u>science reporter</u> would not take too seriously. He had come here, after all, at the <u>United Nations Space Administration's own request</u> . . . — "The Secret" by Arthur C. Clarke

(1) The story takes place in _____

(2) Clues to time are _____

Play the Name Game (9–9)

What's in a name? You can often make a good guess about when and where a story takes place, just by starting from a character's name.

For example, Caleb and Hettie aren't names you'd expect to belong to people today—nor do names like Kim or Dustin seem likely for someone from the past. And what about names like Françoise or Olga? Names such as these offer you a good guess about someone's nationality or where his or her ancestors came from.

Make a list of names that give clues to background—and see how good you are at identifying one another's examples.

_____

_____

_____

_____

_____

_____

_____

_____

_____

_____

_____

_____

_____

_____

_____

_____

_____

_____

_____

From the Points of View of Fiction
(*Reading Selection 9–10*)

Writers of both fiction and nonfiction can choose between two points of view: first person or third person. But the writer of fiction can explore possibilities that the nonfiction writer can't.

How would you like to be able to read someone's mind? It could be both good or bad, depending what you read there, and most people would say that it's not possible anyway. Yet, in fiction, writers may choose to express their characters' thoughts, allowing readers to know their motives and feelings, as well as their words and actions.

Since writers want their readers to know the basic plan and rules of their fictional world, right from the start, they generally alert readers to their chosen point of view in the opening paragraphs.

To determine point of view, it is necessary to consider only words not used as dialogue for, of course, anyone can use "I" in conversation.

FOR EXAMPLE: "I forgot you were coming," Jan admitted. (*third person*)
"I forgot you were coming," I admitted. (*first person*)

In fiction, each of the two main divisions of point of view—first person and third person—have two subdivisions that you need to note.

The Third-Person Point of View in Fiction

A. Third-Person Omniscient

Omniscient means "all-knowing." It identifies a writer's decision to look into a character or characters' minds if this will make the story clearer or more effective. Such statements as the following are clues to *omniscience* (words relating to the character's thought processes are underlined):

1. She <u>hoped</u> no one would notice how close she was to tears.
2. Although the day was dark and gloomy, he felt irrepressibly cheerful, <u>remembering</u> the promised surprise that awaited him.
3. In spite of what happened, he still <u>thought</u> he was right.

What other words can you list that would show the writer had chosen to enter a character's mind?

When using omniscience, writers can permit the reader to know thoughts of as many characters as they wish. The decision is the writer's and depends upon the method chosen to tell each story as clearly and effectively as possible.

(*Reading Selection 9–10 continued*)

B. Third-Person Outside Observer

Reading a story with this point of view is similar to watching a television show or seeing a movie. Using the third person, writers do not reveal what goes on in any of the characters' minds.

Third person, outside observer, is sometimes called "eye of the camera" viewpoint, for it shows what happened in a pictorial way and lets readers judge for themselves—by what characters do and say, how they look, and what other characters say about them. However, writers still provide other clues through description, dialogue, and action to guide the reader and reveal the attitudes and impressions they wish to create.

Be aware that a sentence such as "Larry said he believed Jeff was telling the truth," is not proof of omniscience. It only states what Larry said, which is not necessarily what he actually believed.

A writer carefully chooses the best point of view for telling a particular story—and good readers are aware of the choice because this knowledge enables them to understand the story better.

Omniscient or Outside Observer? (9–10A)

Directions: Read the following and indicate whether they are written in the third-person omniscient or outside-observer point of view. If the author has chosen omniscience, write at least two examples of specific words or phrases that reveal this choice. If outside observer, write "no words to reveal a character's thoughts."

1. Michael Lowes hummed as he shaved, amused by the face he saw—the pallid, asymmetrical face, with the right eye so much higher than the left, and its eyebrow so peculiarly arched, like a "v" turned upside down. Perhaps this day wouldn't be as bad as the last. In fact, he knew it wouldn't be, and that was why he hummed . . . — "Impulse" by Conrad Aiken

    (1) The point of view is _____ person, _____.

    (2) This is revealed by the author's choice of _____

    _____.

    (3) What repeated word shows Lowes feels optimistic? _____

    (4) What had the day before been like? _____

2. As Mr. John Oakhurst, gambler, stepped into the main street of Poker Flat on the morning of the twenty-third of November, 1850, he was conscious of a change in its moral atmosphere since the preceding night. Two or three men, conversing earnestly together, ceased as he approached, and exchanged significant glances. . . .

    Mr. Oakhurst's calm, handsome face betrayed small concern of these indications. Whether he was conscious of any predisposing cause was another question. "I reckon they're after somebody," he reflected; "likely it's me." . . . —
    "The Outcasts of Poker Flat" by Francis Bret Harte

    (1) The point of view is _____ person, _____.

    (2) This is revealed by the author's choice of _____

    _____.

    (3) The paragraph gives the time as _____.

    (4) The place is _____, which is probably a town located in

    _____.

3. It was almost three o'clock when Mary Jane finally found Eloise's house. She explained to Eloise, who had come out of the driveway to meet her, that everything had been absolutely *perfect,* that she had remembered the way *exactly,* until she had turned off the Merrick Parkway. Eloise said, "*Merritt* Parkway, baby," and reminded Mary Jane that she had found the house twice before, but Mary Jane

just wailed something ambiguous, something about her box of Kleenex, and rushed back to her convertible. Eloise turned up the collar of her camel's-hair coat, put her back to the wind, and waited. Mary Jane was back in a minute using a leaf of Kleenex and still looking upset . . . — "Uncle Wiggily in Connecticut" by J. D. Salinger

(1) The point of view is _____ person, _____.

(2) This is revealed by the author's choice of _____

_____.

(3) Indicate whether the story takes place in the past, modern times, or the future. _____ Clues to the story's time period include

_____ and _____.

(4) Does the story probably take place in the country, a small town, or big city?

_____ Clues to this as the setting include _____

_____.

4. Day had broken cold and gray, exceedingly cold and gray, when the man turned aside from the main Yukon trail and climbed the high earth-bank, where a dim and little-traveled trail led eastward through the fat spruce timberland. It was a steep bank, and he paused for breath at the top, excusing the act to himself by looking at his watch. It was nine o'clock. There was no sun nor hint of sun, though there was not a cloud in the sky. It was a clear day, and yet there seemed . . . a subtle gloom that made the day dark, and that was due to the absence of sun. The fact did not worry the man. . . . He knew that a few more days must pass before that cheerful orb, due south, would just peep above the skyline and dip immediately from view.

The man flung a look back along the way he had come. The Yukon lay a mile wide and hidden under three feet of ice. On top of this ice were as many feet of snow. — "To Build a Fire" by Jack London

(1) The point of view is _____ person, _____.

(2) This is revealed by the author's choice of _____

_____.

(3) What word first gives a clue to the place of the setting? _____

(4) What hints that the setting might hold danger for a man traveling alone?

(Give two examples.) _____

and _____

Beginning to Write Fiction (9–11)

Directions: Try your hand at writing the opening paragraphs of short stories. Write two examples, one using the third-person omniscient point of view and another in third-person outside observer. Be sure you label each to indicate the point of view you use.

To write your paragraphs, you will need to choose:

1. A character, facing some sort of conflict or problem
2. A setting—both time and place
3. Where and how you wish to start off your story
4. Which third-person point of view is better to use

Plan to include at least three sentences in each of your examples.

Opening Paragraph #1

_____

_____

_____

_____

_____

_____

Opening Paragraph #2

_____

_____

_____

_____

_____

_____

_____

Just Who Is Telling the Story? *(Reading Selection 9–12)*

Writer $\longrightarrow$ Reader
$\searrow$ $\nearrow$
Characters in Story

When you are reading fiction, it's important to remember that the writer is not speaking for himself or herself but is creating a world that will seem to be happening as the story is read.

You should also remember that, when fiction is told in the first person by someone speaking as "I," it is not the writer telling his or her story. A moment's thought of the differences between fiction and nonfiction should make this clear.

At times authors choose the first-person point of view, even though they are writing about a character very different from themselves . . . perhaps even a liar or a murderer or someone of the opposite sex.

First person, like the third, has two possibilities.

A. First Person, Main Character

In this point of view, the main character—not to be confused with the author—tells his or her own story.

An obvious advantage is that the reader can share in the experiences and thoughts of the main character. It's like getting a first-hand account of all that's happening and also lets the reader learn what the main character says about other people and events in the story.

First-person, main character also can create such a feeling of authenticity that a forgetful or inexperienced reader may have the impression it's the writer's own story—nonfiction instead of fiction.

Good readers remember there's an author "putting words in the character's mouth." The main character, for example, might use improper grammar or incorrect spelling, which the writer chose to show the speaker is young, poorly educated or from the backwoods.

The main character might even be a braggart, coward, or liar. Without stating this directly, the author will provide clues, such as contradictions and misstatements, so readers can catch the first-person speaker in an untruth.

Because the writer has complete control over every word the first-person speaker says, always be alert for clues to help you draw the right conclusions. Count on the author to let you know whether to take the main character seriously or humorously, and what or how much to believe.

B. First Person, Minor Character

An advantage of the first-person minor-character point of view is that the reader gets a vivid, first-hand account of the story through the words of someone participating in it.

Again, although the character speaks as "I," it is not the writer speaking for him- or herself. If it were, the story would be nonfiction.

By revealing the story through the eyes of a minor character, the author can control how much the reader knows as the story unfolds.

The minor-character narrator (or person telling the story) may take an active part or simply be a kind of reporter, observing from the sidelines. Often the reactions of the first-person minor-character narrator show how the author wants the reader to react to events and other characters. This helps the reader understand the truth the writer is trying to illustrate about life and human nature.

Just Who Is Telling the Story? (9–12A)

Writer ———→ Reader

Characters in Story

Directions: Read each of the following paragraphs to determine whether it is told from the first-person, main or minor character, point of view. Also, write your answers to the additional questions that follow each example.

1. I don't have much work to do around the house like some girls. My mother does that. And I don't have to earn my pocket money. George runs errands for the big boys and sells Christmas cards. And anything else that's got to get done, my father does. All I have to do in life is mind my brother Raymond, which is enough.

   Sometimes I slip and say my little brother Raymond. But as any fool can see, he's much bigger and he's older too. But a lot of people call him my little brother 'cause he needs looking after 'cause he's not quite right. And a lot of smart mouths got lots to say about that too, especially when George was minding him. But now, if anybody has anything to say to Raymond, anything about his big head, they have to come by me. — "Raymond's Run" by Toni Cade Bambara

   (1) The point of view is _____ person, _____.

   (2) The reader has this impression because _____

   _____.

   (3) Two clues to Raymond's problem are _____

   and _____.

   (4) Because of the clues, the reader should draw the conclusion that Raymond is

   _____.

   (5) The speaker states she is "not like some girls." In addition, list two expressions that make her seem like a tomboy. _____

   _____ and _____

2. On a stormy night, in the tempestuous times of the French Revolution, a young German was returning to his lodgings, at a late hour, across the old part of Paris. The lightning gleamed, and the loud claps of thunder rattled through the lofty narrow streets—but I should first tell you something about this young German. — "The Adventure of the German Student" by Washington Irving

   (1) The point of view is _____ person, _____.

   (2) The reader has this impression because _____

   _____.

   (3) The story take place in _____ at the time of _____

   _____.

(9–12A continued)

3. There was a man in the island of Hawaii, whom I shall call Keawe; for, the truth is, he still lives, and his name must be kept secret; but the place of his birth was not far from Honaunau, where the bones of Keawe the Great lie hidden in a cave. This man was poor, brave, and active; he could read and write like a schoolmaster; he was a first-rate mariner besides, sailed for some time in the great world and foreign cities, and he shipped on a vessel bound to San Francisco.

   This is a fine town, with a fine harbor, and rich people uncountable; and, in particular, there is one hill which is covered with palaces. . . . — "The Bottle Imp" by Robert Louis Stevenson

   (1) The point of view is _____ person, _____.

   (2) The reader has this impression because _____

   _____.

   (3) The story takes place in _____.

   (4) The probable time period is _____.

   (5) Clues to the time include _____.

4. Through a ten-power glass I was looking upon the face of Alexander the Great. When I saw that distinctive cut upon the cheek, I'd first thought it was an old banker's cut. . . . But then I realized I'd seen this particular coin before. The cut on the cheek. That was the clue.

   The man who had brought the coin into my shop was sitting opposite my desk. We were alone in my shop. I could feel his eyes upon me as I examined the coin.

   "Yes, it's a very rare coin," I said, although he'd not asked for an opinion. — "Archetypes" by Robert Greenwood

   (1) The point of view is _____ person, _____.

   (2) The reader has this impression because _____

   _____.

   (3) The reader could infer there might be danger involved because

   _____ and

   _____.

Writing in First Person (9–13)

Directions: Try your hand at writing the opening paragraphs of short stories. Write two examples, one using the first-person main-character point of view and another in first-person minor character. Be sure you label each to indicate the point of view you chose.

    To write your paragraphs, you will need to choose:

1. A character, facing some sort of conflict or problem
2. A setting—both time and place
3. Where and how you wish to start off your story
4. Which first-person point of view is better to use

Plan to include at least three sentences in each of your examples.

Opening Paragraph #1

_____

_____

_____

_____

_____

_____

Opening Paragraph #2

_____

_____

_____

_____

_____

_____

_____

Doubting the Main Character (9–14)

Writer ⟶ Reader
↘ ↗
Characters in Story

Directions: There are times when the main character of a story may be bragging, telling lies, or simply not understand the truth about a situation—while both the writer and reader do. You might think of it this way. When using the first-person point of view, the writer not only speaks through the characters but also "puts words into the character's mouth" that reveal the truth. With this in mind, read the following paragraphs and answer the questions that follow.

1. I was getting along fine with Mama, Papa-Daddy and Uncle Rondo until my sister Stella-Rondo just separated from her husband and came back home again. Mr. Whitaker! Of course, I went with Mr. Whitaker first, when he first appeared here in China Grove, taking "Pose Yourself" photos, and Stella-Rondo broke us up. Told him I was one-sided. Bigger on one side than the other, which is a deliberated, calculated falsehood: I'm the same. Stella-Rondo is exactly twelve months to the day younger than I am and for that reason she's spoiled. — "Why I Live at the P.O." by Eudora Welty

(1) The point of view is _____ person, _____.

(2) The reader has this impression because _____

_____.

(3) The setting is a place called _____,

which gives the impression of its being _____.

(4) List three accusations the speaker makes against Stella-Rondo:

(a) _____

(b) _____

(c) _____

(5) The speaker mentions the expression "one-sided."

(a) What does she believe it means? _____

_____

(b) How else can a person be "one-sided"? _____

_____

(6) In what way is the speaker being "one-sided"? _____

_____

(9–14 continued)

2. True! nervous—very, very dreadfully nervous I had been and am; but why *will* you say that I am mad? The disease had sharpened my senses—not destroyed—not dulled them. Above all was the sense of hearing acute. I heard all things in the heaven and in the earth. I heard many things in hell. How, then, am I mad? Hearken! and observe how healthily—how calmly I can tell you the whole story. . . . — "The Tell-Tale Heart" by Edgar Allan Poe

(1) The point of view is _____ person, _____.

(2) What two physical problems does the speaker first admit to?

_____

_____

(3) The question "Why will you say that I am mad?" is the writer's way of calling attention to the character's _____.

(4) What two incredible claims does the speaker make about what he has heard? _____

_____

(5) What techniques does the writer use to make the character's manner of speaking seem disturbed and wild? _____

_____

3. (*Continuation of passage 2.*) It is impossible to say how first the idea entered my brain; but once conceived, it haunted me day and night. . . . He had never wronged me. He had never given me insult. For his gold I had no desire. I think it was his yes! yes, it was this! He had the eye of a vulture—a pale blue eye, with a film over it. Whenever it fell upon me, my blood ran cold; and so by degrees—very gradually—I made up my mind to take the life of the old man, and thus rid myself of the eye forever. — "The Tell-Tale Heart" by Edgar Allan Poe

(1) Who is "he"? _____

(2) What three possible reasons for committing murder are referred to in this passage? _____

_____

(3) Why would the author have the character name these reasons? _____

_____

(4) Why did the character want to "get rid" of the old man? _____

_____

(5) Should the reader infer the character was or was not insane? _____ Why or why not? _____

_____

Identifying Point of View (9–15)

Directions: Read each paragraph, and identify its point of view as first-person main or minor character, or third-person omniscient or outside observer. Be prepared to point out the clues that lead to your decision. In addition, write your answers to the other questions relating to each example.

1. It was a fine September day. By noon it would be summer again but now it was true autumn with a touch of chill in the air. As Joseph Howe stood on the porch of the house in which he lodged, ready to leave for his first class of the year, he thought with pleasure of the long indoor days that were coming. It was a moment when he could feel glad of his profession. — "Of This Time, Of That Place" by Lionel Trilling

    (1) The point of view is _____ person, _____.

    (2) Joseph Howe's profession is probably that of _____.

    (3) Clues are the time of year, which is _____

      and his leaving for _____.

    (4) The fact that Howe lives in _____ is a

      clue that his marital status is probably _____.

2. My brother would often get drunk when I was a little girl, but that put a different sort of fear into me from what Mr. Speed did. With Brother it was a spiritual thing. And though it was frightening to know that he would have to burn for all that giggling and bouncing around on the stair at night, the truth was that he only seemed jollier to me when I would stick my head out of the hall door. It made him seem almost my age for him to act so silly . . . But the really frightening thing about seeing Brother drunk was . . . I could always recall my mother's words to him when he was sixteen, the year before she died . . .
    "Son, I'd rather see you in your grave."
    Yet those nights put a scaredness into me that was clearly distinguishable from the terror that Mr. Speed instilled by stumbling past our house two or three afternoons a week . . . — "A Spinster's Tale" by Peter Taylor

    (1) The point of view is _____ person, _____.

    (2) Two facts known about the main character's family are _____

      _____ and _____.

    (3) The story is obviously fiction because the main character is _____

      while the author is _____.

3. In 1830, only a few miles away from what is now the great city of Cincinnati, lay an immense and almost unbroken forest. The whole region was sparsely settled by people of the frontier . . . Among those . . . was one who had been of those first arriving. He lived alone in a house of logs surrounded on all sides by the great forest . . .

   The little house, with its chimney of sticks . . . and its "chinking" of clay, had a single door and, directly opposite, a window. The latter, however, was boarded up—nobody could remember a time when it was not . . . I fancy there are few persons living today who ever knew the secret of that window, but I am one, as you shall see. — "The Boarded Window" by Ambrose Bierce

   (1) The point of view is _____ person, _____.

   (2) The story takes place _____; the time is _____.

   (3) The question in the story is _____.

   (4) Two facts known about the house's owner are _____

   _____

4. Monk and Glennie were playing catch on the side lawn of the firehouse when Scho caught sight of them. They were good at it, for seventh-graders. Monk, wearing a catcher's mitt, would lean easily sidewise and back, with one leg lifted and his throwing hand almost down to the grass, and then lob the white ball straight up into the sunlight. Glennie would shield his eyes with his left hand and, just as the ball fell past him, snag it with a little dart of his glove . . .

   They were going on and on like that, in a kind of slow, mannered, luxurious dance in the sun, their faces perfectly blank and entranced, when Glennie noticed Scho dawdling along the other side of the street and called hello to him . . .
   — "A Game of Catch" by Richard Wilbur

   (1) The point of view is _____ person, _____.

   (2) Monk and Glennie are probably close in age because _____

   _____.

   (3) Are Monk and Glennie friendly or unfriendly to Scho? _____

   (4) Explain the reason for your choice._____

   _____

   (5) Were Monk and Glennie bored with or enjoying their game of catch?

   _____

   (6) Explain the reason for your choice. _____

   _____

UNIT 10

Ready for Action: Plot

In some stories—and to some readers and writers—*plot* matters most.

It's especially true of stories with cookie-cutter characters: romantic heroines whose chance encounters inevitably find true love; worldly-wise heroes who triumph over diabolical forces of evil and crime; the innocent few among throngs of throwaway victims in tales of frenzy and horror.

Good readers also appreciate plot—what happens in a story or novel, yet insights into character and the depth of a writer's theme are valued more.

For accomplished readers, the plot is the framework, and characters' actions are a way of testing, illustrating, and fulfilling the story's theme. So, although they do not focus narrowly upon the plot line of a story, good readers possess an underlying awareness of its twists and turns, its construction and development.

Therefore, this unit introduces the basics of plot, including techniques by which writers develop plots to logical and satisfactory conclusions. It is important for students to think of well-written fiction as a seamless whole, from beginning to end, with each part and detail contributing to the author's essential purpose.

This unit will also introduce several basic types of fiction passages, studied individually to show the effect and purpose of each. Especially obvious in longer works and novels, each kind of paragraph calls for a different approach, questions, and pace of reading. These passages include: Descriptions of Background and Setting; Dialogue; Narrative Action; Descriptive Characterization; and Authorial/ Thematic Comment.

The first three types of paragraphs are presented in this unit in relation to plot. Descriptive Characterization and Authorial/Thematic Comment will be discussed in later units.

Students need to realize that exercises in this unit are not a satisfactory substitute for reading entire works of fiction. Each skill is meant to become part of a student's treasury of resources, to be called upon when needed and enrich his or her future reading experiences.

NOTES ON ACTIVITIES

About Setting and Plot (10–3A)

As a means of teaching the skills of reading, one of the main advantages to this Kate Chopin story, in addition to its unexpected ending, is its unusually short length. When going over the answers with your classes, invite someone to point out the paragraph containing the proper evidence or clue. After everyone has found it, have the class follow along as it's read. This allows students to "see" the answer and prepares them for more successful reading in the future.

To adapt questions to varying abilities, allow less able students to find only one or two clues, while requesting advanced classes to seek multiple ones. When comparing students' answers, explain that the individual reader need not expect to find every clue but needs only one or two solid pieces of support.

With better students, discuss how Chopin carefully "planted" the impression the Mallards were well-to-do. For example: Mrs. Mallard has her own room, the house is large, and, most importantly, she expresses no concern about money when she contemplates a future life alone.

With less able readers, you may wish to read the story orally, then work together with the class to complete answers to the exercise.

Tell "The Story of an Hour" in Six Plot Steps (10–4)

You may find it helpful to work together with your class to write one or two of the plot steps at the chalkboard before they complete this activity on their own.

Learning how to rewrite and edit their work to make it more precise and concise is one of the most important skills students can learn. It not only improves their writing, but it also makes them more aware of the importance and power of a single word.

After they have written plot step one, you might want to write several students' efforts on the board. Then, working from students' suggestions, refine the examples and make them as clear and informative as possible.

Less able students may need a pre-written example such as the following:

First attempt: Mrs. Mallard's sister tells her that her husband was killed in a train wreck. (14 words)
Second draft: Mrs. Mallard gets news that her husband died in a train wreck. (12 words)
Suggestion: Try to make the plot steps sound like a headline or telegram.
Final draft: Mrs. Mallard gets news of husband's death in train wreck. (10 words)

After completing the exercise, have each class create its own set of plot steps. Put examples on the board to show how different students solve the problem each step presents. Then let the class choose the six that most clearly and concisely retell the story.

Plotting How Time Passes (10–7)

Students can easily become confused about what constitutes a flashback. Explain that true flashbacks do more than give details about a character's background and past. Flashbacks are part of the plot itself, portraying the character in action and usually containing dialogue, as well.

Getting Involved in Narrative Action (10–9A)

The purpose of this exercise is to help students see the techniques writers use to convey a sense of movement in paragraphs of narrative action. You might also want to review how each sentence answers "Who or What?" and "Did what?" so that less able readers can see the difference between predicative verbs and verb forms used as adjectives.

Counts of verbs and verb forms are meant to serve mainly as a basis for comparison, not for evaluation of students. You might also point out that certain words, such as "pass" in example one, and "jump" and "rush" in example two, can also be used as either nouns or verbs, so these also lend to the sense of action.

Drawing Conclusions from Dialogue (10–10)

To give students additional help in identifying change of speakers, you may want to review the punctuation of direct quotations, including dialogue that extends for more than one paragraph.

Fiction: The Long and Short of It (Reading Selection 10–13)

In developing students' awareness of the different types of paragraphs in narrative fiction and the different approaches needed, emphasize that all paragraphs and passages cannot be given clear-cut labels. The goal is for students to realize that they should not go "plugging along," reading all passages equally.

Remind students that, in fiction, the writer speaks through characters, but also provides clues that allow readers to be aware of things the characters do not know or realize.

Knowledge of grammar is a valuable asset for readers. Students can note that descriptive paragraphs contain more adjectives than passages of dialogue or action do, while effective narrative action depends greatly upon strong verbs, sometimes allied with adverbs, and contains relatively few adjectives.

Plotting the Action (10–1)

What is the **plot** of a story?

Many times, getting the right answer depends upon asking the right question. Ask, "What's it about?" and someone might tell you, "It's about a girl with a wicked step-mother."

That may be what a story, perhaps "Cinderella," is "about," but it's not the plot. The question to ask about plot is just, "**What happened?**"

1. Bad guy terrorizes city.
2. Good guy chases bad guy.
3. Good guy and bad guy meet face to face.
4. Good guy defeats bad guy.

That could be the **plot line** of a lot of movies. And, the plot is often told in a series of **plot steps,** like those above.

It used to be said that the plot steps of old romantic movies were all the same:

1. Boy meets girl.
2. Boy loses girl.
3. Boy gets girl.

In that case, the plot line of the story about the girl with the wicked stepmother could be stated:

1. Girl meets prince.
2. Girl loses shoe.
3. Girl gets prince.

Directions: Following is a more serious set of plot steps for the story you recognized above as "Cinderella." But, now they're scrambled! Practice working with plot steps. Show their correct order by writing a number from 1 to 7 in each blank space. "1" shows what happens first, "2" shows what happens next, and so on.

_____ a. Hearing midnight strike, Cinderella runs off, losing a glass slipper.

_____ b. The shoe fits Cinderella, and the prince offers his love.

_____ c. Cinderella's fairy godmother magically makes her ball gown and coach.

_____ d. The prince's men search the kingdom for the slipper's owner.

_____ e. Cinderella's wicked stepmother prevents her from going to the ball.

_____ f. The prince and Cinderella love one another at first sight.

_____ g. Cinderella's benefactor warns her to leave the ball by midnight.

Name _____   Date _____   Period _____

Writing Your Own Plot Steps (10–2)

Of course, plot steps leave out many details. They're not the whole story—they're like the **framework** of the story. Yet you need to know *what happened*—the **plot**—to ask and answer the many questions that involve good readers next, such as *how* something happened and *why* it happened.

Did you notice that each of the plot steps to "Cinderella" was written in ten words or fewer? In creating the framework of the plot, it's necessary that each word be strong and precise. If not, someone trying to follow the storyline might get lost and not even know what questions to ask to find the way out.

Directions: Write 5 to 10 plot steps for a story you know. It's yours for the choosing. You might want to pick another familiar fairy tale, like "Little Red Riding Hood" or "Beauty and the Beast."

Perhaps a story you read recently in class comes to mind. Or one you enjoyed at home.

Plots are everywhere—in the movies, on television. For someone very daring—you might want to risk creating a plot of your own. But, remember, someone else will read your plot steps, as well as you, and try to picture them happening, too.

Make each word count. Be aware of word power:

1. State each step as precisely and directly as you can.

2. Choose words that give a clear picture of your meaning.

3. Use no more than ten words per step. (You'll be penalized one point for each word over ten. 14 words = minus 4.)

4. Learning to weigh words carefully and thoughtfully is one of the first steps to becoming a better reader *and* writer.

In Story Form: Setting and Plot (*Reading Selection 10–3*)

Kate Chopin, 1851–1904. American novelist and short story writer. Born in St. Louis, Missouri, and lived 13 years in Louisiana, both in New Orleans and on a plantation in Natchitoches Parish, returning to St. Louis in 1883. Her famous novel *The Awakening* was published in 1899.

It's time to practice your reading skills on a short story by one of America's best-known authors.

To determine setting, use all the clues you can find. It's definitely not cheating to use the facts you learn about the author's life—especially if you decide the writer has set the story in what—then—was the present.

However, if that's your decision, be sure to check and support your "educated guess" with details from the actual story. It's not necessary to be exact, but have good reason for your opinions.

Kate Chopin calls it "The Story of an Hour," but it should take you far less time to read.

The Story of an Hour by Kate Chopin

Knowing that Mrs. Mallard was afflicted with a heart trouble, great care was taken to break to her as gently as possible the news of her husband's death.

It was her sister Josephine who told her, in broken sentences, veiled hints that revealed in half concealing. Her husband's friend Richards was there, too, near her. It was he who had been in the newspaper office when intelligence of the railroad disaster was received, with Brently Mallard's name leading the list of "killed." He had only taken the time to assure himself of its truth by a second telegram, and had hastened to forestall any less careful, less tender friend in bearing the sad message.

She did not hear the story as many women have the same, with a paralyzed inability to accept its significance. She wept at once, with sudden, wild abandonment, in her sister's arms. When the storm of grief had spent itself she went away to her room alone. She would have no one follow her.

There stood, facing the open window, a comfortable, roomy armchair. Into this she sank, pressed down by a physical exhaustion that haunted her body and seemed to reach into her soul.

She could see in the open square before her house the tops of trees that were all aquiver with the new spring life. The delicious breath of rain was in the air. In the street below a peddler was crying his wares. The notes of a distant song which some one was singing reached her faintly, and countless sparrows were twittering in the eaves.

There were patches of blue sky showing here and there through the clouds that had met and piled one above the other in the west facing her window.

She sat with her head thrown back upon the cushion of the chair, quite motionless, except when a sob came up into her throat and shook her, as a child who has cried itself to sleep continues to sob in its dreams.

She was young, with a fair, calm face, whose lines bespoke repression and even a certain strength. But now there was a dull stare in her eyes, whose gaze was fixed away off yonder on one of those patches of blue sky. It was not a glance of reflection, but rather indicated a suspension of intelligent thought.

There was something coming to her and she was waiting for it, fearfully. What was it? She did not know; it was too subtle and elusive to name. But she felt it, creeping out of the sky, reaching toward her through the sounds, the scents, the color that filled the air.

Now her bosom rose and fell tumultuously. She was beginning to recognize this thing that was approaching to possess her, and she was striving to beat it back with her will—as powerless as her two white slender hands would have been.

When she abandoned herself a little whispered word escaped her slightly parted lips. She said it over and over under her breath: "free, free, free!" The vacant stare and the look of terror that had followed it went from her eyes. They stayed keen and bright. Her pulses beat fast, and the coursing blood warmed and relaxed every inch of her body.

She did not stop to ask if it were or were not a monstrous joy that held her. A clear and exalted perception enabled her to dismiss the suggestion as trivial.

She knew that she would weep again when she saw the kind, tender hands folded in death; the face that had never looked save with love upon her, fixed and gray and dead. But she saw beyond that bitter moment a long procession of years to come that would belong to her absolutely. And she opened and spread her arms out to them in welcome.

There would be no one to live for her during the coming years; she would live for herself. There would be no powerful will bending hers in that blind persistence with which men and women believe they have a right to impose a private will upon a fellow-creature. A kind intention or a cruel intention made the act seem no less a crime as she looked upon it in that brief moment of illumination.

And yet she had loved him—sometimes. Often she had not. What did it matter! What could love, the unsolved mystery, count for in face of this possession of self-assertion which she suddenly recognized as the strongest impulse of her being!

"Free! Body and soul free!" she kept whispering.

Josephine was kneeling before the closed door with her lips to the keyhole, imploring for admission. "Louise, open the door! I beg; open the door—you will make yourself ill. What are you doing, Louise? For heaven's sake open the door."

"Go away. I am not making myself ill." No; she was drinking in a very elixir of life through the open window.

Her fancy was running riot along those days ahead of her. Spring days, and summer days, and all sorts of days that would be her own. She breathed a quick prayer that life might be long. It was only yesterday she had thought with a shudder that life might be long.

She arose at length and opened the door to her sister's importunities. There was a feverish triumph in her eyes, and she carried herself unwittingly like a goddess of Victory. She clasped her sister's waist, and together they descended the stairs. Richards stood waiting for them at the bottom.

Some one was opening the front door with a latchkey. It was Brently Mallard who entered, a little travel-stained, composedly carrying his grip-sack and umbrella. He had been far from the scene of accident, and did not even know there had been one. He stood amazed at Josephine's piercing cry; at Richards' quick motion to screen him from the view of his wife.

But Richards was too late.

When the doctors came they said she had died of heart disease—of joy that kills.

About Setting and Plot (10–3A)

Directions: Use your skills in determining setting to answer the following questions as accurately as you can. You may check the story to find the evidence you need to draw correct conclusions.

_____ 1. The setting of the story is (a) France, (b) the United States, (c) South America.

Clues _____

_____

_____ 2. The Mallard house is most likely located (a) in a town or city, (b) on a large cotton plantation, (c) on the edge of a rain forest.

Clues _____

_____

_____ 3. The time of the setting is most logically (a) during the Civil War, (b) at the turn of the century, (c) shortly after World War I.

Clues _____

_____

_____ 4. The point of view is (a) first-person, main character, (b) first-person, minor character, (c) third-person, outside observer, (d) third-person, omniscient.

Clues _____

_____

5. Although the story has a surprise ending, how did the author, Kate Chopin, prepare for its possibility in the very first paragraph?

_____

_____

6. How were the doctors wrong in their diagnosis of the cause of Mrs. Mallard's death?

_____

_____

7. Why should the ending be considered ironic? (Use the story to support your conclusion.) _____

_____

Tell "The Story of an Hour" in Six Plot Steps (10–4)

Directions: How did Kate Chopin "build" the story to its surprise ending? Writing the plot steps can help you see more clearly. Remember, you're writing about **action,** so avoid such words as *be, has,* and *thinks.* And, **do** use action words like *finds, tells,* and *enters.*

If you first draft your plot steps on a scratch sheet of paper, you'll find it easier to change and cut out words in order to state each step clearly in the ten-word limit.

Make each word count. Remember: word power!

1. State each step as precisely and directly as you can.
2. Choose words that give a clear picture of your meaning.
3. Use no more than ten words per step. (You'll be penalized one point for each word over ten. 14 words = minus 4.)

1. _____

   _____

2. _____

   _____

3. _____

   _____

4. _____

   _____

5. _____

   _____

6. _____

   _____

Changes: All in an Hour (10–5)

Directions: When you think about the plot, you see that Mrs. Mallard's feelings about life changed completely in just one hour. The result explains the author's choice of title. Thinking of the plot, answer the following in brief sentences.

1. At the beginning, what did Mrs. Mallard think of her life and future?

   _____

   _____

2. When she heard the news, what change did Mrs. Mallard see in her life and future?

   _____

   _____

3. Even before the final paragraph, how did Mrs. Mallard see her life changing again?

   _____

   _____

   _____

   _____

Then and Now: In Comparison (10–6)

1. How was life during the time portrayed in "The Story of an Hour" different from that of today?
2. How did people then express the same kinds of feelings that people have today?

These are questions worth thinking about, after you have finished "The Story of an Hour." One of the most important skills of the good reader is the ability to make comparisons—both to see how others are different and also the same from themselves.

Consider the questions alone or through group discussions. Then share your ideas in a written or oral presentation.

Plotting How Time Passes (10–7)

On an ordinary day, most people get up in the morning, eat breakfast, go to work or school, have lunch . . . and so on, hour by hour. And many plots in fiction develop that way, too. It's called **chronological order:** going by the clock.

In some fiction, the writer instead tells the plot as a **flashback:** jumping back in time to an earlier event. Think of flashbacks as actual scenes or action concerning an earlier event, inserted into the story, not simply a paragraph giving background.

Directions: Read the following examples, and tell whether the plot order will include a flashback or is written in chronological order. Then, answer the additional questions concerning each. Be prepared to explain the reasons for your answers.

1. People have wondered (there being obviously no question of romance involved) how I could ever have allowed myself to be let in for the East African adventure of Mrs. Diana in search of her husband. There were several reasons. To begin with, the time and effort weren't mine; they were the property of . . . the Society through which Diana's life had been insured, along with the rest of that job-lot of missionaries. . . . In the second place, the wonderers have not counted on Mrs. Diana's capacity for getting things done. . . . — "The Man Who Saw Through Heaven" by Wilbur Daniel Steele

    (1) The probable plot order is _____.

    (2) The action will likely take place in _____
    _____.

    (3) What clues are given to the time period of the story? _____
    _____

    (4) What question about the action is raised in the opening paragraph?
    _____

    (5) The point of view is _____ person*.

2. The kid burned out the rig's brakes on the Corkscrew grade at eleven thirty that night. Then, panicking as the ten-wheel combo—tractor and semi-trailer—gained speed, he raced the diesel, double-clutched, and tried to jam into a lower gear ratio. The stripping grind from the transmission jarred up into the bunk behind him. Barney Conners came awake fast. — "Runaway Rig" by Carl Henry Rathjen

*It is not always possible or necessary to positively identify the precise use of first- and third-person from the opening paragraph alone.

(10–7 continued)

(1) The probable plot order is _____.

(2) The action will likely take place in _____

_____.

(3) What clues are given to the time period of the story? _____

_____

(4) What question about the action is raised in the opening paragraph?

_____

(5) The point of view is _____ person*.

3. I have just read among the general news in one of the papers a drama of passion. He killed her and then he killed himself, so he must have loved her. What matters He or She? Their love alone matters to me; and it does not interest me because it moves me or astonishes me, or because it softens me or makes me think, but because it recalls to mind a remembrance of my youth, a strange recollection of a hunting adventure where Love appeared to me, as the Cross appeared to the early Christians, in the midst of the heavens. . . .

    That year the cold weather set in suddenly toward the end of autumn, and I was invited by one of my cousins, Karl de Rauville, to go with him and shoot ducks on the marshes, at daybreak . . . The hills right and left were covered with woods, old manorial woods. . . . where the rarest feathered game in that part of France was to be found. — "Love: Three Pages from a Sportsman's Book" by Guy de Maupassant

(1) The probable plot order is _____.

(2) The action will likely take place in _____

_____.

(3) What clues are given to the time period of the story? _____

_____

(4) What question about the action is raised in the opening paragraph?

_____

(5) The point of view is _____ person*.

© 1995 by The Center for Applied Research in Education

---

*It is not always possible or necessary to positively identify the precise use of first- and third-person from the opening paragraph alone.

(10–7 continued)

4. On the third day after they moved into the country he came walking back from the village carrying a basket of groceries and a twenty-four-yard coil of rope. She came out to meet him, wiping her hands on her green smock. Her hair was tumbled, her nose was scarlet with sunburn, he told her that already she looked like a born country woman. His flannel shirt stuck to him, his heavy shoes were dusty. She assured him he looked like a rural character in a play. — "Rope" by Katherine Anne Porter

(1) The probable plot order is _____.

(2) The action will likely take place in _____

_____.

(3) What clues are given to the time period of the story? _____

_____

(4) What question about the action is raised in the opening paragraph?

_____

(5) The point of view is _____ person*.

*It is not always possible or necessary to positively identify the precise use of first- and third-person from the opening paragraph alone.

How Writers "Plant" Clues in Plots (10–8)

Foreshadow: to give clues or hints that help the reader make educated guesses about how a story will progress or end.

Imagine reading a story of a house, reportedly haunted, on a dark and stormy night. You'd naturally be disappointed if a ghost, real or imaginary, didn't appear as you were led to expect through foreshadowing.

Or, a character might warn another of a treacherous undertow that made swimming dangerous. It's likely that someone will be caught in that undertow—and this, too, is an example of foreshadowing.

Directions: Read the following examples, and explain how each uses foreshadowing. Then, answer the additional questions concerning each. Be prepared to explain the reasons for your answers.

1. To George Williams went the distinction of being the first to suggest making Sam Billings the new town-treasurer. The moment he made the nomination at the annual town meeting there was an enthusiastic chorus of approval that resulted in the first unanimous election in the history of Androscoggin . . . .

   The election of Sam to the office of town-treasurer pleased everybody. He was a good business man and he was honest. . . . After he was elected everybody wondered why they had been giving the office to crooks and scoundrels for the past twenty years or more when the public money could have been safe and secure with Sam Billings. The retiring treasurer was still unable to account to everybody's satisfaction for about eighteen hundred dollars of the town's money, and the one before him had allowed his books to get into such a tangled condition that it cost the town two hundred and fifty dollars to hire an accountant to make them balance.

   — "The Rumor" by Erskine Caldwell

   (1) The passage and title seem to foreshadow that _____

   _____.

   (2) The probable plot order is _____.

   (3) The action will likely take place in _____.

   (4) What clues are given to the time period of the story? _____

   _____

   (5) What question about the action is raised in the paragraphs given?

   _____

   (6) The point of view is _____ person*.

2. Mary Cochran went out of the rooms where she lived with her father, Doctor Lester Cochran, at seven o'clock on a Sunday evening. It was June of the year nineteen hundred and eight and Mary was eighteen years old. She walked along Tremont to

---

*It is not always possible or necessary to positively identify the precise use of first- and third-person from the opening paragraph alone.

(10–8 continued)

Main Street and across the railroad track to Upper Main. . . . She had told her father she was going to church but did not intend doing anything of the kind. She did not know what she wanted to do. "I'll get off by myself and think," she told herself as she walked slowly along. . . . Her own affairs were approaching a crisis and it was time for her to begin thinking seriously of her future.

   The thoughtful serious state of mind . . . had been induced in her by a conversation she had with her father on the evening before. . . . Quite suddenly and abruptly he had told her that he was a victim of heart disease and might die at any moment . . .

— "Unlighted Lamps" by Sherwood Anderson

(1) The passage and title seem to foreshadow that _____

_____.

(2) The probable plot order is _____.

(3) The action will likely take place in _____.

(4) What clues are given to the time period of the story? _____

_____

(5) What question about the action is raised in the paragraphs given?

_____

(6) The point of view is _____ person*.

3. Pan was a half white, half Chinese girl. Her mother was dead, and Pan lived with her father who kept an Oriental Bazaar on Dupont Street. All her life had Pan lived in Chinatown, and if she were different in any sense from those around her, she gave little thought to it. It was only after the coming of Mark Carson that the mystery of her nature began to trouble her. — "Its Wavery Image" by Sui Sin Far

(1) The passage and title seem to foreshadow that _____

_____.

(2) The probable plot order is _____.

(3) The action will likely take place in _____.

(4) What clues are given to the time period of the story? _____

_____

(5) What question about the action is raised in the paragraphs given?

_____

(6) The point of view is _____ person*.

* It is not always possible or necessary to positively identify the precise use of first- and third-person from the opening paragraph alone.

Three Types of Fictional Paragraphs
(*Reading Selection 10–9*)

All paragraphs in fiction are not alike, and all do not contain the same type of information. For this reason, the good reader learns to approach each type differently—reading at various speeds, asking and expecting answers to different kinds of questions.

Five types of paragraphs are Descriptions of Background and Setting; Dialogue; Narrative Action; Descriptive Characterization; and Authorial/Thematic Comment. The final two will be introduced later.

Descriptions of Background and Setting:

When reading this type of paragraph, try to get a general impression—do not remember every specific detail. Look especially for repeated words, such as "It was a cold night, bitterly cold . . ." Writers use repetition to highlight something important.

In a long paragraph of description, you will often find a brief sentence or part of a sentence that sums up the writer's purpose in clear, direct language. This sentence may be at the end or in the middle, as the beginning. It serves as the topic sentence and helps assure good readers they have drawn the right conclusion.

Dialogue:

Reading dialogue involves more than knowing what a character says. You need to know why he or she says it. And also why the author chose to put these words into the character's mouth. Ask such questions as: (1) Why did the character say it? (2) What does it show about that person's inner feeling and values? (3) What inferences does the writer expect you to make about the speakers and situation?

In writing dialogue, authors omit such words as *Harry said* or *his wife answered* when they think them unnecessary. Such attribution or identification of speaker can get in the way, and dialogue seems more immediate and real when no outside comments interrupt characters' conversations.

If just two characters are involved, they usually speak alternately. If more than two, writers try to provide whatever identification is needed. When additional comments are added to a character's speech, good readers scan quickly to discover what special information it is meant to give.

Narrative Action:

Passages of narrative action are the fastest-paced paragraphs in fiction. They can be read more quickly because they rely on strong verbs and verb forms. Read them to answer the questions "Who or What?" and "Did What?" The reader's goal is to find out what happened.

(Reading Selection 10–9 continued)

To improve your skill at reading narrative action, look for active verbs such as *ran, threw, jumped,* as well as verb forms such as *running, throwing, jumping,* and *to run, to throw, to jump.*

The Importance of Repetition:

Most writers are aware that active readers read quickly and do not read word for word, nor try to remember every detail. They are reading *and* thinking. That's why writers frequently use repetition, especially in descriptive passages, to emphasize their point.

While unintentional repetition makes a paragraph boring, this type of repetition makes it more meaningful and alerts the fast, experienced reader to the writer's underlying purpose. For example, a writer might repeat the word *happy* to describe a party's mood, use a different version of the same word, such as *happiness* or *happily,* or perhaps use one of its synonyms, such as *joy* or *joyous.*

Getting Involved in Narrative Action (10–9A)

Directions: Read the following passages, which illustrate narrative action, and write your answers to the questions following each.

1. The pass was high and wide and he jumped for it, feeling it slap flatly against his hands, as he shook his hips to throw off the halfback who was diving at him. The center floated by, his hands desperately brushing Darling's knee as Darling picked his feet up high and delicately ran over a blocker and an opposing linesman in a jumble on the ground near the scrimmage line. He had ten yards in the clear and picked up speed, breathing easily, feeling his thigh pads rising and falling against his legs, listening to the sound of cleats behind him, pulling away from them. . . . He was sure he was going to get past the safety man. . . . He pivoted away, . . . dropping the safety man as he ran easily toward the goal line, with the drumming of cleats diminishing behind him. — "The Eighty-Yard Run" by Irwin Shaw

   (1) Underline the verbs or verb forms in the paragraph above. (Consider such phrases as *is riding* as a single verb.) How many did you find? _____

   (2) List the descriptive adjectives used in the paragraph. _____

   _____

   (3) The action concerns a _____ as he _____

   _____ and _____.

   (4) Is the action depicted mainly as the spectator would see it or the character would experience it? _____

   (5) List two words that support this conclusion: _____

   (6) The point of view of this passage is _____ person, _____.

2. Suddenly there came to him (the gold miner) a premonition of danger. It seemed a shadow had fallen upon him. But there was no shadow. His heart had given a great jump up into his throat and was choking him. Then his blood slowly chilled and he felt the sweat of his shirt cold against his flesh. . . .

   . . . A loud, crashing noise burst on his ear. At the same instant he received a stunning blow on the left side of the back, and from the point of impact felt a rush of flame through his flesh. He sprang up in the air, but halfway to his feet collapsed. His body crumpled like a leaf withered in sudden heat, and he came down, his face in the dirt and rock . . . — "All Gold Canyon" by Jack London

© 1995 by The Center for Applied Research in Education

(10–9A continued)

(1) Underline the verbs or verb forms in the paragraphs. (Consider such phrases as *is riding* as a single verb.) How many did you find? _____

(2) List the descriptive adjectives used in the paragraphs. _____

_____

(3) The action concerns a _____ as he _____

_____ and _____.

(4) Is the action depicted mainly as the spectator would see it or the character would

experience it? _____

(5) List two words that support this conclusion: _____

(6) The point of view of this passage is _____ person, _____.

Drawing Conclusions from Dialogue (10–10)

Directions: Read the following passages, which illustrate the conclusions that can be drawn from dialogue, and write your answers to the questions following each. Use your own words unless otherwise indicated.

1. (Ben's wife) had warned Mrs. Thayer in advance and Ben was served with coffee.

"Don't you take cream, Mr. Drake?" (1a) _____

"No. Never." (1b) _____

"That's because you don't get good cream in New York." (1c) _____

"No. It's because I don't like cream in coffee." (1d) _____

"You would like our cream. We have our own cows and the cream is so rich that it's almost like butter. Won't you try just a little?" (1e) _____

"No. Thanks." (1f) _____

"But just a little, to see how rich it is." (1g) _____

She poured about a tablespoonful of cream into his coffee-cup . . . — "Liberty Hall" by Ring Lardner

(1) Identify the speaker in the blank spaces after the lines of dialogue that lack attribution.

(2) What had Ben's wife evidently warned Mrs. Thayer about? _____

_____

(3) Why would Ben say, "No. Never," instead of "No, thank you?" _____

_____

(4) Do Mrs. Thayer's words show her to be (a) caring or inconsiderate; (b) generous or self-seeking? (Choose one of each pair, and explain your reasons for making each choice.)

(a) _____

_____

(b) _____

_____

(5) In place of "No. Thanks," what answer might Ben have been tempted to give instead? _____

_____

© 1995 by The Center for Applied Research in Education

(6) Explain two good qualities he showed by answering as he did. _____

_____

_____

2. (The newly married couple) were evidently very happy. "Ever been in a parlour-car before?" he asked, smiling with delight.

"No," she answered. "I never was. It's fine, ain't it?"

"Great! And then, after a while we'll go forward to the diner, and get a big lay-out. Finest meal in the world. Charge a dollar."   (1) _____

"Oh, do they?" cried the bride. "Charge a dollar? Why, that's too much—for us—ain't it, Jack?"

"Not this trip, anyhow," he answered bravely. "We're going to go the whole thing." — "The Bride Comes to Yellow Sky" by Stephen Crane

(1) Identify the speaker in the blank space after the line of dialogue that lacks attribution.

(2) What shows the husband's desire to please his new bride? _____

_____

_____

(3) How does the dialogue show that the bride is not rich or well-educated?

_____

_____

(4) How does the bride show a sensible attitude and concern for their future well-being? _____

_____

(5) What words of the husband prove her concern is justified? _____

_____

(6) Do the words "happy couple" seem justified or unjustified? Explain.

_____

_____

Opening Paragraphs as Dialogue (10–11)

Directions: Read the following passages, which illustrate the conclusions that can be drawn from dialogue, and write your answers to the questions following each. Use your own words unless otherwise indicated.

1. "Father!"   (1a) _____

   "What is it?"   (1b) _____

   "What are them men diggin' over there in
the field for?"   (1c) _____

There was a sudden dropping and enlarging of the lower part of the old man's face, as if some heavy weight had settled therein; but he shut his mouth tight, and went on harnessing the great bay mare. He hustled the collar on to her neck with a jerk.

   "Father!"   (1d) _____
The old man slapped upon the mare's back.
"Look here, father. I want to know what them
men are diggin' over in the field for,
an' I'm goin' to know."   (1e) _____

   "I wish you'd go into the house, mother, an' 'tend to your own affairs," the old man said then. He ran his words together . . . almost as inarticulate as a growl.
   But the woman understood. . . . "I ain't goin' into the house till you tell me what them men are doin' over there in the field," said she. — "The Revolt of 'Mother'" by Mary Wolkins Freeman

  (1) Identify the speaker in the blank spaces after the lines of dialogue that lack attribution.

  (2) How does the man first respond to his wife's question? _____

_____

  (3) What does this show about him? _____

_____

  (4) What words of the woman first show her determination? _____

_____

  (5) What does Father say to give the reader a negative attitude towards him?

_____

_____

  (6) What word, describing how he spoke, reinforces this attitude? _____

(10–11 continued)

(7) What threat does the wife make in her attempt to make him answer her?

_____

_____

(8) Do the opening paragraphs foreshadow his or her giving up? Explain the reasons

for your decision. _____

2. Mrs. Wallace assisted her husband to remove his overcoat and put her warm palms against his red and wind-beaten cheeks.

"I have good news," said she.

"Another bargain sale?"   (1a) _____

"Pshaw, no! A new girl, and I really believe she's a jewel. She isn't young or good-looking, and when I asked her if she wanted any nights off she said she wouldn't go out after dark for anything in the world. What do you think of that?"

                                          (1b) _____

"It's too good to be true."   (1c) _____

            —"Effie Whittlesy" by George Ade

(1) Identify the speaker in the blank spaces after the lines of dialogue that lack attribution.

(2) What does Mr. Wallace's question reveal about his wife's interests?

_____

(3) What will be the position of the "new girl" in the Wallace household?

_____

(4) Write the words that support this conclusion, and explain why they do.

_____

_____

(5) Must Mrs. Wallace be easy or difficult to work for? Explain the reasons for your

choice. _____

_____

(6) Explain how Mr. Wallace's words may serve as foreshadowing.

_____

_____

The Importance of Description (10–12)

Directions: Read the following passages, which illustrate the effects a writer creates through description, and write your answers to the questions following each.

1. The room in which I found myself was very large and lofty. The windows were long, narrow, and pointed and at so vast a distance from the black oaken floor as to be altogether inaccessible from within. Feeble gleams of encrimsoned light made their way through the trellised panes; the eye, however, struggled in vain to reach the remoter angles of the chamber . . . Dark draperies hung upon the walls. The general furniture was profuse, comfortless, antique, and tattered. Many books and musical instruments lay scattered about, but failed to give any vitality to the scene. I felt that I breathed an atmosphere of sorrow. An air of stern, deep, and irredeemable gloom hung over and pervaded all. — *The Fall of the House of Usher* by Edgar Allan Poe

   (1) List four descriptive words that show the room is big in size.

   _____   _____

   _____   _____

   (2) List four words that make the room seem dim and dark.

   _____   _____

   _____   _____

   (3) List four words that describe the condition of furniture and objects in the room.

   _____   _____

   _____   _____

   (4) What conclusion did the speaker draw concerning his feelings towards this place?

   _____

   (5) What might this foreshadow? _____

   _____

2. The idiosyncrasy of this town is smoke. It rolls sullenly in slow folds from the great chimneys of the iron-foundries, and settles down in black, slimy pools on the muddy streets. Smoke on the wharves, smoke on the dingy boats, on the yellow river—clinging in a coating of greasy soot to the house-front, the two faded poplars, the faces of the passers-by. The long train of mules, dragging masses of pig-iron through the narrow street, have a foul vapor hanging to their reeking sides. Here, inside, is a little broken figure of an angel pointing upward from the mantel-shelf; but even its wings

© 1995 by The Center for Applied Research in Education

(10–12 continued)

are covered with smoke, clotted and black. Smoke everywhere! A dirty canary chirps desolately in a cage beside me. Its dream of green fields and sunshine is a very old dream—almost worn out, I think. — "Life in the Iron Mills" by Rebecca Harding Davis

(1) What key word is repeated throughout the paragraph to give a negative impression of this town? _____

(2) List six adjectives the writer uses to describe its effects.

_____   _____   _____

_____   _____   _____

(3) What example does the writer give to illustrate the unpleasant smell that results from the town's problem?_____

_____

(4) What two objects in the house are also affected and how?

_____

_____

_____

_____

(5) In stating "its dream of green fields and sunshine," who or what does "its" refer to? _____

(6) What might the final statement also reveal about the speaker?

_____

_____

3. The (doctor's) waiting-room was carpeted and stiffly furnished, something like a country parlour. The study had worn, unpainted floors, but there was a look of winter comfort about it. The doctor's flat-top desk was large and well made; the papers were in orderly piles, under glass weights. Behind the stove a wide bookcase, with double glass doors, reached from the floor to the ceiling. It was filled with medical books of every thickness and colour. On the top shelf stood a long row of thirty or forty volumes, bound all alike in dark mottled board covers, with imitation leather backs. — *The Sign of the Lark* by Willa Cather

(10–12 continued)

(1) List two details that show the doctor is not wealthy.

_____

_____

(2) List two details that the doctor wished his place to be well-furnished.

_____

_____

(3) List a detail that proves the doctor takes care of his possessions.

_____

(4) What contrast is drawn between the waiting room and study?

_____

(5) What do you feel accounts for this contrast? _____

_____

(6) What do the bookcases and books show about the doctor and his practice?

_____

_____

Fiction: The Long and Short of It
(*Reading Selection 10–13*)

Stories are told in many ways—through film, by word of mouth, on television, in cartoons and comics. And, of course, they can concern any topic imaginable!

In the field of fiction, there are two main categories: the short story and the novel. They're easy to tell apart, for their obvious difference is their length. All other differences between them result from this one.

One definition of the short story is that it's a work of fiction that can be read in one sitting, while a novel takes longer. But, that makes it depend on how long you can sit . . . and how fast you can read!

You might compare a short story to a half-hour or hour show on television while a novel is more like a full-length movie. The movie can contain more scenes, more characters, and a more complicated plot than the television show can, simply because of its greater length. And, even movies based on novels cannot contain all of the ideas the printed work had.

In addition to meaning a story of prose fiction, the word *novel* also means fresh, new, and original—so the aim of the novel is to give you a fresh way of looking at life and human nature.

It's easiest to say that the novel is a book-length work of fiction—or long enough that it might be printed alone as a book, though short novels are sometimes included with other literary works in collections, such as school anthologies.

Novels run from barely one hundred pages to over a thousand. Shorter ones are sometimes called novellas and novelettes, as well as short novels—but there is no precise rule for telling one from the other.

In addition to having more complicated plots and a greater number of scenes, novelists naturally have more space to develop their ideas more fully. Therefore, as a reader, you get to know more about the situations, settings, and characters than is possible in short stories.

As you read the following excerpts from a novel, remember the various types of paragraphs that invite you to employ various reading skills and speeds: Descriptions of Background and Setting, Dialogue, and Narrative Action.

The Novel: Harry Heathcote of Gangoil (10–13A)

Directions: Read the following passages from the novel, subtitled *A Tale of Australian Bush Life,* by Anthony Trollope. It tells of the life of a young squatter, a settler on public land, in the wild Australian bush country in the early days of its settlement. Each illustrates a different type of passage. Answer the questions which follow in your own words. Be able to support your conclusions with proof from the example.

1. **Opening Paragraph:** Just a fortnight before Christmas, 1871, a young man, twenty-four years of age, returned home to his dinner about eight o'clock in the evening. He was married, and with him and his wife lived his wife's sister. At that somewhat late hour he walked in among the two young women, and another much older woman, who was preparing the table for dinner. The wife and the wife's sister each had a child in its lap, the elder having seen some fifteen months of its existence, and the younger three months. "He has been out since seven, and I don't think he's had a mouthful," the wife had just said. "Oh, Harry, you must be half-starved," she exclaimed, jumping up to greet him, and throwing her arms round his bare neck.

   "I'm about whole melted," he said as he kissed her . . . "I never was so hot or so thirsty in my life . . ."

   (1) The point of view is _____ person.

   (2) Explain how Christmastime in Australia is shown to differ from Christmastime in England. _____

   _____

   (3) Who are the two women holding the young children? _____

   _____

   (4) Since the third woman is not important enough to be identified, what conclusion might you draw about her position? _____

   _____

   (5) What does the wife's first speech show about her feelings towards her husband?

   _____

   _____

   (6) How does she react when he enters, and what does this show?

   _____

   _____

(10–13A continued)

2. **Description of Background:** The young man who had just returned home had on a flannel shirt, a pair of moleskin trousers, and an old straw hat, battered nearly out of all shape . . . As he dashed his hat off, wiped his brow, and threw himself into a rocking-chair, he certainly was rough to look at; but by all who understood Australian life he would have been taken to be a gentleman. He was a young squatter, well known west of the Mary River in Queensland. Harry Heathcote of Gangoil, who owned 30,000 sheep of his own, was a magistrate in those parts, and able to hold his own among his neighbours, whether rough or gentle; and some neighbours he had very rough, who made it almost necessary that a man should be able to be rough also, on occasions, if he desired to live among them without injury.

(1) There is a contrast between Harry Heathcote's appearance and his position.

He looks _____ but he is considered _____.

(2) What does Heathcote have that apparently gives him status, when compared to

the other settlers? _____

_____

(3) What descriptive adjective is repeated four times? _____

(4) Explain what this foreshadows about the kind of action you might expect to occur

later in the novel. _____

_____

_____

3. **Dialogue:** Harry jumped from the ground, kissed his wife . . . and got on his horse at the garden gate. Both the ladies came off the verandah to see him start.

"It's as dark as pitch," said Kate Daly.
(Harry's sister-in-law)

"That's because you have just come out
of the light."   (1a) _____

"But it is dark—quite dark. You won't be
late, will you?" said the wife.

"I can't be very early as it's near ten now.
I shall be back about twelve." So saying, he
broke at once into a gallop and vanished into the night . . .

"Why should he go out now?" Kate said to her sister.

"He is afraid of fire."   (1b) _____

"But he can't prevent the fires by riding about
in the dark. I suppose the fires come
from the heat."   (1c) _____

"He thinks they come from enemies, and
he has heard something. One wretched man
may do so much when everything is dried
to tinder. I do so wish it would rain."   (1d) _____

(1) Identify the speaker in the blank spaces after the four lines of dialogue that lack attribution.

(2) Explain how the time of day proves that Harry Heathcote believes he faces dangerous circumstances. _____

_____

_____

(3) Explain what Harry's sister-in-law feels might set the bush afire. _____

_____

_____

(4) What reasons does his wife fear might be the cause of fire? _____

_____

(5) Why does she feel this way? _____

_____

The Novel: Harry Heathcote of Gangoil (10–13B)

Directions: Read the following passages from the novel, subtitled *A Tale of Australian Bush Life,* by Anthony Trollope. It tells of the life of a young squatter, a settler on public land, in the wild Australian bush country in the early days of its settlement. Answer the questions which follow each type of paragraph. Be able to support your conclusions with proof from the example.

1. **Description of Background:** Mr. Giles Medlicot, though at Gangoil he was still spoken of as a new-comer, had already been located for nearly two years on the land which he had purchased immediately on his coming to the colony. He had come out direct from England with the intention of growing sugar, and, whether successful or not in making money, had certainly succeeded in growing crops of sugar-canes and in erecting a mill for crushing them. It probably takes more than two years for a man himself to discover whether he can achieve ultimate success in such an interprise; and Medlicot was certainly not a man like to talk much to others of his private concerns . . . Hitherto, he had hardly made himself popular. He was not either fish or fowl. The squatters regarded him . . . as a man holding opinions directly adverse to their own interests—in which they were right. And the small free-selectors, who lived on the labour of their own hands—or, as was said of many of them, by stealing sheep and cattle—knew well that he was not of their class.

   (1) List the three versions of the same word that is used in reference to Medlicot's accomplishments since coming to Australia:

   _____   _____   _____

   (2) What question about Medlicot remained to be answered? _____

   _____

   (3) What quality of his made this question hard for his neighbors to answer?

   _____

   _____

   (4) What inference is the reader led to make as to the answer? _____

   _____

   (5) Give two facts or details that support that inference. _____

   _____

   _____

   (6) What is the irony and humor in the term "free-selectors"? _____

   _____

(10–13B continued)

(7) Was Medlicot popular or unpopular with his neighbors? _____

Why?_____

_____

2. **Description of Background:** Christmas Day would fall on a Tuesday, and on the Monday before it Jerry Brownbie, the eldest of (the six Brownbie brothers) now at home, was sitting with a pipe in his mouth on a broken-down stool on the broken-down verandah of the house, and the old man was seated on a stuffy, worn-out sofa with three legs, which was propped against the wall of the house and had not been moved for years. Brownbie was a man of gigantic frame . . . a man, too, of will and energy, but he was now worn out and dropsical, and could not move behind the confines of the home station. . . . The verandah was attached to a big room which ran nearly the whole length of the house. . . . The cookery was generally done in the big room. And here also two or three of the sons slept on beds made upon stretchers along the wall. They were not probably very particular as to which owned each bed. . . . Boolabong was certainly a miserable place; and yet, such as it was, it was frequented by many guests. . . .

(1) The reader should infer Boolabong is the name of _____.

(2) Copy the six-word statement that sums up living conditions at the Brownbie

homestead. _____

_____

(3) List six words that support this conclusion, which the author used to describe various elements of the scene. (Some are used more than once.)

_____   _____   _____

_____   _____   _____

(4) With the Brownbies as his enemies, why does it seem that Harry faces an unfair

fight? _____

_____

(5) Would you infer that the Brownbies were squatters or free-selectors?

_____   Why? _____

_____

(6) Considering the description, what inference might you draw about the Brownbies

being "frequented by many guests"? _____

_____

(10–13B continued)

3. **Narrative Action:** As Medlicot still went on putting out the fire, Jerry attempted to ride him down. Medlicot caught the horse by the rein and violently backed the brute in among the embers. The animal plunged and reared, getting his head loose, and at last came down, he and his rider together. In the meantime Joe Brownbie, seeing this, rode up behind the sugar-planter, and struck him violently with his cudgel over the shoulder. Medlicot sank nearly to the ground, but at once recovered himself. He knew that some bone on the left side of his body was broken, but he could still fight with his right hand—and he did fight.

   Boscabel and George Brownbie both attempted to ride over Harry together . . .

   (1) Underline the verbs or verb forms in the paragraphs above. (Consider such phrases as *is riding* as a single verb.) How many did you find? _____

   (2) List the descriptive adjectives used in the paragraphs. _____

   _____

   (3) The paragraphs show the Brownbies fighting against Harry and _____

   _____

   (4) What two phrases indicate that the Brownbies haven't won yet?

   _____

   _____

   (5) Based on your reading of these paragraphs from the novel, what "educated guess" would you make about its outcome? _____

   _____

   (6) Why would you draw this conclusion?

   _____

   (7) What do you judge to be the basic conflict of the novel?

   _____ vs. _____

UNIT 11

Character: The Heart of the Story

It's possible to read a story in which all sorts of potentially exciting things happen—a robbery, a kidnapping, a chase—and still react, "Who cares?"

In another story, the plot contains very little action and still rates high. Why?

It could be that story and reader failed to "meet" at the right time. Because of taste, maturity level, or simply someone's mood, the story does not suit its reader at a particular time. In school, this, of course, is a major reason why literature assignments need to be approached as a means to the end of becoming more accomplished readers instead of a source of enjoyment—although enjoyment is always a welcome effect!

Yet, here's another reason why a story and reader may fail to connect. Fiction is basically about people. If you can't identify with the characters, it's hard to care what happens, no matter how many adventures or dangers figure in the plot.

If you can "put yourself in the character's place," it's natural to become involved in a story's action and ideas—even though the plot is slight. It's similar to caring what happens to yourself and your friends, just because of the closeness of your relationship.

In fiction, then, "the heart of the story" is its characters and the author's characterization of them.

This unit will introduce student readers to the variety of methods by which leading authors, present and past, achieve effective characterization. Paragraphs chosen for study include both passages of descriptive characterization and passages containing dialogue, action, and the use of omniscience that illustrate the various ways writers use to illuminate their characters' inner natures.

In forming their judgments, students can draw upon skills learned in early units, such as recognizing shades of meaning, making inferences, and drawing conclusions.

In preparation for this unit, plan to discuss the ways that students use to form opinions about people in real life. These can be boiled down to four essential options:

1. How someone looks
2. How someone acts or behaves
3. What someone says
4. What others say about this person

Encourage students to discuss why each of these methods can be both helpful and unreliable in determining what someone is really like. For example, "never judge by appearances" is a faulty axiom. Though an often-quoted saying, students will likely admit that they themselves dress with the expectation, and even hope, of being judged by how they look. Discuss how and why it is valid to form opinions about people, not by the expensiveness of their clothing but by their mien and bearing.

Your discussion of the pros and cons of each of these four means of judging people in real life will lead to the introduction of characterization in fiction, where making valid judgments about characters' inner natures is made easier by clues given by writers, speaking through their characters.

NOTES ON ACTIVITIES

Shades of Differences (11–1A)

To go over this exercise, poll students and keep track of how many have labeled each word "positive," "negative," or "neutral." You may wish to do several lists by counting raised hands, and then assign individual students or groups to tally the rest.

In most classes, it should be evident that a majority agree on the designation given each word. Explain that this is the basis by which writers choose descriptive words. However, since there may be individual reactions to certain words, writers rarely depend upon a single word to form an impression. In a descriptive characterization, the total number of descriptive words and phrases, taken together, determine whether a positive or negative impression is formed of a character.

With advanced students, you may also want to discuss the concept of denotation and connotation in connection with this exercise.

Descriptive Characterization (11–2A & 2B)

In working with these passages and those in the following activities, you may want to remind students of the importance of trying to determine the meaning of unfamiliar words through context. It may also prove helpful to have the examples first read orally.

Depth of Character (11–4A)

Students may have difficulty finding synonyms for some of these nouns. Encourage them to avoid such responses as "understanding—lack of understanding" whenever possible. You may want to point out that most of the noun forms used here also have frequently-used adjective forms.

When students fill in numbers 18-20, explain that such words as *friendliness* and *efficiency* do not represent inner values, for they may refer to an outward show. Such words as *patience, calm, bravery,* and *serenity* would be appropriate.

A Change of Character (11–8)

Before beginning the written assignment, you may want to go over the paragraph to pick out the details that create a negative attitude towards Ethan's wife, Zenobia. It may also be helpful to point out how "crimping-pins" create the effect of hard objects poking out of Zeena's head, a negative kind of halo, even though students can't specifically define what such pins are.

To illustrate how choice of words can create a complete change of character, you may want to write the following sentences on the board.

> FOR EXAMPLE: Her friendly, moon-shaped face was lit with smiles.
> Her sullen, hard-edged face grew dark with anger.

It may help to review Reading Selection 11–1, Dickens' description of Mrs. Joe from *Great Expectations* and its rewritten version. The paragraphs of descriptive characterization in activities 11–2A and 11–2B can also provide additional choices of models for this assignment.

Judging by Appearances (*Reading Selection 11-1*)

Compare the following paragraphs:

A. My sister, Mrs. Joe, with black hair and eyes, had such a prevailing redness of skin that I used to wonder whether it was possible she washed herself with a nutmeg-grater instead of soap. She was tall and bony, and almost always wore a coarse apron . . . having a square impregnable bib in front, that was stuck full of pins and needles.
— from *Great Expectations* by Charles Dickens

B. My sister, Mrs. Joe, with dark hair and eyes, had such a fresh rosiness of skin that I used to wonder whether it was possible she washed herself with rose petals instead of soap. She was tall and slender, and almost always wore a snowy-white apron . . . having a lacy, heart-shaped bib in front that was embroidered with rosebuds and daisies.
— modeled on Dickens' original version

Which would you prefer for an older sister and guardian—Mrs. Joe A. or Mrs. Joe B.?

Both have dark hair and eyes, both are tall and thin—yet the reader tends to feel sympathetic with, to like, one and to feel unsympathetic towards, to dislike, the other. For example, although they describe similar qualities, *slender* creates a positive impression, while *bony* creates a negative one.

As a reader, it's important to remember that writers want you to know "what to think" about characters in a story. With the aim of having all readers feel they've had the same experience and read the same story, they provide clues such as those in the paragraphs of descriptive characterization above.

Remember, too—it is the author's fictional world. Nothing happens, no word is used, no character is introduced unless the author wants it that way.

For this reason, it is often easier to judge people in fiction than in real life. In fiction, you can trust that the author is exercising control. So, you need to make a habit of asking "Why?" and "How?" Why did the author choose these words? How am I expected to react to this character?

Good authors know that words have not only literal meanings, but also arouse emotional responses. They use this knowledge to help readers know how to react correctly to their characters.

Shades of Differences (11–1A)

Directions: From the groups of words with similar meanings listed below, decide what kind of reaction each word would arouse if used to describe a fictional character or character's ideas. In the blank spaces, mark (+) if your reaction is positive and (−) if negative. If you are unfamiliar with a word or have no reaction to it, mark (0) for neutral.

There is no right or wrong to individual answers in this exercise, but writers generally count on most readers to react the same way.

1. _____ **calm**
   _____ serene
   _____ unfeeling
   _____ peaceful
   _____ self-controlled
   _____ composed
   _____ cold-blooded
   _____ smooth
   _____ stony
   _____ cool

2. _____ **imaginative**
   _____ creative
   _____ original
   _____ impractical
   _____ innovative
   _____ peculiar
   _____ far-fetched
   _____ bizarre
   _____ ingenious
   _____ inspired

3. _____ **determined**
   _____ bull-headed
   _____ dedicated
   _____ headstrong
   _____ strong-minded
   _____ purposeful
   _____ obstinate
   _____ mulish
   _____ unadaptable
   _____ persistent

4. _____ **short**
   _____ dumpy
   _____ runty
   _____ petite
   _____ tiny
   _____ dwarfish
   _____ wee
   _____ diminutive
   _____ stubby
   _____ spritelike

5. _____ **generous**
   _____ charitable
   _____ extravagant
   _____ high-minded
   _____ big-hearted
   _____ kindly
   _____ wasteful
   _____ spendthrift
   _____ immoderate
   _____ noble

6. _____ **dynamic**
   _____ confident
   _____ powerful
   _____ strong
   _____ pushy
   _____ persuasive
   _____ bossy
   _____ forceful
   _____ quarrelsome
   _____ aggressive

Shades of Differences (11–1B)

Directions: To discover how a change of descriptive words can alter your impression of someone, write original sentences using a pair of words from each list of descriptive words with similar meanings: 1. calm, 2. imaginative, 3. determined, 4. short, 5. generous, 6. dynamic. (See activity 11–1A.)

From each list, choose one word to create a positive response and another, a negative effect. Then, write sentences that show how changing just one word can change the reader's reaction completely.

FOR EXAMPLE: You can count on Pedro for a *creative* idea!
You can count on Pedro for a *far-fetched* idea!

1. a. _____

   b. _____

2. a. _____

   b. _____

3. a. _____

   b. _____

4. a. _____

   b. _____

5. a. _____

   b. _____

6. a. _____

   b. _____

Descriptive Characterization–Part I (11–2A)

Directions: a. Copy the underlined words and phrases.
  b. In the blank space in front of each, mark (+) if positive, (–) if negative, (0) if neutral or the meaning can't be determined.
  c. After counting the majority of marks, tell whether the author creates a positive or negative attitude towards the character.

1. He was a <u>well-built</u> boy with very black, rather curly hair, <u>good teeth</u> and a skin that his sisters envied, and he had a <u>ready and unpuzzled smile</u>. He was fast on his feet and <u>did his work well</u> and he <u>loved his sisters</u>, who seemed beautiful and sophisticated; he <u>loved Madrid</u>, which was still an unbelievable place, and he <u>loved his work</u> which, done under bright lights, with clean linen, the wearing of evening clothes, and abundant food in the kitchen, seemed romantically beautiful. — "The Capital of the World" by Ernest Hemingway

_____ (1) _____   _____ (2) _____

_____ (3) _____

_____ (4) _____   _____ (5) _____

_____ (6) _____   _____ (7) _____

(8) From Hemingway's description, the boy seems a _____ character.

(9) Does the boy seem (a) worldly wise or (b) naive and innocent? _____

(10) The boy must work as a _____.

(11) From the description, what two things should the reader infer about the boy's

hometown and family background? _____

_____

2. The skipper of the *Sephora* had a <u>thin red whisker</u> all round his face, and the sort of complexion that goes with hair of that color; also the particular, rather <u>smeary shade of blue</u> in the eyes. He was not exactly a showy figure; his <u>shoulders were high</u>, his <u>stature but middling</u>—<u>one leg slightly more bandy</u> than the other. He shook hands, <u>looking vaguely around</u> . . . He <u>mumbled</u> to me as if he were <u>ashamed of what he was saying</u>; gave his name . . . his ship's name, and a few other particulars of that sort, in the <u>manner of a criminal</u> making a reluctant and doleful confession. He had had terrible weather on the passage out—<u>terrible—terrible</u>—wife aboard, too. — from *The Secret Sharer* by Joseph Conrad

(11–2A continued)

_____ (1) _____   _____ (2) _____

_____ (3) _____   _____ (4) _____

_____ (5) _____   _____ (6) _____

_____ (7) _____   _____ (8) _____

_____ (9) _____   _____ (10) _____

(11) From Conrad's description, the skipper seems a _____ character.

(12) Does he seem like a good or bad choice to captain a ship? _____

Based on his description, give two reasons to support your opinion.

_____

_____

3. She was <u>not young</u>, as I remember her, but she was <u>still handsome</u>, <u>tall</u>, <u>well-made</u>, and though dark for an Englishwoman, yet wearing always the <u>clearness of health</u> in her brunette cheeks, and its <u>vivacity</u> in a pair of <u>fine, cheerful black eyes</u>. — from
Villette by Charlotte Brontë

_____ (1) _____   _____ (2) _____

_____ (3) _____   _____ (4) _____

_____ (5) _____   _____ (6) _____

(7) From Brontë's description, the woman seems a _____ character.

Descriptive Characterization—Part II (11–2B)

Directions: 1. Copy the underlined words and phrases.
2. In the blank space in front of each, mark (+) if positive, (–) if negative, (0) if neutral or the meaning is unfamiliar.
3. After counting the majority of marks, tell whether the author creates a positive or negative attitude towards the character.

1. Big Liam O'Grady was a <u>great raw-boned sandy-haired</u> man with the <u>strength of an ox</u> and a <u>heart no bigger than a sour apple</u>. An <u>overbearing</u> man <u>given to berserk rages</u>. Though he was a church-goer by habit, the <u>true god of that man was Money—</u> gold, shining silver, dull copper—the trinity that he worshipped in degree. — "The Quiet Man" by Maurice Walsh

_____ (1) _____

_____ (2) _____

_____ (3) _____

_____ (4) _____   _____ (5) _____

_____ (6) _____

(7) From Walsh's description, Big Liam seems a _____ character.

(8) By comparing Liam O'Grady to an ox, what other qualities besides strength does it seem he must have? _____

(9) By comparing O'Grady's heart to a sour apple, what does it show about his attitude and character? _____

_____

2. As they rode up to the door, a man came out, bare-headed, and they saw to their surprise that he was not a Mexican, but an American, of a <u>very unprepossessing</u> type . . . He was <u>tall, gaunt and ill-formed</u>, with a <u>snake-like neck</u>, terminating in a <u>small, bony head</u>. Under his <u>close-clipped hair</u> <u>his repellent head</u> showed a <u>number of thick ridges</u>, as if the skull joinings were overgrown by layers of superfluous bone. With its <u>small, rudimentary ears</u>, this head had a <u>positively malignant look</u>. The man seemed <u>not more than half human</u>, but he was the only householder on the lonely road to Mora.— from *Death Comes for the Archbishop* by Willa Cather

_____ (1) _____   _____ (2) _____

_____ (3) _____   _____ (4) _____

_____ (5) _____   _____ (6) _____

_____ (7) _____   _____ (8) _____

_____ (9) _____   _____ (10) _____

(11) From Cather's description, the man seems a _____ character.

3. And that was how Otoo and I first came together. He was <u>no fighter</u>. He was <u>all sweetness and gentleness</u>, a <u>love-creature</u>, though he stood <u>nearly six feet tall</u> and was <u>muscled like a gladiator</u>. He was no fighter, but he was also <u>no coward</u>. He had the <u>heart of a lion</u>; and in the years that followed I have seen him <u>run risks</u> that I would never dream of taking. What I mean is that while he was no fighter, and while he always <u>avoided precipitating a row</u>, he <u>never ran away from trouble</u> when it started. — "The Heathen" by Jack London

_____ (1) _____   _____ (2) _____

_____ (3) _____   _____ (4) _____

_____ (5) _____   _____ (6) _____

_____ (7) _____   _____ (8) _____

_____ (9) _____   _____ (10) _____

(11) From London's description, Otoo seems a _____ character.

(12) What characteristic does Otoo show by not trying to "precipitate a row"?

_____

By "never running away from trouble"? _____

© 1995 by The Center for Applied Research in Education

The Animal Kingdom for Comparison (11–3)

One writer describes a character with the "strength of an ox," another has the "heart of a lion," and a third, a "snake-like neck." Whether such comparisons are really exact or fair, readers and writers have come to assign certain characteristics to certain animals—and they have become a kind of shorthand method for describing what a character is like.

Directions: After each of the animals listed, write the human qualities that people have assigned to it and that are understood when used in a comparison to someone.

1. mouse _____

2. ox _____

3. donkey _____

4. fox _____

5. pig _____

6. chicken _____

7. eagle _____

8. mule _____

9. coyote _____

10. deer _____

What other animals do people use to portray human characteristics? Name the animal, and list the qualities it represents.

11. _____

12. _____

13. _____

14. _____

15. _____

Depth of Character (*Reading Selection 11–4*)

Personality: friendliness; charm; awareness of what to say at the right time; poise; the ability to get along with other people

Status: wealth; social prominence; popularity; fame; success in business, entertainment, or sports; the ability to buy whatever you want

What Ingredients Make Up a Positive Character?

Of course, a writer invites you to judge the people in a story by their descriptive characterizations. Yet their descriptions are merely a way to discover what characters are *really* like—their inner values and beliefs, their moral standards, and ethical principles.

In fact, the dictionary first defines *character* as all the features and traits that make up the individual nature of a person or thing. The word *character* comes from a Greek word meaning *engrave* or *mark,* and some believe that your innermost thoughts and beliefs sooner or later leave their mark on your appearance.

By trying to form a positive or negative attitude toward a character, good authors are not simply trying to get you to "like" him or her. The greater goal is to help you understand the character's inner nature—what motivates or moves her to act as she does, what causes him to react in a certain way to the problems he faces.

If you have a *positive* attitude, it means you can sympathize with the character and the character's problems, whether or not you actually "like" her or him.

Negative denotes a character with whom you don't sympathize.

What's a Character Like Inside?

Through descriptive characterization, the characters' words and actions, plus the possible use of omniscience, a writer tries to expose a character's inner beliefs and values.

These include the character traits and qualities most people admire. Some are *courage, determination, loyalty, thoughtfulness, understanding, pride, concern for others, forgivingness, unselfishness,* and *generosity.*

In most novels and stories, the author offers evidence early in the story to give you a basis for forming your attitude, and this attitude holds true throughout the selection.

Toward minor characters, the author may not build a definite attitude, and occasionally an author purposely creates an *ambivalent* attitude towards someone. *Ambi* means both, and in such cases, you would have *both* positive and negative feelings or feel undecided. If so, your goal will be to discover why the author causes you to have such conflicting feelings.

If a character is developed as positive, the writer wants you to be "on his or her side." This does not mean positive characters, being human, are always right or never make mistakes. It does invite you to identify yourself with positive characters, their feelings, and their problems.

Fiction is chiefly about people. Because of an author's careful characterization, you can often "know" people in a fictional world better than you know the people around you—and also to learn more about yourself and others through fictional experiences.

Depth of Character (11–4A)

Directions: Listed below are the character traits that most people admire and which are either possessed or honored by positive characters. Yet, each of these positive traits has an opposite, showing a lack of good inner values and beliefs.

In the blank space following each positive character trait, write a word or phrase naming its opposite. For numbers 18-20, write any additional inner values or beliefs that you think are important. Be sure that they represent worthy inner qualities, not outward signs of status or personality.

Positive Value	**Negative Trait**
1. courage	1. _____
2. loyalty	2. _____
3. thoughtfulness	3. _____
4. understanding	4. _____
5. honesty	5. _____
6. pride	6. _____
7. concern for others	7. _____
8. determination	8. _____
9. forgivingness	9. _____
10. unselfishness	10. _____
11. generosity	11. _____
12. compassion	12. _____
13. modesty	13. _____
14. trustworthiness	14. _____
15. sense of duty	15. _____
16. nobility	16. _____
17. gentleness	17. _____
18. _____	18. _____
19. _____	19. _____
20. _____	20. _____

A Gathering of Famous Characters—Part I (11–5A)

The Scarlet Letter by Nathaniel Hawthorne

Directions: Copy the underlined words and phrases, then mark (+) if positive, (–) if negative, (0) if neutral, and tell if the attitude created is positive or negative. Also, answer the additional questions concerning the inner values and character traits revealed by the passage.

1. Hester Prynne

The young woman was tall, with a figure of <u>perfect elegance</u> on a <u>large scale</u>. She had <u>dark and abundant hair</u>, so glossy that it <u>threw off the sunshine</u> with a gleam, and a face which, beside being <u>beautiful</u> from <u>regularity of feature</u> and <u>richness of complexion</u>, had the <u>impressiveness</u> belonging to a <u>marked brow</u> and <u>deep black eyes</u>. She was <u>lady-like,</u> too . . . characterized by a certain <u>state and dignity</u>. . . . And never had Hester Prynne appeared more lady-like, in the antique interpretation of the term, than as she issued from the prison. Those who had before known her, and had expected to behold her dimmed and obscured by a disastrous cloud, were astonished, and even startled, to perceive how her <u>beauty shown out</u>, and <u>made a halo</u> of the misfortune and ignominy in which she was enveloped. . . .

_____ (1) _____ _____ (2) _____

_____ (3) _____ _____ (4) _____

_____ (5) _____ _____ (6) _____

_____ (7) _____ _____ (8) _____

_____ (9) _____ _____ (10) _____

_____ (11) _____ _____ (12) _____

_____ (13) _____ _____ (14) _____

(15) From her description, Hester Prynne seems a _____ character.

(16) Considering her description, what surprises the reader about the place that

Hester has been? _____

_____

(17) Based on the description, name two character traits Hester seems to exhibit in this first appearance after her "misfortune."

_____

(11–5A continued)

2. Roger Chillingworth

. . . a man <u>well-stricken in years</u>, a <u>pale, thin, scholar-like visage</u>, with <u>eyes dim and bleared</u> by the lamplight that had served them to pour over many ponderous books. Yet these same <u>bleared optics</u> had a <u>strange, penetrating power</u>, when it was their owner's purpose to <u>read the human soul</u>. This figure of the study and the cloister . . . was <u>slightly deformed</u>, with the <u>left shoulder a trifle higher</u> than the right.

_____ (1) _____   _____ (2) _____

_____ (3) _____   _____ (4) _____

_____ (5) _____   _____ (6) _____

_____ (7) _____   _____ (8) _____

(9) From this description, Roger Chillingworth seems a _____
    character.

3. A Further View of Roger Chillingworth

. . . There was a remarkable intelligence in his features, as of a person who had so cultivated his mental part that it could not fail to mould the physical itself. . . .

At his arrival . . . and some time before she saw him, the stranger had bent his eyes on Hester Prynne. It was carelessly, at first. . . . Very soon, however, his look became <u>keen and penetrative</u>. A <u>writhing horror twisted</u> itself across his features, like a <u>snake gliding swiftly</u> over them. . . . His <u>face darkened</u> with some powerful emotion, which nevertheless, he so <u>instantaneously controlled</u> . . . that, save at a single moment, its expression might have <u>passed for calmness</u>. After a brief space, the <u>convulsion</u> grew almost imperceptible, and finally subsided in the depths of his nature.

(1) According to paragraph one, what effect has Chillingworth's inner nature had on

his physical self? _____

_____

(2) Upon seeing Hester, what emotion appears upon his face? _____

(3) What comparison does Hawthorne make to describe this emotion?

_____

(4) By stating that the "convulsion . . . subsided into the depths of his nature," Hawthorne refers to Chillingworth's inner qualities. Name two character traits that you infer might be part of Chillingworth's inner nature.

_____

A Gathering of Famous Characters—Part II (11–5B)

The Scarlet Letter by Nathaniel Hawthorne

Directions: In *The Scarlet Letter,* Arthur Dimmesdale is a character toward whom Hawthorne creates an ambivalent attitude. This means his description guides you to have *both* positive and negative feelings or be undecided how to feel about him.

First, list the underlined words and phrases that cause you to have positive feelings towards him. Then list those that show an inner weakness of character. Also, answer the additional questions, concerning the inner values and character traits revealed by the passage.

Arthur Dimmesdale

. . . a young clergyman, who had come from one of the great English universities. . . . His <u>eloquence and religious fervor</u> had already given the earnest of <u>high eminence</u> in his profession. He was a person of <u>very striking</u> aspect, with a <u>white, lofty, and impending brow</u>, <u>large, brown, melancholy eyes</u>, and a mouth which, unless when he forcibly compressed it, was <u>apt to be tremulous</u>, expressing both <u>nervous sensibility</u> and a <u>vast power of self-restraint</u>. Notwithstanding his <u>high native gifts</u> and <u>scholar-like attainments</u>, there was an air about this young minister,—an <u>apprehensive, half-frightened</u> look,—as of a being who felt himself <u>quite astray</u>, and <u>at a loss</u> in the pathway of human existence. . . . Therefore, so far as his duties would permit, he trod in the shadowy by-paths, and thus kept himself <u>simple and childlike</u>; coming forth, when occasion was, with a <u>freshness, and fragrance</u>, and <u>dewy purity of thought</u>, which, as many people said, affected them like the <u>speech of an angel</u>.

1. List twelve words and phrases that create a positive attitude:

(1) _____   (2) _____

(3) _____   (4) _____

(5) _____   (6) _____

(7) _____   (8) _____

(9) _____   (10) _____

(11) _____   (12) _____

2. List five words and phrases that show a weakness of character.

(1) _____   (2) _____

(3) _____   (4) _____

(5) _____

3. Does Arthur Dimmesdale seem to be basically a positive or negative character?

_____ Explain the reasons for your choice. _____

_____

4. Name two character traits that Dimmesdale seems to possess or admire.

_____

A Gathering of Famous Characters (11–6)

Ethan Frome by Edith Wharton

Directions: Answer the questions concerning the following passages from the novel *Ethan Frome*.

A. Ethan Frome

Even then he was the <u>most striking figure</u> in Starkfield, though he was but the <u>ruin of a man.</u> It was not so much his <u>great height</u> that marked him . . . it was the <u>careless powerful look</u> he had, in spite of a <u>lameness checking each step</u> like the jerk of a chain. There was something <u>bleak and unapproachable</u> in his face, and he was so <u>stiffened and grizzled</u> that I took him for <u>an old man</u> and was surprised to hear that he was not more than fifty-two. . . .

"He's looked that way ever since he had his smash-up; and that's twenty-four years ago come next February," Harmon threw out between reminiscent pauses . . . .

"It was a pretty bad smash-up?" I questioned Harmon . . . thinking how <u>gallantly</u> his <u>lean brown head</u>, with its shock of light hair, must have sat on his <u>strong shoulders</u> before they were <u>bent out of shape</u>.

1. List six underlined words and phrases that portray Ethan as positive and strong.

    (1) _____   (2) _____

    (3) _____   (4) _____

    (5) _____   (6) _____

2. List six underlined words and phrases that show the effects of the accident.

    (1) _____   (2) _____

    (3) _____   (4) _____

    (5) _____   (6) _____

3. Considering Ethan's appearance, what was the speaker surprised to learn?

    _____

4. What question is raised in the paragraphs given?

    _____

(11–6 continued)

B. What a Townsperson Says About Ethan

    Harmon drew a slab of tobacco from his pocket, cut off a wedge and pressed it into the leather pouch of his cheek. "Guess he's been in Starkfield too many winters. Most of the smart ones get away."

    "Why didn't he?"

    "Somebody had to stay and care for the folks. There warn't ever anybody but Ethan. Fust his father—then his mother—then his wife."

    "And then the smash-up?"

    Harmon chuckled sardonically. "That's so. He had to stay then."

    "I see. And since then they've had to care for him?"

    Harmon thoughtfully passed his tobacco to the other cheek. "Oh, as to that: I guess it's always Ethan done the caring."

1. Does the passage imply that Ethan was dumb or smart? _____ Explain

    your reason for choosing this answer. _____

    _____

2. Name two character traits Ethan seems to possess and explain how he exhibits each.

    (1) _____

    (2) _____

C. Ethan Frome drove in silence, the reins loosely held in his left hand, his browned seamed profile, under the helmet-like peak of the cap, relieved against the banks of snow like the bronze image of a hero.

1. What comparison sums up the attitude the author wants you to have towards

    Ethan? _____

2. In addition to the traits you have named, list two other traits this leads you to

    think he possesses. _____

    _____

A Gathering of Famous Characters (11–7)

The Great Gatsby by F. Scott Fitzgerald

Directions: Answer the questions concerning the following passages depicting characters from the novel *The Great Gatsby*.

A. Tom Buchanan

He had changed since his New Haven years. Now he was a <u>sturdy straw-haired man</u> of thirty with a <u>rather hard mouth</u> and a <u>supercilious manner</u>. Two <u>shining arrogant eyes</u> had established dominance over his face and gave him the appearance of <u>always leaning aggressively forward</u>. Not even the <u>effeminate swank</u> of his riding clothes could hide the <u>enormous power</u> of that body—he seemed to fill those <u>glistening boots</u> until he strained the top lacing, and you could see a <u>great pack of muscle</u> shifting when his shoulder moved under his thin coat. It was a body capable of <u>enormous leverage</u>—a <u>cruel body</u>.

1. List four underlined phrases showing Tom Buchanan to possess physical strength and endurance.

   (1) _____   (2) _____

   (3) _____   (4) _____

2. List two underlined phrases that make Buchanan seem expensively dressed.

   (1) _____   (2) _____

3. List five other underlined phrases that add up to create a negative attitude toward Tom Buchanan.

   (1) _____   (2) _____

   (3) _____   (4) _____

   (5) _____

4. Name two character traits that Buchanan seems likely to possess.

   _____

B. Jay Gatsby

If personality is an unbroken series of <u>successful gestures</u>, then there was <u>something gorgeous</u> about him, some <u>heightened sensitivity</u> to the promises of life, as if he were <u>related to one of those intricate machines</u> that register earthquakes ten thousand miles away. This <u>responsiveness</u> had nothing to do with that flabby impressionability which is dignified under the name of the "creative temperament"—it was an <u>extraordinary gift for hope</u>, a <u>romantic readiness</u> such as I have never found in any

(11–7 continued)

other person and which it is not likely I shall ever find again. No—Gatsby <u>turned out all right</u> in the end; it is what preyed on Gatsby, what foul dust floated in the wake of his dreams that temporarily closed out my interest in the abortive sorrows and short-winded elations of men.

1. List the eight underlined phrases, and mark (+) for positive, (−) for negative, and (0) for neutral in the blank space before each.

   _____ (1) _____

   _____ (2) _____

   _____ (3) _____

   _____ (4) _____

   _____ (5) _____

   _____ (6) _____

   _____ (7) _____

   _____ (8) _____

2. List two phrases describing a negative kind of responsiveness that do *not* fit

   Gatsby. _____

3. Does Gatsby seem to be basically a positive or negative character?

   _____ Explain the reasons for your choice. _____

   _____

4. Does "something gorgeous" refer to Gatsby's outward appearance or inner nature?

   _____ Explain the reasons for your choice.

   _____

   _____

5. List two phrases that imply that all Gatsby problems were not of his own making.

   _____

6. Explain what effect the experience of knowing Gatsby had on the speaker. (Use

   your own words.) _____

   _____

A Change of Character (11–8)

Directions: Following is the description of a famous character, the wife of Ethan Frome, from the novel by Edith Wharton. Read it carefully, noting the words the author has chosen to create a positive or negative impression.

Then, write an original character sketch, using this description as a model. You may base your description on someone you know or create an imaginary character. Your character may be positive or negative, male or female. In the place of "she," write a name that reinforces the attitude you wish your reader to have.

Model:

Against the dark background of the kitchen she (Zeena) stood up tall and angular, one hand drawing a quilted counterpane to her flat breast, while the other held a lamp. The light, on a level with her chin, drew out of the darkness her puckered throat and the projecting wrist of the hand that clutched the quilt, and deepened fantastically the hollows and prominence of her high-boned face under its ring of crimping-pins. — from *Ethan Frome* by Edith Wharton

A Character of Your Own

_____

_____

_____

_____

_____

_____

_____

_____

_____

_____

_____

_____

Characterization Through Action and Dialogue—Part I (11–9A)

Directions: You can learn of characters' inner natures and values through dialogue, narrative action, and the use of omniscience as well as descriptive characterization. Read the following examples from well-known writers, and answer the questions relating to each passage.

1. (*Scout is a 9-year-old girl; Jem, her 13-year-old brother; and Atticus, her father.*)

   "I'll send him home," a burly man said, and grabbed Jem roughly by the collar. He yanked Jem nearly off his feet.
   "Don't you touch him!" I kicked the man swiftly. Barefooted, I was surprised to see him fall back in real pain. I intended to kick his shin, but aimed too high.
   "That'll do, Scout." Atticus put his hand on my shoulder. "Don't kick folks. No—" he said, as I was pleading justification.
   "Ain't nobody gonna do Jem that way," I said. — from *To Kill a Mockingbird* by Harper Lee

   (1) The point of view is _____ person, _____.

   (2) Why doesn't Jem seem to be engaged in a fair fight? _____

   _____

   (3) Name two of Scout's character traits, and explain how they are shown through the action and dialogue.

   (a) _____

   (b) _____

   (4) From this incident, does Scout seem like a "proper little girl" or more like a

   tomboy? Explain why. _____

   _____

2. (*Before the end of the Civil War, a 10- or 11-year-old slave girl yearns for personal freedom.*)

   . . . All of a sudden my mistress was out there and she had grabbed me by the shoulders.
   . . . I raised my head high and looked her straight in the face and said: "You called me Ticey. My name ain't no Ticey no more, it's Miss Jane Brown. . . ."
   . . . That night when the master and the rest of them came in from the swamps she told my master I had sassed her in front of the Yankees. My master told two of the other slaves to hold me down. One took my arms, the other one took my legs. My

(11–9A continued)

master jecked up my dress and gived my mistress the whip and told her to teach me a lesson. Every time she hit me she asked me what I said my name was. I said Jane Brown. She hit me again: what I said my name was. I was Jane Brown.

My mistress got tired beating me and told my master to beat me some. He told her that was enough. . . . — *The Autobiography of Miss Jane Pittman* by Ernest J. Gaines

(1) Name two of Jane's character traits, and explain how they are shown through the action and dialogue.

(a) _____

(b) _____

(2) The point of view is _____ person, _____.

(3) This novel is called *The Autobiography of Miss Jane Pittman*. If you compare the point of view with the name of the author, why can't this possibly be true?

_____

_____

(4) This scene also foreshadows what Jane will do when freed from slavery. When given the choice of staying and working for her former master or setting out on

her own, what will Jane likely choose? _____

What foreshadows her choice? _____

_____

Characterization Through Action
and Dialogue—Part II (11–9B)

Directions: You can learn of characters' inner natures and values through dialogue, narrative action, and the use of omniscience as well as descriptive characterization. Read the following examples from well-known writers, and answer the questions relating to each passage.

1. (*Ralph is a 12-year-old boy, one of a group of boys stranded on an island.*)

   No one said anything but the faces turned to Ralph were intent. . . . He had learnt as a practical business that fundamental statements like this had to be said at least twice, before everyone understood them. One had to sit, attracting all eyes to the conch*, and drop words like heavy round stones among the little groups that crouched or squatted. He was searching his mind for simple words so that even the littluns would understand what the assembly was about. — *The Lord of the Flies* by
   William Golding

   (1) The point of view is _____ person, _____.

   Write a phrase that serves as proof. _____

   _____

   (2) Name a positive character trait Ralph reveals in this passage. _____

   How is it shown? _____

   _____

   (3) What quality of a good leader does Ralph also display? _____

   _____

   (4) What problem might make it hard for Ralph to convince his listeners, no matter

   what he says? _____

   _____

© 1995 by The Center for Applied Research in Education

---

*a huge seashell, serving as a sign of leadership

(11–9B continued)

2. He (Heathcliff) seemed a sullen, patient child, hardened, perhaps, to ill-treatment; he would stand Hindley's blows without winking or shedding a tear, and my pinches moved him only to draw in a breath and open his eyes, as if he had hurt himself by accident and nobody was to blame.

   This endurance made old Ernshaw furious, when he discovered his son persecuting the poor, fatherless child, as he called him. He took to Heathcliff strangely, believing all he said (for that matter, he said precious little, and generally the truth). . . . — from *Wuthering Heights* by Emily Brontë

   (1) What positive character trait does Heathcliff exhibit in paragraph one when

   beaten and pinched? _____ How does he exhibit it?

   _____

   (2) According to paragraph two, what are two other positive traits that are part of

   Heathcliff's character? _____

   _____

   (3) What are two factors that would make Heathcliff's inner nature difficult to know

   or understand? _____

   _____

   (4) What element in Heathcliff's background might make the reader sympathize

   with him? _____

Interpreting Character (11–10)

Writer ——→ Reader

↘   ↗

Characters in Story

The Grapes of Wrath by John Steinbeck

Directions: Remember that writers of fiction speak through characters. Yet, often, writers provide clues that allow the reader to understand more than the character does. Keep this in mind as you read the following passages, and answer the questions relating to each.

Ma Joad (*The Joads are a homeless family, one of thousands heading west in search of work.*)

1-A. . . . Ma was heavy, but not fat; thick with child-bearing and work. She wore a loose Mother Hubbard of gray cloth in which there had once been colored flowers, but the color was washed out now, so that the small flowered pattern was only a little lighter gray than the background. The dress came down to her ankles, and her strong, broad, bare feet moved quickly and deftly over the floor. . . . Strong, freckled arms were bare to the elbow, and her hands were chubby and delicate, like those of a plump little girl. She looked out into the sunshine. Her full face was not soft; it was controlled, kindly. Her hazel eyes seemed to have experienced all possible tragedy and to have mounted pain and suffering like steps to a high calm and a superhuman understanding. She seemed to know, to accept, to welcome her position, the citadel of the family, the strong place that could not be taken.

(1) In reference to Ma Joad, the author uses "strong" three times to describe her

_____, _____, and _____ in the family.

(2) Name three characteristics that make Ma seem feminine and dainty.

(a) _____

(b) _____

(c) _____

(3) According to Steinbeck, two character traits that show in Ma's face are

_____ and _____.

(4) What character traits have resulted from Ma's experiences with pain and suffering? _____

(5) To describe her position in the family, Steinbeck compares Ma to

_____ and _____.

© 1995 by The Center for Applied Research in Education

1-B. (*continued*) And since old Tom* and the children could not know hurt or fear unless she acknowledged hurt and fear, she had practiced denying them in herself. And since, when a joyful thing happened, they looked to see whether joy was on her, it was her habit to build up laughter out of inadequate materials. But better than joy was calm. Imperturbability could be depended upon. And from her great and humble position in the family she had taken dignity and a clean calm beauty. From her position as healer, her hands had grown sure and cool and quiet; from her position as arbiter she had become as remote and faultless in judgment as a goddess. She seemed to know that if she swayed the family shook, and if she ever really deeply wavered or despaired the family would fall, the family will to function would be gone.

(1) What was Ma's response in the face of hurt and fear? (Use your own words.)

_____

(2) Why was it important that Ma responded this way? _____

_____

(3) How could Ma "build up" joy? _____

_____

(4) What, according to Steinbeck, was better than joy? _____

(5) In view of the family's situation, why was this important? _____

_____

_____

(6) After describing Ma's position as "great and humble," what does Steinbeck give as two additional services Ma performs for her family?

(a) _____

(b) _____

(7) To describe Ma with regard to these services, Steinbeck compares her to

_____. What word in passage A foreshadows this comparison? _____

(8) Explain how passages A and B support Ma's right to be called "great."

_____

(9) Explain how passages A and B show that Ma deserves to be called "humble."

_____

_____

---

* Ma's husband

(11-10 continued)

2. **Feeding the Children** (*At a camp where the Joads stop, a group of hungry children gather around as Ma cooks for the family.*)

. . . The strange children stood close to the stew pot, so close that Ma brushed them with her elbows as she worked. . . .

Ma said helplessly, "I dunno what to do. I got to feed the fambly. What'm I gonna do with these here?" The children stood stiffly and looked at her. Their faces were blank, rigid, and their eyes went mechanically from the pot to the tin plate she held. Their eyes followed the spoon from pot to plate . . .

"I can't send 'em away. I don't know what to do. . . . I can't rob the fambly. I got to feed the fambly. . . ." She looked apologetically at the waiting children. "There ain't enough," she said humbly. "I'm a-gonna set this here kettle out, an' you'll all get a little tas', but it ain't gonna do you no good." She faltered, "I can't he'p it. Can't keep it from you." She lifted the pot and set it down on the ground. . . .

(1) Explain both sides of the conflict Ma faces as she looks at the children:

whether to _____ or _____.

(2) Explain the feelings that underlie each side of Ma's conflict.

_____

yet _____

(3) Name four character traits that Ma exhibits during this incident.

(a) _____   (b) _____

(c) _____   (d) _____

UNIT 12

Something to Think About

As concluding activities in this exploration of higher-level reading, this unit will concentrate on three types of passages that require close reading: authorial comments, elements of symbolism, and thematic references.

All are closely related. All help to reveal the author's purpose in writing the story or novel: its theme, its main idea, and the question about life or human nature the author has chosen to expose and explore.

Becoming an accomplished reader cannot be achieved through exercises and activities, no matter how stimulating. It can only be achieved through reading.

It is hoped that student readers will understand that working with examples and passages of short stories and novels can provide them with the right mind-sets for various types of reading and arm them with the right questions to ask and seek to answer as they read.

The goal is to develop active, alert readers who can read better, faster, and with greater insight and understanding because they know how to pace their reading, what they wish to discover in different types of passages, and what they are reading for—the essence of fiction, its idea or theme.

For the good reader, one of the chief attractions of reading is that it provides a unique opportunity to enter into the mind of another—via good literature, which presents continually new discoveries and ideas, new worlds to explore, and the opportunity to "experience" life without living it in the ordinary sense. For those who have learned to accept the challenges of literature, it's the chance to discover what people are like, what makes them tick.

NOTES ON ACTIVITIES

What Is Fiction "About"? (Reading Selection 12–1)

When discussing a story and its theme, discourage conjecture, such as "Maybe the boy's mother died in childbirth," that lacks actual proof. If an author thinks something is relevant to the story, proof will be there—generally in more than one place because of its importance.

Often one student will find a piece of valid proof that others did not note. Good reading does not require students to catch every detail so long as they understand the point an author is making.

Assuming a Persona (12–2A)

You may want to use or adapt this exercise for other stories and novels you are teaching. It is a valuable tool for helping students to develop the habit of putting themselves in someone else's place and thus become more insightful.

Tuning in to Theme (Reading Selection 12–3)

The definitions in this selection relate to a number of exercises following. Instead of going over each element intensively as an introduction, you may prefer to highlight pertinent definitions as you introduce individual exercises or present definitions orally for students to write in their notebooks.

"A World of Ideas," Authorial Comment—Part II (12–5B)

With regard to the passage by Rose Macaulay, you might want to discuss why the author chose to present this thematic comment through a series of questions, not as statements. Point out that she naturally could only judge by herself. She could not know if everyone would agree, but only assume that others felt as she did. Ask students how Ray in the quotation from *Banjo* makes a similar, important assumption made by storytellers about their readers and listeners.

Symbols: The Extra Dimension in Reading (12–7A through 12–7C)

These activities are designed to serve as self-contained exercises to introduce students to the depth of ideas conveyed by a writer's use of symbolism. Studying passages separately from the novels can help enhance students' understanding and allow them the pleasure of recognition when reading the full works later.

The passages may also be used in direct correlation with assigned reading of the novels themselves.

Symbols and Theme—Part I (12–8A)

In your introduction or discussion, you may want to refer to certain types of religions, such as the Aztecs of Mexico, that required human sacrifice and thus might be considered to have "blood-swollen gods."

Symbols and Theme—Part II (12–8B)

Before working with this activity, it should be helpful to review some of the characteristics of a hero, such as *courage, determination, loyalty, thoughtfulness, understanding, pride, concern for others, forgivingness, unselfishness,* and *generosity.* This will help students understand that being a true hero requires having more positive qualities than prowess in battle, alone.

Beginnings and Endings (12–9A through 12–9C)

In working with the exercises, which contain the opening and closing paragraphs of three distinguished novels, some students might fear that it "ruins" a story to know how it ends. Remind them that many people like to see popular movies again and again. With a good film or story, knowing what happens adds to the pleasure and allows the viewer or reader to concentrate on other things, equally or more important and interesting.

What Is Fiction "About"? (*Reading Selection 12–1*)

A piece of fiction is not just a number of parts; it's a whole.

And, authors want readers to share an experience as similar as possible to the one they had in mind and to have the same feelings and reactions at their stories' end.

When you think of the contradictory testimony given in a trial, you know that even eyewitness accounts often don't agree. Yet authors of fiction have an advantage: absolute control over the worlds they create.

Nothing gets into a story unless the author wants it there. No word of dialogue is spoken, no descriptive word is used, no bit of action occurs without a reason.

Everything fits the author's purpose—to direct the reader to have the experience and impression the author wishes to achieve.

Why? Because a fictional work is a created whole, there should be a reason for everything in a piece of fiction—from the choice of title to the decision to end the plot at a particular place and time.

Why? Once the key to the story is found, once the questions raised by the author are discovered, every answer will point in the same direction, the pieces fit together, and the wholeness of the story become clear.

To discover how it works, consider the following imaginary story:

The main character is a man who had an unhappy boyhood. When he was young, his father made fun of him and laughed at his ambition to get a good education and make something of himself. Because he felt his father didn't care for him, he dropped out of school and ran away from home.

As an adult and father himself, the main character has a steady job but no chance for advancement. Remembering his own father's attitude, he tries to give his son all the encouragement and support he can.

As a father, however, he pays such close attention to his son that the boy feels he is never allowed to make a decision of his own.

The father, who never went to college and didn't even finish high school, wants to give his son the advantages he lacked. He insists that the boy go to college, even though his son doesn't like the idea. After an argument the boy runs away from home. His final words to his father are, "You don't really care about me."

The father remembers telling his own father the same thing, but this time he knows it isn't true. He can only ask himself, "Why?"

The story might be titled "A Different Kind of Father."

What Is Fiction "About"? (12–1A)

Directions: Answer the following questions concerning the imaginary story, "A Different Kind of Father."

1. Why does the father feel his own father didn't care for him? (Give two reasons.)

   a. _____

   b. _____

2. Why does the father give his son so much encouragement and support?

   _____

3. Why does the boy feel unhappy? _____

4. About what future plan do the father and son disagree? _____

   _____

5. When the boy says, "You don't really care about me," why does the father feel the boy's accusation isn't true? _____

   _____

6. Why, in one sense, is the accusation true? _____

   _____

7. After reading the entire story, the reader would see that the title, "A Different Kind of Father," is ironic.

   a. Why, in one sense, does the father behave differently from his own father?

   _____

   b. Why, in another sense, does the father make the same mistake that his own father made? _____

   _____

Filling in the Story (12–1B)

Directions: Write a passage or paragraph that would fit the details given for "A Different Kind of Father." You may wish to write a passage containing a description of setting or background, dialogue, narrative action, or descriptive characterization.

Before beginning to write, you should settle on details such as the characters' names, the time and place of the story's setting, the father's occupation, the boy's ambition, and other members of the family. If you wish, you may write several types of passages—or even the entire story.

A Different Kind of Father

_____

_____

_____

_____

_____

_____

_____

_____

_____

_____

_____

_____

_____

_____

Thinking About Theme (*Reading Selection 12–2*)

When fiction is carefully written and read, questions and answers lock together to form a whole, and the answer to one question answers others the story raises.

Good readers trace the patterns woven into a story. If something seems out of place, they should ask themselves "Why?" and be sure the answer fits with everything given before.

In "A Different Kind of Father," the main character's feelings about his father caused him to go to the opposite extreme and make his own son unhappy. Every detail in the story would lead to the same realization or conclusion: Sometimes people hurt another person while trying to do what's right.

That is the **theme:** the idea, realization, or question about life or human nature which the story explores.

Even good readers would not be able to state the theme so plainly until the story's end, and, of course, there are many ways to express the same idea. In fact, you can understand a theme without stating it in so many words. Often put into a sentence, the theme seems much less than the story itself, which is meant to be a whole "experience," not a cold, flat statement.

Why did the story end as it did?

It ends when an author has fulfilled the story's purpose, has made the desired impact on the reader, has said everything needed to express the theme. Take again "A Different Kind of Father." It ended with the father asking, "Why?"

It's not appropriate to ask what happened next. Did the boy run away and never come back, did he join the army, or return home and go to college? The question and its answer are not important to the theme. If they were, the author would give clues to let the reader know the answer or end the story differently.

The key is the question "Why?" so the reader understands the terrible feeling the father must have, knowing he has failed but not knowing what he's done wrong. And the reader has the additional experience of knowing the answer to the father's question, although the main character doesn't.

A good work of fiction ends when it has made its point. The theme will be fully appreciated by looking back through the story to its beginning, rather than trying to guess what happens next.

Often, by reading again the opening paragraphs, you'll discover clues to the theme or outcome that you hadn't noticed at first. You'll see how everything contributed to the author's purpose and theme.

As you read, don't expect to know all the answers immediately, but ask the right questions as you go along, and you'll find yourself becoming more and more able to participate fully in the experience of reading fiction.

Assuming a Persona (12–2A)

Directions: One way of fully experiencing a story and its theme is to put yourself in the place of its major character and try to share his or her feelings. Imagine yourself as the father or son in "A Different Kind of Father." Or, since the story is an imaginary one, you might want to "create" a mother, sister, girl-friend, or some other character.

   Write an interior monologue at least 8-10 sentences long, expressing the thoughts and feelings that would be going through this person's mind at the end of the story.

A Different Kind of Father

Choice of character: _____

Monologue: _____

_____

_____

_____

_____

_____

_____

_____

_____

_____

_____

_____

_____

© 1995 by The Center for Applied Research in Education

Tuning in to Theme (*Reading Selection 12–3*)

Good readers know the importance of varying their reading speeds according to the type of passage and its purpose.

Although you need support for conclusions you draw from a story, you need not catch every specific detail. When authors make points essential to their readers' understanding, they generally provide proof in more than one paragraph and place—all contributing to the same conclusion.

Yet certain passages and paragraphs do require greater concentration and attention, called **close reading.** Here are some terms that will help you understand the deeper goals and passages that require close reading.

Insight: looking inside; an instance of apprehending (grasping or understanding) the true, inner, and deeper nature of a person or thing. *For example, though someone seems uncaring, you might have insight into that person's true motives.*

Theme: the realization or question about life or human nature that the author wishes to present and explore; the idea or conclusion about the characters in the story that the author wants the reader to draw, based on the story or novel as a whole.

(1) Look back to consider the entire story, from ending to title.

(2) Interpretations will vary, but all should be related to the same ideas.

(3) Themes should be stated as a sentence or question.

(4) An understanding of theme can sometimes be reached by consideration of the main conflict.

Moral: the practical lesson or advice about the right way to live that is contained in a story or experience. *For example: crime doesn't pay.* Although morals are a common element of children's stories, higher-level reading rarely leads to such simple morals but to themes that represent an observation about life, or even a question. *For example: Sometimes people hurt another person while trying to be helpful and supportive.*

Authorial comment: Speaking as the narrator of a story or through one of their characters, authors sometimes include passages relating to theme in the course of a story. Although the theme cannot be fully understood until the end, such paragraphs guide readers to an awareness of the story's purpose.

Symbol: Everyone understands and uses symbols everyday. *For example: 1 + 1 = 2* Can you explain what each of its elements stands for? A symbol is simply something that stands for something else. In a work of literature, a symbol is a type of comparison. Yet it is more than a metaphor because it has a wider significance. Serving as a point of reference throughout the story, novel, poem, or play, a symbol not only helps you picture the writer's meaning more clearly but also leads to an insightful understanding of the story's purpose and theme.

And the Moral Is . . . (12–4)

Directions: Below are short summaries of five familiar Aesop fables, which are famous for having simple, practical morals. Even if you haven't heard a story before, it should be easy to recognize the truth it is trying to teach.

From the sentences listed below, choose the moral that fits each story, and write it in the blank space following.

a. Trying to please everyone can result in pleasing no one.
b. It's easy to criticize what you can't get.
c. Slow and steady wins the race.
d. People don't believe known liars, though they're telling the truth.
e. Use good times to save for bad times ahead.

1. Bored with his job, a shepherd boy thought it would be fun to fool all the villagers by pretending a wolf was attacking the flock. He cried "Wolf," and everyone immediately rushed to his aid. Fooling them was so much fun, he tried it again. And, he fooled them once more. Then a real wolf attacked. But when he cried "Wolf," nobody came.

Moral _____

2. Seeing some plump, ripe grapes growing high on a vine, a hungry fox thought they were the sweetest, most delicious-looking grapes he had ever seen. He jumped and he leaped, but they were out of his reach. After much effort, he felt too tired to try again and finally said, "There's no use trying. They're probably sour anyway."

Moral _____

3. All summer, while the grasshopper chirruped and hopped, sang and enjoyed the warm, sunny weather, the ant worked busily to store and save enough grain to last through the winter. When winter came, the grasshopper was cold and hungry. He went to the ant and begged for something to eat. The ant said, "You knew in the summer that winter was to come. It's your own fault you're hungry now."

Moral _____

(12–4 continued)

4. A miller decided to sell his donkey at market. Putting his young son on the donkey's back, he headed to town. Some people said it wasn't fair for a boy to ride and his old father to walk. So they traded places. Then others said that wasn't fair either. So both rode. As they neared town, someone cried, "How terrible to overload a donkey so!" Hearing this, the miller tied the donkey's legs and slid a pole between them. Then he and his son carried the donkey, swinging upside down. The sight caused such commotion that the frightened donkey kicked free as they were crossing a bridge, fell into the water, and was lost.

Moral _____

5. The hare made fun of the tortoise for being so slow. The tortoise said he didn't need to go fast, for his shell kept him safe. Yet the hare kept making fun of the tortoise, who was provoked into a race. When the distance was set, the hare judged it would take hours for the tortoise to make what the hare could run in minutes. After running out of sight, the hare decided to rest for a while to make the race seem more exciting. Then he fell asleep, but the tortoise just kept going. When the hare awoke, it was too late to catch up. The tortoise won.

Moral _____

"A World of Ideas," Authorial Comment—Part I (12–5A)

Directions: Although a selection's theme is only fulfilled at its ending, authors frequently provide clues through authorial comment. Such passages require close reading, inviting the reader to ask questions that go beyond the story itself and provide insight into life and human nature in general, as well as the characters.

Read the following examples, and answer the questions that relate to them—the type of questions you, as a reader, should make it a habit to ask.

1. Fifteen is of all ages the most difficult to locate—to put one's fingers on and say, "That's the way I was." . . . All one can know is that somewhere between thirteen, boyhood's majority, and seventeen, when one is a sort of counterfeit young man, there is a time when youth fluctuates hourly between one world and another—pushed ceaselessly forward into unprecedented experiences and vainly trying to struggle back to the days when nothing had to be paid for. Fortunately none of our contemporaries remember much more than we do of how we behaved in those days. . . .
— "He Thinks He's Wonderful" by F. Scott Fitzgerald

   (1) The "two worlds" a boy of 13 and 17 goes back and forth between must be

   _____ and _____.

   (2) Thirteen can be considered "boyhood's majority" because that is the age when

   someone becomes a _____.

   (3) Why might someone of 15 be a sort of "counterfeit" young man?

   _____

   _____

   (4) Before age 13, why might it be true that "nothing had to be paid for"?

   _____

   _____

   _____

   (5) Why would it be so difficult for an older person to remember what being 15 was

   like? _____

   _____

   (6) Are Fitzgerald's observations true for boys or girls, now as then? Why or why

   not? _____

   _____

2. There is a time in the life of every boy when he for the first time takes the backward view of life. Perhaps that is the moment when he crosses the line into manhood. The boy is walking through the street of his town. He is thinking of the future and of the figure he will cut in the world. Ambitions and regrets awake within him. Suddenly something happens; he stops . . . and waits as for a voice calling his name. Ghosts of old things creep into his consciousness, the voices outside of himself whisper a message concerning the limitations of life. From being sure of himself and his future he becomes not at all sure. If he be an imaginative boy a door is torn open and for the first time he looks out upon the world, seeing . . . the countless figures of men who before his time have come out of nothingness into the world, lived their lives and again disappeared into nothingness. The sadness of sophistication has come to the boy. . . . The eighteen years he has lived seem but a moment, a breathing space in the long march of humanity. — "Sophistication" by Sherwood Anderson

(1) This passage concerns a change taking place in someone who has reached age

_____ and is at the beginning of _____.

(2) Up until this time the person has been thinking of _____.

(3) "The figure he will cut in the world" must mean _____

_____ and _____.

(4) When the change comes over him he begins to think of _____

and _____.

(5) Instead of thinking of his own "ambitions and regrets," how does he change his

attitude about the future? _____

_____

(6) Anderson titles his story "Sophistication" and writes of its sadness coming to the

boy. What must he mean by the word *sophistication*?

_____

_____

_____

(7) Are these ideas true for boys or girls, now as then? Why or why not?

_____

_____

"A World of Ideas," Authorial Comment—Part II (12–5B)

Directions: Although a selection's theme is only fulfilled at its ending, authors frequently provide clues through authorial comment. Such passages require close reading, inviting the reader to ask questions that go beyond the story itself and provide insight into life and human nature in general, as well as the characters.

Read the following examples, and answer the questions that relate to them—the type of questions you, as a reader, should make it a habit to ask.

1. *(Ray is a vagabond seaman and writer, talking to friends in a cafe in west Africa.)*
   ". . . I think about my race as much as you. I hate to see it kicked around and spat on by the whites, because it is a good earth-loving race. I'll fight with it if there's a fight on, but if I am writing a story—well, it's like all of us in this place here, black and brown and white, and I telling a story for the love of it. Some of you will listen, and some won't. If I am a real story-teller, I won't worry about the differences in complexion of those who listen and those who don't, I'll just identify myself with those who are really listening and tell my story . . ." — from *Banjo* by Claude McKay

   (1) What reason does the speaker give for telling his stories?

   _____

   (2) In what kind of situation does race matter to the speaker and make him willing

   to fight for it? _____

   _____

   (3) In what situation doesn't race matter to the speaker? _____

   _____

   (4) As a storyteller, what matters to the speaker more than someone's race?

   _____

   (5) As a comment upon life and human nature, what idea does the author wish to ex-

   press? _____

   _____

2. *(Finny is a prep school student, a talented athlete, who has been permanently crippled in an accident.)*
   "I like the winter," Finny assured me for the fourth time, as we came back from chapel that morning.
   "Well, it doesn't like you." Wooden plank walks had been placed on many of the school paths for better footing, but there were icy patches everywhere on them. A crutch misplaced and he could be thrown down upon the frozen wooden planking, or into the ice-encrusted snow. . . .
   "The winter loves me," he retorted, and then, disliking the whimsical sound of that, added, "I mean as much as you can say a season can love. What I mean is, I love winter, and when you really love something, then it loves you back, in whatever way it has to love." . . . — from *A Separate Peace* by John Knowles

(12–5B continued)

(1) Explain why winter might seem not to "like" someone like Finny.

_____

_____

(2) Finny says he loves winter. If someone loves winter, what are two things a person might especially like about it? _____

_____

(3) Select a detail in the passage that describes its being the kind of weather Finny must like. _____

_____

(4) In relation to the theme, the passage involves the true meaning of love. In Finny's eyes, if you truly love someone, should you want to (a) change or (b) not change the person or thing you loved? _____

(5) How could winter best show its love for Finny? _____

_____

3. . . . Had everyone, then, some different self, that only a few people, that sometimes only they themselves, knew? How know anyone? She (Daisy) had put the same question to herself the other day, when reading the published diary of a man of letters, who revealed in his daily records a self strangely hidden from his friends. They had known him as one kind of person, and he was, between himself and his diary, quite another. Which was the more real? Not necessarily the secret, hidden self. . . . Further, if they all had these queer hidden selves, need they so much mind showing them to one another, need they be afraid?

  Well, it all depended. . . . — *Keeping Up Appearances* by Rose Macaulay

(1) When was the "man of letters" (or author's) secret self revealed to the world?

_____

(2) What conclusion did Daisy draw from this discovery?

_____

_____

(3) What about Daisy herself would make her draw this conclusion?

_____

_____

(4) In order to agree with Daisy's conclusion, what would also have to be true of the reader? _____

_____

Name _____ Date _____ Period _____

Identifying Familiar Symbols (12–6)

Directions: A symbol is something that stands for something else. In relation to literature, the idea of symbols and symbolism at first may seem strange and
confusing. Yet you use symbols every day with never a problem. Just for
practice and fun, answer the following questions about commonplace symbols.

1. Name what each of the following symbols stands for when posted along a road.

   a. _____   b. _____

2. Name three things a ring on someone's finger might symbolize.

   a. _____   b. _____   c. _____

3. What five symbols are commonly used in school in reference to grades?

   _____

4. Write a word or draw a symbol used in school or pro athletics.

   _____

5. Write a symbol used in a school subject, such as chemistry or algebra.

   Symbol: _____   **Meaning:** _____

6. A medal may be given as a symbol to someone outstanding in such areas as

   _____ and _____.

7. Name the three chief colors that are used as symbols with regard to traffic, and tell
   what each one stands for.

   a. _____   b. _____   c. _____

8. A blue ribbon symbolizes _____.

9. Name three things flags of different colors and designs may symbolize.

   a. _____

   b. _____

   c. _____

10. In the slogan "I ♡ NY," ♡ stands for _____.

11. is a symbol meaning _____.

12. Name three occupations a badge can symbolize.

    a. _____   b. _____   c. _____

13. The dove is a bird symbolizing _____

14. Draw a symbol used in music.

Symbols: The Extra Dimension in Reading—Part I (12–7A)

The Scarlet Letter by Nathaniel Hawthorne

Directions: The following example illustrates how awareness of symbols in great works of literature brings you a better understanding of an author's purpose and theme. After close reading, answer the questions concerning the passage.

The founders of a new colony, whatever Utopia of human virtue and happiness they might originally project, have invariably recognized it among their earliest practical necessities to allot a portion of the virgin soil as a cemetery, and another portion as the site of a prison. In accordance with this rule, it may safely be assumed that the forefathers of Boston had built the first prison-house somewhere in the vicinity of Cornhill, almost as seasonably as they marked out the first burial ground. . . . Certain it is, that, some fifteen or twenty years after the settlement of the town, the wooden jail was already marked with weather-stains and other indications of age, which gave a yet darker aspect to its beetle-browed and gloomy front. . . . Like all else that pertains to crime, it seemed never to have known a youthful era. Before this ugly edifice . . . was a grass-plot much overgrown with burdock, pigweed, apple-peru and such unsightly vegetation, which evidently found something congenial in the soil that had so early borne the black flower of civilized society, a prison. But, on the one side of the portal, and rooted almost at the threshold, was a wild rose-bush, covered, in this month of June, with its delicate gems, which might be imagined to offer their fragrance and fragile beauty to the prisoner as he went in, and to the condemned criminal as he came forth to his doom, in token that the deep heart of Nature could pity and be kind to him.

(1) No matter how perfect its founders want it to be, what are two negative things that all new colonies must provide space for?

_____

(2) The first serves as a symbol that all humans must _____.

(3) The second symbolizes the fact that all human societies have _____.

(4) Hawthorne is writing of the early settlement of _____.

(5) List three words Hawthorne uses to describe the appearance of the prison.

a. _____ b. _____ c. _____

(6) Since weeds such as burdock, pigweed, and apple-peru find a "congenial" atmos-

phere near the prison, Hawthorne implies that the prison is a type of _____

in society and symbolizes this by comparing it to a _____.

(12–7A continued)

(7) Beside the door of the prison grows a wild rose-bush. Does Hawthorne intend "wild" to mean (a) savage and hard to tame or (b) growing naturally, without having been planted there?

_____

Explain the reason for your choice. _____

_____

(8) Besides offering its fragrance and beauty, the rose-bush is a symbol that Nature will

_____ and _____

to those found guilty of crimes.

(9) Name two factors that show personification of nature.

a. _____

b. _____

(10) Give an example of a law of nature and a law of society.

a. _____

b. _____

(11) According to the passage and its symbols, which type of law seems more fair and

why? _____

_____

_____

Name _____   Date _____   Period _____

Symbols: The Extra Dimension in Reading—Part II (12–7B)

A Tale of Two Cities by Charles Dickens

Directions: The following examples show how awareness of symbols in great works of literature brings you a better understanding of an author's purpose and theme. After close reading, answer the questions concerning each passage.

1. *A Tale of Two Cities* concerns the French Revolution and the conditions leading to its days of violence and rebellion. Of the Paris suburb of Saint Antoine, Dickens writes "cold, dirt, sickness, ignorance, and want, were the lords in waiting of the saintly presence."

   (1) What is ironical about the suburb's name of Saint Antoine and Dickens' calling it a "saintly presence"? _____

   _____

   _____

   (2) Considering other words used to describe Saint Antoine's condition, must "want" mean (a) hope and desire or (b) poverty and neediness? _____

2. A large cask of wine had been dropped and broken in the street. The accident had happened in getting it out of a cart; the cask had tumbled out . . . and it lay on the stones just outside the door of the wine-shop, shattered like a walnut-shell.
   . . . The rough, irregular stones of the street . . . had dammed it into little pools; these were surrounded, each by its own jostling group or crowd, according to its size. Some men kneeled down, made scoops of their two hands joined, and sipped. . . . Others, men and women, dipped in the puddles with little mugs of mutilated earthenware, or even with handkerchiefs from women's heads, which were squeezed dry into infants' mouths . . . others devoted themselves to the sodden and lee-dyed pieces of the cask, licking, and even champing the moister wine-rotted fragments with eager relish. There was no drainage to carry off the wine, and not only did it all get taken up, but . . . much mud got taken up along with it. . . .
   The wine was red wine, and had stained the ground of the narrow street in the suburb of Saint Antoine, in Paris, where it was spilled. It had stained many hands, too, and many faces, and many naked feet, and many wooden shoes. . . . Those who had been greedy with the staves of the cask, had acquired a tigerish smear about the mouth; and one tall joker so besmirched . . . scrawled upon a wall with his finger dipped in muddy wine-lees—BLOOD.

(12–7B continued)

(1) List two details about the people and their possessions that show how poor they are.

a. _____

b. _____

(2) List two details that show the bad condition of the suburb itself.

a. _____

b. _____

(3) Describe three things the people do that show their desperate wish to have and share the wine.

a. _____

b. _____

c. _____

(4) Give an example that reveals the ignorance and possible source of sickness existing in Saint Antoine, and explain why.

a. _____

b. _____

(5) From the act of the "tall joker," what does the spilled red wine clearly symbolize?

_____

(6) After having the wine, how does the appearance of the people also fit this symbolism? (Give two examples.)

a. _____

_____

b. _____

_____

(7) What does this symbolism foreshadow about the people's behavior, once the revolution has begun? _____

_____

© 1995 by The Center for Applied Research in Education

Symbols: The Extra Dimension in Reading—Part III (12–7C)

A Tale of Two Cities by Charles Dickens

Directions: The following examples show how awareness of symbols in great works of literature brings you a better understanding of an author's purpose and theme. After close reading, answer the questions concerning the passage.

(Defarge and his wife, wine-shop owners who are helping plot the revolution, take a recruit from the country, the mender of roads, to see the King and Queen.)

. . . The crowd waited to see the carriage of the King and Queen.

. . . Soon the large-faced King and the fair-faced Queen came in their golden coach, attended by . . . a glittering multitude of laughing ladies and fine lords, and in jewels and silks and powder and splendour and elegantly spurning figures, and handsomely disdainful faces of both sexes, the menders of roads bathed himself, so much to his temporary intoxication, that he cried Long live the King, Long live the Queen, Long live everybody and everything! . . . During the whole of this scene, which lasted some three hours, he had plenty of shouting and weeping and sentimental company. . . .

The mender of roads was now coming to himself, and was mistrustful of having made a mistake in his late demonstrations; but no.

"You are the fellow we want," said Defarge, in his ear; "you make these fools believe that it will last forever. Then they are the more insolent, and it is nearer ended."

Madame Defarge . . . nodded in confirmation.

"If you were shown a great heap of dolls, and were set upon them to pluck them to pieces and despoil them to your own advantages, you would pick out the richest and gayest. Say! Would you not?"

"Truly yes, madame."

"Yes. And if you were shown a flock of birds, unable to fly, and were set upon to strip them of their feathers for your own advantage, you would set upon the birds of the finest feathers, would you not?"

"It is true, madame."

"You have seen both dolls and birds to-day," said Madame Defarge, with a wave of her hand towards the place where they had last been apparent; "Now, go home!"

(12–7C continued)

(1) What did the mender of roads do that made him seem "temporarily intoxicated" when he saw the royal procession? _____

_____

(2) What was the actual cause of this "temporary intoxication"?

_____

(3) Why would Defarge say the mender of roads's behavior helped fool the rulers of France? _____

_____

(4) Who are the "dolls and birds" that the mender of roads had seen?

_____

Why are these fitting symbols? _____

_____

(5) How does Madame Defarge wish to see the "dolls and birds" treated?

_____

_____

(6) What is Madame Defarge's true goal? _____

_____

_____

Symbols and Theme—Part I (12–8A)

The Red Badge of Courage by Stephen Crane

Directions: The following examples show how awareness of symbols in great works of literature brings you a better understanding of an author's purpose and theme. After close reading, answer the questions concerning each passage.

1. *(After enlisting with dreams of glory, the youth, Henry Fleming, discovers the reality of war.)*

     . . . In the darkness he saw visions of a thousand-tongued fear that would babble at his back and cause him to flee, while others were going about their country's business. He admitted that he would not be able to cope with this monster. He felt that every nerve in his body would be an ear to hear the voices, while other men would remain solid and deaf.

   (1) The author uses the word _____ as a symbol for the kind of fear that war

       inspires.

   (2) Explain why such fear might seem a "thousand-tongued."

       _____

       _____

   (3) How does "thousand-tongued" help carry out Crane's symbol for fear?

       _____

       _____

2. . . . They (the soldiers) were going to look at war, the red animal—war, the blood-swollen god.

   (1) Name the two symbols Crane uses to stand for war.

       a. _____

       b. _____

   (2) Explain why each is an appropriate piece of symbolism for war.

       a. _____

       b. _____

3. Presently he began to feel the effects of the war atmosphere—a blistering sweat, a sensation that his eyeballs were about to crack like hot stones. A burning roar filled his ears. . . .

     There was a blare of heated rage mingled with a certain expression of intentness on all faces. Many of these men were making low-toned noises with their mouths, and these subdued cheers, snarls, imprecations, prayers, made a wild, barbaric song that went as an undercurrent of sound, strange and chantlike with the resounding chords of the war march. . . .

(12–8A continued)

    (1) List three words or phrases that fit the symbolism of war as a pagan religion.

        a. _____   b. _____   c. _____

    (2) Crane describes the soldiers' expressions of "heated rage" and "low-toned noises." Does this make them seem (a) self-controlled and courageous or (b) controlled by forces outside themselves?

    _____

4. To the youth it was an onslaught of redoubtable dragons. He became like the man who lost his legs at the approach of the red and green monster. He waited in a sort of horrified, listening attitude. He seemed to shut his eyes and wait to be gobbled.

    (1) List three phrases that reinforce or carry out Crane's symbol for the fear that war inspires.

        a. _____

        b. _____

        c. _____

5. At times he regarded the wounded soldiers in an envious way. He conceived persons with torn bodies to be peculiarly happy. He wished that he, too, had a wound, a red badge of courage.

    (1) To the youth, what symbolized courage? _____

    (2) Explain why this can be compared to a sort of red badge. _____

    _____

    _____

    (3) Why doesn't this type of red badge necessarily represent courage?

    _____

    _____

Symbols and Theme—Part II (12–8B)

The Red Badge of Courage by Stephen Crane

Directions: In the title of Steven Crane's novel, the "red badge" stands for a wound received in battle, as if it were a symbol of courage. And, this leads you to ask, "What is true courage?"

Although you can't really express the theme until you have read an entire story, often symbols and authorial comments will help you pose the right questions. Keep this in mind as you read the following passages and write your answers.

1. *(Among a group of wounded men, the unwounded youth and another man observe a mortally-wounded soldier, lurching along in the agonies of death.)*

   They began to have thoughts of a solemn ceremony. There was something rite-like in these movements of the doomed soldier. And there was a resemblance in him to a devotee of a mad religion, blood-sucking, muscle-wrenching, bone-crushing. They were awed and afraid. They hung back lest he have a command of a dreadful weapon.

   (1) List four phrases that refer to the symbol of war as god of a pagan religion.

   a. _____   b. _____

   c. _____   d. _____

   (2) List two phrases that refer to the symbol of war as a red animal.

   a. _____   b. _____

   (3) Why would the youth and other soldier react with awe and fear?

   _____

2. To the youth the fighters resembled animals tossed for a death struggle into a dark pit. There was a sensation that he and his fellows, at bay, were pushing back, always pushing fierce onslaughts of creatures who were slippery. . . .

   When, in a dream, it occurred to the youth that his rifle was an impotent stick, he lost sense of everything but his hate, his desire to smash into pulp the glittering smile of victory which he could feel upon the faces of his enemies. . . .

   The flames bit him, and the hot smoke broiled his skin. His rifle barrel grew so hot that ordinarily he could not have borne it upon his palms; but he kept on stuffing cartridges into it. . . . If he aimed at some charging form through the smoke, he pulled his trigger with a fierce grunt. . . .

   When the enemy seemed falling back before him and his fellows, he went instantly forward, like a dog who, seeing his foes lagging, turns and insists upon being pursued. And when he was compelled to retire again, he did it slowly, sullenly, taking steps of wrathful despair.

   (1) List four phrases that make soldiers on both sides seem more like animals than men when engaged in battle.

   a. _____   b. _____

   c. _____   d. _____

(2) List four phrases that show the youth is not thinking clearly nor acting normally during the heat of fighting. (Do not repeat phrases used in [1].)

a. _____

b. _____

c. _____

d. _____

3. These incidents made the youth ponder. It was revealed to him that he had been a barbarian, a beast. He had fought like a pagan who defends his religion. Regarding it, he saw that it was fine, wild, and in some ways, easy. He had been a tremendous figure, no doubt. To this struggle he had overcome obstacles which he had admitted to be mountains. . . . And he had not been aware of the process. He had slept and, awakening, found himself a knight.

(1) List four words or phrases that refer to Crane's symbols for war.

a. _____   b. _____

c. _____   d. _____

(2) After the battle, the youth felt he "had slept" when fighting and that it had actually been easy. In what sense might this be so? _____

_____

4. (But) There was a frenzy made from this furious rush. The men, pitching forward insanely, had burst into cheerings, moblike and barbaric, but tuned in strange keys that can arouse the dullard and the stoic. It made a mad enthusiasm that, it seemed, would be incapable of checking itself before granite and brass. There was the delirium that encounters despair and death, and is heedless and blind to the odds. . . .

Presently the straining pace ate up the energies of the men. As if by agreement, the leaders began to slacken their speed. . . . Since much of their (the soldiers') strength and their breath had vanished, they returned to caution. They were becoming men again.

(1) List four words or phrases that refer to Crane's symbols for war.

a. _____   b. _____

c. _____   d. _____

(2) How and why did the soldiers "become men again"?

_____

_____

(3) One definition of the word *man* is the creature, *Homo sapiens,* the wise, characterized especially by a highly-developed brain. With this in mind, discuss what Crane's symbols lead the reader to feel about the type of courage and heroism shown in the heat of battle.

_____

_____

_____

_____

Beginnings and Endings—Part I (12–9A)

Directions: When you have finished reading a story or novel, you can understand it better by going back to the beginning. There you will often find clues and connections, unnoticed at first reading, that now reveal the author's purpose more clearly. Doing this will help you discover that fiction is not just a string of incidents but a created whole. In fact, the title can help, too.

To realize the importance of beginnings and endings, read the following passages and answer the accompanying questions concerning each.

A Tale of Two Cities by Charles Dickens

(**A Tale of Two Cities** *concerns the French Revolution and the conditions leading to its days of violence and rebellion, as well as characters from England involved in the plot.*)

1. It was the best of times, it was the worst of times, it was the age of wisdom, it was the age of foolishness, it was the epoch of belief, it was the epoch of incredulity, it was the season of Light, it was the season of Darkness, it was the spring of hope, it was the winter of despair, we had everything before us, we had nothing before us, we were all going direct to Heaven, we were all going direct the other way—in short, the period was so far like the present period, that some of its noisiest authorities insisted on its being received, for good or for evil, in the superlative degree of comparison only.

   (1) In this opening paragraph, Charles Dickens uses a series of seven antitheses. In the blank spaces below, list the two sides of each element he contrasts.

   a. _____ <> _____

   b. _____ <> _____

   c. _____ <> _____

   d. _____ <> _____

   e. _____ <> _____

   f. _____ <> _____

   g. _____ <> _____

   (2) The setting of this story includes both Paris and London. Does Dickens intend this paragraph to apply to Paris, London, or both? _____

   Explain the reason for your choice. _____

   _____

(12–9A continued)

(3) Dickens states that period of the story was like the present. Choose one of the analogies in the opening paragraph, and give examples to show why both sides of it are still true now.

_____

_____

2. *(At the end of the story, one of the major characters, a Londoner, sacrifices his life for the woman he loves. He takes the place of her husband, a condemned French noble-man, and dies on the revolutionaries' guillotine in Paris. As he stands on the guillo-tine, his last words end the novel.)*

"It is a far, far better thing that I do, than I have ever done; it is a far, far better rest that I go to than I have ever known."

(1) In what way does this last paragraph emphasize the period of the revolution also exemplified as "the best of times" and "the worst of times"?

_____

_____

_____

_____

(2) Explain how the title pertains both to the ending and the idea expressed in the

opening paragraph. _____

_____

_____

© 1995 by The Center for Applied Research in Education

Beginnings and Endings—Part II (12–9B)

Directions: When you have finished reading a story or novel, you can understand it better by going back to the beginning. There you will often find clues and connections, unnoticed at first reading, that now reveal the author's purpose more clearly. Doing this will help you discover that fiction is not just a string of incidents but a created whole. In fact, the title can help, too.

To realize the importance of beginnings and endings, read the following passages and answer the accompanying questions concerning each.

The Secret Sharer by Joseph Conrad

(Setting: aboard a sailing ship anchored at the head of the gulf of Siam.)

1. Opening Paragraph

It must be said . . . that I knew very little of my officers. In consequence of certain events of no particular significance, except to myself, I had been appointed to the command only a fortnight before. Neither did I know much of the hands forward. All these people had been together for eighteen months or so, and my position was that of the only stranger on board. I mention this because it has some bearing on what is to follow. But what I felt most was my being a stranger to the ship; and if all the truth must be told, I was somewhat of a stranger to myself. The youngest man on board (barring the second mate) and untried as yet by a position of the fullest responsibility, I was willing to take the adequacy of the others for granted. They had simply to be equal to their tasks; but I wondered how far I should turn out faithful to that ideal conception of one's own personality every man sets up for himself secretly.

(1) The novel's point of view is _____ person, _____.

(2) What is the speaker's position on the ship? _____

(3) Name the three ways in which the speaker considers himself a stranger, and explain the reason each is true.

    a. He is a stranger to _____ because _____

    _____.

    b. He is a stranger to _____ because _____

    _____.

    c. He is a stranger to _____ because _____

    _____.

2. Final Paragraph

Already the ship was drawing ahead. And I was alone with her. Nothing! No one in the world should stand now between us, throwing a shadow on the way of silent knowledge and mute affection, the perfect communion of a seaman with his first command.

(1) The final paragraph reveals how the captain changes during the course of the novel. Explain two ways he has changed and how the passage makes this clear.

a. He must no longer be _____

because _____

_____.

b. He must no longer be _____

because _____

_____.

(2) Although the novel's title, *The Secret Sharer,* is important to the theme, the questions about its purpose can only be answered by reading the entire novel. What are two questions raised by this title?

a. _____

b. _____

Beginnings and Endings—Part III (12–9C)

Directions: When you have finished reading a story or novel, you can understand it better by going back to the beginning. There you will often find clues and connections, unnoticed at first reading, that now reveal the author's purpose more clearly. Doing this will help you discover that fiction is not just a string of incidents but a created whole. In fact, the title can help, too.

To realize the importance of beginnings and endings, read the following passages and answer the accompanying questions concerning each.

The Ponder Heart by Eudora Welty

1. Opening Paragraphs

My Uncle Daniel's just like your uncle, if you've got one—only he has one weakness. He loves society and he gets carried away. If he hears our voices, he'll come right down those stairs, supper ready or no. When he sees you sitting . . . , he'll take the other end of the sofa and then move closer up to see what you've got to say for yourself; and then he's liable to give you a little hug and start trying to give you something. Don't do you any good to be bashful. He won't let you refuse. All he might do is forget tomorrow what he gave you today, and give it to you all over again. Sweetest disposition in the world. That's his big gray Stetson hanging on the rack right over your head—see what a large head size he wears?

Things I could think of without being asked that he's given away would be—a string of hams, a fine suit of clothes, a white-face heifer calf, two trips to Memphis, pair of fantail pigeons, fine Shetland pony (loves children), brooder and incubator, good nanny goat, bad billy, cypress cistern, field of white Dutch clover, two iron wheels and some laying pullets (they were together), cow pasture during drouth (he has everlasting springs), innumerable fresh eggs, a pick-up truck—even his own cemetery lot, but they wouldn't accept it. And I'm not counting this week. He's been a general favorite all these years.

(1) The point of view is _____ person, _____.

(2) In the novel, "you" are being asked to play the role of _____.

(3) The speaker says "Uncle Daniel's just like your uncle." In the light of the first two paragraphs, is the reader likely to agree or disagree? _____

Why? _____

_____.

(4) How does he get "carried away" and display his "one weakness"?

_____.

(5) How does saying Uncle Daniel has the "sweetest disposition in the world" contradict

the first sentence? _____

_____.

(6) Name six things of considerable value that Uncle Daniel has given away.

_____   _____

_____   _____

_____   _____

(7) Name four things of questionable value Uncle Daniel has given or tried to give away.

_____   _____

_____   _____

(8) Is the novel likely to be serious or humorous? _____

Explain two reasons behind your choice. _____

_____

_____

2. *Final Paragraphs*

I'm going to holler—*Uncle Daniel!*
I'd like to warn you again, he may try to give you something—may think he's got something to give. If he does, do me a favor. Make out like you accept it. Tell him thank you.
Uncle Daniel? Uncle Daniel! We've got company!
Now he'll be down.

(1) What favor does the speaker ask "you" to agree to? _____

_____

(2) What must have happened that Uncle Daniel apparently doesn't realize?

_____

(3) Judged by the opening and closing paragraphs, does it seem more likely that the novel is told in (a) chronological order or (b) flashback?

_____

(4) What question must the plot of *The Ponder Heart* answer?

_____

(5) Uncle Daniel's last name is Ponder, which helps account for that word in the title, *The Ponder Heart,* but the title also contains symbolism.
  a. Considering the opening and closing paragraphs, explain what "heart" must symbolize in relation to Uncle Daniel's one "weakness." _____

_____

  b. Name two other ways in which the word *heart* might serve as a symbol or clue about the rest of the story. _____

_____

_____

© 1995 by The Center for Applied Research in Education

Theme: What It Means to Be Human (12–10)

Directions: Frank Stockton's "The Lady, or the Tiger" is one of the world's most memorable short stories. Read the following passages from the story, along with its plot steps, to discover why the story ends in a way that's hard to forget.

1. *(The setting is a semibarbaric kingdom in olden times, where the fate of a man accused of a major crime was decided by chance, in public, in the King's arena.)*

   When a subject was accused of a crime of sufficient importance to interest the king, public notice was given that . . . the fate of the accused person would be decided in the king's arena.

   When all the people had assembled . . . he (the king) gave a signal . . . and the accused subject stepped out into the amphitheater. Directly opposite him . . . were two doors, exactly alike and side by side. It was the duty and the privilege of the person on trial to walk directly to these doors and open one of them. He could open either door he pleased. If he opened the one, there came out of it a hungry tiger, the fiercest and most cruel that could be procured, which immediately sprang upon him and tore him to pieces, as a punishment for his guilt. . . .

   But if the accused person opened the other door, there came forth from it a lady, the most suitable to his years and station that His Majesty could select among his fair subjects; and to this lady he was immediately married, as a reward of his innocence.

   (1) Since *barbaric* means savage and uncivilized, explain what a semibarbaric king-

   dom must be. _____

   _____

   (2) In what way might the king's form of punishment be considered fair?

   _____

   (3) In what way was it unfair? _____

   _____

2. **Plot Steps**
   a. The King's daughter loves a young man beneath her station.
   b. The King discovers the princess's secret romance.
   c. Her lover is arrested, sentenced to trial in the arena.
   d. The kingdom's fiercest tiger crouches behind one door.
   e. One of the kingdom's loveliest damsels waits behind the other.
   f. The royal party and public arrive for the trial.
   g. The princess possesses the secret of the doors.
   h. She also knows the lady who waits as the prize.
   i. The accused glances up, realizing the princess knows the secret.
   j. The princess and he exchange glances, his asking "Which?"
   k. She makes an almost imperceptible gesture to the right.
   l. The young man without hesitation opens the door she indicates.

(12–10 continued)

(1) For what crime is the young man sent to the arena?

_____

(2) What two secrets has the princess learned?

_____

_____

(3) What important question do the plot steps leave unanswered?

_____

3. **A Passage About the Princess**

Possessed of more power, influence, and force of character than anyone who had ever before been interested in such a case, she (the princess) had done what no other person had done—she had possessed herself of the secret of the doors. . . .

And not only did she know in which room stood the lady, ready to emerge, all blushing and radiant, should her door be opened, but she knew who the lady was. . . . Often she had seen, or imagined that she had seen, this fair creature throwing glances of admiration upon the person of her lover, and sometimes she thought these glances were perceived and even returned. . . . The girl was lovely, but she had dared to raise her eyes to the loved one of the princess; and, with all the intensity of the savage blood transmitted to her through long lines of wholly barbaric ancestors, she hated the woman who blushed and trembled behind that silent door.

(1) What reason did the princess have for being jealous of the lady behind the door?

_____

_____

(2) What in the passage implies that the girl behind the door might be innocent of flirting glances? _____

_____

4. **Final Paragraphs**

Her decision had been indicated in an instant, but it had been made after days and nights of anguished deliberation. She had known she would be asked, she had decided what she would answer, and without the slightest hesitation, she had moved her hand to the right.

The question of her decision is one not to be lightly considered, and it is not for me to presume to set up myself as the one person able to answer it. And so I leave it with all of you: Which came out of the opened door—the lady, or the tiger?

(1) Although the young man is described as "handsome and brave to a degree unsurpassed in the kingdom," the story contains no descriptive characterization of the princess. Why would the author omit his description?

_____

_____

364

(12–10 continued)

(2) The title and ending ask the same question. What comment does the narrator make about the answer? _____
_____

(3) Does this imply that the reader should or should not feel qualified to answer the title question? _____ Why or why not?
_____

(4) The final paragraphs speak of the princess's "anguished decision" and her decision "not to be lightly considered." Thoughtfully explain what the princess's feelings must be, both for and against having the young man she loved choose the lady or the tiger.

   a. Against his choosing the lady: _____
_____

      For this choice: _____
_____

   b. Against his choosing the tiger: _____
_____

      For this choice: _____
_____

(5) The princess's "agonizing decision," along with the title and final question, indicate the story's theme concerns how people make decisions.

   a. The king wanted his prisoners' guilt or innocence to be decided by
_____.

   b. The princess made her decision on the basis of the strength of conflicting character traits: _____
versus _____

   c. The princess's lover made his decision on the basis of
_____

Assuming a Persona—"The Lady, or the Tiger?" (12–11)

Directions: One way of fully experiencing a story and its theme is to put yourself in the place of a major character and try to share his or her feelings. Imagine yourself as the princess or young prisoner in "The Lady, or the Tiger?" Or perhaps you might wish to choose the king or the lady waiting behind the door. Write an interior monologue of at least 8-10 sentences long, expressing the thoughts and feelings that would be going through this person's mind just before the chosen door was opened.

Your choice of character: _____

_____

_____

_____

_____

_____

_____

_____

_____

_____

_____

_____

_____

_____

_____

_____

Answer Key

UNIT 1, THE GOOD READER IN ACTION

What's Missing? (1–2)

1. A stitch in time saves nine.
2. Waste not, want not.
3. A penny saved is a penny earned.
4. Look before you leap.
5. Honesty is the best policy.
6. It's better to be safe than sorry.

Filling in Famous Quotations (1–3)

1. 'Tis the good reader that makes the good book.
2. Almost everything that is great has been done by youth.
3. Making peace is harder than making war.
4. The appetite grows by eating.
5. After all, tomorrow is another day.
6. A house is a living-machine.
7. A riot is at bottom the language of the unheard.
8. Education makes us what we are.
9. No time like the present.
10. You can't step twice into the same river.
11. There was an old owl liv'd in an oak
    The more he heard, the less he spoke;
    The less he spoke, the more he heard
    O, if men were all like that wise bird!
12. If all the good people were clever,
    And all the clever people were good,
    The world would be nicer than ever
    We thought that it possibly could. . .

Another Kind of Reading . . . For Fun (1–5)

Mystery Word = VICTORY

A Crossword with a Difference (1–7)

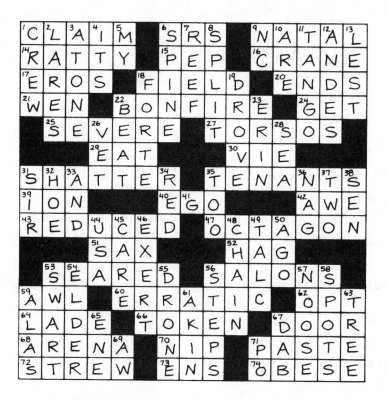

Guide to Taking Notes: Australia—
A Penal Colony (1–8A)

Part I.

1. Cook discovers Australia
2. first convicts transported from England
3. total of 83,000 people sent to Tasmania , New South Wales

A. In time of penal colonies

1. stealing a rabbit; seven years in penal colony
2. stealing silver spoons; 300 lashes

   3. not flogging hard enough; being flogged oneself

   4. murdering another convict; hanging

   5. witness to a convict's murder; hanging

   6. stealing 26 cents' worth of bacon; hanging

B. In England during Twain's earlier visit

   1. wife-beating; 25 lashes

   2. choking to rob someone; 25 lashes

Part II. Here is a sample of what might be included in a student report:

Eighteen years after its discovery, Australia become an English penal colony. From 1788-1831, England transported a total of 83,000 men, women, and children to be imprisoned in the states of New South Wales and Tasmania. People were sent to Australia for crimes that ranged from petty to serious. The sentence for stealing a rabbit was seven years there. A convict stealing silver spoons might receive 300 lashes while a convict who witnessed another convict's murder could be hanged himself. These are typical of the cruel punishments inflicted at this time.

More Than Just the Facts (1–8B)

A. Sample quotes reveal Twain's attitude. Students may choose other quotes or portions thereof.

   1. Quoting one who called it " the cruelest discipline ever known"

   2. "Convict life. . . so unendurable"

   3. The term "civilized" could not be applied

   4. "Not advanced toward a high grade of civilization"

   5. ". . . Between convict and master . . . a noticeable monotony of sameness"

B. With what two words did Twain describe the effect being punished with 25 lashes had on wife-beaters and garroters?

   1. great

   2. wholesome

Dialogue with an Author (1–9A)

   1. selling them; giving them away

   2. Yes (You may also allow *Probably* as a correct answer.)

   3. The pressure to study for college and feeling it necessary to read would help explain why the books felt like "a million bricks on my heart."

4. Hughes was less likely to be seen throwing away the books at night.

5. True

6. True

7. Hughes felt he was not in control of what he read. He was forced to read for college.

8. Hughes was young and had no experience at sea. His college credits did not qualify him for an officer's job.

9. Yes

10. Going to sea offered a chance for adventure. It also allowed a chance to travel—and get paid for it. *Note: Other valid answers include:* Experiencing life firsthand, not just in the pages of books, and the opportunity to meet many different kinds of people

UNIT 2, ALL WORDS ARE NOT CREATED EQUAL

Reading for Proof (2–1)

Sample corrected version: On Saturday, Oct. 7th, we set out early in the morning, and being somewhat unacquainted with the way, asked it of some people we met. They told us we must ride a mile or two and turn down a lane on the right hand. By their direction we rode on, but not yet coming to the turning, we met a young fellow and asked him how far it was to the lane which turned down towards Guilford. He said we must ride a little further and turn down by the corner of Uncle Sam's lot.

Spelling Dosent Madder—Or Dose It? (2–2)

Sample corrected version:

The Proof Is in the Proofreading

Spelling doesn't matter so long as it's right.

Most of the time when you're reading, nothing could be farther from your mind than looking for errors in spelling, punctuation, and grammar. That's because you expect it to be correct.

A piece of writing isn't really ready to be read until it's proofread.

That's because sloppy or even unintentional mistakes create a bad impression right from the start.

If the writer doesn't care enough to correct his or her errors, readers will decide that he or she can't have much worth saying. Someone who doesn't care about the details that make it possible to read more easily also probably hasn't bothered to get facts straight, hasn't thought through his or her ideas, and doesn't know how to express them interestingly and well.

Discussing "Royal Exile" (2–3A)

1. Man is unpopular with eagles and rabbits because he hunts and kills them. Cattle have reason to dislike man because he feeds and protects them, but only to slaughter them later for food and leather. Big game like elephants are also on man's "hit list" to be killed for sport or ivory. (Students might also name other animals, like tigers and pandas, that are endangered species because humans have taken their territory as well as capturing and killing them.)

2. Markham must mean "dumb" in the sense of unable to talk because dogs and horses can't explain how they really feel, and the man is trying to pay them a compliment by using words like "noble" and "loyal" to describe them.

3. The advantages for horses and dogs are that man feeds and takes care of them. The disadvantages are that they have to obey humans as their masters, give up their freedom, and sometimes suffer cruel treatment.

4. Markham was delighted with Camciscan, but he had been forced to come to a new place, accept new masters, and a new way of life so perhaps it was not so delightful for him.

Note: Markham does not provide the meaning or pronunciation of Camciscan in her book.

What's the Difference? (2–3B)

1. S	6. D
2. S	7. D
3. S	8. S
4. D	9. S
5. S	10. D

Counting on Strong Words (2–4A)

Nouns	Verbs	Adjectives
1. eagle	1. must seem	1. masterful
2. owl	2. has	2. forlorn
3. rabbit	3. points	3. two
4. man	4. are	4. universal
5. animal	5. believes	5. peculiar
6. friends	6. are	6. proud
7. unpopularity	7. says	7. alleged
8. pride	8. look	8. two
9. two	9. are	9. noble
10. dog	10. are	10. dumb

11. horse	11. have suspected	11. loyal
12. innocence	12. are	12. tolerant
13. confraternity	13. have depended	13. suspecting* (verbal/participle)
14. friends	14. were	14. past
15. years	15. should feel	15. gentle
16. tolerance	16. had lost	16. kind
17. life	17. have been	17. alike
18. dog	18. remember	
19. horse	19. is	
20. keeping	20. can(not) recall	
21. contact	21. owned	
22. earth	22. owned	
23. Horses	23. knew	
24. particular	24. were	
25. part	25. were	
26. life	26. was	
27. birthdays		
28. phase		
29. childhood		
30. remembering* (gerund)		
31. horse		
32. one		
33. father		
34. one		
35. Camciscan		
36. one		

Comparison of Totals: Nouns *36*   Verbs *26*   Adjectives   *17*

Counting Strong Words in "A Passionate Shepherd to His Love" (2–5A)

Nouns	**Verbs**	**Adjectives**
1. love	1. come	1. steepy
2. pleasures	2. live	2. seeing[†] (verbal/participle)
3. hills	3. be	3. shallow
4. valleys	4. ill prove	4. melodious
5. dales	5. yields	5. thousand
6. fields	6. will sit	6. fragrant
7. woods	7. feed	7. embroidered[†] (verbal/participle)
8. mountain	8. sing	8. made[†] (verbal/participle)
9. shepherds	9. will make	9. finest
10. flocks	10. pull	10. pretty
11. rivers	11. may move	11. fair-lined[†] (verbal/participle)

---

*These can also be considered verb forms.
[†]May be considered verb forms, as well as participial adjectives

12. falls	12. come	12. purest
13. birds	13. live	13. coral
14. madrigals	14. be	14. amber
15. beds	15. shall dance	15. May
16. roses	16. sing	
17. posies	17. may move	
18. cap	18. live	
19. flowers	19. be	
20. kirtle		
21. leaves		
22. myrtle		
23. gown		
24. wool		
25. slippers		
26. cold		
27. buckles		
28. gold		
29. belt		
30. straw		
31. ivy-buds		
32. clasps		
33. studs		
34. shepherd-swain		
35. delight		
36. morning		
37. delights		
38. mind		

Comparison of Totals: Nouns *38* Verbs *19* Adjectives *15*

Kangaroo: Symbol of Australia (2–6A)

Sample rewritten version:

Australia is the land of the kangaroo. For centuries, aboriginal tribes have depicted kangaroos on totems and used them as the subject of rituals. Today its image is on the national coat of arms. To foreigners the kangaroo is the symbol of Australia. It is incorrect to speak of it as if it were a single species. There are 90 varieties. Some are no larger than rats. Others are as tall as humans. Some of them are essentially inhabitants of deserts. Others live in the eastern rain forest. All are vegetarians, except for the musky rat kangaroo, which also feeds on insects.

Not Equal, but Genuinely Needed (2–7)

The following is one way of restating the over-written paragraph.

A Case of Selling Too Hard*

Some corporations that do business with many different countries around the world try to influence people in underdeveloped lands to buy products for which they have no real need. Such companies try to encourage the purchase of "quick-fix" and convenience items that are better-suited to the lives of people living in technologically advanced societies than the lives of those in the third world, whose basic needs go unmet.

Discussion: From Forewords & Afterwords *(2–8A)*

1. Except for the example, Auden consistently uses the words *children* and *child*, showing that he means his words to apply to both girls and boys.

2. Auden thinks it is harmful to expect a child to be a top student if the child is stupid. (*Note*: You might wish to discuss Auden's use of the word *stupid,* which would not be used by modern educators. Do students think he is being too blunt? Have them compare his bluntness with such modern terms as "learning disabled" or "learning disadvantaged" and decide whether or not Auden's point is sound but would be better if put in a more diplomatic way.)

3. Auden believes it is wrong to encourage children to follow in their parents' footsteps if their talents and abilities are not suited for this field. If they are, he feels there is nothing wrong with parents having such ambitions.

4. Auden believes it is helpful for parents to demand high standards. His proof is that, in his experience, the majority of children with parents who were ambitious for them become successful and credit their parents for much of their success.

5. Students will have their own opinions and reasons for their beliefs.

How Good Writers Use Strong Words (2–8B)

Most *modern books* on *bringing* up *children warn parents* against *projecting* their *own ambitions* onto their *children* and *demanding* of them a *high standard* of *achievement*. It *seems* to me that this *warning* is *merited only* in *cases* where there is *no relation* between the *parents' ambition* and the *child's* actual *endowments*. If the *child* is *stupid,* it is obviously *harmful* to *show anger* or *shame* because he is *not* at the *top* of the class, just as it is *wrong* for a *father* to *try* to *force* a *son* with a *talent* for, say *engineering,* into the *family grocery business*. But there are *many cases* in which a *parent's ambition* is quite *justified*—if his *child* is *talented* in the *way* which the *parent believes*. From *my* own *experience,* I would say that, in the *majority* of *cases,* the *children* of *parents*

---

*You might discuss whether the "Hard Sell" refers to the multinational companies or to the fact that the writer is trying too hard to sell himself as a superior person with a superior vocabulary.

who were *ambitious* for them *are successful* and, *whatever* the *conflicts* and *mistakes* may have been, they *recognize* in *later life* how *much* they *owe* their *success* to the *high standards* of *achievement* which was *demanded* from them at *home*.

by W. H. Auden

Search and Scan Exercise (2–9A)

1. 1670, 1713, 1734, 1740, 1713, 1754, 1713, 1730, 1733
2. Nova Scotia, Georgia, Pennsylvania, North Carolina, Maryland, Pennsylvania
3. 85,000; 360,000
4. Philadelphia, Charleston, Norfolk, Baltimore, Philadelphia
5. 12

UNIT 3, WHEN TO USE A DICTIONARY

Making the Educated Guess (3–1)

Note: Credit student "educated guesses" if they are on the right track.

1. i. a kind of flower
2. f. a breed of dog
3. d. act of going backward, getting worse
4. e. soundness of moral character, including honesty
5. b. very small, tiny
6. j. wishing harm or evil to others
7. h. to scold severely
8. o. temporary, lasting only briefly
9. g. doubt or disbelief
10. l. acting on sudden impulse
11. n. a sign; one that announces
12. k. amusement and/or laughter
13. c. unmindful, unaware
14. m. period of time between
15. a. poor; lacking fullness

How Writers Help You Make Educated Guesses (3–2)

1. seen; heard
2. money
3. curiosity
4. never-ending
5. much wild activity and noise
6. fear
7. harmony
8. fish
9. vague
10. alike; umbrella

Turning to the Dictionary for Help (3–3)

1. fairs
2. calves
3. monkeys
4. moose

5. tomatoes   8. empresses
6. skies   9. fish or fishes
7. witches   10. humans

Finding It in the Dictionary (3–4A)

1. A. 3; B. 6; C. 9
2. a. C - Random House
   b. found at the end, not
      near the beginning
3. a. A. 1; B. 4; C. 3
   b. to show
   c. idea, notion
4. a. A
   b. Music, Psychology
5. a. phantasy
   b. A
6. C
7. Grotesque means ugly;
   unreal means non-existent
8. a. imaginative poem, play, etc.; A or B
   b. daydreams, usually pleasant; B
      (may also use "daydream" from C)
   c. hallucinations; C

Words with Two Meanings (3–5)

1. a. the rank below sergeant; a non-commissioned officer
   b. bodily; of the body
2. a. strong and offensive in smell or taste
   b. an official grade of military service
3. a. a city that is the seat of government of a state or nation
   b. involving loss of life; giving a sentence of death
4. a. to appeal to; woo; act as a suitor to
   b. to go to court against in an attempt to right an alleged wrong
5. a. crushed into fine particles
   b. the solid surface of the earth
6. a. a strip of stiffening material
   b. to remain; continue in the same place
7. a. a deer less than one year old
   b. to cringe and flatter, treating another as a superior
8. a. seriousness
   b. the pull of all bodies on the earth's surface towards its center
9. a. on purpose, carefully thought out beforehand
   b. consider carefully, as in a court case
10. a. to divide by a blow; split
    b. cling (to); be faithful (to)

Words with a Past (3–6)

Definition in Sentence	Other Sense
1. i	belonging to a count or earl
2. h	a spike road barrier preventing passage until toll is paid; also used in time of war

3. e	graze; feed on pasture; nibble at leaves, shoots, etc.
4. j	terror or awe; also admiration, dread, reverence
5. c	travelers or pilgrims; also gypsies, pioneers in wagon trains, desert peoples on camels
6. d	to scatter or spread over an area, as seeds
7. g	rooster or other fowl
8. b	to chew the cud as . . . cattle, deer, and camels do
9. a	a shepherd
10. f	to gather or collect grain left by reapers or regular gatherers

Context Clues to "Little, But Tricky" Words (3–7)

A. Over
1. c
2. e
3. f

C. Up
1. f
2. a
3. c

E. By
1. d
2. c
3. f

G. Too
1. d
2. a

B. Through
1. b
2. d
3. a

D. For
1. e
2. f
3. b

F. Along
1. b
2. e

H. Off
1. a
2. f
3. d

Recognizing Shades of Meaning (3–8)

A. Journey
1. expedition
2. trek
3. voyage
4. outing
5. tour
6. pilgrimage

B. Slow
1. deliberate
2. gradual
3. lackadaisical
4. sluggish
5. leaden
6. dawdling

C. Produce
1. construct
2. generate
3. compose
4. assemble
5. develop

Choosing the Right Synonyms (3–9)

A. Journey
1. tour
2. pilgrimage
3. expedition
4. outing
5. trek
6. voyage

B. Slow
1. lackadaisical
2. leaden
3. gradual
4. deliberate
5. sluggish
6. dawdling

C. Produce
1. develop
2. construct
3. assemble
4. composed
5. generate

More Practice with Synonyms (3–10)

   A. *Clear*

   1. readily observed; conspicuous
   2. easy to see or understand
   3. cannot be mistaken or misinterpreted
   4. that can be seen
   5. clearly marked off; not alike
   6. perfectly clear; transparent

   B. *Flow*

   1. to cause to flow in a continuous stream; to flow freely, abundantly
   2. to make or flow with a bubbling sound
   3. to move or cause to move with a whirling motion
   4. to move with a sudden, strong increase of power
   5. to move in a circuit or a circle and return, as the blood does

   C. *Ordinary*

   1. dull; monotonous
   2. done or acquired by habit; steady
   3. likely to occur or appear
   4. done as a regular procedure; customary or prescribed
   5. having the same characteristics as others of a group, class, etc.
   6. handed down from generation to generation or done by custom

Putting Synonyms in Their Places (3–11)

A. *Clear*	B. *Flow*	C. *Ordinary*
1. visible	1. swirl	1. expected
2. distinct	2. gurgle	2. habitual
3. unmistakable	3. pour	3. typical
4. obvious	4. circulate	4. traditional
5. noticeable	5. surge	5. humdrum
6. limpid		

What's in a Name? (3–12A)

Example 1	*Example 2*	*Example 3*
face	home	wisdom
look	house	good sense
features	household	intelligence
kisser	dwelling	judgment
countenance	residence	prudence

mien	domicile	sagacity
visage	abode	acumen
physiognomy	habitation	perspicacity

Discussing "Discontent" (3–13A)

1. The man was ashamed of being poor and thought using the embroidered coat would make him look better off.

2. Even though their loves caused them grief, they were too much in love to get rid of their painful burdens.

3. One man wanted to get rid of his memory so he could forget his guilt and all of the crimes he'd committed. Another gave up his modesty so he wouldn't be ashamed or embarrassed when he revealed his ignorance. Perhaps he was also too ignorant to know better.

4. Students will differ about what is humorous. The serious point is that one should not envy others who seem better off, for their misfortunes might seem worse than yours if you traded places. Also, people should try to bear their misfortunes with patience to make them seem less troublesome.

5. Much of the people's unhappiness was due to imagination—their fantasies or fancies that others were more fortunate than themselves.

Discontent: Understanding Meaning Through Context (3–13B)

Note: Accept students' interpretations from context if they fit the basic idea of its usage in the passage.

1. thrown; throw, fling, hurl
2. collection, group; supply of goods or items
3. thinking; (from an earlier exercise)
4. announced, declared; announced officially
5. misfortunes, troubles; great misfortunes, disasters
6. huge; wonderful, amazing, enormous
7. strange; confused, not concentrating
8. person, human being; one who doesn't live forever
9. amusement, enjoyment; entertainment, amusement
10. bundle, burden; bundle, burden (Archaic)
11. a great number; a large number
12. unusual, unexpected; oddly out of the ordinary
13. (See no. 5)
14. (See no. 11)
15. bad tempers, diseases; disorders of mind, body/diseases

16. combination; complicated or involved state or condition/complex combination

17. known; that can happen, likely to happen

18. a kind of disease; a human organ once thought as responsible for certain emotions, making *disease* valid

19. bad, nasty, mean; irritable/short-tempered

20. bad trait, error; foolishness/a senseless act

21. weaknesses, bad traits; moral weaknesses

22. bad, evil; recklessly wasteful, immoral

23. worthless, no-good fellow; scoundrel/wicked person

24. width; width

25. sorts, mood; "out of humor"/bad mood

26. face; face, expression

27. face; face, look

28. order, announcement; official announcement

29. misfortune, calamity, grief, misery, etc.; pain, suffering

30. home; home/dwelling

31. sickness; a mild illness

32. bratty, delinquent, bad; lacking sense of what is proper

33. trading, swapping; trade by exhanging without money

34. trading, swapping; exchange, barter

35. visage; (See no. 27)

36. strange, funny; distorted, ridiculous

37. aware, sensitive; aware

38. long, standing out; sticking out, conspicuous

39. long, thin sticks; a stick used in trap-ball*

40. fatty part of legs below knees in back; fleshy back part of leg below the knee

41. sad, pitiful; deserving or causing pity

42. complaints, sorrowing; expressions of grief

43. did, completed; performed a duty

44. place; place as filled by a substitute

45. manner, appearance; the way one appears

46. comfortable, satisfactory; convenient, adequate†

47. complain; show discontent, complain

48. sympathy, understanding; deep sympathy, pity

---

*Probably not in most students' dictionaries
†(from etymology) Student guesses in this context might be more accurate than modern dictionaries as this word's meaning has undergone changes

UNIT 4, A MEETING OF MINDS

Identifying a Writer's Point of View (4–1A)

Part A

1. Third Person	6. Third Person
2. First Person	7. Third Person
3. First Person	8. First Person
4. Third Person	9. Third Person
5. First Person	10. First Person

Part B

1. "You" is anyone planning or thinking about taking a trip abroad.
2. The person reading may not do this or may no longer be in school.
3. (1) c
   (2) b
   (3) Although many students may agree they feel this way, there may also be differences of opinion. If so, it will show one of the weaknesses of using "you" in this non-specific sense.

Writing in First- and Third-Person Points of View (4–1B)

Students' sentences should include a variety of first-person pronouns and at least two direct quotations.

Always the First Person (4–2)

1. W	6. N
2. N	7. N
3. W	8. N
4. W	9. W
5. W	10. N

A Meeting of Minds (4–3)

Part A

1. b, c
2. a
3. b

Part B

1. O	4. O
2. SP	5. SP
3. SP	6. O

7. SP	10. SP
8. O	11. SP
9. SP	12. O

A Matter of Opinion (4–5)

1. a. T	2. a. T	3. a. O
b. T	b. T	b. O
c. O	c. O	c. T
d. O	d. T	d. O

Recognizing "Charged" Words (4–6)

Part A.
1. claimed
2. *Mob* makes the people seem likely to riot; a *crowd* is just a large group of people so the word does not suggest it is about to turn violent.
3. (1) An *attitude* is simply an opinion, while a *belief* is deeply felt and held.
   (2) take the attitude
4. (1) a
   (2) *Responsible* merely indicates the person did it, perhaps unintentionally; *guilty* makes it seem likely to be criminal or immoral.

Part B.
1. did not accept
2. inappropriate
3. plain
4. unwise
5. questioned

Dealing with Doublespeak (4–7)

1. e. method of discipline; ways to make kids behave
2. d. handicapped; having a disability
3. h. not favoring either sex, male or female
4. k. prisons
5. b. broken; not working
6. n. the poor section of a town
7. c. firing workers to increase profits
8. o. people getting rid of a group of people they hate

9. l. a test
10. f. an item *not* free because you must buy another item to get it
11. j. poor, needy
12. m. the act of being fired from a workplace
13. a. teacher
14. i. one well above or below average
15. g. a word or words not found offensive by a member of the group it refers to

Fancy Words, Simple Ideas (4–8)

1. f
2. d
3. e
4. a
5. c

In Other Words: Familiar Sayings in Disguise (4–9)

1. A bird in the hand is worth two in the bush.
2. A fool and his money are soon parted.
3. A penny saved is a penny earned.
4. The early bird gets the worm.
5. Better late than never.

A Taste of Humor (4–10A)

A. (1) "How do you manage to do it?" "Don't you find it difficult?" (Or similar types of questions.)
   (2) It's likely no one ever asked this, so "often" draws attention to how ridiculous the question is.
B. (1) It is a kind of prison.
   (2) Since a teacher corrects compositions, he's punning that a schoolhouse is also a kind of house of correction.
C. (1) He said so himself.
   (2) He could be lying.
   (3) Opinion. Animals communicate, but there are questions about whether they actually talk in a human sense.
D. (1) They don't really use words as humans do.
   (2) using comparison and flowery figures (ready and fluent delivery is another possibility)
   (3) showing off; liking to talk a great deal; acting conceited and interested in no one but themselves

E. (1) You love the other person and want to be sure he or she loves you.
   (2) "I forgot" seems to indicate the other's feelings aren't very important to the asker.
   (3) It seems a contradiction to ask this question if you don't care enough to remember the answer.
   (4) Answer can vary widely.

A Taste of Humor (4–10B)

A. (1) The first method is technical, but the second is just a matter of opinion, which can't be taken as a serious way of classifying sonnets.
   (2) Anyone who can read the paragraph can undoubtably count to 14. The idea that they might not be able to is clearly ridiculous.
   (3) This contradicts the statement about sonnets having 14 lines. Anything longer or shorter wouldn't be a sonnet.
   (4) Any poem with more than 14 lines isn't a sonnet, so paying a sonnet writer by the line can't be taken seriously.
B. (1) Good. *Example:* a chance to travel to Europe; an offer of a job at good wages; etc. (Students' answers will vary.)
   (2) No. Acquiring something new to worry about is not generally thought to be good or a genuine opportunity.
   (3) It would be floating scientific equipment, perhaps a burned-out satellite, too large to be casually dropped in a trash bin.
   (4) He compares it to the way he felt when he was blamed for his sister's messiness.
C. (1) The negative approach is typical of adults, who always seem to tell kids what not or never to do, at least as kids see it.
   (2) It makes it seem as if he would swallow bones or choke on purpose, not by accident.
   (3) (a) The usual expression is "play with fire," not flames.
       (b) "Flames" rhymes with James.
   (4) Kids are often accused of thinking their parents dull and old-fashioned.
   (5) Good. All either would be dangerous, or show lack of consideration and concern for others.
D. (1) Tim says they weighed two pounds and had a 15-inch wingspan.
   (2) No, he is not accurate. A mosquito's wingspan is only a fraction of an inch, so he exaggerates greatly.
   (3) Their reason for going outside was their desire to spit.
   (4) He calls mosquitoes more dangerous than wolves, bears, and bobcats.
E. (1) Sound travels at a set speed, not affected by the noise, its kind, or volume.
   (2) Most people would rather eat than have to get up.
   (3) It's based on common sense of human behavior, not scientific knowledge.

In All Seriousness (4–11)

A. (1) first person
   (2) university career
   (3) becoming a sailor; acquiring a boat
   (4) building a boat
   (5) "I ought to have known better."
B. (1) third person
   (2) The Spanish word *Señora*, not the English *Mrs.*
   (3) Felipe Moreno. Upon his father's death, he became the head of the ranch as he was the eldest son.
   (4) Felipe was ill.
C. (1) third person
   (2) a. everyone
       b. To be true, it needs to apply to more than one specific person.
   (3) b
D. (1) third person
   (2) become accustomed or used to something
   (3) hits or attacks
   (4) a. poor food; b. a long road; c. a hard lot
E. (1) first person
   (2) country
   (3) They were taken to be slaves.
   (4) "When shall I forget . . ."

Serious or Humorous? Determining the Difference— Part I (4–12)

A. (1) serious
   (2) third person
   (3) the beginnings of modern medicine; or revolution in modern medicine
B. (1) serious
   (2) third person
   (3) the joys of having and using a baseball
C. (1) humorous
   (2) third person
   (3) surprise or unexpected twists
D. (1) serious
   (2) first person
   (3) the extent of someone's love
E. (1) humorous
   (2) first person
   (3) flaws in logic

Serious or Humorous? Determining the Difference—Part II (4–13)

A. (1) serious
   (2) third person
   (3) time as a discovery
B. (1) humorous
   (2) third person ("Ah" or I is in quotes)
   (3) exaggeration (also, dialect, although not given as a choice)
C. (1) humorous
   (2) first person
   (3) surprise; an unexpected twist
D. (1) humorous
   (2) first person
   (3) making fun of human nature (Students may wish to discuss this attitude of a mother towards her obviously teenage son, both pro and con.)
E. (1) serious
   (2) first person
   (3) what it's like to swim in a pond

UNIT 5, THE READER AS REPORTER

In the News: The 5 W's and an H (5–1A)

1. **Who or What?** Xavier Powers
   Did What? was named Athlete of the Year
   When? Friday
   Where? at all-city sports banquet
   Why? because of record-breaking scoring in basketball
   How? ———-

2. **Who or What?** Betina Everett, psychologist
   Did What? warns teenagers about false goals
   When? recently
   Where? in her book *Fads and Fantasies*
   Why? ———-
   How? by exposing twisted standards

3. **Who or What?** opponents of sports arena
   Did What? plan to stage protest
   When? tonight
   Where? at council meeting
   Why? hoping to convince members to vote "no"
   How? by showing signed petitions

4. **Who or What?** Spunky, a dog
   Did What? alerted Garcia family (to a fire)
   When? early this morning
   Where? in their Sloane Avenue home
   Why? (because of the fire)
   How? by barking, whining, and pawing

5. **Who or What?** Eastgate's 86-85 win
   Did What? strengthened Eastgate's chances
   When? Tuesday night

Where? at home
Why? ———
How? by putting Eastgate in a tie for first (could be considered "why")

In the News: The 5 W's and an H (5–1B)

1. **Who or What?** Rayman Webster
Did What? received the top award
When? today
Where? in Capital City
Why? his painting was best of 2,000 entries*
How? by winning the statewide Young Artists contest*
2. **Who or What?** Toni Grace
Did What? saved a 4-year-old girl from drowning
When? yesterday
Where? in a neighbor's pool
Why? because she felt somebody had to do it
How? (by going to her help—only implied so may be left blank)
3. **Who or What?** sunken Spanish galleon
Did What? was discovered
When? Saturday
Where? off Mexico's coast
Why? because of map, equipment, and luck
How? by divers
4. **Who or What?** police
Did What? issued a warning about con men
When? today
Where? in Carlton
Why? to prevent further robberies
How? (by publishing the news—only implied so may be left blank)

5. **Who or What?** Clarissa Kraft
Did What? said her job looks more glamorous than it is
When? today
Where? in an interview
Why? because of long hours and difficult rehearsals
How? speaking to local media

Textbook Topics: The Five W's and an H (5–4)

1. **Who or What?** Calvin Coolidge
Did What? became 30th U.S. President
When? in 1923
Where? United States
Why? President Harding died suddenly
How? by having been vice president (also has a sense of "Why")
2. **Who or What?** osteopathic medicine
Did or Does What? treats patients by manipulation
When? since 1874
Where? in the United States
Why? because of its theory about the cause of ailments
How? by manipulating affected bones and muscles
3. **Who or What?** Eskimos
Did or Do What? rarely live in igloos
When? in winter
Where? in cold far north
Why? live in sod, wood, or stone shelters
How? ———
4. **Who or What?** pony express riders
Did What? carried mail some 2,000 miles in about eight days
When? in 1860

---

*How and Why are closely related and could be switched.

Where? Saint Joseph, Missouri, to Sacramento, California
Why? for fast delivery
How? by riding in relays, changing horses and riders

5. **Who or What?** plate tectonics
Did or Does What? envisions Earth as once one super-continent
When? 100 million years ago
Where? on planet Earth
Why? because of jigsaw fit of coastlines
How?——

The Five W's and an H in Prose Literature (5–5)

Note: Allow credit for answers that vary somewhat but can be justified by the text.

1. **Who or What?** Mr. and Mrs. Delahanty
Did What? lingered at breakfast table
When? Saturday morning at six o'clock
Where? on their ranch
Why? Mrs. Delahanty was talking about the hat
How? ——

2. **Who or What?** Durante
Did What? rode slowly
When? —— (give credit for educated guesses)
Where? on the way to Tony's house (in the desert)
Why? he thought there was no hurry
How? (on horseback—not stated, but implied)

3. **Who or What?** Harriet Beecher Stowe
Did What? went to see President Lincoln
When? November, 1863
Where? in the President's study

Why? to see about the Emancipation Proclamation
How? ——

4. **Who or What?** I — first-person speaker (Agnes's mother?)
Did What? left on a long journey
When? before dawn on a frosty morning
Where? at a farm, heading into the wilderness
Why? anxious to arrive before dark
How? ——

5. **Who or What?** I—a boy with a paper route
Did What? hurried to finish job to get home
When? in September, before daybreak
Where? in a town
Why? the circus was in town
How? by rushing madly

More Practice with Prose Literature (5–6)

Note: Allow credit for answers that vary somewhat but can be justified by the text.

1. **Who or What?** William
Did What? remembered he had nothing for children
When? on way to the station
Where? on way to station
Why? ——
How? with a pang of disappointment

2. **Who or What?** I—first-person speaker
Did What? was arrested
When? December in 1949
Where? Paris
Why? as a receiver of stolen goods
How? through an American tourist

3. **Who or What?** Krueger

Did What? felt something gone wrong
When? as the steamer was getting ready to leave
Where? from Brazil
Why? for reasons he didn't understand
How? because of a vague sense of trouble

4. **Who or What?** a cowboy
Did What? swore bitterly
When? in winter
Where? in Nebraska
Why? remembered small boys followed him
How? ——

5. **Who or What?** Molly
Did What? kept thinking her husband had changed
When? over and over during the train ride
Where? in Canada
Why? his face seemed different
How? with the thought thudding hollowly through her mind

Using the 5 W's and an H in Poetry, Too (5–7)

1. **Who or What?** Kubla Khan
Did What? decreed (or ordered) a pleasure dome
Where: in Xanadu (also possibly where the river Alph ran)

2. **Who or What?** the embattled farmers
Did What? stood and fired the shot heard round the world
When: in April; **Where:** by the bridge

3. **Who or What?** the harp
Did or Does What? hangs mute or silent
Where: in Tara's walls; **Why:** the souls seem to have fled

4. **Who or What?** I—first-person speaker

Did What? have reached these lands
When: but newly; **How:** by a lonely route
Where: also possible to answer "these lands"

5. **Who or What?** a pause
Did What? comes
When: between dark and daylight (or in the evening)
Why: to be known as the Children's Hour

6. **Who or What?** I—first-person speaker
Did What? stand
Where: at the prow of a ship
Why: because the speaker is tired of feeling pressured and is going over the sea

Identifying the "You's" in Poems (5–8A)

Note: Allow credit for answers that vary somewhat but can be justified by the text.

1. **Who or What?** You
Did or Does What? (have) heard of the one-hoss shay
Is *you* stated or unstated? stated
What does *you* mean? the reader

2. **Who or What?** You
Did or Does What? sing no sad songs for me
Is *you* stated or unstated? unstated
What does *you* mean? "my dearest," someone the speaker loves

3. **Who or What?** You
Did or Does What? hear the bells
Is *you* stated or unstated? unstated
What does *you* mean? anyone

able to hear or imagine hearing the bells

4. **Who or What?** You (good people)
   Did or Does What? give ear or hear my song
   Is *you* **stated or unstated?** stated
   What does *you* **mean?** good people

5. **Who or What?** What immortal hand or eye
   Did or Does What? could frame thy fearful symmetry
   Is *you* **stated or unstated?** stated as "thy"; not stated as "you"

What does *you* **mean?** the tiger

6. **Who or What?** You (ladies)
   Did or Does What? sigh no more
   Is *you* **stated or unstated?** unstated
   What does *you* **mean?** ladies

7. **Who or What?** a maiden (named Annabel Lee)
   Did or Does What? lived with no other thought, etc.
   Is *you* **stated or unstated?** stated
   What does *you* **mean?** used as a way to involve the reader or average person

Outlining "Specialists in Sleep" (5–10A)

I. Major in sleep offered Bowling Green State University students
   A. Don't earn degree dozing in class
      1. Are candidates for doctoral degree
      2. Studying to be sleep specialists in field of psychology
   B. Likely to spend nights in speech lab
      1. Seek to discover what happens during sleep
      2. Stay awake while others are sleeping

II. Sleep not fully understood, according to lab director Dr. Pietro Badia
   A. Scientists unable to specify what is normal and abnormal
   B. Total loss of memory experienced during sleep
   C. Difference between scientific results and people's honest beliefs
      1. Some monitored as sleeping soundly contrary to their opinions
      2. Others reporting sound sleep monitored awakening up to 500 times

III. How lab and students obtain accurate information
   A. Sleepers recorded by sleep-monitoring instruments
      1. Scored and evaluated by students
      2. 1,000–1,500 feet of paper recorded in one night
   B. Cameras also focused on volunteer sleepers
      1. Able to "see" in total darkness
      2. Videotapes allow observation from control center
   C. Volunteers "wired" to electrodes recording wave patterns in six areas
      1. Knowledge needed of proper placement and interpretation of results
      2. Graphs, mounds of paperwork—with own stories to tell

Outlining "The Background of Mythology" (5–11A)

I. Religions of Greece and Rome now extinct
   A. No worshippers left among living men
      1. Not part of theology or religion
      2. Belongs to literature and thought
   B. Holds a lasting place
      1. Closely connected with poetry and art, ancient and modern
      2. Will not pass into oblivion
II. Earth a flat, circular disk to Greeks
   A. Greece in middle
   B. Two possibilities for central point
      1. Olympus, home of gods
      2. Delphi, famous for oracle
III. Greeks' picture of the Earth
   A. Divided into equal parts by the *Sea*, or Mediterranean
   B. Surrounded by *River Ocean*
      1. Flowing south to north on the west
      2. Flowing in opposite direction to the east
      3. Always with a steady, even current
IV. Special races at Earth's edge
   A. The Hyperboreans
      1. Inhabited northern portion of Earth
      2. Dwelt in everlasting bliss and spring
   B. The Ætheopians
      1. Lived on south, close to the stream of Coacean
      2. Both happy and virtuous
      3. Favored by gods, who sometimes visited them
   C. People of the Elysian Plain
      1. On western side, by the stream of Ocean
      2. Transported to immortality without tasting death
      3. Region also called Fortunate Fields and Isles of the Blessed
V. Knew little of real peoples other than Greeks
   A. Imagined western part of sea held giants, monsters, enchantresses
   B. Believed peoples favored by gods lived around the Earth's disk

Drawing Valid Conclusions (5–12A)

A.	B.	C.	D.
(1) +	(1) +	(1) +	(1) +
(2) o	(2) +	(2) +	(2) o
(3) o	(3) o	(3) +	(3) o
(4) +	(4) +	(4) o	(4) +
(5) o	(5) o	(5) o	(5) o

Drawing Conclusions About Literature (5–13)

A. (1) o　　B. (1) +　　C. (1) o　　D. (1) +
　 (2) +　　　 (2) +　　　 (2) +　　　 (2) o
　 (3) o　　　 (3) o　　　 (3) +　　　 (3) +
　 (4) +　　　 (4) o　　　 (4) o　　　 (4) +
　 (5) o　　　 (5) o　　　 (5) o　　　 (5) o

Drawing Conclusions About Literature (5–14)

A. (1) +　　B. (1) +　　C. (1) +　　D. (1) +
　 (2) +　　　 (2) +　　　 (2) o　　　 (2) +
　 (3) o　　　 (3) o　　　 (3) +　　　 (3) o
　 (4) o　　　 (4) +　　　 (4) +　　　 (4) o
　 (5) +　　　 (5) o　　　 (5) o　　　 (5) o

UNIT 6, WHEN COMPLICATIONS ARISE

Note: Student answers in this unit will vary. Allow credit if they contain the right basic elements and make proper sense. Some possible additions are noted in parentheses, although others may also be valid.

Breaking Up Busy Sentences (6–1A)

A. Who or What?	**Did or Does What?**
(1) We	saw the first faint blushes (of morning)
(2) the sun	would rise
(3) the day	promised to be a good one

B. Who or What?	**Did or Does What?**
(1) Tony	waited
(2) Cindy	asked the teacher (about . . . assignment)
(3) they	headed (for the cafeteria and lunch)

C. Who or What?	**Did or Does What?**
(1) We	left the movie
(2) Both Chet and I	agreed
(3) we	expected it to end (differently)
(4) everything	pointed (to a happy ending)

D. Who or What?	**Did or Does What?**
(1) Coach Andrews	is well-respected
(2) he	treats everyone (fairly)
(3) he	demands discipline
(4) he	cares (about his players)

E. Who or What?	Did or Does What?
(1) I	believe
(2) most people	want to do well
(3) they	(often) become confused and discouraged
(4) they	don't get the kind of results
(5) they	want
(6) they	(just) quit trying

Breaking Up Busy Sentences (6–1B)

A. Who or What?	Did or Does What?
(1) Daisy	stood
(2) Billy	climbed (frantically) (over Elmer)
(3) the little one	toddled (smilingly about)

B. Who or What?	Did or Does What?
(1) We	began to see symptoms of vegetation
(2) we	had reached a pretty Indian village
(3) we	stopped to change mules
(4) the light	had broken in
(5) we	seemed to have been transported

C. Who or What?	Did or Does What?
(1) I	mean
(2) they	read (slowly and with effort)
(3) it	tires them
(4) they	do not read (as easily [as they breathe])
(5) they	breathe

D. Who or What?	Did or Does What?
(1) He (Ishmael Bush)	boasted
(2) he	had never dwelt (in a place)
(3) he	might not (safely) fell every tree
(4) he	could view (from his own threshold)
(5) the law	had (rarely) been known to enter his clearing
(6) his ears	had never (willingly) admitted the sound of a church bell

E. Who or What?	Did or Does What?
(1) We	hold these truths to be self-evident
(2) all men	are created equal
(3) they	are endowed (by their creator) with certain . . . rights
(4) life, liberty, and the pursuit of happiness	are (among these)

The Real Meanings of There and It (6–2A)

A. Who or What?   **Did or Does What?**

(1) no satisfactory answers   were given to the questions
(2) that (questions)   had been bothering us
(3) we   left the meeting (angrily)
(4) our time   had been wasted (by attending)

B. Who or What?   **Did or Does What?**

(1) a time of celebration   was (it)
(2) everyone   awaited the return of our hometown hero
(3) who (the hero)   won two gold medals

C. Who or What?   **Did or Does What?**

(1) The explorers   started off (on their expedition)
(2) many well-wishers   were (on hand)
(3) everyone   knew
(4) they   faced a journey
(5) that (the journey)   was bound to be both long and dangerous

D. Who or What?   **Did or Does What?**

(1) the snake   looked harmless
(2) no sense   was (in taking chances)
(3) good reason   was for doing so
(4) the woodsman   did not wish to disturb a creature
(5) that (the creature)   was hurting no one

E. Who or What?   **Did or Does What?**

(1) no way   is to tell
(2) method   will work out (best)
(3) you   will have to try one out
(4) that (one)   isn't successful
(5) you   can try the other

The Real Meanings of There and It (6–2B)

A. Who or What?   **Did or Does What?**

(1) Old Caesar   lifted up his voice
(2) he (Old Caesar)   was fat and sleepy
(3) yellow rings   were (around his dim old eyes)
(4) which (the yellow rings)   looked (like spectacles)
(5) a neighbor   was
(6) who (the neighbor)   bore (on his hand) the imprint . . . of Caesar's . . . teeth
(7) he (Caesar)   had lived (at the end of a chain . . .)

B. Who or What? | **Did or Does What?**

(1) three sisters — were (fair and bright)
(2) they (the three sisters) — loved one valiant knight
(3) the dove — flies (over the mulberry-tree)

C. Who or What? | **Did or Does What?**

(1) a summer evening — was (it)
(2) Old Kaspar's work — was done
(3) he (Kaspar) — was sitting
(4) his little grandchild Wilhelmine — sported (by him) (on the green)

D. Who or What? | **Did or Does What?**

(1) the whole town — took a lively interest (in the hunger artist)
(2) excitement — mounted
(3) everybody — wanted to see him
(4) people — were (there)
(5) who (people) — bought season tickets . . . and sat
(6) visiting hours — were (there)
(7) the whole effect — was heightened (by torch fires)
(8) the cage — was set (out)
(9) the children's special treat — was to see the hunger artist
(10) he (the hunger artist) — was often just a joke (to their elders)
(11) that (joke) — happened to be in fashion
(12) the children — stood (open-mouthed)

Supplying Understood Words (6–3A)

A. Who or What? | **Did or Does What?**

(1) I — thought of the clean, comfortable surroundings
(2) I — had been reared (in which)
(3) a wave of homesickness — swept (over me)
(4) that (wave of home-sickness) — made me feel faint

B. Who or What? | **Did or Does What?**

(1) I — looked (at the cot)
(2) I — was to sleep (in which [the cot])
(3) (I) — suspected
(4) I — should not be the first to use the sheets and pillowcases
(5) they (sheets and cases) — had come (from the laundry)

C. Who or What? | **Did or Does What?**

(1) The trapper — did not allow his companions time to hesitate

(2) he (the trapper)   (was) dragging them both
(3) he (the trapper)   nearly buried his person (in the fog)
(4) he (the trapper)   was speaking

D. Who or What?   **Did or Does What?**

(1) the three   were (scarcely) bowed (to the ground)
(2) their ears   were saluted
(3) the whizzing of . . . lead   was heard
(4) (the whizzing of . . . lead)   was buzzing

Supplying Understood Words (6–3B)

A. Who or What?   **Did or Does What?**

(1) 1868   was
(2) (I)   (was) looking (at a map of Africa)
(3) (I)   (was) putting my finger (on the . . . space . . .)

(4) I   said to myself (with . . . assurance and . . . audacity)

(5) which (assurance and
      audacity)   are no longer (in my character)
(6) I   grow up
(7) I   shall go (there)

B. Who or What?   **Did or Does What?**

(1) I   wandered (lonely as a cloud)
(2) That (cloud)   floats (on high o'er vales and hills)
(3) I   saw a crowd . . . of golden daffodils
(4) (The daffodils)   (were) fluttering
(5) (The daffodils)   (were) dancing (in the breeze)

C. Who or What?   **Did or Does What?**

(1) I   pondered (. . . over many a volume . . .)
(2) I   nodded
(3) (I)   (was) nearly napping
(4) a tapping   came (suddenly)
(5) some one   (was) gently rapping, rapping

D. Who or What?   **Did or Does What?**

(1) Bailey   didn't look up
(2) she (the grandmother)   wheeled around
(3) (she [the grandmother])   faced the children's mother
(4) whose face   was . . . broad and innocent
(5) (whose face)   was tied around (with a green head-kerchief)

(6) that (the head-kerchief)   had two points (on the top) (like rabbit's ears)

Supplying Understood Words (6–3C)

A. Who or What? **Did or Does What?**

(1) He (Frederic Woolley) was not (without wit)

(2) he (Frederic Woolley) had great knowledge and considerable taste

(3) he (Frederic Woolley) had won a . . . respect for his refusal to accept it

(4) *It* stands for "the movement of the 'new' literature"

B. Who or What? **Did or Does What?**

(1) the scene was altogether (picturesque and striking)

(2) the huts (were) composed (of bamboo)

(3) (the huts) (were) thatched (with palm leaves)

(4) the Indian women . . . (were) standing (at the doors)

(5) the mules (were) rolling themselves (on the ground)

(6) the snow-white goats (were) browsing (amongst the palm trees)

(7) the air (was) soft and balmy

(8) the dew-drops (were) glittering (on the broad leaves . . .)

(9) all around (was) so quiet, cool and still

C. Who or What? **Did or Does What?**

(1) I heard the foxes

(2) they (the foxes) range (over the snow crust . . .)

(3) (the foxes) (were) barking

(4) (the foxes) (were) laboring [as if] (with some anxiety)

(5) (the foxes) (were) seeking expression

(6) (the foxes) (were) struggling (for light and to . . . run freely . . .)

(7) we take the ages (into account)

(8) a civilization may be going on (among the brutes)

D. Who or What? **Did or Does What?**

(1) I heard the learned astonomer

(2) the proofs, the figures were ranged (before me)

(3) I was sitting

(4) I heard the astonomer

(5) he (the astronomer) lectured

(6) I became sick and tired

(7) (I) (was) rising

(8) (I) (was) gliding

(9) I wandered off

(10) (I) looked up (in perfect silence) (at the stars)

A Challenge for "Understanding" Readers (6–4)

A. Who or What? **Did or Does What?**

(1) Paul was a Herculean logger

(2) who (Paul)	combed his beard (with a young tree)
(3) who (Paul)	skidded his timber (with Babe the Blue Ox . . .)
(4) who (Babe)	measured forty-two ax handles . . .
(5) who (Paul)	operated a camp cook house
(6) the flapjack griddle	was greased by twenty-four Arabs
(7) (the Arabs)	(were) imported from the Sahara Desert
(8) they (the Arabs)	could stand the heat
(9) (the Arabs)	(were) skating (to and fro . . .)
(10) slab of bacon	(were) strapped to their feet
(11) who (Paul)	tamed the Mississippi
(12) it (the Mississippi)	was young and wild
(13) who (Paul)	ruled the American country
(14) it (the American country)	was only a timberland . . .

B. Who or What?   **Did or Does What?**

(1) The prairie schooners	first became visible . . .*
(2) (The prairie schooners)	(were) rigged (with canvas tops)*
(3) which (the tops)	gleamed whitely
(4) one	might almost imagine them to be seagulls
(5) (the seagulls)	(were) perched (far, far away)
(6) one	continued to watch
(7) the dots	grew
(8) they (dots or schooners)	came drifting (across the prairie)
(9) they (dots or schooners)	floated (out of the haze . . .)
(10) they (dots or schooners)	proved to be veritable wagons
(11) horses	(were) hitched ahead
(12) folk and all their possessions	(were) inside
(13) a whole herd of cattle	(were) following (behind)

Shorter, but Not Always Better (6–5)

Answers will vary. Allow credit if students have written clear, correct, and understandable sentences. They should include not only Who or What, Did or Does What, but also answers to Where, When, Why, and How, if included in the original. Students may need to use adverbs or adverbial phrases to maintain the meaning of adverbial clauses. However, this will not always be possible. If not, it will help students understand the value of combining sentences.

---

* Accept (1) and (2) if given in transposed order.

Practice in Paraphrasing (6–6A)

1. How much you can play depends upon how much you can pay.

2. Eighty-seven years ago our ancestors created a new country on the North America continent. It began from a concern for freedom and it is devoted to the belief that all people are born equal.

3. On a summer evening
   Old Kaspar had finished his work
   And he was sitting in the sun
   In front of the door of his cottage.
   His little granddaughter Wilhelmine
   Was playing near him in the yard.

4. Human beings are made of more than one element, including spiritual and physical, mental and emotional ones. When people concentrate on one element and ignore the others, they do not develop all of their human capacities. A one-sided person is unaware of half of the opportunities and possibilities that are available in life and exist in the world.

Practice in Paraphrasing (6–6B)

1. Are there any people alive with so few deep feelings
   That they have never told themselves,
   "This is my own country, the nation were I was born!"

2. With respect to reading, it is good to decide upon the outcome you seek and your purpose for reading.* The more clearly you know your own reasons and interests concerning your reading, the more certain and lasting will be your success in achieving your reading goals.

3. The private life of every self-educated person, from Benjamin Franklin on, proves that all were alike because all of them were not only sincere but also careful in their choice of reading matter. In fact, people who educate themselves often do better than those who are told what to read by others. The reading of self-educated people is more effective and successful because they know why they read and what they want to read whenever books concern them.

4. I feel sudden joy whenever I see
       A rainbow in the sky;
   I felt this way as a young child,
   I feel the same way now that I'm an adult,
   I hope to feel the same when I'm old,
       Or I'd rather not live.

5. People hold in their minds one theory of politics which has found its expression in both their laws and their revolutions. This is the theory

---

* Students may choose to paraphrase this paragraph using first-person plural. However, second person is a more natural-sounding choice by current standards.

that governments exist to protect two things: people and property. Concerning people, this theory maintains that all people have equal rights because all are alike in nature. If this goal is to be achieved completely, democracy is the form of government needed to reach it.

A Challenge in Paraphrasing (6–7)

Times like this test what people's inner selves are like. Some people are willing to fight for and support their country when things are going well, but they try to avoid serving it in a time of crisis. The person who will stand up for it now should have the love and thanks of everyone. Abuse of power, like hell, is not easy to overcome. Yet, it is good to know that the more difficult the fight, the greater the victory. If something comes too easily, we think it has little value. Only something that costs a great deal is considered to have true worth.

Paraphrasing a Speech by Shakespeare (6–8)

(Yet it is commonly accepted as true,
That being in a low position makes a young person wish to climb the ladder of success,)
As someone climbs upward, he or she keeps looking toward the top;
But when a person gets to the top and achieves success,
He or she then ignores the steps necessary for getting there
And keeps looking even higher, feeling too good and important to notice the steps
By which he or she made it to a top-level position.

UNIT 7, COMING TO TERMS WITH TECHNIQUES OF LITERATURE

What Others Imply, You Infer (7–1A)

1. **Literal:** Once milk has been spilled, it is almost impossible to wipe it up in a way that will make it usable, and crying won't help solve the problem.

   Figurative: When something goes wrong that can't be made right, you won't change the situation by crying.

2. **Literal:** Sweetness attracts flies, sour things don't, so flies will hover near honey and be easier to catch.

   Figurative: Acting sweet and nice will get you what you want faster than acting bad-tempered and sour.

3. **Literal:** If you repair or sew up a hole when it's small, it won't grow larger—so you save effort, or "one stitch" will "save nine."

> **Figurative:** If you take care of a problem when it's small, it won't have a chance to grow larger.

4. **Literal:** Few highways are completely straight. If they were, travel on them would be dull, tiresomely difficult, and seemingly endless.

   Figurative: Even though you seem to be in a rut or a bad situation seems without an ending, eventually things will change or "take a turn" for the better (or worse?).

5. **Literal:** Don't bother a sleeping dog, unless you're prepared to cope with it—from taking it out or dodging its bite.

   Figurative: If a situation has calmed down, don't start anything unless you're prepared to deal with whatever happens as a result.

Colloquial, Colorful, or Cliché (7–2)

1. to have a lot of money
2. to be very touchy; ready to take offense; likely to believe any comment is an insult
3. not to feel well
4. describing someone who does not feel like eating as he or she normally does
5. to feel oneself in the best of health
6. implying a situation is finished and best forgotten
7. describing something that was once part of one's plans but has been discarded or forgotten
8. to take a very short nap
9. to stay away from something as if it could give you a terrible, communicable disease
10. to be in a very shaky situation, involving a great risk and facing great difficulty in getting out of it

Making Thoughtful Inferences (7–3)

A. (1) out of style; (2) worn out or in poor condition
B. (1) use old books instead of new ones; (2) make sure children can and do read
C. (1) health and appearance; (2) how they feel about themselves; whether they are greedy, finicky, anorexic, and so on
D. (1) guilty of something worse; (2) that she does not want to face a jury or trial because she knows she could not win
E. (1) are educated as scientists; (work in) laboratories; (2) almost everyone, everyday life; (3) the present and the past; (4) everyone ought to know that is used in everyday life
F. (1) stay up late or make their own rules (disobey their parents' orders); (2) United States; (3) he writes of "American" mothers, not just mothers

(also, he writes of traveling on the "western continent" and calls his book *North America*); (4) being spanked once in a while makes children happier and perhaps healthier

Creating Mental Pictures with Metaphors (7–4A)

Note: Students may find other valid reasons for finding metaphors fitting.

A. (1) road, a ribbon of silver; (2) metaphor; (3) A ribbon, like a road, is long and narrow *and*, because it is reflecting moonlight, it must gleam like pale silver.
B. (1) my heart, a singing bird; (2) simile; (3) The metaphor shows happiness because the bird is singing *and* its being free and able to fly creates a light-hearted feeling.
C. (1) truth, a shadow; (2) metaphor; (3) A shadow, like the truth, is impossible to pin down and hold *and,* like a shadow, the truth can seem to vanish or disappear.
D. (1) a poet, a beacon; (2) metaphor; (3) A good poet, like a beacon, stands out from his or her surroundings *and* a poet can inspire and guide people as a beacon's light does.
E. (1) Assyrian army, wolves attacking a sheepfold; (2) simile; (3) The army is like a wild beast coming down to attack its prey *and* the Assyrians will show no mercy, just as the wolf will kill innocent lambs.
F. (1) shame, Pride's cloak; (2) metaphor; (3) People use shame to cover their feelings as a cloak covers a person's body *and* people who have no pride would not feel bad about doing something shameless, so would not need a cloak.

Creating Mental Pictures with Metaphors (7–4B)

Note: Students may find other valid reasons for finding metaphors fitting.

A. (1) stately pines, two cathedral towers; (2) simile; (3) The trees, like cathedral towers, are tall and slender, tapering to points *and* they stand out from their surroundings as cathedral towers do.
B. (1) she (a woman), a phantom of delight; (2) metaphor; (3) The woman, like a phantom, must not seem quite real—but like a vision of loveliness *and* the speaker seems to feel she might disappear any instant, for he calls her "a lovely apparition" and a "moment's ornament."
C. (1) she (a woman), a cloudless night; (2) simile; (3) The starry, cloudless night is clear and lovely, like the woman *and* the stars imply a heavenly kind of beauty and the darkness a kind of mystery.
D. (1) good prose, a window pane; (2) metaphor; (3) Good writing, like a window pane, should be clear *and* writing allows the reader to see through or understand something else, as a person looks through a window pane to see something else.

E. (1) whistle of a boat, calls and cries of a lost child; (2) simile; (3) The whistling sounds lost and unhappy because the boat is alone in the fog, like a lost child *and* the whistling comes from afar, it keeps repeating itself, and its direction is hard to determine.

Quotations with More than One Metaphor (7–5)

Note: Students may find other valid reasons for finding metaphors fitting.

1. a. (1) a house, a castle; (2) Like a castle to a king or queen, each person's home is his or her headquarters *and* in a home people can "rule" as royalty rules in a castle.
   b. (1) a house, a fortress; (2) A home is a place where someone feels (or wants to feel) safe and protected, as in a fortress *and* in a fortress you can shut out those who aren't wanted, which is also true of a house. (3) metaphors
2. a. (1) a brain, something made of feathers; (2) Feathers are light and fluffy as this person's brain matter must be *and* the person must be "soft in the head" or "scatter brained" like something filled with feathers. (Feathers also float if they escape from a pillow case.)
   b. (1) a heart, something made of lead; (2) Lead is both dull and heavy as this person's heart must be *and* a heart of lead would be "hard to move" as lead is so it would feel little emotion or sympathy. (3) metaphors
   Note: This comparison must refer to a specific person or type, not people in general.
3. a. (1) the snowfall, a silence deep and white; (2) The snow, like silence, makes the entire scene seem soundless and still *and* the snow, like silence, also seems deep and hard to penetrate.
   b. (1) snow-covered trees, someone wearing ermine; (2) The snow is white, soft, and fluffy like an ermine's fur *and* this ermine is "too costly for an earl" because the beauty of this snowfall can't be purchased at any price.
   c. (1) snow covering twigs, an inch-deep coating of pearl; (2) The snow on the twig is gleaming, smooth, and white like pearl *and* is also compared to something costly and precious, as the snow on the trees was. (3) metaphors
4. a. (1) hope, spring; (2) Hope gives you something to look forward to, as spring does *and* both make you feel carefree and light-hearted.
   b. (1) despair, winter; (2) Despair is dark and gloomy as winter often is *and* winter is cold and brings a heavy heart, as despair does. (3) metaphors.

Seeing the Logic in an Analogy (7–7)

Note: Students may find other valid points for comparison.

A. (1) sport and war
   (2) a. One side envies the other's wealth, depth, abilities, and power.
       b. Participants and supporters in both war and sports brag about being "number one" and their confidence of victory.
       c. The "rules" of sports are broken, as the need for referees proves; in war, the "other side" is always accused of disobeying the "rules of war."
       d. In sports, fans may cheer rival players' injuries and players brag of "taking out" another player; in war, people cheer the destruction of the enemies, and their heroes are those who kill the most.
   (3) The opponents in war are openly trying to kill or put the other side permanently out of action; this is either not true or not admitted in sports.

B. (1) crimes and virtues
   (2) Virtue or goodness gives people a clear conscience, making them feel good about themselves because they know they did what was right.
   (3) Crime can give someone a guilty conscience and make him or her have negative feelings about himself and his own behavior.

C. (1) the Japanese concept of work and a form of beauty
   (2) The actual job one performs is less important than the way a person does it.
   (3) When people are doing a job, they are not really actors or artists, involved in a creative process or solely engaged in a performance.
   (4) It might be a spectacle in the sense that it is done in a style worth watching, even if it can't be called art.

D. (1) a computer and a moron
   (2) The period after 3, inside the quotation marks, was left out.
   (3) a. The computer could not think well enough to supply the period inself.
       b. The computer replied with a lot of senseless gibberish.
       c. When you ask why it does this, it hasn't brains enough to explain or answer.
   (4) a. A human being would supply the missing period.
       b. A person would at least have some answer for the question.

E. (1) writing and talking
   (2) A person should know how to read with understanding and have acquired knowledge through reading.
   (3) It does not say all those who talk a lot are idiots, only that idiots talk a lot. To conclude the first is a logical fallacy. (See notes on activities.)
   (4) The idiot lacks knowledge and understanding, so cannot talk sensibly, just as a person can't write well without the knowledge gained from reading.

Personification Makes Things *Almost Human—* *Part I (7–8A)*

A. (1) April
(2) a. Laugh thy girlish laughter
b. Weep thy girlish tears
B. (1) Night
(2) a. trailing garments (of Night)
b. (Sweep through) *her* marble halls
c. her sable skirts
C. (1) Freedom
(2) a. her mountain height
b. (Unfurled) her standard
c. She tore . . . and set (the stars . . .)
(3) night
D. (1) hares; (2) merry; (3) clover and corn; (4) lay sleeping

Personification Makes Things *Almost Human—* *Part II (7–8B)*

A. (1) the flower; (2) modest and Thou's (you've) met me
B. (1) toad; (2) knows; (3) butterfly; (4) preaches
C. (1) Four young oysters
(2) a. hurried up
b. all eager (for the treat)
c. their coats (were brushed)
d. their faces washed
e. Their shoes (were neat and clean)
D. (1) Pride; (2) it wears a cloak; (3) metaphor

How Antithesis Attracts Attention (7–9)

A. (1) Life on a farm requires dealing with genuine problems, the forces of nature, and real-life situations.
(2) The school-house is separate from the world; its situations are "set up" and artificially created for teaching purposes, not real.
B. (1) There are things more important than winning.
(2) Winning is all there is. (Students may have other versions.)
(3) "It's everything" comes as a surprise.
C. (1) Rice implies a player's attitude, spirit or "heart," sense of fair play, and good sportsmanship are more important than winning.
(2) Lombardi states winning is everything; Rice believes that winning is far less important than playing one's best.

D. (1) carefree, unthinking attitude of boys and the serious, actual death of the frogs

    (2) Young people can take part in destructive actions "just for fun" without thinking of the harmful, hurtful consequences. (Students may want to extend this to the behavior of certain adults.)

E. (1) The author lists more than nine activities for summer, only one for winter.

    (2) There was much to do outside in summer; in winter, only one thing: school.

    (3) Summer and country are always sensual living, while winter was always compulsory learning. (Point out the relationship between *sensual* and the five senses; then ask students how the summer activities involved these five.)

Three Useful Literary Terms (7–11)

A. 1. most unhappy; 2. atrocious; 3. most unkindest; 4. heaven was falling and earth's foundation fled. (Have students explain why each is exaggerated.)

B. 1. O, World; 2. Age of Gold; 3. Western wind; 4. thou deep and dark blue ocean

C. 1. (1) ring; (2) It can mean a piece of jewelry for your finger or to "ring someone up" by calling on the telephone.

    2. (1) ran into; (2) It can mean having an accident or happening to meet.

    3. (1) to pass; (2) It can mean hand in or throw, as a quarterback would a football.

    4. (1) never and always; (2) If the speaker means these words, this must be a lie—which would be telling the truth, which means the statement is a lie, so. . . (Students may try to rewrite this statement, clarifying its meaning.)

Recognizing Irony in Words and Situations (7–12A)

A. (1) lucky; (2) Meg must mean "unlucky" because her day was going badly.

B. (1) (how) loyal and faithful; (2) He must mean "disloyal and unfaithful" because his former friends were snubbing him. ("How" calls attention to the irony.)

C. (1) the "art" of killing men; (2) "Killing men" cannot be called an art, which implies creating beauty, not destroying lives.

D. (1) majestic equality; (2) This is not true "equality" since the rich do not want or need to sleep under bridges or steal bread because they have homes and food. The word "majestic" implies the law considers itself too far above ordinary people to be aware of this and "majestic" is an ironic opposite of *equal*.

E. (1) policy of peace and Peace to End Peace; (2) Neither of these phrases means what it says because the policy of peace was not successful, having ended in war, and the purpose of peace is the opposite of a time period intended to end peace. (Students can validly list "War to End War" and "very successful" as ironic if they provide logical reasons for their choices.)

F. (1) did mischief enough and called a great man; (2) This man did things too terrible to be called mere mischief and does not deserve to be called great. (Students can validly list "triumphantly" if they qualify his acts as worthy only of failure.)

Dramatic Irony: "The Blind Men and the Elephant" *(7–13A)*

Part I. 1. side to wall; 2. tusk to spear; 3. trunk to snake; 4. knee to tree; 5. ear to fan; 6. tail to rope. 7. Each was judging the entire elephant from the knowledge of just one part.

Part II. 1–6. *Stanza 1:* by observation; *stanza 3:* t'is very clear; *stanza 4:* I see; *stanza 5:* Is very plain and 'T's clear enough; *stanza 6:* E'en the blindest man can tell; 7. Anyone reading the poem or knowing about elephants would be able to deny it. 8. The poem is dramatic irony because the speakers don't realize what they are saying; the reader does.

Part III.
1. Each made an accurate comparison concerning the part of the elephant he knew about.
2. None of them were aware of the other 5/6 of the animal they hadn't described.
3. Each felt he himself was the only one who was right, so they all were wrong.
4. People get in arguments or fights without having all the facts, but believe they are completely right about a subject or situation. (Examples could include politics, marital or family problems, even international relations.)
5. The results include arguments, fights, smear campaigns, divorce, and even war.
6. The poet hopes readers will see how they themselves or those they know may be part of the problem, but won't be offended because they are being asked to laugh, not given a sermon or lecture.

Identifying Literary Techniques (7–15)

1. personification; 2. hyperbole* and metaphor; 3. personification, apostrophe, and metaphor; 4. personification, metaphor, and antithesis; 5. personifica-

---

* Some students may feel "ruthless" is not an exaggeration; you may want to credit "analogy" in its place.

tion and antithesis; 6. cliché and metaphor; 7. personification, apostrophe, and metaphor; 8. metaphor and hyperbole; 9. ambiguity; 10. antithesis and cliché.

Matching Test: Literary Terms (7–16)

1. g	5. d	9. a	13. f	17. e
2. n	6. i	10. j	14. p	18. l
3. c	7. h	11. o	15. r	
4. q	8. b	12. m	16. k	

UNIT 8, THE TRUTH IN LITERATURE

One Topic: Two Approaches (8–2A)

1. Hover homes and the future

2. *Example I:* third person; *Example II:* third person

3. to describe what life will be like in the future (details may include homes, gardening, transportation)

4. Example II tells about a family of the future, while Example I is an impersonal account.

5. future; *verb possibilities:* will (no longer) live, will allow, will have, will be

6. past; *verb possibilities:* had, steered, were, was filled, refused

7. Example I; "It will be a simple matter."

8. Example II; This is about people and invites the reader to "see" the Hover homes as the family members did, looking down from space. (Students may state a similar idea in their own words.)

9. Example II; "Filled with impatience" describes the way most people would feel when approaching a new place to live.

10. No one really knows what life will be like in the future, so both are really products of the imagination.

11. *Example I:* This can be true if it expresses someone's true opinion about life in the future. It might also turn out to be true if the writer has guessed right.

    Example II: This is true in the sense that it expresses the way that fathers and children often truly feel and behave. Some might feel it offers as true a vision of the future as Example I does.

12. Example I; Example II; Example II.

Identifying Fiction and Nonfiction—Part I (8–5A)

Note: From first reading the paragraphs, it may not be possible for students to name precisely who the main character will be. Additional allowable names are in parentheses.

1. (1) for himself
   (2) butterflies and superstrings
   (3) first person
   (4) nonfiction
2. (1) through characters
   (2) Julio (his brother Luis and mother)
   (3) third person
   (4) fiction
3. (1) through characters
   (2) Tom and Grace Carter (Junior and Grace)
   (3) third person
   (4) fiction
4. (1) for himself
   (2) William James
   (3) third person
   (4) nonfiction

Identifying Fiction and Nonfiction—Part II (8–5B)

1. (1) for himself
   (2) the writer's decision to go to France
   (3) first person
   (4) nonfiction
2. (1) through characters
   (2) Pop Apling or Beech Cartwright (exact choice uncertain)
   (3) third person
   (4) fiction
3. (1) for herself
   (2) childhood play
   (3) third person
   (4) nonfiction
4. (1) through characters
   (2) the speaker "I" as a child (Not identified by name and, since fiction, assumed not to be the author, but a character.)
   (3) first person
   (4) fiction

Taking Sides in Conflict (8–6A)

1. (1) Jerry Armytage versus the bush fire
   (2) She is all alone against a fast-moving, widespread, raging fire that meant "red death."
   (3) Man vs. Nature
2. (1) Chee versus his father-in-law
   (2) Old Man Fat is so angry he won't listen.
   (3) Man vs. Man

3. (1) Leiningen versus an army of man-eating ants
   (2) There is a vast number of ants that can destroy everything in its path.
   (3) Man vs. Nature
4. (1) Carter Druse versus the Southern land of his birth in the Civil War
   (2) He must fight against his own family and is considered a traitor to the Confederate states in which he was born.
   (3) Man vs. Society

Taking Sides in Conflict (8–6B)

1. (1) the speaker versus himself
   (2) He must go into the Army, has little time, and can't do as he wants.
   (3) Man vs. Self
2. (1) Ellie or Tommy versus the white people who object to Tommy's going to the school (Choice of main character is uncertain.)
   (2) Tommy is just a child, and adults are physically threatening him.
   (3) Man vs. Society
3. (1) Ulrich von Gradwitz versus George Znaneym
   (2) The feud was long standing; it was a dark, cold winter night in the forest.
   (3) Man vs. Man
4. (1) Jean Valjean versus himself
   (2) He is armed and seems ready to kill; he feels extreme terror but also love towards his intended victim, so his mind is truly a battleground.
   (3) Man vs. Self

Considering Conflict (8–7)

Note: Student answers may be developed differently or express other original, but valid ideas.

A. Man vs. Nature

1. (a) status in society; (b) wealth; (c) race (Nationality, religion, and sex are among other possibilities.)
2. (a) hurricanes; (b) earthquakes; (c) blizzards (Students may list others.)
3. Humans can't stop these things from happening. (A person "wins") by managing to survive, escape from, or protect him- or herself, property, loved ones.
4. (a) going hunting for dangerous game, such as lions; (b) attempting to climb a mountain (or defy the ocean, etc.)

5. (a) courage; (b) determination; (c) forethought—planning ahead

B. Man vs. Man

1. (a) husband vs. wife; (b) brother (sister) vs. brother (sister); (c) daughter (son) vs. mother (father) (Plus, all other possible combinations of these relationships.)

2. No human being is as great or powerful as Nature. People can usually communicate with one another and at least have an idea of human thought processes, abilities, and limitations.

3. (a) love; (b) jealousy; (c) hate (Also greed, misunderstanding, selfishness, etc.)

C. Man vs. Society

1. It often involves a person who disagrees with a belief, such as the oppression of one group by another, or another type of group action he or she feels is wrong.

2. There are many possibilities: someone seeking democracy in a dictatorship; someone opposing a prejudiced majority.

3. (a) It is intellectual when someone uses words, intelligence, and political means to win over the other side. (b) It is physical when the person against society becomes a rebel or revolutionary, and is willing or feels it necessary to use force.

4. The main character must stand alone or as a member of a small minority, facing a struggle against a more powerful majority. Therefore, this conflict requires both moral and physical courage. It also involves conflicting emotions.

D. Man vs. Self

1. Often the conflict comes from someone's being torn between what she or he was told to do or believe was right and that person's own beliefs or wishes.

2. The problem is that the reader knows which side is best and may find it difficult to understand or sympathize fully with the character's indecision.

3. A character might have to go against someone close, which is wrong, to do what is right.

4. When a character is called upon to testify for a friend, it would be wrong to lie and right to tell the truth. But it is also right to protect a friend and wrong to get a friend in trouble, as telling the truth might do.

Creating Conflicts (8–9)

This exercise allows students to develop the conflicts in a variety of ways, so answers will vary.

"The Blanket"—Questions of Conflict and Heroism
(8–10A)

1. Petey versus his father
2. Petey is an 11-year-old boy, while his father has authority, age, power, and responsibility over him.
3. Man vs. Man
4. Petey won by convincing his father to let Granddad stay; his Dad won because he realized the truth about the girl he was about to marry, and because he really loved and wanted his father at home.
5. "hard . . . face" or "(she) said to him coldly" (possibly "slobbered over him")
6. a. It took moral courage for Petey to stand up to his Dad. Some fathers would be angry or cruel to a son who stood up to them this way.
   b. Petey realized his Granddad was just pretending to look forward to going. He also thought to show his Dad how Granddad felt by suggesting the possibility of cutting the blanket in two.
   c. Petey truly cared for his Granddad and wanted what was best for him.
   d. Petey understood how his Granddad felt. He knew how hard it would be to live in the old house after Granddad was gone, and understood that, in time, his father might be in the same situation as Granddad was now.
   e. Petey would not cry, even though he felt like it. He also didn't beg or coax his father, trying to get his own way.
   f. Even though Granddad was to leave the next morning, Petey didn't give up on trying to find a way to show his father that Granddad should stay.
7. Some students might feel Petey risked a whipping if his Dad took his actions the wrong way. Others might decide Petey must know his father well enough not to fear physical punishment.

UNIT 9, SETTING THE STAGE FOR ACTION: SETTING & POINT OF VIEW

Creating a Time Line (9–2)

Student versions of the effects may differ somewhat.

Event	Effect
1. Age of Knights and Chivalry	A world divided into royalty and peasants, glorifying courage in battle and noble behavior

2. Discovery of America	Opened up a new continent of hope and opportunity to the world's people
3. American Revolutionary War	Brought home the idea that people's voices, ideas, and happiness ought to matter in their governing
4. American Civil War	Resulted in the end of slavery and a reunited national government
5. Turn of the Century	A period when the effects of the industrial revolution brought visible changes to life
6. World War I	Called "the war to end all wars" but brought disillusionment to many
7. The Great Depression	A time of hopelessness, lost jobs, and bread lines
8. World War II	Sought to "make the world safe for democracy," led to greater awareness of international interdependence
9. Viet Nam to Present	An era marked by technological change and social questions

"How You Say It"—Clue to Setting (9–7A)

1. Modern time period: A and C; students' reasons may vary

2. Before turn of century: B and D; students' reasons may vary

3. Southern setting: C; students' reasons may vary

4. Set in England: D; students' reasons may vary

Working with Opening Paragraphs—Part I (9–8A)

1. (1) in the American West (*clues*: cattle, ranch, ridge crests)
   (2) comparison of clouds to puffs of cannon smoke, old methods of farming

2. (1) on a sailing ship in the South Pacific
   (2) type of ship and conditions indicate the past

3. (1) a poor section of a city in USA (*clues*: basement apartment, cockroach)
   (2) modern living conditions and language

4. (1) a town in England (*clues*: street address, use of language)
   (2) old-fashioned language and attitude of mother

Working with Opening Paragraphs (9–8B)

1. (1) in the midwestern United States (*clue:* the canal, which must be the Erie as American speech pattern eliminates the Suez or Panama)
   (2) The use of the Erie Canal and speech patterns indicate the past.

2. (1) a town in the American South (*clues:* cotton mill, bus, office building)
   (2) modern details like the bus and push-button umbrella

3. (1) a large city, probably London, England (*clues:* use of language, such as elder, bystreet, fashionably-placed, West End.) *Note:* Compare to American English
   (2) a shop that custom makes boots, one that's "now no more" indicate the past

4. (1) a rural area, probably in a small village (*clues:* farm noises in the distance yet a number of people nearby)
   (2) the word "laborers," the peaceful, old-fashioned atmosphere

5. (1) the moon
   (2) a science reporter living two weeks on the moon proves it's set in the future

Omniscient or Outside Observer? (9–10A)

1. (1) third, omniscient
   (2) "amused by the face he saw" and "knew"
   (3) hummed
   (4) bad

2. (1) third, omniscient
   (2) "was conscious" and "reflected" (The second "conscious" is in a question.)
   (3) November, 1850
   (4) Poker Flat, probably in the American West

3. (1) third, outside observer
   (2) no words to reveal a character's thoughts
   (3) modern times; the Parkway and Kleenex
   (4) city; the system of roads and Mary Jane's trouble finding the house

4. (1) third, omniscient
   (2) excusing the act to himself; the fact did not worry the man; he knew
   (3) Yukon (perhaps cold)
   (4) the day is "exceedingly cold" and the three feet of ice plus three feet of snow

Just Who Is Telling the Story? (9–12A)

1. (1) first, major character
   (2) the girl speaks mostly of her feelings and what she does and thinks

    (3) "he's not quite right" and he has a big head

    (4) retarded

    (5) "as any fool can see" and "smart mouths" (Also, "they have to come by me")

2. (1) first, minor character

    (2) the speaker uses "I," but his subject is "this young German"

    (3) Paris; the French Revolution

3. (1) first, minor character

    (2) Keawe seems to be the main character

    (3) Hawaii

    (4) the 19th century

    (5) sailing ships, palaces

4. (1) first, main character

    (2) the speaker is talking about his opinion and suspicions

    (3) the speaker mentions himself and the man being alone, and the stranger is watching closely (Also, the coin is rare)

Doubting the Main Character (9–14)

1. (1) first, main character

    (2) the speaker concentrates on herself, her feelings and ideas

    (3) China Grove; a small town

    (4) (a) Stella-Rondo stole the speaker's boyfriend

        (b) Stella-Rondo accused the speaker of being one-sided

        (c) Stella-Rondo tells lies (and, she's spoiled)

    (5) (a) that she is physically bigger on one side than the other

        (b) by having only one interest in life or concentrating mainly on one idea or thing

    (6) She is telling only one side of the story, her own, so Stella-Rondo's side won't be given.

2. (1) first, main character

    (2) being nervous and having had a disease

    (3) strangeness and probably insanity

    (4) He claimed to have heard all things in heaven and many things in hell.

    (5) He speaks in short, jerky sentences and phrases; he also contradicts himself by claiming to be calm, while speaking in a frantic manner. (Also repeats himself and speaks too emphatically—for example, "why *will* you" and "Hearken!")

3. (1) the old man whom the speaker plans to kill

    (2) having been wronged or insulted; wanting another's money

    (3) to show that the old man was innocent of any wrong and the speaker had none of the normal reasons for murdering him

    (4) He can't stand the old man's one blue eye because it reminds him of a vulture's.

    (5) was insane; It must be called crazy to kill a man because of one of his eyes.

Identifying Point of View (9–15)

1. (1) third, omniscient
   (2) professor or teacher
   (3) fall; his first class
   (4) boarding house; single
2. (1) first, main character
   (2) she is younger than her brother and her mother is dead
   (3) female; male
3. (1) first, main character
   (2) near Cincinnati; 1830
   (3) why the window was boarded up
   (4) he was one of the first settlers and lived alone
4. (1) third, outsider
   (2) both are seventh-graders
   (3) friendly
   (4) Scho was across the street when Glennie called to him
   (5) enjoying it
   (6) Their game of catch was called "luxurious" and they looked "entranced."

UNIT 10, READY FOR ACTION: PLOT

Plotting the Action (10–1)

a. 5; b. 7; c. 2; d. 6; e. 1; f. 4; g. 3

About Setting and Plot (10–3A)

1. (b) the United States; **Clues:** Since the author gives no direct clues as to place, students should use the details of Kate Chopin's background to determine this element of setting. Ask advanced students to decide whether the author wants the reader to "see" the midwest of St. Louis or the southern New Orleans. Because there are no hints of a French influence in the story, St. Louis seems the better choice.
2. (a) in a town or city; **Clues:** The nearness of the newspaper office and telegraph service, the open square before the house and the peddler are characteristic of a city or town.
3. (b) at the turn of the century; **Clues:** The author's lifetime (1851–1904) is a valid clue. Also, mention of rail travel and telegramming.
4. (d) third person, omniscient; **Clues:** Such words as "she felt it" and "she knew," plus the writer's ability to tell what's going on in Mrs. Mallard's mind and soul.
5. Chopin prepares for the main character's sudden death by stating that

Mrs. Mallard has "a heart trouble" and it was important to "break the news gently."

6. The doctors felt Mrs. Mallard had died of joy. In reality, she died of shock and horror at finding her new hope and happiness gone as suddenly as it came.

7. The ending is ironical because the true cause is the opposite of what the other characters believe and would expect. Because of this, it can be considered an example of dramatic irony.

Tell "The Story of an Hour" in Six Plot Steps (10–4)

1. Mrs. Mallard gets news of husband's death in train wreck.
2. She expresses sudden grief, then goes alone to her room.
3. In her soul, she loves Mallard yet feels joyously free.
4. Transformed, Mrs. Mallard rejoins her sister and husband's friend downstairs.
5. Someone unlocks the front door and Mallard arrives home, alive.
6. The sister screams; Mrs. Mallard falls dead of shock.

Note: The examples above are not meant to be definitive versions.

Changes: All in an Hour (10–5)

1. At the beginning, Mrs. Mallard had dreaded living a long life, bending to her husband's "powerful will," even though she knew him to be kind and loving.
2. When she heard the news, Mrs. Mallard felt herself free to live her own life, welcoming the future, and hoping to live many years more.
3. Upon seeing her husband alive, Mrs. Mallard must have known her freedom did not exist and, again, must have felt a dread of living a long time. In an ironical sense, of course, her wish was granted.

Plotting How Time Passes (10–7)

Note: Accept students' answers to questions 4 and 5 if logically based on the details given.

1. (1) flashback
   (2) East Africa
   (3) Such expressions as "job-lot of missionaries" and "Mrs. Diana in search of her husband" make the setting seem an earlier time, long ago to students.
   (4) Does Mrs. Diana find her husband? Why was he "lost"?
   (5) first

2. (1) chronological
   (2) a highway—the Corkscrew grade—somewhere in the United States
   (3) The fact that the boy is driving a ten-wheeler shows the story is modern.
   (4) Does the truck crash? Does the kid stop the truck safely?
   (5) third
3. (1) flashback
   (2) the marshes near the speaker's cousin's place in France
   (3) Such phrases as "strange recollection" and mention of the Cross appearing to early Christians makes it seem a story of the early part of this century.
   (4) Who was killed? What was strange about what happened?
   (5) first
4. (1) chronological
   (2) a place in the country near a village; rural United States
   (3) The fact that they are merely "playing" at being country people make it seem that they are modern city people who feel rural life is wonderful, not real work.
   (4) Why did he need 24 yards of rope? Why did they move to the country?
   (5) third

How Writers "Plant" Clues in Plots (10–8)

Note: Accept students' answers to questions 4 and 5 if logically based on the details given.

1. (1) Something will go wrong as it has before and some rumor will make it seem Sam Billings is crooked, as the others were.
   (2) chronological
   (3) a small town called Androscoggin, U.S.A.
   (4) The town meeting and the attitude of the townspeople, plus expressions like "crooks and scoundrels" make it seem as if the time is the early part of this century—the past but not the distant past.
   (5) Why did the town have such trouble with elections?
   (6) third
2. (1) Mary's father will die, and she will be left alone.
   (2) chronological
   (3) a small town in the U.S.A.
   (4) The passage states the year was 1908. The railroad track is another way to fix the time if the date were omitted.
   (5) What kind of future faces Mary?
   (6) third
3. (1) Pan will be torn between her white and oriental heritages.
   (2) chronological
   (3) Chinatown, U.S.A.—possibly San Francisco
   (4) The hint of Pan's getting to know Mark Carson, which seems an

American name, means this story allows her more freedom than would be expected if the time were far in the past.

(5) Can Pan come to terms with her two heritages? Will she choose one or the other?

(6) third

Getting Involved in Narrative Action (10–9A)

1. The pass <u>was</u> high and wide and he <u>jumped</u> for it, <u>feeling</u> it <u>slap</u> flatly against his hands, as he <u>shook</u> his hips to <u>throw</u> off the halfback who <u>was diving</u> at him. The center <u>floated</u> by, his hands desperately <u>brushing</u> Darling's knee as Darling <u>picked</u> his feet up high and delicately <u>ran</u> over a blocker and an <u>opposing</u> linesman in a jumble on the ground near the scrimmage line. He <u>had</u> ten yards in the clear and <u>picked</u> up speed, <u>breathing</u> easily, <u>feeling</u> his thigh pads <u>rising</u> and <u>falling</u> against his legs, <u>listening</u> to the sound of cleats behind him, <u>pulling</u> away from them . . . He <u>was</u> sure he <u>was going</u> to get past the safety man . . . He <u>pivoted</u> away, . . . <u>dropping</u> the safety man as he <u>ran</u> easily toward the goal line, with the <u>drumming</u> of cleats <u>diminishing</u> behind him. (*Note:* Plan to allow a certain amount of leeway in determining verbs and verb count as this is a reading, not grammar exercise, and meant mainly to increase awareness of action.)

(1) 27

(2) high, wide, (opposing), thigh, safety, goal

(3) football player (as he) catches a pass (and) runs for a goal line (Accept variations if logically based on the details given.)

(4) character

(5) "feeling," "listening," also "sure (he was going to get past . . .)"

(6) third, omniscient

2. Suddenly there <u>came</u> to him (the gold miner) a premonition of danger. It <u>seemed</u> a shadow <u>had fallen</u> upon him. But there <u>was</u> no shadow. His heart <u>had given</u> a great jump up into his throat and <u>was choking</u> him. Then his blood slowly <u>chilled</u> and he <u>felt</u> the sweat of his shirt cold against his flesh . . .

. . . A loud, <u>crashing</u> noise <u>burst</u> on his ear. At the same instant he <u>received</u> a <u>stunning</u> blow on the left side of the back, and from the point of impact <u>felt</u> a rush of flame through his flesh. He <u>sprang</u> up in the air, but halfway to his feet <u>collapsed.</u> His body <u>crumpled</u> like a leaf <u>withered</u> in sudden heat, and he <u>came</u> down, his face in the dirt and rock . . . (*Note: Jump, sweat, impact, and rush are action-showing words as well.*)

(1) 17

(2) no, cold, loud, (crashing), same, left, (withered), sudden

(3) miner (as he) senses danger or is attacked (and) receives a blow or is shot in the back

      (4) character

      (5) "came (to him)," "premonition," also " felt"

      (6) third, omniscient

Drawing Conclusions from Dialogue (10–10)

1. (1) (a) Mrs. Thayer, (b) Ben, (c) Mrs. Thayer, (d) Ben, (e) Mrs. Thayer, (f) Ben, (g) Mrs. Thayer

    (2) She must have warned Mrs. Thayer that Ben didn't like cream in his coffee.

    (3) He wanted to emphasize his dislike of cream to avoid further pressure.

    (4) a. *inconsiderate:* She should have paid attention to his wishes instead of rudely pushing him to take what he obviously didn't want.

        b. *self-seeking:* She is paying herself compliments on the richness of her cream, trying to making herself look special.

    (5) I don't want your cream! I hate cream! Stop bothering me! What do I have to say to get the idea through your thick skull. (Maybe your cream may be thick but your head is thicker.)

    (6) 1. He showed self-restraint by not getting mad.

        2. He showed more consideration of her than she did of him.

2. (1) the husband, Jack

    (2) He was willing to spend what was for him a large amount of money in order to please his new bride.

    (3) Her not having been in a dining car and attitude towards money prove she's not rich. "Ain't" shows she's not well-educated.

    (4) She shows she is sensible by not wanting to be extravagant with their money when she says, "It's too much for us," proving she thinks they might need it later.

    (5) He says it isn't too much "this trip, anyhow," meaning it usually would be. He also says this "bravely," showing he knows it will strain his finances.

    (6) The words seem justified for they are both concerned for one another's welfare and show they care about each other.

Opening Paragraphs as Dialogue (10–11)

1. (1) (a) wife, (b) husband, (c) wife, (d) wife, (e) wife

    (2) He says nothing but just goes on harnessing his horse.

    (3) He's stubborn and thinks his wife has no right to pry into "his" business.

    (4) "I want to know . . . an' I'm goin' to know."

    (5) He says "tend to your own affairs" or mind your own business. He also wants her to go into the house.

    (6) growl

(7) She says she will not go inside until he tells her what the men are digging.

(8) his giving up; She has shown determination and seems to be in control.

2. (1) (a) husband, (b) husband

(2) She likes to go shopping and spend money.

(3) She will be a servant or housekeeper.

(4) "I asked her if she wanted any nights off." This proves she would be working and living in the house.

(5) difficult; Mrs. Wallace sounds as if she has found fault with other girls who worked for her, and her husband acts as if it's hard to believe she has found someone she will like.

(6) It likely foreshadows that it really *is* too good to be true, and there will be problems this time, also.

The Importance of Description (10–12)

1. (1) large, lofty, long, vast (remoter)

(2) black, feeble, dark, gloom

(3) comfortless, antique, tattered, scattered

(4) It had "an atmosphere of sorrow."

(5) Something bad or sad had happened and would happen again.

2. (1) smoke

(2) black, slimy, dingy, greasy, foul, dirty (among others)

(3) The mules "reek" and give off a foul odor.

(4) The figure of an angel is covered with smoke; the canary is dirty because of smoke.

(5) the canary

(6) The speaker has also dreamed of getting away but now fears it's not possible.

3. (1) the unpainted floors of the study, the imitation leather bindings of the books

(2) The waiting room is carpeted; the desk is well-made.

(3) The papers are in orderly piles.

(4) The waiting room seems stiffly formal, in contrast to the comfortable study.

(5) The waiting room is for visitors, the doctor's patients, while the study is for his personal use.

(6) The doctor seeks to learn as much as he can about medicine and wants to be a good physician.

The Novel: Harry Heathcote of Gangoil (10–13A)

1. (1) third

(2) The Australian weather is so hot that Harry says, "I'm about whole melted," while Christmas is colder in England.

(3) One is Harry's wife, and the other is her sister.

(4) The other woman is probably a housekeeper.

(5) It shows that she is concerned about him and worries about his not eating.

(6) She throws her arms around him, showing how much she loves him.

2. (1) rough and poorly-dressed (but considered) a gentleman [He *is* a magistrate.]

(2) He owns 30,000 sheep which seems to be an impressive holding.

(3) rough

(4) It foreshadows the likelihood of a clash or fight between Harry Heathcote and some of his neighbors.

3. (1) (a) Harry; (b) Harry's wife; (c) Kate; (d) Harry's wife

(2) He has been out all day, was leaving at 10, and wouldn't be home till midnight. He must be tired and wouldn't go out unless he expected trouble.

(3) Harry's sister-in-law feels the heat might cause the bush to catch fire by spontaneous combustion.

(4) His wife feels a fire might be set by some of Harry's enemies.

(5) She feels this way because she knows Harry overheard something that alerted him to danger.

The Novel: Harry Heathcote of Gangoil (10–13B)

1. (1) successful; succeeded; success

(2) Did he make money? Was he financially successful?

(3) Medlicot did not like to talk much to others about his business.

(4) He is successful financially.

(5) Medlicot grew good crops and owned his own mill.

(6) The fact that some of these "freely" selected or took other's cattle and sheep "for free" makes this term ironical. *Free* usually refers to something good; this is just plain stealing.

2. (1) the Brownbie homestead or station

(2) Boolabong was certainly a miserable place.

(3) broken-down, broken-down, worn-out, worn-out, dropsical, miserable; also possibly "stuffy" and "not particular"

(4) There are six Brownbie brothers versus Harry Heathcote and whoever works for him. Blood ties are stronger than others, as well.

(5) free-selectors; They don't seem the type of men who would work hard for a living.

(6) It seems suspicious because there are few attractions at Boolabong unless someone wanted to share in some "free selecting."

3. As Medlicot still <u>went</u> on <u>putting</u> out the fire, Jerry <u>attempted</u> to <u>ride</u> him down. Medlicot <u>caught</u> the horse by the rein and violently <u>backed</u> the brute in among the embers. The animal <u>plunged</u> and <u>reared</u>, <u>getting</u> his head loose, and at last <u>came</u> down, he and his rider together. In the meantime Joe Brownbie, <u>seeing</u> this, <u>rode</u> up behind the sugar-planter, and <u>struck</u> him violently with his cudgel over the shoulder. Medlicot <u>sank</u> nearly to the ground, but at once <u>recovered</u> himself. He <u>knew</u> that some bone on the left side of his body <u>was broken,</u> but he <u>could</u> still <u>fight</u> with his right hand—and he <u>did</u> <u>fight</u>.

Boscabel and George Brownbie both <u>attempted</u> to <u>ride</u> over Harry together. . . .

(1) 21

(2) left, right

(3) Medlicot

(4) He could still fight; He did fight.

(5) Harry will win.

(6) Harry is introduced as the hero. The reader sides with him, and he seems smart, brave, and capable of winning.

(7) Man vs. Man

UNIT 11, CHARACTER: THE HEART OF THE STORY

Descriptive Characterization—Part I (11–2A)

Students may differ on individual words and phrases, if they have logical reasons, but should agree about the passage being positive or negative.

1. (1) + (well-built); (2) + (good teeth); (3) + (ready and unpuzzled smile); (4) + (good teeth); (5) + (loved his sisters); (6) + (loved Madrid); (7) + (loved his work); (8) positive; (9) (b) naive and innocent; (10) waiter; (11) The boy comes from a small town; his family is poor. (Also, has several sisters and is unused to "abundant food.")

2. (1) – (thin red whiskers); (2) – (smeary shade of blue); (3) – (shoulders were high); (4) – or 0 (stature but middling); (5) – (one leg slightly more bandy); (6) – (looking vaguely around); (7) – (mumbled); (8) – (ashamed of what he was saying); (9) – (manner of a criminal); (10) – (terrible—terrible); (11) negative; (12) "Looking around vaguely" and "ashamed" make him seem too weak to command. His mumbling means his orders would be hard to hear.

3. (1) 0 (not young); (2) + (still handsome); (3) + (tall, well-made); (4) + (clearness of health); (5) + (vivacity); (6) + (fine, cheerful black eyes); (7) positive

Descriptive Characterization—Part II (11–2B)

1. (1) – or 0 (great raw-boned, sandy-haired); (2) – (strength of an ox); (3) – (heart no bigger than a sour apple); (4) – (overbearing); (5) – (given

to berserk rages); (6) – (true god of that man was money); (7) negative; (8) He seems stupid and clumsy; (9) He seems bad-tempered and stingy with his money.

2. (1) – (very unprepossessing); (2) – (tall, gaunt, and ill-formed); (3) – (snake-like neck); (4) – (small, bony head); (5) – or 0 (close-clipped hair); (6) – (repellent head); (7) – (number of thick ridges); (8) – (small, rudimentary ears); (9) – (positively malignant look); (10) – (not more than half human); (11) negative

3. (1) + or 0 (no fighter); (2) + (all sweetness and gentleness); (3) + (love-creature); (4) + or 0 (nearly six feet tall); (5) + (muscled like a gladiator); (6) + (no coward); (7) + (heart of a lion); (8) + or 0 (run risks); (9) + (avoided precipitating a row); (10) + (never ran away from trouble); (11) gentleness, understanding; (12) courage, determination

The Animal Kingdom for Comparison (11–3)

1. quiet, timid, fearful
2. strong, clumsy, stupid
3. stubborn, patient
4. sly, sharp
5. fat, lazy, greedy
6. cowardly, dumb
7. brave, powerful, free
8. stubborn
9. thieving, untrustworthy
10. shy, gentle

11–15. Possibilities include lamb, tiger, bee, elephant, rat.

Depth of Character (11–4A)

1. cowardice
2. disloyalty
3. thoughtlessness
4. blindness, prejudice
5. dishonesty
6. abjectness, lowliness
7. indifference, lack of concern
8. indecision, inaction
9. vengefulness
10. selfishness
11. stinginess, greed
12. mercilessness, coldness
13. conceit
14. untrustworthiness
15. unreliability
16. baseness
17. cruelty

18–20. Possibilities include calm, self-control, kindness.

A Gathering of Famous Characters—Part I (11–5A)

1. **Hester Prynne**
   (1) + (perfect elegance)
   (2) 0 or + (large scale)
   (3) + (dark and abundant hair)
   (4) + (threw off sunshine)
   (5) + (beautiful)
   (6) + (regularity of feature)
   (7) + (richness of complexion)
   (8) + (impressiveness)
   (9) 0 or + (marked [clearly-defined] brow)
   (10) + (deep black eyes)

(11) + (lady-like)
(12) + (state and dignity)
(13) + (beauty shown out)
(14) + (made a halo)

(15) positive
(16) It is surprising that someone so lady-like and beautiful would have been in prison
(17) courage and pride

2. Roger Chillingworth

(1) – (well-stricken in years)
(2) – (pale, thin, scholar-like visage)
(3) – (eyes dim and bleared)
(4) – (bleared optics)
(5) – (strange, penetrating power)

(6) – (read the human soul)
(7) – (slightly deformed)
(8) – (left shoulder a trifle higher)
(9) negative

3. A Further View of Roger Chillingworth

(1) Chillingworth's mental part has "moulded" or affected his physical self, causing him to look as he does.
(2) horror

(3) The look of horror is compared to a snake gliding over his face.
(4) cruelty and untrustworthiness (Also, hatred, anger)

A Gathering of Famous Characters—Part II (11–5B)

Arthur Dimmesdale

1. (1) eloquence and religious fervor
(2) high eminence
(3) very striking
(4) white, lofty and impending brow
(5) large, brown, melancholy eyes
(6) vast power of self-restraint

(7) high native gifts
(8) scholar-like attainments
(9) simple and childlike
(10) freshness and fragrance
(11) dewy purity of thought
(12) speech of an angel

2. (1) apt to be tremulous
(2) nervous sensibility
(3) apprehensive, half-frightened
(4) quite astray
(5) at a loss

3. Positive; there are more positive traits given than negative ones.
4. self-restraint and sense of duty

A Gathering of Famous Characters (11–6)

A. Ethan Frome

1. (1) most striking figure
(2) great height
(3) careless powerful look

(4) gallantly
(5) lean brown head
(6) strong shoulders

2. (1) ruin of a man
(2) lameness checking each step
(3) bleak and unapproachable

(4) stiffened and grizzled
(5) an old man
(6) bent out of shape

3. that Ethan was not an old man, no more than 52 years old
4. What caused the accident? How, where, and why did it happen?

B. What a Townsperson Says About Ethan
1. smart; saying "most" means not all of the smart ones left and implies Ethan was one of these
2. (1) caring—for his parents and wife; (2) sense of duty—He stayed in Starkfield. (Other possibilities include loyalty, compassion, concern for others, unselfishness.)

C. 1. "like the bronze image of a hero"
   2. courage and nobility

A Gathering of Famous Characters (11–7)

A. Tom Buchanan
1. (1) sturdy straw-haired man
   (2) enormous power
   (3) great pack of muscle
   (4) enormous leverage
2. (1) effeminate swank
   (2) glistening boots
3. (1) rather hard mouth
   (2) supercilious manner
   (3) shining arrogant eyes
   (4) always leaning aggressively forward
   (5) cruel body
4. cruelty and selfishness

B. Jay Gatsby
1. (1) + (successful gestures); (2) + (something gorgeous); (3) + (heightened sensitivity); (4) + (related to one of those intricate machines); (5) + (responsiveness); (6) + (extraordinary gift for hope); (7) + (romantic readiness); (8) + (turned out all right)
2. flabby impressionability and "creative temperament"
3. Positive; the phrases are all (or mainly) complimentary, including "Gatsby turned out all right."
4. inner nature; the "something" gorgeous is directly related to "heightened sensitivity" and in fact is in apposition to it.
5. what preyed on Gatsby and foul dust
6. It disillusioned the speaker and made him lose interest in people for a while.

Characterization Through Action and Dialogue— Part I (11–9A)

1. (1) first, major character
   (2) Jem is only 13; his opponent is a burly man, almost able to lift Jem by the collar.
   (3) (a) loyalty—by coming to the aid of her brother; (b) courage—in attacking a full-grown man

       (4) tomboy—because of her readiness to fight and also such language as "Ain't nobody gonna do Jem that way."

  2. (1) (a) courage—able to endure the beating without giving in

          (b) determination—continuing to insist her name was Jane Brown

      (2) first, main character

      (3) Ernest J. Gaines, the author, is a man and, if truly an autobiography, it would be written by a woman, Jane Pittman herself.

      (4) setting out on her own; she showed courage, determination, and an independent spirit with regard to her name.

Characterization Through Action and Dialogue—Part II (11–9B)

  1. (1) third, omniscient; "searching his mind"

      (2) (a) thoughtfulness—Ralph considered the "fundamentals" and searched for the words that needed to be said.

          (b) understanding—Ralph understood his audience of little children and the difficulties in communicating with them.

      (3) The group consisted of "littluns," boys who seemed little to Ralph, who himself was only 12. Such small boys might not comprehend a complex problem.

  2. (1) courage—Heathcliff does not wink or cry when beaten.

      (2) endurance and generally truthful

      (3) Heathcliff seemed sullen and spoke little.

      (4) He was poor and fatherless.

Interpreting Character (11–10)

1–A. (1) feet, arms, and place in the family

      (2) (a) Ma's dress has a small flowered pattern.

          (b) Her hands are chubby and delicate.

          (c) Ma is compared to a plump little girl.

      (3) self-control and kindliness

      (4) (high) calm and (superhuman) understanding

      (5) a citadel and a strong place

1–B. (1) Ma would not admit she was hurt or afraid.

      (2) The family would react as Ma did.

      (3) Ma tried to look on the bright side and find laughter in small things.

      (4) joy

      (5) Because they were poor, out of work, and homeless, the family could not afford to let themselves be overwhelmed by their problems.

      (6) (a) Ma is the healer.

          (b) She is also the arbiter, whose judgment the others trust.

      (7) goddess; superhuman

(8) Ma is the inner strength of the family, the one the others turn to.

(9) Ma serves the family quietly and calmly. (Also, she is poor and homeless.)

2. (1) share the food with the children or give it all to her family

(2) Ma fears her own family hasn't enough to eat, yet she wants to help the hungry children.

(3) (a) generosity

(b) loyalty to her family

(c) understanding

(d) compassion (also, sense of duty, thoughtfulness)

UNIT 12, SOMETHING TO THINK ABOUT

What Is Fiction "About"? (12–1A)

1. a. His father made fun of him.

   b. His father discouraged his ambition to get an education.

2. He doesn't want to make the mistakes his father did.

3. The boy feels his father won't let him make his own decisions.

4. They disagree about whether or not the boy should go to college.

5. The father was only trying to keep his son from feeling the kind of rejection his father had shown him.

6. The father was more concerned with his own feelings as a boy than with his son's true feelings in the present.

7. a. He tried to show how much he cared for his son; his father didn't.

   b. The father didn't consider how his son truly felt and so drove him away.

And the Moral Is . . . (12–4)

1. d. People don't believe known liars, though they're telling the truth.

2. b. It's easy to criticize what you can't get.

3. e. Use good times to save for bad times ahead.

4. a. Trying to please everyone can result in pleasing no one.

5. c. Slow and steady wins the race.

"A World of Ideas," Authorial Comment—Part I (12–5A)

1. (1) childhood and adulthood

(2) teenager

(3) He wants to be thought of as nearly grown up but still has many feelings and qualities of a child.

(4) Children aren't expected to "know better" as adults are, and even

the law traditionally has treated juvenile offenders differently from adult criminals.

   (5) In some ways a 15-year-old faces a conflicting pull between the worlds of childhood and adulthood, so later a person finds it hard to remember exactly how they thought and felt.

   (6) a matter of individual opinion

2. (1) 18; manhood

   (2) the future

   (3) what others will think of him and the level of success he'll reach

   (4) the limitations of life and the people who have lived and died before

   (5) Instead of being sure of himself and the future, he becomes not at all sure.

   (6) the awareness that one's self is not all important; the individual is only one of many individuals who live and have lived

   (7) a matter of individual opinion

"A World of Ideas," Authorial Comment—Part II (12–5B)

1. (1) He tells stories for the love of it.

   (2) He'll fight when his race is "kicked around and spat on"—insulted and attacked.

   (3) Race doesn't matter when he's writing a story.

   (4) Whether or not someone is listening matters more than race.

   (5) People of any race can identify with characters of another race if only they want to. (All people are basically alike if they give one another a chance.)

2. (1) Finny was on crutches so the icy weather made walking dangerous and more difficult.

   (2) the cold, invigorating weather and the snow for its beauty and winter sports

   (3) "the ice-crusted snow"

   (4) b. not change

   (5) Winter could best show its love by being itself: cold and snowy

3. (1) His diary was published.

   (2) That everyone probably has a secret self that no one or only a few others know about.

   (3) Daisy herself must have a secret, hidden self.

   (4) The reader must also have a secret self.

Identifying Familiar Symbols (12–6)

Note: Students may have other valid examples for some of these questions.

1. a. stop   b. railroad crossing

2. a. engagement; b. wedding; c. school or class

3. A, B, C, D, F

4. Tigers, Steelers, Cowboys (any team insignia)

5. *example*: x in algebra means unknown; au means gold

6. athletics and valor in war

7. a. red—stop; b. green—go; c. yellow—caution

8. first prize/ first place

9. a. stars and stripes—U.S.A.; b. checkered flag—winner of race; c. flags to symbolize army battalion, scout troop, school, etc.

10. love

11. no smoking

12. a. firefighter, b. police officer, c. someone supporting a cause, such as a political party or fund-raising campaign

13. peace

14. (music)

Symbols: The Extra Dimension in Reading— Part I (12–7A)

(1) prison and cemetery

(2) die

(3) crime

(4) Boston

(5) a. beetle-browed; b. ugly; c. gloomy (also, wooden; marked with weather stains)

(6) weed or evil; black flower

(7) growing naturally; a rosebush can't act savagely or hard to tame

(8) pity and be kind

(9) a. saying nature has a heart
    b. saying nature can pity and be kind (also, capitalizing Nature)

(10) a. the law of gravity—nature
     b. a law against stealing, etc.—society

(11) The laws of nature seem more fair because nature's laws apply equally to everyone, no matter if someone is rich or poor, of any race, kind, or belief.

Symbols: The Extra Dimension in Reading— Part II (12–7B)

1. (1) a saint represents holiness and goodness, but this suburb is its opposite—a vile place to live
   (2) b. poverty and neediness

2. (1) a. Some use broken mugs; b. Some have bare feet. (Also, their willingness to drink wine spilled on the dirty street.)
   (2) a. The street is poorly paved with rough, irregular stones.
   b. There is no proper drainage in the street.
   (3) a. The people scoop up wine with their hands.
   b. Women sop up wine in their kerchiefs.
   c. People lick and suck wine-soaked fragments of the barrel.
   (4) Drinking wine mixed with dirt from the street shows ignorance about the importance of sanitation and is a possible source of disease.
   (5) blood
   (6) a. The people's hands, faces, and feet are stained with the wine, symbolizing the blood stains to come during the revolution.
   b. Wine smears give people's faces a "tigerish" look, symbolizing their blood-thirsty desire for revenge during the revolution.
   (7) This foreshadows that the people will be just as greedy for blood once the revolution begins as they are now for wine.

Symbols: The Extra Dimension in Reading—
Part III (12–7C)

(1) The mender of roads began to shout "Long live the King . . . ," the opposite of his true aim as a revolutionary.

(2) The procession was so magnificent, he forgot himself, seeing it.

(3) If France's rulers felt the people loved them, they wouldn't suspect a revolution was brewing.

(4) The "dolls and birds" are the royalty and nobility. The symbol fits because they are showily dressed and wearing "fine feathers." They also seem unreal, like dolls "toying" with life.

(5) Madame Defarge wants them to be torn apart, stripped of their finery, and treated mercilessly.

(6) She is willing for the revolution to go to any extreme to destroy the royalty and nobility.

Symbols and Theme—Part I (12–8A)

1. (1) monster
   (2) The boy continually hears inner warnings about the awfulness of war, as if coming from a thousand different tongues.
   (3) A monster is a grotesque creature having abnormal characteristics such as a thousand tongues.
2. (1) a. the red animal
   b. the blood-swollen god
   (2) a. War, like an animal, can be brutal and savage, and red symbolizes blood.

    b. In war, soldiers go to death like sacrifices to a god that demands blood.

3. (1) a. prayers
      b. barbaric
      c. chantlike (also, imprecations; resounding chords)
  (2) (b) controlled by forces outside themselves

4. (1) a. (onslaught of) redoubtable dragons
      b. red and green monster
      c. wait to be gobbled

5. (1) a wound
  (2) The red would represent the spilled blood, and the wound would be like a badge or medal, showing the soldier's bravery in battle.
  (3) Instead of acting with true courage, the soldier could simply have been wounded from being in the wrong place at the wrong time.

Symbols and Theme—Part II (12–8B)

1. (1) a. solemn ceremony; b. rite-like; c. mad religion; d. awed and afraid (Also, blood-sucking)
  (2) a. muscle-wrenching; b. bone-crushing (Also, blood-sucking)
  (3) The two were awed and afraid because they knew they were in the presence of a man who was dying as a victim of war.

2. (1) a. resembled animals; b. fierce onslaught of creatures; c. a fierce grunt; d. glittering smile
  (2) a. in a dream; b. lost sense of everything but his hate; c. ordinarily he could not have borne it; d. desire to smash into a pulp the smile of victory

3. (1) a. barbarian; b. beast; c. pagan; d. defends his religion (Also, wild)
  (2) In the heat of battle, he was overcome by the fury of war, not thinking or acting normally. This made it seem easy, as if it were all a dream.

4. (1) a. frenzy; b. barbaric; c. tuned in strange keys; d. delirium (Also, mad enthusiasm)
  (2) When the leaders slowed the soldiers' pace and their energies failed, the soldiers started to be more careful and were "men" again.
  (3) Crane leads the reader to feel that soldiers in battle acted like beasts, not men. Instead of using their "highly developed brains," they seemed in a trance so their courage came from unthinking rage or a kind of madness, not thoughtful purpose and patriotism.

Beginnings and Endings—Part I (12–9A)

1. (1) a. best of times   worst of times
      b. age of wisdom   age of foolishness
      c. epoch of belief   epoch of incredulity
      d. season of Light   season of Darkness
      e. spring of hope   winter of despair

f. everything before us   nothing before us
g. all going direct to Heaven   all going direct the other way
(2) both; If that time was like the present, it also means this must be true everywhere.
(3) open for choice
2. (1) It was the worst of times because of the horror of the guillotine and the blood-thirsty violence; but the best side of someone also showed, when a man was willing to sacrifice his life for someone else.
(2) The ending shows that characters from both cities are involved in this act, while the idea behind the story is that the extremes of good and evil exist in both places, as in any "two cities."

Beginnings and Endings—Part II (12–9B)

1. (1) first, main character
(2) captain; in command of the ship
(3) a. his ship because he had only been appointed to it two weeks earlier
b. his crew because they had been together about 18 months, while he was new
c. himself because he is not sure he can live up to his image of an ideal captain
2. (1) a. a stranger to his ship because he says nothing or no one would stand between them
b. a stranger to himself because he is alone and feels a "perfect communion" so he must know that he has the qualities needed to command it
(2) a. Who was the secret sharer mentioned in the title?
b. Why was it necessary to keep his identity secret?

Beginnings and Endings—Part III (12–9C)

1. (1) first, minor character
(2) a visitor
(3) disagree; Uncle Daniel seems like a "one of a kind" character
(4) He continually tries to give things away.
(5) If he has the "sweetest disposition in the world," he can't be like anyone else, let alone every reader's uncle.
(6) a. fine suit of clothes; b. heifer calf; c. two trips to Memphis; d. fine Shetland pony; e. field of white clover; f. pick-up truck (Student choices may vary slightly.)
(7) a. pair of pigeons; b. bad billy goat; c. two iron wheels; d. his own cemetery lot (Student choices may vary slightly.)
(8) humorous; Some of the items given away seem ridiculous, and Uncle Daniel's character traits are greatly exaggerated.
2. (1) The speaker asks "you" to accept something if Uncle Daniel offers it to you.

(2) Uncle Daniel must not realize that he no longer has anything to give away.

(3) flashback

(4) Why doesn't Uncle Daniel have anything left to give away?

(5) a. "Heart" symbolizes generosity. Uncle Daniel is big-hearted because he freely gives away his possessions, both big and small, to everyone he meets.

b. The word *heart* also serves as a symbol of love, and it could also stand for his having a heart problem or illness.

Theme: What It Means to Be Human (12–10)

1. (1) A semibarbaric kingdom must be half savage and half civilized.
   (2) The King treated every person accused of an important crime equally, which is fair.
   (3) An innocent person could easily pick the tiger and a guilty one the lady, which is unfair.

2. (1) loving the princess, someone superior to his rank
   (2) who or what is behind each door and the identity of the "prize" lady
   (3) who or what was behind the chosen door and what happened when it was opened

3. (1) The lady had dared to look admiringly at the man the princess loved.
   (2) The passage states that the princess might merely have imagined seeing these glances of admiration.

4. (1) Descriptive characterization, positive or negative, would provide a clue to the princess's decision.
   (2) The narrator says he does not believe himself qualified to answer it.
   (3) should not; If the author can't answer it, the reader can't know either—which is exactly as the author wants it.
   (4) a. *Against choosing the lady:* The princess hated the lady and would suffer greatly, seeing the two married and living together.
      For this choice: The princess loved the young man and wished him to be alive and happy.
      b. *Against choosing the tiger:* The princess loved the man and would hate seeing him die so horribly.
      For this choice: If he were dead, she need not be miserable, knowing another woman was his wife and having to see them together.
   (5) a. chance or luck; b. jealousy vs. unselfishness (Other choices could include generosity vs. selfishness; love vs. hate.); c. his trust in the princess